CAMBRIDGE STUDIES ON THE AMERICAN SOUTH

Series Editors:

Mark M. Smith, *University of South Carolina, Columbia*
Peter Coclanis, *University of North Carolina at Chapel Hill*

Editor Emeritus:

David Moltke-Hansen

Interdisciplinary in its scope and intent, this series builds upon and extends Cambridge University Press's longstanding commitment to studies on the American South. The series offers the best new work on the South's distinctive institutional, social, economic, and cultural history and also features works in a national, comparative, and transnational perspective.

Titles in the Series

Old Age and American Slavery

DAVID STEFAN DODDINGTON

Cardiff University

CAMBRIDGE
UNIVERSITY PRESS

CAMBRIDGE
UNIVERSITY PRESS

Shaftesbury Road, Cambridge CB2 8EA, United Kingdom

One Liberty Plaza, 20th Floor, New York, NY 10006, USA

477 Williamstown Road, Port Melbourne, VIC 3207, Australia

314–321, 3rd Floor, Plot 3, Splendor Forum, Jasola District Centre, New Delhi – 110025, India

103 Penang Road, #05–06/07, Visioncrest Commercial, Singapore 238467

Cambridge University Press is part of Cambridge University Press & Assessment, a department of the University of Cambridge.

We share the University's mission to contribute to society through the pursuit of education, learning and research at the highest international levels of excellence.

www.cambridge.org
Information on this title: www.cambridge.org/9781009123082

DOI: 10.1017/9781009127974

First published 2024

Printed in the United Kingdom by TJ Books Limited, Padstow Cornwall

A catalogue record for this publication is available from the British Library.

Library of Congress Cataloging-in-Publication Data
NAMES: Doddington, David Stefan, 1986– author.
TITLE: Old age and American slavery / David Stefan Doddington, Cardiff University.
DESCRIPTION: Cambridge ; New York, NY : Cambridge University Press, 2024. | Series: Cambridge Studies on the American South | Includes bibliographical references and index.
IDENTIFIERS: LCCN 2023015897 (print) | LCCN 2023015898 (ebook) | ISBN 9781009123082 (hardback) | ISBN 9781009124256 (hardback) | ISBN 9781009127974 (ebook)
SUBJECTS: LCSH: Enslaved older people – United States – Social conditions. | Slaveholders – United States – Social conditions. | Older people – United States – Social conditions. | Slavery – United States – History. | United States – Race relations – History.
CLASSIFICATION: LCC E443 .D634 2024 (print) | LCC E443 (ebook) | DDC 306.3/620973–dc23/eng/20230425
LC record available at https://lccn.loc.gov/2023015897
LC ebook record available at https://lccn.loc.gov/2023015898

ISBN 978-1-009-12308-2 Hardback

Catrin, Idris, ac Anwen. Chi yw'r peth gorau sydd erioed wedi digwydd i mi.

Contents

Figures

Tables

Acknowledgments

I wanted to acknowledge the horrific global impact of COVID-19, but could not do justice to the enormity of it all. New parenthood in a pandemic, and losing precious time with loved ones, has been difficult, but my experiences are minor with the suffering of so many. I simply express my deepest condolences to all those who lost family and loved ones in this pandemic.

* * *

The research for this book was completed with a Leverhulme Trust Research Fellowship awarded for 2018–19, and I am truly grateful for the support this provided. Work using the *Slavery and the Law* database was undertaken in 2019 following an award from the Roosevelt Institute for American Studies, Middelburg, Netherlands, and I appreciate Damian Alan Pargas's guidance here (as well as his generosity with beer and *bitterballen*). I was also fortunate to receive the Founders' Award from the British Association of American Studies in 2018, which funded research abroad and for which I express sincere thanks.

Cardiff University's History Department houses outstanding scholars and, more importantly, generous friends. I want to thank, particularly, Emily Cock, Matthew Grant (honorary Cardiffian), Rachel Herrmann, Bronach Kane, James Ryan, and Stephanie Ward for feedback on this work. Mark Williams heard me bang on about this book at such length – and gave such helpful commentary throughout – that he deserves particular praise. I genuinely don't know if I could have written this book without Lloyd Bowen. The workshop he delivered on writing – and the use of the "power hour" – was transformative. I have had one year of research leave since completing my PhD in 2013, but Lloyd's workshop, and his continuous support afterwards, gave me the confidence to write this book despite my teaching and administrative load. Keir Waddington gave far too much of his already-pressed-upon time to help me with reviewing the manuscript, and I am immensely (and selfishly) grateful to him for doing so and for his nuanced observations throughout. Pints of Rev. James with Bill Jones and Stephanie Ward were a balm through trying times, and my plan to simply not accept Bill's retirement has worked quite nicely. Tracey Loughran has once again proven herself the most incredibly generous scholar and friend, not only with editing support but also in thinking through the wider significance of this project. Her guidance is invaluable and I owe her big-time. In various formats, I have received support on this research, and I would like to thank Aviva Ben-Ur, Maria Cannon, Corinne T. Field, Jeff Forret, Rebecca Fraser, David Hitchcock, Gad Heuman, David Lewis, Andrea Livesey, Tim Lockley, Rosie Narayan, Damian Alan Pargas, Lydia Plath, Thomas Strong, Emily West, Nick Witham, and Fay Yarbrough. I would also like to thank the anonymous reviewers and editorial teams at *Slavery & Abolition*, *Journal of Global Slavery*, and *Journal of Southern History*.

Research was conducted in archives across the South and I am indebted to historians, archivists, and librarians at these institutions. Particular thanks go to Mark M. Smith and Matt D. Childs at the University of South Carolina, Columbia, for drinks, lunch, and research seminars that proved stimulating and productive. Connie Schultz is a legend of the BrANCH research community and her house-share arrangement was hugely appreciated for this trip. In Mississippi, Clinton Bagley and Carter Burns were the very definition of Southern hospitality and I am enormously grateful for the effort they put in to showing me around, helping with research, and keeping me well entertained. I am also indebted to Cambridge University Press, with Mark M. Smith and Peter Coclanis's enthusiasm for this project providing great encouragement throughout these difficult years. Cecelia A. Cancellaro and Victoria Phillips have been wonderful editors, and their guidance and astute suggestions, along with those of the anonymous readers, have only improved the book. Bharathan Sankar and Laheba Alam have provided outstanding support with production, and I am very grateful for their excellent work. Helen B. Cooper's copy-editing has been superb and her keen eye has both improved the prose and caught many an error. Any that remain are my own.

Finally, I want to express my thanks to my family. My parents are so incredibly loving and kind, and I could not wish for a more supportive safety net back home, even if mostly via Zoom these past few years. The McStewington/Doddos mean the world to me, even if the ever-expanding cast list makes Christmas unaffordable. Catrin Doddington is simply the most wonderful partner; she is loving, generous, intelligent, and kind, and I'm the luckiest man alive to be able to share a life with her. My two children, Idris and Anwen, were born during the course of writing this book and, sleepless nights notwithstanding, nothing has made me happier. I always wanted to be a dad but nothing could have prepared me for the sheer intensity of the love I feel for them, and the joy (terror/tiredness) that parenthood brings. Every night before bed Idris asks "what was your favorite part of the day" and demands I provide three options. He claims to be getting sick of my repetitive answer of "playing with you two," but it is the truth. This book is for Catrin, Idris, ac Anwen: *Chi yw'r peth gorau sydd erioed wedi digwydd i mi.*

* * *

Some arguments used in this book have appeared in article form elsewhere. I am extremely grateful to *Journal of Southern History*, *Slavery & Abolition*, and *Journal of Global Slavery* for allowing me to republish them here. See David Stefan Doddington, "Old Age, Mastery, and Resistance in American Slavery," *Journal of Southern History*, 88.1 (2022), 111–44; "Age, Resistance, and Solidarity in US Slave Communities," *Slavery & Abolition*, 42.4 (2022), 710–32; "'Old Fellows': Age, Identity, and Solidarity in Slave Communities of the Antebellum South," *Journal of Global Slavery* 3.3 (2018), 286–312.

Introduction

Old Age and American Slavery

On June 30, 1814, in Botetourt, Virginia, an enslaved woman named Fan was murdered by Ralph, a fellow slave. Ralph sought to cover his tracks by claiming that Fan had accidently drowned, but he failed to convince his enslaver and was quickly taken to jail. Under the threat of torture, and with evidence from Black and white witnesses mounting up, Ralph confessed that "he had struck [Fan] with his Fist, choked her & threw her into the creek." This first assault did not suffice and Ralph determined to finish the job: "observing she was swimming & making to the opposite side of the creek, he got a stick, followed her & struck her on the head & finished her." When asked why he had killed Fan, Ralph claimed that "she was very quarrelsome & told lies on him." The brutality of the assault perhaps speaks to the violence that permeated a slave society, and there may have been motives left unsaid. Ralph's willingness to use extreme force to settle this grudge, however, also reflected the belief that he could get away with it. According to Ralph, Fan was too old to be of any concern to her enslavers: "she was such a trifling old negroe he did not expect he would be hung for killing her."[1] Formerly enslaved people commonly claimed they tried to protect Black elders in slavery; Frederick Douglass, the most famous Black activist of the nineteenth century, insisted that the aged enslaved found solace and support among their own: "there is not to be found, among any people, a more rigid enforcement of the law of respect to elders."[2] Ralph, however, had not received this message.

---

[1] Executive papers, James Barbour, July 1814, Box 13, Folder 1, Misc. Reel, 5522, 0241–0244, Library of Virginia (LVA). Ralph was mistaken.

[2] Frederick Douglass, *My Bondage and My Freedom: Part* I. – *Life as a Slave. Part* II. – *Life as Freeman* (New York: Miller, Orton & Mulligan, 1855), 69.

White southerners also understood age was a vector of power. Writing to his sister in 1858, North Carolina enslaver William Pettigrew explained how the process of aging inevitably entailed a loss of sorts: "he who has attained 50 must soon expect the inexorable hand of time to soften that vigour which is all important in a ruler and without which he soon permits some stronger spirit than his own to assume the mastery over him."[3] White male enslavers lauded authority and independence and were supposed to exert dominance over "dependents" – whether women, children, or those whom they enslaved, while Stephanie Jones-Rogers shows that white women also sought to "acquire and exercise mastery over enslaved people."[4] But Pettigrew's fear that some "stronger spirit" would "assume the mastery over him" indicates wider fears among antebellum whites that age-related decline did not necessarily inspire collective social or familial support, but could be seized upon by rivals looking to assert themselves.

In *Old Age and American Slavery*, I explore perceptions of old age and attitudes toward "old" people in the US South. I focus on the experiences and identities of enslavers and enslaved alike and reveal the implications of aging on the institutional and ideological structures underpinning the so-called Peculiar Institution. As both a system of economic exploitation and a contested site of personal domination, slavery was shaped by concerns with age. In revealing how enslavers and enslaved people negotiated

[3] Robert Starobin (Ed.), *Blacks in Bondage: Letters of American Slaves* (New York: New Viewpoints, 1974), 34–5.

[4] Examples of this work include: Dickson D. Bruce Jr., *Violence and Culture in the Antebellum South* (Austin: University of Texas Press, 1979); Bertram Wyatt-Brown, *Southern Honor: Ethics and Behavior in the Old South* (New York: Oxford University Press, 1982); Edward L. Ayers, *Vengeance and Justice: Crime and Punishment in the 19th-Century American South* (New York: Oxford University Press, 1984); Kenneth S. Greenberg, *Honor and Slavery: Lies, Duels, Noses, Masks, Dressing as a Woman, Gifts, Strangers, Humanitarianism, Death, Slave Rebellions, the Proslavery Argument, Baseball, Hunting, and Gambling in the Old South* (Princeton: Princeton University Press, 1996); Bertram Wyatt-Brown, *The Shaping of Southern Culture: Honor, Grace, and War, 1760s–1890s* (Chapel Hill: University of North Carolina Press, 2001); Craig Thompson Friend and Lorri Glover (Eds.), *Southern Manhood: Perspectives on Masculinity in the Old South* (Athens: University of Georgia Press, 2004); Lorri Glover, *Southern Sons: Becoming Men in the New Nation* (Baltimore: Johns Hopkins University Press, 2007); John Mayfield, *Counterfeit Gentlemen: Manhood and Humor in the Old South* (Gainesville: University of Florida Press, 2009); Bertram Wyatt-Brown, *A Warring Nation: Honor, Race, and Humiliation in America and Abroad* (Charlottesville: University of Virginia Press, 2014); Robert Elder, *The Sacred Mirror: Evangelicalism, Honor, and Identity in the Deep South, 1790–1860* (Chapel Hill: University of North Carolina Press, 2016); Thavolia Glymph, *Out of the House of Bondage: The Transformation of the Plantation Household* (New York: Cambridge University Press, 2008); Stephanie Jones-Rogers, *They Were Her Property: White Women As Slave Owners in the American South* (New Haven: Yale University Press, 2019), 62.

pressures associated with aging, and how their communities addressed these issues, this book develops vital and ongoing debates on power, resistance, and survival. In doing so, it deepens our understanding of the structures of American slavery, and of the most personal experiences of those enmeshed in it.

* * *

This book developed out of questions arising from my first monograph, *Contesting Slave Masculinity in the American South*.[5] I could not move past the case of Moses, "a feeble old man," murdered by King, a fellow slave, in Richmond, 1848. During the beating Moses tried to protect himself by making explicit reference to his age: "King I ain't fit to die. I don't want to go to Hell King, don't kill such an old creature as I." Moses even offered King "every cent of money I have got." Neither these pleas nor his advanced age saved him. King taunted and beat his elder before drowning him in a puddle of muddy water.[6]

I was struck by the cruelty of the assault, during which King repeatedly mocked his overmatched opponent, interspersing the beating with the pointed request Moses acknowledge "how come his name was King." The terror and sadness in Moses's cries led me to critically reappraise existing work on old age in enslaved communities. From the revisionist historiography of the 1970s onwards, scholars have overwhelmingly emphasized communal support, even reverence, for Black elders.[7] There has been a wave of important new scholarship on age in slavery which

---

[5] David Stefan Doddington, *Contesting Slave Masculinity in the American South* (New York: Cambridge University Press, 2018).

[6] Executive Papers, William Smith, Box 7, Folder 4, March 18, 1848, LVA.

[7] Examples here include: John Blassingame, "Status and Social Structure in the Slave Community: Evidence From New Sources," in Harry P. Owens (Ed.), *Perspectives and Irony in American Slavery* (Jackson: University of Mississippi Press, 1976), 137–51, 151; Herbert Gutman, *The Black Family in Slavery and Freedom, 1750–1925* (Oxford: Basil Blackwall, 1976), 198–9, 218; Eugene Genovese, *Roll, Jordan, Roll: The World the Slaves Made* (New York: First Vintage Books Edition, 1976), 522–3; Leslie Pollard, "Aging and Slavery: A Gerontological Perspective," *Journal of Negro History*, 66.3 (1981), 228–34; Deborah Gray White, *Ar'n't I A Woman? Female Slaves in the Plantation South* (New York: W.W.Norton & Company, 1999 [1985]), 114–18; Brenda Stevenson, *Life in Black and White: Family and Community in the Slave South* (New York: Oxford University Press, 1996), 227; Stacey Close, *Elderly Slaves of the Plantation South* (London: Routledge, 1997); Sharla Fett, *Working Cures: Healing, Health, and Power on Southern Slave Plantations* (Chapel Hill: University of North Carolina Press, 2002), 26, 55–88; Dorothy Smith Ruiz, *Amazing Grace: African American Grandmothers as Caregivers and Conveyors of Traditional Values* (Westport: Praeger 2004); Daina Ramey Berry, *The Price for Their Pound of Flesh: The Value of the Enslaved from Womb to Grave in the Building of the Nation* (Boston: Beacon

emphasizes the exploitation of slavers, and which argues that in the face of this violence enslaved communities respected their aged and lauded their guidance.[8] As Daina Ramey Berry explains, "despite low external values, their soul values excelled. They carried great wisdom and stability for the community and were respected by younger enslaved family and friends."[9]

I kept encountering material, however, that suggested peers viewed enslaved elders in more complex ways than some of this historiography allows, and that elders themselves did not always believe due reverence had been granted. Moreover, "respect" granted on account of advanced years could seem condescending, being based on a perception of reduced abilities or accommodation on account of age. On Solomon Northup's Louisiana plantation, "Old Abram ... [was] a sort of patriarch among us." Northup also emphasized, however, that "age and unremitting toil" had "somewhat shattered [Abram's] powerful frame and enfeebled his mental faculties." Northup's respect for Abram was predicated on pity, not parity. Indeed, he later used the trope of aging to reflect his own fear of remaining enslaved and his desire to avoid transitioning into the "patriarch" of the plantation: "The summer of my life was passing away; I felt I was growing prematurely old; that a few years more, and toil, and grief, and the poisonous miasma of the swamps would accomplish their work on me – would consign me to the grave's embrace, to moulder and be forgotten."[10] Associations of old age with physical decline, social isolation, and even submission to bondage shaped personal identities and community dynamics in slavery. Enslaved people perceived as old by others sometimes resented or resisted such reasoning, and this led to tension in enslaved communities.

* * *

Press, 2017), ch. 5; Jason Eden and Naomi Eden, *Age Norms and Intercultural Interaction in Colonial North America* (Lanham: Lexington Books, 2017), ch. 6.

[8] See, for example: Nathaniel Windon, "Superannuated: Old Age on the Antebellum Plantation," *American Quarterly*, 71.3 (2019), 767–77; Frederick Knight, "Black Women, Eldership, and Communities of Care in the Nineteenth-Century North," *Early American Studies*, 17.4 (2019), 545–61; Corinne T. Field, "Old-Age Justice and Black Feminist History: Sojourner Truth's and Harriet Tubman's Intersectional Legacies," *Radical History Review* 139.1 (2021), 37–51; Jenifer L. Barclay, *The Mark of Slavery: Disability, Race, and Gender in Antebellum America* (Urbana: University of Illinois Press, 2021), 41.

[9] Berry, *Price for Their Pound of Flesh*, 131. On page 132, Berry notes that there are generally two positions on enslaved elders. At one end, they "were revered and treated with respect." At the other, "they were isolated and disregarded." Berry's focus is on the former, and I hope to further the debate by emphasizing the latter.

[10] Solomon Northup, *Twelve Years a Slave: Narrative of Solomon Northup, a Citizen of New York, Kidnapped in Washington City in 1841, and Rescued in 1853* (Auburn: Derby & Miller, 1853), 185–6, 235.

"Old age" is not a self-evident category, and it is worth outlining the demographic context of the US South. For both enslaved and white people, the US Census of 1850 designated "infancy" as under five, "youth" from five to twenty, and "maturity" as between twenty to fifty. Those aged from fifty to one hundred were in "old age," with "extreme old age" being one hundred plus.[11] Nevertheless, Berry rightly states that "during enslavement, those who reached age forty were considered elderly"; her outstanding work on the declining financial values placed on people in their late thirties underscores the physical depreciation associated with time's onward march, and the violence of slavery itself.[12]

The enslaved population in the antebellum years generally trended young: in 1820, where age ranges encompassed twenty-six to forty-four, and then forty-five plus, the percentage of enslaved people in the latter category was only 10 percent. Seventy percent of the enslaved population were twenty-five or younger. In 1830 and 1840, where classifications encompassed thirty-six to fifty-four, and then fifty-five plus, 16 percent of the overall population were thirty-six or older; only 4 percent were over fifty four. From 1850 age categories were structured by decade, and the percentage of enslaved people aged forty plus was 14 percent in 1850 and 1860. This same cohort made up 17 and 18 percent of the total white population in 1850 and 1860 (see Table I.1).[13]

---

[11] See Table XXXIII – "Proportion of White Males to Females, for 1850"; Table LXXXV – "Proportion of Male Slaves to Female, for 1850," in United States Census Bureau, *1850 Census: Compendium of the Seventh Census* (Washington, DC: Beverley Tucker, Senate Printer, 1854), 56, 91.

[12] Berry, *Price for Their Pound of Flesh*, 130. Daina Ramey Berry, "Berry Slave Value Database" (Ann Arbor: Inter-university Consortium for Political and Social Research [distributor], 2017-10-30). https://doi.org/10.3886/E101113V1. See also Genovese, *Roll, Jordan, Roll*, 521; Robert Fogel and Stanley Engerman, *Time on the Cross: The Economics of Negro Slavery* (New York: W. W. Norton, 1989 [1974]), 72–5.

[13] Categories for 1820 census: 0–13, 14–25, 26–44, 45+. For 1830 and 1840: 0–9, 10–23, 24–35, 36–54, 55–100, 100+. For 1850 and 1860: 0–4, 5–9, 10–14, 15–19, and then by decade until 100+. Data from Michael R. Haines, "Slave Population, by Sex and Age: 1820–1860," Table Aa2093-2140, in Susan B. Carter, Scott Sigmund Gartner, Michael R. Haines, et al. (Eds.), *Historical Statistics of the United States, Earliest Times to the Present: Millennial Edition* (New York: Cambridge University Press, 2006). Census material from 1790 to 1810 does not distinguish enslaved people by age.

For comparison to white population, see Michael R. Haines, "White Population, by Sex and Age: 1790–1990." Table Aa287-364 in Carter, Gartner, Haines, et al. (Eds.), *Historical Statistics of the United States*.

I have not disaggregated by gender as for the white and enslaved population there was c. 1 percent difference between men and women in these age categories. From the ages of twenty to fifty – Black and white – this favored men, while "for very old persons the excess

TABLE I.I *Slave population by age/sex.*

1820	M	F	Total	% of pop
0–13	343852	324344	668196	43.44
14–25	203088	202336	405424	26.36
26–44	163723	152693	316416	20.57
45+	77365	70637	148002	9.62
Total	788028	750010	1538038	
% 45+	9.82	9.42	9.62	

1830	M	F	Total	% of pop
0–9	353498	347665	701163	34.90
10–23	312567	308770	621337	30.93
24–35	185585	185786	371371	18.48
36–54	118880	111887	230767	11.49
55–100	41545	41436	82981	4.13
100+	748	676	1424	0.07
Total	1012823	996220	2009043	
% 36+	15.91	15.46	15.69	
% 55+	4.18	4.23	4.20	

1840	M	F	Total	% of pop
0–9	422584	421465	844049	33.93
10–23	391206	390117	781323	31.41
24–35	235386	239825	475211	19.10
36–54	145260	139204	284464	11.44
55–100	51331	49746	101077	4.06
100+	750	581	1331	0.05
Total	1246517	1240938	2487455	
% 36+	15.83	15.27	15.55	
% 55+	4.18	4.06	4.12	

For both 1850 and 1860, I have included the n/a in the total population used to calculate the percentages

1850	M	F	Total	% of pop
0–4	267088	273406	540494	16.87
5–9	239163	239925	479088	14.95
10–14	221480	214712	436192	13.61
15–19	176169	181113	357282	11.15
20–29	289595	282615	572210	17.86
30–39	175300	178355	353655	11.04
40–49	109152	110780	219932	6.86

(continued)

(continued)

1850	M	F	Total	% of pop
50–59	65254	61762	127016	3.96
60–69	38102	36569	74671	2.33
70–79	13166	13688	26854	0.84
80–89	4378	4740	9118	0.28
90–99	1211	1473	2684	0.08
100+	606	819	1425	0.04
Age n/a	1870	1822	3692	0.12
Total	1602534	1601779	3204313	
% 40+	14.47	14.35	14.41	
% 50+	7.66	7.43	7.55	
% 60+	3.59	3.58	3.58	
% 70+	1.21	1.29	1.25	
% 80+	0.39	0.44	0.41	
% 90+	0.11	0.14	0.13	

1860	M	F	Total	% of pop
0–4	322156	331010	653166	16.52
5–9	287299	288650	575949	14.57
10–14	276928	264320	541248	13.69
15–19	220365	228481	448846	11.35
20–29	355018	343023	698041	17.66
30–39	218346	220520	438866	11.10
40–49	140791	139002	279793	7.08
50–59	79776	75926	155702	3.94
60–69	46219	44124	90343	2.28
70–79	15433	15724	31157	0.79
80–89	4627	5334	9961	0.25
90–99	1317	1714	3031	0.08
100+	671	900	1571	0.04
Age n/a	13679	12407	26086	0.66
Total	1982625	1971135	3953760	
% 40+	14.57	14.34	14.46	
% 50+	7.47	7.29	7.38	
% 60+	3.44	3.44	3.44	
% 70+	1.11	1.20	1.16	
% 80+	0.33	0.40	0.37	
% 90+	0.10	0.13	0.12	

Data drawn from Haines, Michael R., "Slave population, by sex and age: 1820–1860." Table Aa2093-2140 in *Historical Statistics of the United States, Earliest Times to the Present: Millennial Edition*, edited by Susan B. Carter, Scott Sigmund Gartner, Michael R. Haines, Alan L. Olmstead, Richard Sutch, and Gavin Wright. New York: Cambridge University Press, 2006.

There are some points of geographical variation to address. The emerging states and territories in the southwest typically skewed younger than elsewhere. In the 1820 census, 7 percent of enslaved people in Mississippi, and 6 percent in Alabama, were over the age of forty-five, as compared to 11 percent in Maryland, Virginia, and South Carolina, 10 percent in North Carolina, and 9 percent in Georgia.[14] In the 1840 census, 13 percent of enslaved people in Alabama and Tennessee, 12 percent in Mississippi, 11 percent in Arkansas, and 10 percent in Missouri were aged thirty-six or older. In Maryland, Virginia, the Carolinas, and Georgia, the proportion of enslaved people aged thirty-six or older ranged from 15 to 19 percent.[15] In both the 1850 and 1860 census, in Texas, the newest slave state, 11 percent of the enslaved population were recorded as forty plus; the oldest slave state, Virginia, had the same cohort at 18 percent in 1850, and 17 percent in 1860.[16] Notwithstanding regional distinctions, a sizable minority of the antebellum enslaved might have been considered by their peers, if not invariably recognizing themselves, as having entered – or as soon to be entering – the chronological boundaries of "old age" in slavery.

For the white population, scholars frequently pinpoint *around* sixty as the beginning of old age. W. A. Achenbaum notes that, "in virtually every historical moment and site, old age was said to commence around age sixty-five, give or take fifteen years on either end."[17] Using this expanded range allows us to address conflicts surrounding the aging process and its

is with the females, the exceptions being chiefly in the new states." United States Census Bureau, *1850 Census: Compendium of the Seventh Census*, 54.

[14] "Aggregate Amount of Each Description of Persons in the United States and their Territories, according to the Census . . .," in United States Census Bureau, *Census for 1820* (Washington, DC: Gales & Seaton, 1821), 18.

[15] Data drawn from individual state returns in United States Census Bureau, *1840 Census: Compendium of the Enumeration of the Inhabitants and Statistics of the United States, as Obtained at the Department of State, from the Returns of the Sixth Census* (Washington, DC: Thomas Allen, 1841), 24–100.

[16] Data drawn from Table LXXXII – Ratio of Ages of the Slaves in 1850," in United States Census Bureau, *1850 Census: Compendium of the Seventh Census*, 89–90; "Slave Population by Age and Sex," United States Census Bureau, *1860 Census: Recapitulation of the Tables of Population, Nativity, and Occupation* (Washington, DC: Beverley Tucker, Senate Printer, 1864), 594–5.

[17] W. Andrew Achenbaum, "Delineating Old Age: From Functional Status to Bureaucratic Criteria," in Corinne T. Field and Nicholas L. Syrett (Eds.), *Age in America: The Colonial Era to the Present* (New York: New York University Press, 2015), 301–20, 301. See also Stephen Katz, Kavita Sivaramakrishnan, and Pat Thane, "'To Understand All Life as Fragile, Valuable, and Interdependent': A Roundtable on Old Age and History," *Radical History Review*, 139 (2021), 13–36, 17–18; Susannah Ottaway, "Medicine and Old

attendant social impacts. Fifty not only designated "old age" in census material, but was commonly portrayed as a transition point in cultural representations of the life-course. James Baillie's 1848 prints – *The Life and Age of Man* and *The Life and Age of Woman* – used long-standing metaphors of the life-course as a rising and falling staircase, and presented both men and women as atop the steps aged fifty.[18] Yet while the fifty-year-old woman was described as a "blessing to the earth," there was a clear sense of shifting powers for men: "strength fails at Fifty, but with wit/fox like he helps to manage it."[19] Nonetheless, even managed decline could only delay the inevitable. In an 1846 lecture to the University of Louisville Medical Department, Charles Caldwell explained that the period from twenty-five to forty-five constituted a (white) man's "chief season of business, enterprise, and action." After this "commences his period of decline. Having reached the mid-day of his life, and basked for a time in the enjoyment of its sunlight, he must now descend, through its afternoon and evening, to its night in the grave."[20]

Pat Thane argues that old age has commonly been divided into "'green' old age, a time of fitness and activity with some failing powers, and the last phase of sad decrepitude," and Corinne T. Field notes that nineteenth-century Americans believed (or hoped) only "the very last steps of life are full of suffering."[21] Such attitudes and demarcations clearly existed among antebellum whites. However, so too did the understanding that aging brought losses – both physical and mental – that came faster than one hoped for, and which occasioned no little strife. Nathanael Emmons, an influential antebellum theologian, lamented that "old age begins so soon

---

Age," in Mark Jackson (Ed.), *The Oxford Handbook of the History of Medicine* (Oxford: Oxford University Press, 2013), 338–55, 341.

[18] Corinne T. Field, *The Struggle for Equal Adulthood: Gender, Race, Age, and the Fight for Equal Citizenship in Antebellum America* (Chapel Hill: University of North Carolina Press, 2014), 99–102. For wider discussion on temporal metaphors associated with the life cycle, see Mark Schweda, "The Autumn of My Years: Aging and the Temporal Structure of Human Life," in Mark Schweda, Michael Coors, and Claudia Bozzaro (Eds.), *Aging and Human Nature: Perspectives from Philosophical, Theological, and Historical Anthropology* (Cham: Springer Nature, 2020), 143–59.

[19] James Baillie, *The Life and Age of Woman, Stages of Woman's Life from the Cradle to the Grave* (New York, ca. 1848); James Baillie, *The Life and Age of Man, Stages of Man's Life from the Cradle to the Grave* (New York, ca. 1848). Consulted at www.loc.gov/item/2006686266/ and www.loc.gov/item/2006686267/.

[20] Charles Caldwell, *Thoughts on the Effects of Old Age on the Human Constitution: A Special Introductory* (Louisville: John C. Noble Printer, 1846), 14.

[21] Pat Thane, *Old Age in English History: Past Experiences, Present Issues* (Oxford: Oxford University Press, 2000), 4; Field, *The Struggle for Equal Adulthood*, 102.

FIGURE I.I James Baillie, *The Life and Age of Man. Stages of Man's Life from the Cradle to the Grave* (New York, c. 1848). Courtesy of the Library of Congress, Washington, DC.

FIGURE I.2 James Baillie, *The Life and Age of Woman. Stages of Woman's Life from the Cradle to the Grave* (New York, c. 1848). Courtesy of the Library of Congress, Washington, DC.

after the meridian of life"; the Reverend John Stanford seemingly concurred: "You gradually ascended from infancy to youth, and from youth to manhood, till you reached the summit of fifty. Now you equally mark the steps of descent to old age, and cannot fail to recollect the animating pleasure of the one contrasted with the feebleness of the other."[22] Time's relentless march could inspire denial, with Emmons claiming "almost every person desires to be young rather than old, and therefore is unwilling to know and realize that he has passed the meridian of life, and is descending to old age, with great but insensible rapidity."[23] It might also entail reflection. David Golightly Harris, aged forty-three, stoically accepted the inevitably of his own decline: "It is a sad thought to know that old age is creeping on me so fast, but sad as it is, it must be borne."[24] Another antebellum writer noted the necessary anguish at realizing:

that you have had your fair half at least of the ordinary term of years allotted to mortals; that you have no right to expect to be any handsomer or stronger than you are now; that you have climbed to the summit of life, whence the next step must necessarily be decadence. Ay, though you do not feel it; though the air may be as fresh, and the view as grand – still, you know that it is so. Slower or faster, you are going down-hill.[25]

Emmons's suggestion that "there seems to be no impropriety however in calling any man old rather than young, who has passed the meridian of life, which is commonly supposed to be at about forty-five," indicates how even in a "green" old age, nineteenth-century Americans started perceiving themselves or others as beginning their downwards march from around this time.[26] That others (and scholars now) might dispute this designation is part of the story worth telling.

Returning to the numbers, nineteenth-century census data shows a similarly youthful white population, albeit with higher life expectancy than enslaved people. The 1850 census showed that "nearly two-fifths of the whole are between the ages of twenty and fifty, and less than one-tenth

---

[22] Nathanael Emmons, "Piety, a Peculiar Ornament to the Aged," in Jacob Ide (Ed.), *The Works of Nathanael Emmons, D.D., Late Pastor of the Church in Franklin, Mass., with a Memoir of His Life* (6 vols.; Boston: Crocker & Brewster, 1842), 2: 492–505, 499; John Stanford, *The Aged Christian's Companion* (New York: Stanford & Swords, 1855), 11.

[23] Emmons, "Piety, a Peculiar Ornament to the Aged," 499.

[24] Philip N. Racine (Ed.), *Piedmont Farmer: The Journals of David Golightly Harris, 1855–1870* (Knoxville: University of Tennessee Press, 1990), 426.

[25] By a woman [anon], "Growing Old," *The Ladies' Repository: A Monthly Periodical, Devoted to Literature, Arts, and Religion*, 18.5 (May 1858), 276–82, 276.

[26] Emmons, "Piety, a Peculiar Ornament to the Aged," 492.

over fifty; whilst more than one-half are under twenty years of age."[27] Ralph
Waldo Emerson's claim that "America is the country of young men" is borne
out in earlier data too.[28] Between 1800 and 1820, 12 percent of whites were
recorded as forty-five or older. From 1830 onwards age categories were set
by decade. In 1830, fifteen percent of white people were over the age of forty,
and this had risen to eighteen percent by 1860. By 1860, 10 percent of the
white population were over fifty, 4 percent sixty plus, 1 percent seventy or
more, and below 1 percent for the age ranges from eighty to one hundred
plus (see Table I.2).[29]

The antebellum satirist Joseph Baldwin's statement that "in the new
country, there are no seniors" was an exaggeration, but it spoke to
regional trends identified earlier.[30] In 1820, 8 and 9 percent of the white
population in Alabama and Mississippi were over the age of forty-five; in
comparison, 12 percent of whites in Maryland, Virginia, and North
Carolina were forty-five or older, with South Carolina and Georgia having
11 and 10 percent of their population within this age cohort.[31] In 1840,
9 percent of whites were fifty or older in Maryland, Virginia, and North
Carolina, with the same group making up 8 and 7 percent of South
Carolina and Georgia's white population. In Alabama, Mississippi, and
Missouri, the fifty-plus cohort made up 5 percent of the population; in
Arkansas this dropped to 4 percent.[32] In Texas, for 1850 and 1860, 5 and
6 percent of whites were over the age of fifty; the same age cohort
represented 10 percent of Virginia's white population.[33] A sizable minority of white people in the antebellum slave states would thus have been
considered as having passed "the meridian of life" and, perhaps controver-
sially, beginning their "[descent] to old age, with great but insensible

---

[27] "Table XXVIII – Per Cent of the Several Ages of the White Population to the Total Whites,
1850," in United States Census Bureau, *1850 Census: Compendium of the Seventh
Census*, 51.

[28] Ralph Waldo Emerson, "Old Age," *The Atlantic Monthly* (January, 1862).

[29] Data drawn from Haines et al., "White population, by sex and age: 1790–1990."

[30] Joseph G. Baldwin, *The Flush Times of Alabama and Mississippi: A Series of Sketches*
(New York: D. Appleton and Co., 1854), 234.

[31] "Aggregate amount of each description of persons in the United States and their
Territories, according to the Census ...," in United States Census Bureau, *Census for
1820*, 18.

[32] Data drawn from individual state returns in United States Census Bureau, *Compendium
of the Enumeration of the Inhabitants and Statistics of the United States*, 1840.

[33] "Table XXVIII – Per Cent of the Several Ages of the White Population to the Total
Whites – 1850," 51; Data drawn from "White Population by Age and Sex," United
States Census Bureau, *1860 Census: Recapitulation of the Tables of Population,
Nativity, and Occupation*, 592–3.

TABLE 1.2 *White population by age/sex.*

For 1790, only broad age categories for males were given: age 0–15, 802, 327; age 16 and older, 813, 298. No age data for females were given.

1800	M	F	Total	% of pop
0–9	764118	715197	1479315	34.37
10–15	353071	323648	676719	15.72
16–25	393156	401499	794655	18.46
26–44	431589	411694	843283	19.59
45+	262487	248030	510517	11.86
N/A	0	0	0	0.00
Total	2204421	2100068	4304489	
% 45+	11.91	11.81		11.86

1810	M	F	Total	% of pop
0–9	1035058	981421	2016479	34.40
10–15	468083	448322	916405	15.63
16–25	547597	561956	1109553	18.93
26–44	571997	544256	1116253	19.04
45 +	364836	338478	703314	12.00
N/A	0	0	0	0.00
Total	2987571	2874433	5862004	
% 45+	12.21	11.78		12.00

1820	M	F	Total	% of pop
0–9	1345220	1280570	2625790	33.40
10–15	612515	605375	1217890	15.49
16–25	776030	781371	1557401	19.81
26–44	766283	736600	1502883	19.12
45 +	495065	462888	957953	12.18
N/A	0	0	0	0.00
Total	3995113	3866804	7861917	
% 45+	12.39	11.97		12.18

From 1830–1860, I have included the n/a in the total population used to calculate the percentages

1830	M	F	Total	% of pop
0–4	972980	921934	1894914	17.99
5 to 9	782075	750741	1532816	14.55

(continued)

(continued)

1830	M	F	Total	% of pop
10 to 14	669734	638856	1308590	12.43
15–19	573196	596254	1169450	11.10
20–29	956487	918411	1874898	17.80
30–39	592535	555531	1148066	10.90
40–49	367840	356046	723886	6.87
50–59	229284	223504	452788	4.30
60–69	135082	131307	266389	2.53
70–79	57772	58336	116108	1.10
80–89	15806	17434	33240	0.32
90–99	2041	2523	4564	0.04
100+	301	238	539	0.01
N/A	5318	0	5318	0.05
Total	5360451	5171115	10531566	
% 40+	15.08	15.27	15.17	
% 50+	8.21	8.38	8.30	
% 60+	3.94	4.06	4.00	
% 70+	1.42	1.52	1.47	
% 80+	0.34	0.39	0.36	
% 90+	0.04	0.05	0.05	

1840	M	F	Total	% of pop
0–4	1270743	1203319	2474062	17.43
5–9	1024050	986940	2010990	14.17
10–14	879530	836630	1716160	12.09
15–19	756106	792223	1548329	10.91
20–29	1322453	1253490	2575943	18.15
30–39	866452	779120	1645572	11.59
40–49	536606	502183	1038789	7.32
50–59	314528	304852	619380	4.36
60–69	174238	173329	347567	2.45
70–79	80067	80565	160632	1.13
80–89	21677	23962	45639	0.32
90–99	2508	3232	5740	0.04
100+	476	316	792	0.01
N/A	6100	0	6100	0.04
Total	7255534	6940161	14195695	

(continued)

(continued)

1840	M	F	Total	% of pop
% 40+	15.58	15.68	15.63	
% 50+	8.18	8.45	8.31	
% 60+	3.84	4.05	3.95	
% 70+	1.44	1.56	1.50	
% 80+	0.34	0.40	0.37	
% 90+	0.04	0.05	0.05	

1850	M	F	Total	% of pop
0–4	1472053	1424405	2896458	14.81
5–9	1372438	1331690	2704128	13.83
10–14	1225575	1176554	2402129	12.29
15–19	1041116	1087600	2128716	10.89
20–29	1869092	1758469	3627561	18.55
30–39	1288682	1128257	2416939	12.36
40–49	840222	748566	1588788	8.13
50–59	498660	459511	958171	4.90
60–69	264742	256480	521222	2.67
70–79	111416	112648	224064	1.15
80–89	31243	34403	65646	0.34
90–99	3653	4499	8152	0.04
100+	357	430	787	0.00
N/A	7153	3154	10307	0.05
Total	10026402	9526666	19553068	
% 40+	17.46	16.97	17.22	
% 50+	9.07	9.11	9.09	
% 60+	4.10	4.29	4.19	
% 70+	1.46	1.60	1.53	
% 80+	0.35	0.41	0.38	
% 90+	0.04	0.05	0.05	

1860	M	F	Total	% of pop
0–4	2091460	2025985	4117445	15.29
5–9	1788711	1739387	3528098	13.10
10–14	1590472	1523281	3113753	11.57
15–19	1400536	1452045	2852581	10.60
20–29	2497210	2420139	4917349	18.26
30–39	1867378	1636213	3503591	13.01

(continued)

(continued)

1860	M	F	Total	% of pop
40–49	1224086	1058246	2282332	8.48
50–59	740429	659246	1399675	5.20
60–69	400862	380011	780873	2.90
70–79	153649	156583	310232	1.15
80–89	38001	42753	80754	0.30
90–99	4135	5634	9769	0.04
100+	385	542	927	0.00
N/A	14073	11085	25158	0.09
Total	13811387	13111150	26922537	
% 40+	18.55	17.57	18.07	
% 50+	9.68	9.49	9.59	
% 60+	4.32	4.47	4.39	
% 70+	1.42	1.57	1.49	
% 80+	0.31	0.37	0.34	
% 90+	0.03	0.05	0.04	

Data drawn from Haines, Michael R., "White population, by sex and age: 1790–1990." Table Aa287-364 in *Historical Statistics of the United States, Earliest Times to the Present: Millennial Edition*, edited by Susan B. Carter, Scott Sigmund Gartner, Michael R. Haines, Alan L. Olmstead, Richard Sutch, and Gavin Wright. New York: Cambridge University Press, 2006.

rapidity."[34] Despite regional distinctions, then, demographic trends show sufficient continuity to allow for a wide-ranging discussion on old age in the American South.

* * *

My concern is less, however, with chronological age than with exploring intersubjective perceptions of the aging process and intergenerational dynamics – in other words, showing how people understood embodied time in a relational and functional context, used temporal language to position themselves and others in social hierarchies – and considering the consequences

[34] Individual state returns drawn from 1820, 1840, 1850, and 1860 censuses. The national average for whites aged fifty plus from 1830 to 1860 was 9 percent. Average drawn from data presented in Haines, "White population, by sex and age: 1790–1990." Quote: Emmons, "Piety, a Peculiar Ornament to the Aged," 499.

of such positioning.[35] Theologian and philosopher Michael Coors argues that "understanding aging is not only about understanding the embodied Self, but always about understanding how the embodied Self interacts with other embodied Selves,"[36] and Kirsi Pauliina Kallio and Mary E. Thomas show that age is an identity that "gains sensibility through performative experiences, struggles, and intersections through a range of social meaning." They insist that age can only be "experienced in relation to others and made specific and contingent through contexts of encounter."[37] These wider theoretical positions are of value when assessing antebellum perceptions of, and experiences relating to, old age. Contemporary discussions on aging were situational and intersubjective. People may have been considered "old" in some settings, and by some observers, but not in or by others; these unstable categorizations could inspire reflection or, indeed, tension.[38] Emmons noted, for example, "How many have been startled the first time they heard themselves called old, or the first time they realized themselves to be so!" Contemporaries used terms such as "old" or "elder" fluidly, and so do I. As Emmons pithily put it, "Children always think their parents are old."[39]

Moreover, the hardships of slavery, commonly said to have sped up the physical effects of aging, detached the concept of old age from consistent chronological moorings and underscored the embodied nature of time's passage. Josiah Henson recalled stopping at a Vicksburg plantation on the way to New Orleans, where he faced sale from his conniving enslaver. Some of his "old companions" now lived there and Henson was devastated by their decline: "It was the saddest visit I ever made. Four years in an unhealthy climate and under a hard master had done the ordinary work

---

[35] On chronological, functional, and comparative readings to "old age," see Thane, *Old Age in English History*, 4; Steven Mintz, "Reflections on Age as a Category of Analysis," *Journal of the History of Childhood and Youth*, 1.1 (Winter, 2008), 90–4; Corinne T. Field and Nicholas L. Syrett (Eds.), "AHR Roundtable: Chronological Age: A Useful Category of Historical Analysis," *American Historical Review* 125 (April 2020), 371–459; Alexander R. Schwall, "Defining Age and Using Age-Relevant Constructs," in Walter C. Borman and Jerry W. Hedge (Eds.), *The Oxford Handbook of Work and Aging* (Oxford: Oxford University Press, 2012), 170–86. On age and intergenerational dynamics as relational, see Kirsi Pauliina Kallio and Mary E. Thomas, "Intergenerational Encounters, Intersubjective Age Relations," *Emotion, Space, and Society*, 32 (2019), 1–4, 2. On embodied time, see Michael Coors, "Embodied Time: The Narrative Refiguration of Aging," in Schweda et al. (Eds.), *Aging and Human Nature*, 129–41, 133.
[36] Coors, "Embodied Time," 133.
[37] Kallio and Thomas, "Intergenerational Encounters," 2.
[38] Schwall, "Defining Age and Using Age-Relevant Constructs," 172–7.
[39] Emmons, "Piety, a Peculiar Ornament to the Aged," 493, 492.

of twenty."[40] Enslaved people were thus commonly depicted as "prematurely worn out by labor, and the whip, hunger, and the branding iron."[41] Henson's former companions may not have been chronologically old, but their experience of body, health, and self told a different story. Henson became convinced of the need to escape after seeing their premature aging, telling himself: "If this is to be my lot, I cannot survive it long. I am not so young as those whose wretched condition I have but just seen, and if it has brought them to such a condition, it will soon kill me."[42] Such subjective elements of perception – both personal and public – are critical to this book and to wider understandings of embodied time. I examine age as a functional category, metaphor, and symbol, as a means of comparatively constructing identities, and ultimately as a relation of power, rather than exploring the demographics of antebellum slavery or medicalized understandings of aging.[43] In delineating the contexts and consequences of assessments of "old age" among enslaved people and their enslavers, I underscore how far age factored into the conflict and negotiations within enslaved communities, and between enslaved people and their enslavers.

The book therefore also contributes to work on enslavers and notions of mastery itself. Much existing work stresses the significance enslavers and their peers accorded to public demonstrations of power, dominance

---

[40] Josiah Henson, *"Uncle Tom's Story of His Life."An Autobiography of the Rev. Josiah Henson (Mrs. Harriet Beecher Stowe's "Uncle Tom")* ... (London: Christian Age Office, 1876), 67.

[41] William G. Hawkins, *Lunsford Lane; or, Another Helper from North Carolina* (Boston: Crosby & Nichols, 1863), 187–8.

[42] Henson, *"Uncle Tom's Story of His Life,"* 69–70.

[43] On these topics, see Fogel and Engerman, *Time on the Cross*; Michael Tadman, *Speculators and Slaves: Masters, Traders, and Slaves in the Old South* (Madison: University of Wisconsin Press, 1996 [1989]); Steven Deyle, *Carry Me Back: The Domestic Slave Trade in American Life* (Oxford: Oxford University Press, 2005); Todd L. Savitt, *Medicine and Slavery: The Diseases and Health Care of Blacks in Antebellum Virginia* (Urbana: University of Illinois Press, 1981); Peter McCandless, *Slavery, Disease, and Suffering in the Southern Lowcountry* (New York: Cambridge University Press, 2012); Jim Downs, *Sick from Freedom: African American Illness and Suffering During the Civil War and Reconstruction* (Oxford: Oxford University Press, 2012); Marie Jenkins Schwartz, *Birthing a Slave: Motherhood and Medicine in the Antebellum South* (Cambridge, Mass.: Harvard University Press, 2006); Marli F. Weiner, *Sex, Sickness, and Slavery: Illness in the Antebellum South* (Urbana: University of Illinois Press, 2012); Dea H. Boster, *African American Slavery and Disability: Bodies, Property, and Power in the Antebellum South, 1800–1860* (New York: Routledge, 2013); Stefanie Hunt-Kennedy, *Between Fitness and Death: Disability and Slavery in the Caribbean* (Urbana: University of Illinois Press, 2020); Barclay, *The Mark of Slavery*.

of others, and independence, increasingly including women in these analyses.[44] Scholars have examined the transition from infancy to adolescence then maturity, the roles of white men and women in the "prime of life," and death in the antebellum South.[45] Few have considered, however, how the march of time affected the performance of mastery. General studies on old age in American history, moreover, rarely examine the US South. Instead, most studies focus on northern states, moving rapidly through earlier periods before concentrating on the late nineteenth and early twentieth centuries.[46] In contrast, I emphasize how enslavers – men and women – adapted to, resisted, or failed to overcome changes associated with age, both real and imagined. I show the consequences of these actions and choices in southern communities, Black and white.

* * *

Gender, to paraphrase Joan Scott, is everywhere.[47] However, although I address gender and age throughout the text, I do not foreground it. The book hopes to lay the groundwork for future studies of age as crucially determining multiple aspects of the experience of slavery. I have thus

---

[44] See note 4.

[45] See, for example, Greenberg, *Honor and Slavery*, 91–97; Glover, *Southern Sons*; Stephen Berry, *Princes of Cotton: Four Diaries of Young Men in the South, 1848–1860* (Athens: University of Georgia Press, 2007); Craig Thompson Friend and Lorri Glover (Eds.), *Death and the American South* (New York: Cambridge University Press, 2014); Jones-Rogers, *They Were Her Property*.

[46] See, for example, W. Andrew Achenbaum, *Old Age in the New Land: The American Experience since 1790* (Baltimore: Johns Hopkins University Press, 1978); David Hackett Fischer, *Growing Old in America* (New York: Oxford University Press, 1978); Howard P. Chudacoff, *How Old Are You? Age Consciousness in American Culture* (Princeton: University of Princeton Press, 1989); Thomas R. Cole, *The Journey of Life: A Cultural History of Aging in America* (New York: Cambridge University Press, 1992); Susannah R. Ottaway, Lynn A. Botelho, and Katharine Kittredge, *Power and Poverty: Old Age in the Pre-Industrial Past* (Westport: Greenwood Press, 2002); Gregory Wood, *Retiring Men: Manhood, Labor, and Growing Old in America, 1900–1960* (Lanham: Lexington Books, 2012); Field and Syrett (Eds.), *Age in America*; Field and Syrett (Eds.), "Chronological Age: A Useful Category of Historical Analysis." Field's *Struggle for Equal Adulthood* predominantly refers to slavery in the context of youth/maturity. Work that covers the US South has not addressed aging in the context of mastery. See Carole Haber and Brian Gratton, "Old Age, Public Welfare and Race: The Case of Charleston, South Carolina 1800–1949," *Journal of Social History*, 21. 2 (1987), 263–79; Carole Haber and Brian Gratton, *Old Age and the Search for Security: An American Social History* (Bloomington: Indiana University Press, 1994).

[47] Joan Scott, "Gender: A Useful Category of Analysis," *American Historical Review*, 91.5 (1986), 1053–75, 1067.

taken a macro-level approach where the focus is explicitly on demonstrating the importance of age to structuring slavery as a system of exploitation. However, if we recognize gender as coalescing around specific attributes and behaviors, rather than specifically related to sex-based identity, then the book reveals that negative characterizations of old age, such as dependency and frailty, had much in common with antebellum characterizations of femininity/effeminacy. The thrust of much gender history is to portray these characteristics as inherently gendered, and then to argue outward from that position, so that gender is the primary relation of power within this analytic framework. As Jeanne Boydston argues, however, it can be more productive to think in terms of power and then work outward to understand how different subject positions are aligned upon the axis of weak/strong – and therefore what they have in common – rather than awarding any one subject position primacy.[48] This approach enables recognition of commonalities in how the dominant discourse perceives Black/feminine/old age but does not assume that gender (or race) is always prior to age. My focus on age does not preclude others training the lens on gender, and I hope perhaps to illuminate aspects of gendered experience by refracting gender through the less well-studied lens of age.

Old Age and American Slavery suggests, in fact, that within particular contexts age can be more important than gender: in some cases of neglect and abandonment of enslaved elders, younger white slavers overriding the power of old white slavers, or younger Black people gaining positions of authority over old enslaved people there are obviously differences in the specifics of the experience according to gender, but they do not affect the pattern of experience at the same fundamental level as age. In many of the cases noted herein, the power play was predicated on loss of power or authority due to age, rather than gendered differences; the male and female white slavers/enslaved people alike were judged on their age and challenged by those younger than them, and the difference gender makes was only in the form the power play took. In arguing thus, I hope to further establish age as an important category of analysis in its own right.[49]

* * *

[48] Jeanne Boydston, "Gender as a Question of Historical Analysis," *Gender & History*, 20.3 (2008), 558–83, 573.
[49] My thinking in this paragraph has been developed in conversation with Tracey Loughran and in private correspondence, 16/08/22.

This book is deliberately polemical. Aging is, of course, "a multi-faceted phenomenon which includes processes of gain and processes of loss, experiences of competence and experiences of deficit."[50] Here, however, I prioritize *only* the disruptions contemporaries associated with aging, the difficulties people believed they faced as they grew older, and moments of intergenerational tension. This was not the only type of relationship between generations, or between Black and white, and growing older was not always and inevitably perceived as a negative. Yet in focusing near entirely on intergenerational support systems among the enslaved, the overall effect of the scholarship to date has been to flatten the necessarily complex relationships enslaved people forged with one another in the context of oppression.[51] I deliberately focus on tension in the hope not only of inspiring conversation, disagreement, and debate, but also of demonstrating in new ways the corrosive effects of slavery on the identities and experiences of all within the system.

There is more variation in relation to perceptions of white aging, but W. A. Achenbaum's recent statement that "being old and becoming older in antebellum America did not connote loss of functionality" serves as an intriguing point to start interrogating the significance of age and intergenerational conflict in the context of slavery and enslaver identity.[52] Accordingly, I again focus entirely on those occasions when enslavers believed that advanced age meant they, or others, were unable to "function" as "masters." This approach forces deeper reflection on social tension in white communities and on how age, as much as gender, race, and class, shaped hierarchies and power dynamics in the American South. Indeed, it disrupts static notions of mastery. Historians have done tremendous work in exploring the violence enslavers practiced for profit.[53] In presenting

---

[50] Heinz Rüegger, "Beyond Control: Dependence and Passivity in Old Age," in Schweda et al. (Eds.), *Aging and Human Nature*, 47–57, 48.

[51] See note 7. Scholars who have emphasized conflict in the community, albeit without foregrounding age, include Peter Kolchin, "Re-Evaluating the Antebellum Slave Community," *Journal of American History*, 70.3 (1983), 579–601; Stevenson, *Life in Black and White*; William Dusinberre, *Them Dark Days: Slavery in the American Rice Swamps* (New York: Oxford University Press, 1996); Orlando Patterson, *Rituals of Blood: Consequences of Slavery in Two American Centuries* (Washington, DC: Civitas/Counterpoint, 1998); Dylan Penningroth, *The Claims of Kinfolk: African American Property and Community in the Nineteenth Century South* (Chapel Hill: University of North Carolina Press, 2003); Jeff Forret, *Slave Against Slave: Plantation Violence in the Old South* (Baton Rouge: Louisiana State University Press, 2015).

[52] Achenbaum, "Delineating Old Age," 303.

[53] See, in particular, Walter Johnson, *River of Dark Dreams: Slavery and Empire in the Cotton Kingdom* (Cambridge, Mass.: Harvard University Press, 2013); Edward E. Baptist, *The Half*

enslavers as such dominant figures, however, there is a danger that we confirm their mythology of dominance even while rejecting their claims of benevolence. Enslavers, however cruel and capricious, could not stop time from marching on. The pressures associated with aging, both real and imagined, could wreak havoc on their public and private claims to power. These old slavers are not objects of pity. Their struggles with "time's relentless hand," however, deepen understanding of the interpersonal mechanisms of slavery as an exploitative system; they show how age operated as a vector of power that intersected with race, gender, and class, and which shaped wider concerns over control, exploitation, resistance, and survival in a slave society.[54] Their fates further reveal the all-encompassing effects of the culture of exploitation that drove life in antebellum slavery.

* * *

Sowande' M. Mustakeem's work on the terrors of the Middle Passage reveals how far age-related concerns factored into the dynamics of slavery and resistance in the colonial era.[55] Here, I focus on the early republic and antebellum decades of American slavery, when age categories were explicitly used to manage manumission in the aftermath of the American Revolution. These laws revolved around the assumption that those above a certain age – ranging from thirty-five to forty-five – would be unable to care for themselves. They provide a wealth of material on approaches to age in the context of slavery, and broader understandings of body, health, and self.[56] Antebellum enslavers could adapt, reject, or

---

Has Never Been Told: Slavery and the Making of American Capitalism(New York: Basic Books, 2014); Sven Beckert, *Empire of Cotton: A Global History* (Cambridge, Mass.: Harvard University Press, 2014); Jones-Rogers, *They Were Her Property*.

[54] Henry Clay, and Felix Octavius Carr Darley, *Odd Leaves from the Life of a Louisiana "Swamp Doctor." In "The Swamp Doctor's Adventures in the South-West. Containing the Whole of the Louisiana Swamp Doctor; Streaks of Squatter Life; and Far-Western Scenes; in a Series of Forty-Two Humorous Southern and Western Sketches ..."* (Philadelphia: T. B. Peterson, 1858), 141–3.

[55] Sowande' M. Mustakeem, *Slavery at Sea: Terror, Sex, and Sickness in the Middle Passage* (Urbana: University of Illinois Press, 2017).

[56] Of the twenty-four manumission by "certificate" acts passed between 1777 and 1864, only five had no age limit: Connecticut in 1777, South Carolina in 1800, New Jersey in 1846, Virginia in 1846, and Missouri in 1864. Connecticut's was changed in 1792 to limit manumission to those under forty-five. New Jersey limited manumission to those between twenty-one to thirty-five in 1786, and changed this to twenty-one to forty in 1798, before scrapping the law in 1846; both Missouri and Virginia limited manumission to those between eighteen and forty-five in 1782 and 1804 and then shifted the categories to twenty-one and forty-five. South Carolina simply eliminated the law in 1820. A number of states also used bond requirements to provide insurance in case of aged and infirm free

resist this type of legislation, but in all cases contemporaries were forced to address the significance of age appertaining to identity, ability, and embodied experience in slavery.

This chronology also places enslavers' protestations around the treatment of elders in the context of the geographic and economic expansion of slavery and the growing political tensions over slavery in the antebellum decades. In this era, existing claims as to the "good" treatment of elders achieved new importance as the politics of paternalism and its associated promises of support from cradle to grave became a vital component of proslavery literature during the antebellum era, and one that was heavily contested by Black activists and abolitionists.[57] In the form of received or denied care for Black elders, age attained crucial political importance in this period.

Across the period, contemporaries showed concern that the process of aging would hinder enslavers' performances of mastery. Cases from the revolutionary era up to the Civil War associated old age with inevitable physical decline, and possibly weakened mental faculties. Antebellum cases sometimes relied on the idea that aged enslavers were incapable of fulfilling the paternalistic bargain. With quite striking consistency, intergenerational disputes revolved around a concern that the aged could not

---

Blacks becoming a "drain" on resources, and/or required emancipated Black people to leave the state. On the breakdown on manumission statutes by age, see Benjamin Joseph Klebaner, "American Manumission Laws and the Responsibility for Supporting Slaves," *Virginia Magazine of History and Biography* 63.4 (1955), 443–53. For wider literature on manumission, see, for example Thomas D. Morris, *Southern Slavery and the Law, 1619–1860* (Chapel Hill: University of North Carolina Press, 1996); T. Stephen Whitman, *The Price of Freedom: Slavery and Manumission in Baltimore and Early National Maryland* (Lexington: University Press of Kentucky, 1997); Bernie D. Jones, *Fathers of Conscience: Mixed-Race Inheritance in the Antebellum South* (Athens: University of Georgia Press, 2009); Yvonne Pitts, *Family, Law, and Inheritance in America: A Social and Legal History of Nineteenth-Century Kentucky* (New York: Cambridge University Press, 2012); Kelly M. Kennington, *In the Shadow of Dred Scott: St Louis Freedom Suits and the Legal Culture of Slavery in Antebellum America* (Athens: University of Georgia Press, 2017); Loren Schweninger, *Appealing for Liberty: Freedom Suits in the South* (New York: Oxford University Press, 2018).

[57] See, for example, Thomas Jefferson, *Notes on the State of Virginia* (Philadelphia: Richard and Hall, 1788), 151. On the cultural and political symbolism of representations of elderly slaves in the postbellum era, see David W. Blight, *Race and Reunion: The Civil War in American Memory*(Cambridge, Mass.: Harvard University Press, 2001), 284–91; Nathaniel Windon, "A Tale of Two Uncles: The Old Age of Uncle Tom and Uncle Remus," *Common-Place*, 17.2 (2017), http://commonplace.online/article/a-tale-of-two-uncles/; Lydia Ferguson, "Pro-Slavery Appropriations and Inadvertent Agencies: The Elder(ly) 'Uncle' in Plantation Fiction," *American Studies*, 58.1 (2019), 49–72.

control the enslaved, and both families and communities were willing to publicly state these fears. These cases therefore reveal broader tensions inherent to slavery; regardless of the proslavery claims of mutual obligations, enslavers understood the "simmering violence inherent to mastery," the attendant need to demonstrate dominance, and the personal and political dangers if individuals were no longer capable of doing so.[58] Throughout the book I show how this mentality fundamentally shaped the contested nature of mastery and resistance, as well as broader concerns with the aging process in a slave society.

The Civil War–era is a natural end-point for this study, but the Conclusion addresses David Blight and Jim Down's recent imperative to "disrupt the history of emancipation" and to recognize "freedom" as a perilous process.[59] This was particularly true for those most vulnerable, including Black elders who had left "their best days behind them."[60] Violet Guntharpe poignantly recalled the aftermath of the Civil War in her Works Progress Administration (WPA) interview: "Lots of de chillun die, as did de old folks."[61] In setting out the problems elders faced in the aftermath of emancipation, the book ends by underscoring the long-lasting violence of American slavery.

* * *

To assess social and cultural constructions of "old" age and their impacts on enslaved and enslaver alike, I draw on diverse textual and visual sources. I analyze contemporaries' uses of chronological markers, temporal metaphors, and discursive labels such as "old," "aged," and "elderly" to describe and evaluate people's abilities and identities, and consider the intersubjective dimensions of embodied time. Michael Coors writes that "we learn to recognize ourselves as bodies by reference to there being other embodied selves like ourselves and we recognize among those others many embodied selves of different bodily appearance." These bodies may be "larger, have different shapes, probably grey hair," and we thus "experience that the other bodies change in time, and we experience that others perceive a change in our bodily appearance. Those differences and changes

---

[58] Vincent Brown, *Tacky's Revolt: The Story of an Atlantic Slave War* (Cambridge, Mass.: Harvard University Press, 2020), 4.

[59] Jim Downs and David Blight (Eds.), *Beyond Freedom: Disrupting the History of Emancipation* (Athens: University of Georgia Press, 2017).

[60] Sterling N. Brown, *My Own Life Story* (Washington, DC: Hamilton Printing, 1924), 7.

[61] George P. Rawick (Ed.), *The American Slave: A Composite Autobiography*, 2.2 (Westport: Greenwood Press, 1972), 217.

are expressed by using the words 'older,' 'younger,' and 'aging.'"[62] My discursive and textual examination thus illuminates contemporaries' feelings about and treatment of people they categorized as old, the changes they associated with aging, and their personal considerations and comparisons on age, health, and self.

I make extensive use of slave testimonies, including nineteenth-century published narratives, postbellum memoirs, and oral histories collected from the Works Progress Administration (WPA) project.[63] The antebellum narratives provide remarkable insight into the structures of slavery, social interactions, personal and public identities, and the politics of abolitionism and emancipation. Their inherent subjectivity, and the complex politics of their production, is less of a burden and more of a boon to scholars seeking to interrogate identities and community dynamics.[64] Critical and creative assessment of the language employed in these texts reveals how elders viewed themselves and were viewed by others, how age affected experiences in – and responses to – bondage, and how abolitionists and Black activist writers figuratively and literally applied concepts of age. The discursive construction of old age in functional, relational, and subjective terms in these texts speaks to the significance of ideas on aging to broader debates surrounding agency, resistance, and survival in (and out of) slavery.

There have been numerous critiques of the WPA interviews conducted with formerly enslaved people in the 1930s, centering on the age of

---

[62] Coors, "Embodied Time," 133.

[63] All published slave narratives cited were sourced at "North American Slave Narratives," *Documenting the American South* (University Library, University of North Carolina at Chapel Hill), https://docsouth.unc.edu/neh/texts.html. The WPA narratives are sourced from George P. Rawick (Ed.), *The American Slave: A Composite Autobiography*, Series *1–2*. 19 Vols. (Westport: Greenwood Press, 1972); Rawick (Ed.), *The American Slave: A Composite Autobiography, Supplement, Series 1*. 12 Vols. (Westport: Greenwood Press, 1977); Rawick (Ed.), *The American Slave: A Composite Autobiography, Supplement, Series 2*. 10 Vols. (Westport: Greenwood Press, 1979); and *Federal Writers' Project: Slave Narrative Project* (1936), Manuscript/Mixed Material. www .loc.gov/collections/slave-narratives-from-the-federal-writers-project-1936-to-1938/about-this-collection/. FWP volumes are organized by state/interviewee name. Hereafter cited as Rawick (Ed.), *AS*, with volume/edition number, and FWP by state.

[64] The case for their usage has been exhaustively made. On the debates, see John Blassingame, "Using the Testimony of Ex-Slaves: Approaches and Problems," *Journal of Southern History*, 41.4 (1975), 473–92; Charles T. Davis and Henry Louis Gates Jr. (Eds.), *The Slave's Narrative* (New York: Oxford University Press, 1985); essays in John Ernest (Ed.), *The Oxford Handbook of the American Slave Narratives* (New York: Oxford University Press, 2014); David Stefan Doddington and Elizabeth Maeve Barnes, "Engaging with Sources: Slave Narratives," *Bloomsbury History: Theory and Method Articles* (London: Bloomsbury Publishing, 2021). http://dx.doi.org/10.5040/9781350970892.089

respondents – both in terms of their youth while enslaved and their advanced age at point of interview – and the impact of segregation, racial violence, and the Depression on the stories relayed and recorded.[65] As with fugitive narratives, however, the subjectivity and selective memories of the respondents should be embraced in the present context. Many of the formerly enslaved repeated stories told by or about their families; this suggests that the oral tradition was not simply a means by which Black Americans interpreted and attempted to understand the collective legacy of slavery, but that it also framed their most personal memories and identities.[66] A critical reading of the testimonies illuminates tropes and ideas that enslaved people used to make sense of their lives and provides insight into relationships between enslaved people and their enslavers. The testimonies are particularly useful in exploring the quotidian elements of enslavement: suggested questions for case workers typically focused on the day-to-day activities of enslaved people. Moreover, because the majority of interviewees were legally emancipated in 1865, the interviews are not bound by the necessary emphasis on permanent flight in the fugitive narratives and their subsequent teleological construction.[67]

WPA respondents were typically enslaved in childhood and therefore predominantly over the age of seventy when interviewed. Scholars have suggested this limits their usefulness.[68] However, this age-related concern is helpful in the context of this book. As shall be discussed, elders frequently held responsibilities over children deemed too young for work, and thus many respondents recorded their encounters with Black elders and addressed intergenerational relationships in some detail. The

---

[65] On the WPA narratives, see Blassingame, "Using the Testimony of Ex-Slaves"; Paul D. Escott, *Slavery Remembered: A Record of Twentieth Century Slave-Narratives* (Chapel Hill: University of North Carolina Press, 1979); David Thomas Bailey, "A Divided Prism: Two Sources of Black Testimony on Slavery," *Journal of Southern History*, 46.3 (1980), 381–404; Donna Spindel, "Assessing Memory: Twentieth-Century Slave Narratives Reconsidered," *Journal of Interdisciplinary History*, 27.2 (Autumn, 1996), 247–61; Sharon Ann Musher, "Contesting 'The Way the Almighty Wants It': Crafting Memories of Ex-Slaves in the Slave Narrative Collection," *American Quarterly*, 53.1 (2001), 1–31; Edward E. Baptist, "'Stol' and Fetched Here': Enslaved Migration, Ex-slave Narratives, and Vernacular History," in Edward E. Baptist and Stephanie M. H. Camp (Eds.), *New Studies in the History of American Slavery* (Athens: University of Georgia Press, 2006), 243–74.

[66] Baptist, "Stol' and Fetched Here," 245.

[67] Charles L. Perdue Jr., Thomas E. Barden, and Robert K. Phillips (Eds.), *Weevils in the Wheat: Interviews with Virginia Ex-Slaves* (Charlottesville: University of Virginia Press, 1992), xxxiv–xxxvi, 367–76.

[68] Spindel, "Assessing Memory."

experiences of aging are not timeless, but respondents frequently made reference to their own advanced age, openly voiced their anger at a perceived lack of respect from the younger generation, and also compared their experiences and ailments while enslaved and free. Used in conjunction with contemporaneous records, the WPA narratives enable the identification of similarities in recollections and representations of aging across time, which in turn suggests continuities in approaches to age and subsequent intergenerational tension in southern communities, Black and white, over the longer period.

I also engage with a wide range of material from white society, including plantation journals, letters, travel accounts, diaries, medical treatises, and political and prescriptive literature for and by enslavers. This material demonstrates how age factored into enslavers' identities, and their private and public performances of dominance and mastery – both over enslaved people and within the white community. I use legal records – civil and criminal – to explore tensions between white southerners and to illuminate how age shaped broader concerns with authority and control. Although legal conventions mean that testimony was often deliberately antagonistic, scholars have shown that the courts were an important site for the construction of a sociocultural and legal discourse around body, health, and self.[69] Kimberly Welch reiterates how, even if we cannot be certain of the "truth" claims of petitioners, litigants, and defendants, tales told in a courtroom "had to be recognizable to the other participants. They had to be plausible and fit into other narratives."[70] Participants in the legal process had to speak to and through a recognizable discourse to make their case, whether true or false. The courtroom was thus an arena where ideas on the aging process were applied, contested, and reinforced when making judgments on the actions and identities of enslavers.

* * *

[69] Ariela J. Gross, *Double Character: Slavery and Mastery in the Antebellum Southern Courtroom* (Princeton: Princeton University Press, 2000), 98. Wider scholarship on the complexity to, dangers of, and riches within, legal records, including both depositions and courtroom testimony, which has influenced me includes Natalie Zemon Davis,*Fiction in the Archives: Pardon Tales and Their Tellers in Sixteenth-Century France* (Stanford: Stanford University Press, 1987), 5, 21; Carolyn Steedman, *Dust* (Manchester: Manchester University Press, 2001), esp. ch. 3; Frances E. Dolan, *True Relations: Reading, Literature, and Evidence in Seventeenth-Century England* (Philadelphia: University of Pennsylvania Press, 2013), 113–18.

[70] Kimberly M. Welch, *Black Litigants in the Antebellum American South* (Chapel Hill: University of North Carolina Press, 2018), 46.

The book is split in two. Part I shows how understandings of the aging process affected the dynamics of slavery, with particular attention to the continued exploitation of elders and the efforts of enslavers to rid themselves of responsibilities and costs by selling, abandoning, or neglecting Black elders. Proslavery polemicists – antebellum and beyond – sought to "portray a civilization now obsolete, to picture the relations of mutual attachment and kindness which in the main bound together master and servant." In doing so, they frequently claimed that "no tillers of the soil, in ancient or modern times, received such ample compensation for their labors."[71] This section underscores the mendacity of such paternalistic claims, with chapters showing the continued work expected of elders, the abuse of enslaved people deemed unsound on account of advanced age, and enslavers' cynical efforts to sell, abandon, or neglect those whom they believed were no longer productive. I then consider how age shaped social hierarchies and interpersonal relations among the enslaved themselves, looking at intergenerational struggles in work, leisure time, and community affairs. In contrast to existing scholarship, this section shows how support for Black elders was conditional and sometimes contested. The section concludes with a provocative challenge to the dominant historiographical vision of unquestioned respect for Black elders among the enslaved and considers how survival strategies might conflict with rather than reinforce notions of resistance.

Part II focuses on the pressures enslavers faced as they aged. Proslavery writers commonly presented an image of mastery as innate and inviolable. Patrick Hues Mell noted that "God, in his wisdom, has instituted the family gradations, has established the relation of master and servant, of governor and governed, and commanded each to be content with the situation in which he is placed."[72] Rhetoric was not reality, and this section reveals the concerns of white southerners when they felt "the infirmities of age growing upon [them] very sensibly."[73] I begin by showing how far enslaved people understood that mastery was

---

[71] R. Q. Mallard, *Plantation Life Before Emancipation* (Richmond: Whittet & Shepperson, 1892), vi, 36.

[72] Patrick Hues Mell, *Slavery: A Treatise, Showing That Slavery Is Neither a Moral, Political, nor Social Evil* (Penfield: Printed by Benj. Brantly, 1844), 21.

[73] Diary of Benjamin Leonard Covington Wailes, August 1, 1861, *Records of Antebellum Southern Plantations from the Revolution through the Civil War*, Series N: *Selections from the Mississippi Department of Archives and History* (microfilm; Frederick, Md., 1985–), reel 19. All references from the *Records of Antebellum Southern Plantations* were consulted at Library of Congress (LOC).

embodied, not innate, and that, as the enslaver's body grew "withered by time," so too might their pretensions of control.[74] The subsequent chapters demonstrate how antebellum whites responded to fears of a loss of mastery on account of age, exploring both enslavers' efforts to exploit this for their own gain and the actions of those who were forced to respond to the depredations of others. The final chapter reveals how, when elderly enslavers proposed emancipation, rivals utilized a discourse that conflated old age with weakness, both of body and mind, to challenge this final expression of mastery. Their efforts to do so, whether successful or not, serve to underscore the personal and political concerns with aging in a society built on exploitation and expressions of power. The recognition of enslaved and enslaver alike that "the ravages of time" came for all shaped the dynamics of American slavery.[75]

Old Age and American Slavery reveals how antebellum southerners adapted to, resisted, or failed to overcome changes associated with age, both real and imagined. It connects concerns with aging to wider debates over strategies of control, survival, and dominance in slavery. In examining how individuals, families, and communities felt about the aging process and dealt with elders, I emphasize the complex and contested social relations that developed in a slave society. Showing how old age ran through the arguments of Black activists, abolitionists, proslavery propagandists, and enslavers, I reveal how representations – and the realities – of aging spoke to wider debates on the politics of paternalism and resistance. Ultimately, by illuminating age as a crucial aspect of the complex web of relations that bound together enslavers and enslaved, this book asks readers to rethink existing narratives relating to networks of solidarity in the American South. It emphasizes the all-encompassing violence and exploitation of American slavery.

[74] Diary of Benjamin Leonard Covington Wailes, July 17, 1860.
[75] W. A. Riddlemoser, "Conception in the Human Female," 1843–4, Box 150, Part II, Joseph Meredith Toner Collection of Manuscripts (Manuscript Division, LOC, Washington, DC).

PART I

THE ENSLAVED

"As to those more advanced in life"

Old Age in Slavery

American slavery was a brutal system of exploitation in which white enslavers forced Black people to work for them. Debates continue to rage over whether enslavers were capitalists or how far the US – and the global – economy was shaped by slavery in the Americas, but there is general consensus among scholars that enslavers were profit-driven and focused on extracting the maximum labor from the people whom they enslaved. This manifested in violence, strategic "management," commercial and capital investment, crop innovations, and the forging of global financial trade networks.[1] It also meant that enslavers sought to exploit enslaved people "from youth to grey hairs."[2] Enslavers were cruelly adept

---

[1] On these debates, see, for example, Eric Williams, *Capitalism and Slavery* (Chapel Hill: University of North Carolina Press, 1944); Fogel and Engerman, *Time on the Cross*; Johnson, *River of Dark Dreams*; Baptist, *The Half Has Never Been Told*; Beckert, *Empire of Cotton*; Berry, *The Price for Their Pound of Flesh*; Caitlin Rosenthal, *Accounting for Slavery: Masters and Management* (Cambridge, Mass.: Harvard University Press, 2018); Scott Reynolds Nelson, "Who Put Their Capitalism in My Slavery?" *Journal of the Civil War Era*, 5.2 (2015), 289–310; John E. Murray, Alan L. Olmstead, Trevon D. Logan, Jonathon B. Pritchett, and Peter L. Rousseau, "The Half Has Never Been Told: Slavery and the Making of American Capitalism," *Journal of Economic History*, 75.3 (2015), 919–31; James Oakes, "Capitalism and Slavery and the Civil War," *International Labor and Working-Class History*, 89 (2016), 195–220; Peter Coclanis, "Slavery, Capitalism, and the Problem of Misprision," *Journal of American Studies*, 52 (2018), 1–9; John Clegg, "A Theory of Capitalist Slavery," *Journal of Historical Sociology*, 33.1 (2020), 74–98; Gavin Wright, "Slavery and Anglo-American Capitalism Revisited," *Economic History Review*, 73.2 (2020), 353–83.

[2] Mary L. Cox and Susan H. Cox, *Narrative of Dimmock Charlton, a British Subject, Taken from the Brig "Peacock" by the US Sloop "Hornet," Enslaved while a Prisoner of War, and Retained Forty-Five Years in Bondage* (Philadelphia: The Editors, 1859), 1.

at assessing the temporal rhythms of the life cycle and adapting to the demands of embodied time when structuring their workforce. As with enslavers' other interactions with Black elders, this flexibility stemmed from economic self-interest and a desire for dominance, not concern for enslaved peoples' well-being – and it came at a great cost for these individuals and the wider slave community.

Within the emerging political rhetoric of paternalism, proslavery propagandists proclaimed enslavers' support for elderly slaves was "an example and mark of fidelity of the master, in consideration for the fidelity and loyalty of his servant."[3] Enslavers, however, were attuned to the temporalities of the aged body and adept at developing flexible work regimes designed to maximize the labor of those whom they enslaved.[4] Elizabeth Fox-Genovese and Eugene Genovese argued that, in theory, "when [enslavers'] interest and humanity clashed, piety and honor demanded a decision for humanity."[5] Nevertheless, minding Michael Tadman's injunction in his exploration of "key slaves" to explore what enslavers "did to slaves, rather than what they said they did," it is clear that proslavery claims of a leisurely retirement for the aged were mostly baseless.[6] When Abram Childress of Henrico County, Virginia, explained

---

[3] James H. Easterby and Daniel C. Littlefield (Eds.), *The South Carolina Rice Plantation, as Revealed in the Papers of Robert F. W. Allston* (Columbia: University of South Carolina Press, 2004), 348. On paternalism and cultural hegemony, see Genovese, *Roll, Jordan, Roll*, 25–49, 147–9, 597. Further development of this thinking includes Elizabeth Fox-Genovese and Eugene Genovese, *The Mind of the Master Class: History and Faith in the Southern Slaveholder's Worldview* (New York: Cambridge University Press, 2005) and *Fatal Self-Deception: Slaveholding Paternalism in the Old South* (New York: Cambridge University Press, 2011). On the nineteenth-century development of paternalism as a political ideology, see Lacy Ford, *Deliver Us from Evil: The Slavery Question in the Old South* (New York: Oxford University Press, 2009), especially chapters 5–6. On paternalism and historiography, see Kathleen M. Hilliard, *Masters, Slaves, and Exchange: Power's Purchase in the Old South* (New York: Cambridge University Press, 2014), 2–5, 184–5; Walter Johnson, "A Nettlesome Classic Turns Twenty-Five," *Common-Place*, 1.4 (2001); Tadman, *Speculators and Slaves*, xix–xxxvii; Windon, "Superannuated," 768.

[4] The "fixed-cost" character of slavery meant that "owners strove to keep slaves busy at all times of the year," but this has rarely been tied directly into assessments of strategies toward elders. See Ralph V. Anderson and Robert E. Gallman, "Slaves as Fixed Capital: Slave Labor and Southern Economic Development," *Journal of American History*, 64.1 (1977), 24–46; Wright, "Slavery and Anglo-American Capitalism Revisited," 372.

[5] Fox-Genovese and Genovese, *Mind of the Master Class*, 368.

[6] Tadman, *Speculators and Slaves*, xx–xxi and xxxi–xxxvi. Tadman explains that select individuals, usually drivers or senior domestic figures, are overrepresented in archival (slaver) sources on enslaved/enslaver relations, and that these figures had a degree of privilege that served a practical function in plantation management, but also an ideological

that "depreciation, natural to slaves in the decline of life," meant his slaves were "diminishing in value every year," he did not tenderly care for them because of a "bond of interest" between master and slave.[7] Instead, Childress proposed to sell Martin and Elizabeth, two enslaved people who were passed down to his children from their grandfather. He wanted rid of those "in the decline of life" before they became "worthless and a charge upon their owners."[8] The courts granted his request and Martin and Elizabeth were sold. The profits were presumably used to purchase the bodies of those increasing in value.

* * *

The rhythms of agricultural labor shaped the lives of most enslaved people across the US South.[9] On plantations, farms, and smallholdings, the work enslaved people did from "the dawn of day in the morning, till the darkness was complete in the evening" required stamina, skill, and strength.[10] This physically, mentally, and emotionally taxing labor required reckoning with the inevitability of aging and its bodily effects. Enslavers typically measured the laboring qualities of enslaved people through a dynamic system wherein "prime" or "full hand" described the ideal worker. Antebellum slavers were desperate to obtain and utilize these "prime hands," conjuring up neat images of people as "a commodity: alienable, easily sold, and, in important ways, rendered effectively identical for white entrepreneurs' direct manipulation."[11] Enslavers understood, however, that enslaved people

role for enslavers. As Tadman explains, "the favoring of key slaves had the critically important role of allowing a slaveholder to tell himself or herself that he or she treated slaves well. The all-important thing was that, by considering that they treated 'worthy' and 'more sensible' slaves (key slaves) well, they could treat the rest with racist indifference – and could still maintain a self-image of benevolence" (p. xxxii).

[7] Fox-Genovese and Genovese, *Mind of the Master Class*, 368.

[8] Petition of Abram Childress, November 5, 1855, Franklin County Virginia, #21685519, Race and Slavery Petitions Project, Series 2. Race and Slavery Petitions Project (University Libraries, University of North Carolina at Greensboro), accessed via the "Slavery and the Law (1775–1867)" module of the subscription database ProQuest History Vault; hereinafter cited as RSPP. For an accessible searchable index of the RSPP, see http://library .uncg.edu/slavery/petitions.

[9] Enslaved people worked in urban and industrial environments but the production and sale of commercial cash-crops – cotton, rice, grains, sugar – were the main drivers of the slave economy. For overviews, see Richard Follett, Sven Beckert, Peter Coclanis, and Barbara Hahn, *Plantation Kingdom: The American South and Its Global Commodities* (Baltimore: Johns Hopkins University Press, 2017).

[10] Douglass, *My Bondage and My Freedom*, 215.

[11] Baptist, *The Half Has Never Been Told*, 101; Rosenthal, *Accounting for Slavery*, 144; Berry, *Price for Their Pound of Flesh*, 68.

were not bloodless commodities. As Frederick Douglass wrote, slavers knew they "had to deal not with earth, wood, and stone, but with men; and by every regard they had for their safety and prosperity they had need to know the material on which they were to work."[12]

An aging workforce was a problem for enslavers seeking "prosperity," as they knew that the physical deterioration of enslaved people over time would lead to ever-diminishing returns. Thomas Chaplin of South Carolina was disgusted at the thought of having to provide for those who did nothing to profit him. After listing the nine hands he was able to use in the fields, he listed the elderly slaves and children as "those that eat & do nothing in the world for me."[13] Benjamin Boulware, also of South Carolina, pleaded the necessity of offloading a group of enslaved people from his nephew's estate because they were "growing old" and he did not want such obligations. Boulware, who served as trustee, argued that these elders were "in a deteriorating condition and depreciating in value every day."[14] Time's march was measured in dollars lost, and Boulware successfully rid himself of those who did "nothing" for him.

The desire to replace those who had given the "best years and the best strength of [their] life," as Frederick Douglass described one elder, with children born in (and of) oppression brings home the cyclical horrors of enslavement.[15] As the executors of William Locke, a Tennessee enslaver, explained when trying to sell his land instead of enslaved people, although his five old slaves were "worthless," the youngsters were "fast increasing in Value and in a few years will be worth more to the Heirs than the whole of the land."[16] Daina Ramey Berry and Jennifer Morgan, to name but a few, have clearly demonstrated that enslaved women's (re)productive exploitation was shaped by age and embodied time.[17] In 1857 Rachel Jane

[12] Frederick Douglass, *Life and Times of Frederick Douglass, His Early Life as a Slave, His Escape from Bondage, and His Complete History to This Time* ... (Hartford: Park Publishing Co., 1881), 156.

[13] Theodore Rosengarten (Ed.), *Tombee: Portrait of a Cotton Planter* (New York: Quill/William Morrow, 1986), 488.

[14] Petition of Benjamin Boulware, July 12, 1859, Fairfield District, South Carolina, #21385955, Series 2, RSPP.

[15] Douglass, *My Bondage and My Freedom*, 112–14.

[16] Petition of Elizabeth Locke et al., c. 1832, Jackson County, Tennessee, #11483213, Series 1, RSPP.

[17] Berry, *Price for Their Pound of Flesh*, especially ch. 1. On reproductive exploitation and slavery more generally, see Jennifer Morgan, *Laboring Women: Gender and Reproduction in the Making of New World Slavery* (Philadelphia: University of Pennsylvania Press, 2004); Jennifer Morgan, *Reckoning with Slavery: Gender, Kinship, and Capitalism in the early Black Atlantic* (Durham: Duke University Press, 2020).

Boland sought permission to sell an enslaved woman who was "old and of very little value." She wanted to replace her with a younger woman "whose labor & increase will greatly promote their interest." The request was granted and, aged fifty-eight, Rebecca was sold.[18] Louise Mathews, enslaved in Texas, emphasized the naked self-interest of enslavers in making decisions about age and productivity; her enslaver counselled to "take good care de young'uns, 'cause de old ones gwine play out some-time, and I wants de young'uns to grow strong."[19]

FIGURE 1.1 *Louise Mathews, ex-slave, Ft. Worth.* United States Fort Worth Texas, 1937. Nov. 9. Photograph. Courtesy of the Library of Congress, Washington, DC.

[18] Petition of Rachel Jane Boland, December 7, 1857, Wilkinson County, Mississippi, #21085706, Series 2, RSPP.
[19] Rawick (Ed.), *AS*, 5.3, 65.

Enslavers implicitly and explicitly acknowledged the inevitability of the aging process, while enslaved people were all too aware that their "masters" connected age with ability. Charles Ball overheard a conversation between two enslavers who were relocating to Georgia. One noted that now was the optimum time to do so: "prime hands were in high demand . . . the boys and girls, under twenty, would bring almost any price at present." Ball was left with no illusions as to the relative lack of interest in elders: "As to those more advanced in life, he seemed to think the prospect of selling them at an unusual price, not so good, as they could not so readily become expert cotton-pickers."[20] They would, however, still be sold. In a letter to his son, Charles Manigault, a leading rice planter in South Carolina, bemoaned the qualities of the aged while revealing they remained subject to the auction block: "I have seen the Lists of Carsons 210 Negroes also Capt. Ingrahams 70. Carsons are inferior most of them old very few single & prime. Ingrahams but little better. I am on the Constant look out, & hope in a few weeks at furthest to pick up 10 or 12 Prime."[21] Manigault "pick[ed] up" fourteen "prime hands" three days later. His dismissive postscript – "there is an old man & an old woman thrown in for nothing, as they wish to go with their family" – indicates both the low value of elders to enslavers and their continued exploitation.[22]

* * *

The "hands" system demonstrates how enslavers viewed and managed the dynamic effects of aging when assessing their body of workers. Daniel Hundley, a prominent proslavery writer, explained the system:

> On most plantations a certain amount only of work is daily required of each competent person, men, women, and children or youths; the "task" prescribed being graduated in accordance with age and condition, from the "quarter-hand" of the youngest to the "half hand" and the "three-quarter hand" of older years, up to the "full-hand" of mature and healthful adult strength; thence retrograding, in like degrees, toward declining force and years.[23]

Of course, it was enslavers who had the prerogative to determine what constituted reasonable tasks for those declining in "both force and years."

---

[20] Charles Ball, *Fifty Years in Chains or, The Life of an American Slave* (New York: H. Dayton; Indianapolis: Asher & Co, 1859), 45.

[21] James M. Clifton (Ed.), *Life and Labor on Argyle Island: Letters and Documents of a Savannah River Rice Plantation, 1833–1867* (Savannah: The Beehive Press, 1978), 239.

[22] Clifton (Ed.), *Life and Labor*, 240.

[23] Daniel R. Hundley, *Social Relations in Our Southern States* (New York: H. B. Price, 1860), 339–40.

Enslavers claimed these arrangements were applied on a day-to-day level. In a memo to the State Executive Department, South Carolina rice planter Robert Allston asserted that "the task is allotted to each slave in proportion to his age and physical ability."[24] Ben Sparkman's journal for his South Carolina rice plantation shows what these distinctions looked like in practice. On November 28, 1833, Sparkman recorded that "the 6 fellows commenced cutting wood." While the "fellows" were employed as such, "the women & two old fellows" assisted "in caning & winnowing Rice." Age-related distinctions appear regularly in Sparkman's diary. Enslaved men labelled "old" were moved out of the all-male gangs undertaking the most vigorous physical labor, such as plowing, wood-cutting, and log-rolling, and moved into mixed-sex groups with comparatively lighter tasks. On December 11, 1834, Sparkman recorded that "The six fellows went to cut wood, the women & two old fellows to cut down corn stockins in negro House field."[25] James Henry Hammond of South Carolina recorded similar distinctions, writing in his 1857–8 plantation book that "those, who from age & infirmities are unable to keep up with the prime hands are put in the suckler's gang."[26] Advanced age was conflated with infirmity, while placing all elders with nursing mothers shows that age operated alongside, and sometimes overruled, gender when shaping work and status. Hammond's specific claim that these aged individuals were unable to "keep up with the prime hands" underscores the relational elements to these negative assessments of aging's effects on the laboring qualities of enslaved people.

The task labor that predominated on rice plantations and across the Lowcountry was perhaps easiest to organize according to strength, age, and endurance. Differential work targets, however, were also set for individual workers on farms and on plantations where the gang system predominated. Charles Ball remembered how in South Carolina, "prime" hands were expected to pick fifty pounds of cotton, and women with children forty, while "twenty-five pounds was assigned as the daily task

---

[24] Easterby and Littlefield (Eds.), *The South Carolina Rice Plantation*, 346.

[25] Ben Sparkman Plantation Journal, 1848–1859, November 28, 1833, and December 11, 1834, #3574-z, Southern Historical Collection, The Wilson Library, University of North Carolina at Chapel Hill (SHC).

[26] Plantation Book 1857–8, James Henry Hammond Papers, Records of Antebellum Southern Plantations from the Revolution through the Civil War, Series A, South Caroliniana Library (University of South Carolina [SCL]), Part 1: *The Papers of James Henry Hammond, 1795–1865*, Reel 13–15.

of old people, as well as a number of boys and girls."[27] Prince Smith, aged 100, neatly summarized to his WPA interviewer how the dynamics of slave labor were attuned to the rhythms of the life cycle:

Dere wus three kinds of days work on de plantation: One is de whole tas', meanin' a whole han' or a person een his prime. He wus given two tas' fur his day's wurk. A tas' carried frum twenty four to twenty five rows which wus thirty-five feet long en twenty five feet wide. De three fourth han' wus given one whole tas' which consists of twelve rows. All de young chillun wus included in dis group. De half han' was de old slaves who did a half tas' for dere day's work. When it was time to pick cotton, de three fourth han' had to pick thirty pound an' de half han' twenty fur dere day's work.[28]

Ball saw the old and the young as occupying the same "step," but Smith understood that the logic of aged decline already marked elders as inferior; they, unlike the young, promised ever-diminishing returns and thus occupied the lowest rung of plantation life.

* * *

The toll that aging took on enslaved peoples' powers of endurance and abilities sometimes led to a shift in roles. Describing her memories of a slave auction to her WPA interviewer, Mary Gaines noted how the seller acknowledged this woman "*has* been a good worker in the field," but that her use now lay elsewhere: "He said this old woman can cook." Regardless, "they sold her off cheap."[29] Some enslavers thus separated elders from the main workforce and tasked them alternatively. John Carmichael Jenkins of Natchez described one such arrangement: "All hands in Saragossa field yet, will finish cutting out there this forenoon- Dan & old Bob diging out p[o]nd near Garden."[30] John Nevitt, in the same region, similarly noted: "This day all hands picking cotton Except old Sam & Dan geting picketts for scaffolds." Sam and Dan were frequently set apart from others. While the main workforce picked cotton from dawn to dusk during the harvesting months, the two men were separately set to ginning, cutting, splitting, and hauling wood.[31]

---

[27] Ball, *Fifty Years in Chains*, 217.   [28] Rawick (Ed.), *AS*, 3.4, 117.

[29] Rawick (Ed.), *AS*, 9.3, 7. Italics mine.

[30] Dr. John Carmichael Jenkins Journal, Elgin Plantation Records, June 7–8, 1843, Historic Natchez Foundation, Natchez, Mississippi (HNF).

[31] John Nevitt Diary, September 11, 1827 and October 30, 1828, *Records of Antebellum Southern Plantations*, Series J, *Selections from the Southern Historical Collection*, Part 6, Reel 3, 72, 160.

Certain plantation roles appear predominantly reserved for elders. One enslaver who sought to sell Jenny explained to the prospective buyer that she was a "good nurse, could work in a garden," and stressed the generic expectations of aged working conditions: "[Jenny] could do and perform all the usual services of a female servant advanced in years."[32] Plantation records from across the South indicate a range of jobs were viewed as "usual services" for elders. Charles Manigault's 1854 listing of slaves at his Gowrie and East Hermitage plantations labelled most enslaved people as "P" or "1/2," indicating their work in the field. Several slaves had their age or the label "old" listed alongside their role. These included fifty-year-old George and Flora, serving as "Trunk Minder" and "Nurse," respectively; "Hannah (Old, Minding Children)"; and "Joe (Old Watchmen)."[33] Manigault's instructions to his overseer eight years earlier suggest these arrangements were part of a long-standing system for dealing with elderly slaves. According to Manigault, "anyone who has nothing else to do (such as 'Old Ned') who would attend to it would add much to their health & comfort" so should maintain the garden.[34] Manigault claimed this task provided comfort to an elderly man, but he also ensured there were no idle bodies on the plantation. Thomas Chaplin, of St. Helena Island, South Carolina, more directly stated how otherwise useless workers could be employed through shifting roles: "Put [Old] Judge to do some work in the garden. I intend to take him for a gardener altogether. He is ruptured, and not fit for other work."[35] Sympathy for Judge's "ruptured" condition was subordinate to the desire to ensure he was still "fit" for *some* work.

Enslaved elders were frequently put in childcare roles. These positions were commonly identified with enslaved women, with the ubiquitous image of "mammy" in antebellum and postbellum lore reflecting this association of childcare.[36] An 1851 *De Bow's Review* article on the

---

[32] In this instance it was a lie. Jenny was "labouring under long previous and permanent disability from chronic rheumatism & other disease," required "constant attention," and was now a "heavy charge" on Mitchell's funds. Petition of Thadeus Mitchell, November 11, 1833, Lancaster County, Virginia, #21683322, Series 2, RSPP.

[33] Clifton (Ed.), *Life and Labor*, 183–5.   [34] Clifton (Ed.), *Life and Labor*, 62.

[35] While no age is provided for Judge, he is elsewhere listed as "Old Judge." See Rosengarten (Ed.), *Tombee: Portrait of a Cotton Planter*, 555, 742.

[36] On the politics of figures such as "Mammy," see, for example, Micki McElya, *Clinging to Mammy: The Faithful Slave in the Twentieth Century America* (Cambridge, Mass.: Harvard University Press, 2007). For general discussions on childcare and enslaved women, see Marie Jenkins Schwartz, *Born in Bondage: Growing Up Enslaved in the Antebellum South* (Cambridge, Mass.: Harvard University Press, 2000), 86; Stevenson, *Life in Black and White*, 227; Brenda Stevenson, "Gender Conventions, Ideals and Identity among Antebellum Virginia Slave Women," in David Barry Gaspar and

"Management of Negroes on Southern Estates" described childcare arrangements:

A large house is provided as a nursery for the children, where all are taken at daylight and placed under the charge of a careful and experienced woman, whose sole occupation is to attend to them, and see that they are properly fed and attended to, and above all things to keep them as dry and as cleanly as possible, under the circumstances.[37]

The structuring of this work from daylight, when prime workers took to the field, and the reference to "experience" suggest this was work for the elderly. Benjamin Woolsey, executor of Calvin Norris's Alabama estate, explained directly how the use of elders in this role spoke to planter convenience: "Some of the said negroes are old & only serviceable as nurses of the younger negro children."[38] Louis Manigault was simply dismissive when detailing his plans to deal with two aged arrivals: "The Woman Harriet is (as list says) ¾ Hand, so I'll put her in the field. The other old Woman is not much. She can mind all these Children."[39] A nursery for unproductive younger workers staffed by unproductive older workers allowed enslavers to maximize parents' productive labor and to protect their "investments" for the future. The old woman was "not much," but she could still be put to work.

In establishing the future interests of enslavers, childrearing was commonly framed as "the most profitable part of plantation business," but using elders here also extracted maximum value from those who were "worn-out."[40] As William Green, enslaved in Maryland, put it: "all the

Darlene Clark Hine (Eds.), *More Than Chattel: Black Women and Slavery in the Americas* (Bloomington:Indiana University Press,1994),169–93, 174–5; Wilma King, "'Suffer with them till death': Slave Women and Their Children in Nineteenth-Century America," in Gaspar and Hine (Eds.), *More Than Chattel*, 145–68; Wilma King, *Stolen Childhood: Slave Youth in Nineteenth-Century America* (Bloomington: Indiana University Press, 1995), 64; Philip D. Morgan, *Slave Counterpoint: Black Culture in the Eighteenth-Century Chesapeake and Lowcountry* (Chapel Hill: University of North Carolina Press, 1998), 474; White, *Ar'n't I A Woman?*, 114.

[37] [Anon], "Management of Negroes upon Southern Estates," *De Bow's Review*, 10.6 (1851), 621–7, 624. See, also, Hammond, Plantation Book, 1857–8.

[38] Petition of Benjamin Woolsey, March 2, 1858, Dallas County, Alabama, #20185821, Series 2, RSPP.

[39] Clifton (Ed.), *Life and Labor*, 140.

[40] Andrew Flinn Plantation Book, 1840, Rules for Overseers, No. 14, Manuscripts Plb, SCL; Lewis Garrard Clarke and Milton Clarke, *Narratives of the Sufferings of Lewis and Milton Clarke, Sons of a Soldier of the Revolution, During a Captivity of More than Twenty Years Among the Slaveholders of Kentucky, One of the So-Called Christian States of North America* (Boston: Bela Marsh, 1846), 108.

children and old people that are past labor, are kept in the quarters. The old people are to mind the children and to keep them out of the fire, and to get their food."[41] On Josephine Cox's Mississippi plantation, women "too old" to "work in the field" and therefore in charge of the children were dismissively called "the Drop Shot Gang."[42]

Elderly men were also tasked with childcare. Abner Green of Georgia told his interviewer that "dey had one old man to see after de little chillun like," and that "de old people made us behave."[43] David Gavin, an enslaver from South Carolina, noted upon the death of "old man Friday" how this man's work had changed over a lifetime. In his early days Friday "carried my keys and attended to feeding the horses and attending to my cattle, hogs and stock generall as long as he was able." As Friday aged, "he was unable to do any such thing much." Instead, he "noticed the yard and the little negroes and would remind me of many little matters to be attended to."[44] Although women more frequently held childcare roles, Charlie Aarons noted that "the old men and the women looked after the children of the slaves while their parents worked in the fields."[45] Rebecca Jane Grant, enslaved in South Carolina, confirmed that limited utility on account of age was the main consideration here and indicated how advanced age cut across, and occasionally shifted, gendered norms relating to work and caring responsibilities: "all of us chillun, too little to work, used to have to stay at de 'Street.' Dey'd have some old folks to look after us – some old man, or some old woman."[46]

* * *

Care-giving responsibilities frequently extended into cooking and nursing roles. As Litt Young of Mississippi explained, "old women what was too old to work in the field done the cookin' and tended the babies."[47] Slaver records show that age and gender were key here: seven of the eleven cooks listed in Alonzo White's auction books between 1853 and 1863 were women aged between fifty and eighty years old. Charles Manigault's

[41] William Green, *Narrative of Events in the Life of William Green (Formerly a Slave). Written by Himself* (Springfield: L. M. Guernsey, Book, Job, & Card Printer, 1853), 9.

[42] Rawick (Ed.), *AS, Supp.*, Ser. 1, 7.2, 525.

[43] Rawick (Ed.), *AS, Supp.*, Ser. 1, 3.1, 271.

[44] David Gavin Diary, 1855–1874, September 13, 1856, #1103-z, SHC.

[45] Rawick (Ed.), *AS*, 6, 2. On gendered caring roles, see Damian Alan Pargas, "From the Cradle to the Fields: Slave Childcare and Childhood in the Antebellum South," *Slavery & Abolition*, 32.4 (2011), 477–3, 482.

[46] Rawick (Ed.), *AS*, 2.2, 179.   [47] Rawick (Ed.), *AS*, 5.4, 228.

cook at the Gowrie plantation was Charity, whose rating as ½ hand likely indicates advanced age, while his overseer at Encampment recorded in 1849 "the Death of an old woman by the name of Binah, who acted as plantation cook for the Hermitage hands."[48] On the Georgia plantation of Frances Kemble's husband, "an old woman, whose special business this is," distributed food to the workers.[49] Anne Simon Deas's postbellum paean to the "Lost Cause" expanded upon these arrangements. Deas created composite characters in a partly fictionalized account of life in antebellum South Carolina, including "old Maum Beck . . . who keeps the keys of the store room, gives out the meals, and exercises a general – and I should say a very lenient – supervision over the other servants," and Plenty, "an admirable cook" who was "getting quite old."[50]

Notwithstanding claims of elders' authority, it is evident that these roles were a way for enslavers to maximize productivity. On Jamie Parker's plantation, Aunt Mag did the cooking because she "was too 'old and useless' to work in the field." Indeed, "the women working in the field, of course had no time to attend to baking their bread."[51] Labor considerations in the round shaped such compartmentalization, with enslavers reorienting the workforce to suit their requirements and to maximize returns on their "investments." Charles Ball recounted that on one plantation, enslaved families previously cooked for themselves, but as this adversely affected time spent in the field, the overseer "made it the duty of an old woman, who was not capable of doing much work in the field, to stay at the quarter, and bake the bread of the whole gang."[52] The emphasis on *made* underscores how limited capacity in some fields did not limit the potential for exploitation elsewhere.

Alongside caring and cooking, experienced elders commonly provided healthcare. Enslaved women in these roles were often skilled midwives, responsible for administering care for Black and sometimes white women before, during, and after birth. Ned Chaney of Mississippi described his mother's skills here: "Ever'body call her 'mammy,' white folks an' black

---

[48] Alonzo White Slave Auction Book, 1853–63, *Records of Antebellum Southern Plantations* Series B, *Selections from the South Carolina Historical Society*, Reel 8, 00001-00078; Clifton (Ed.), *Life and Labor*, 3–4, 70–1.

[49] Frances Ann Kemble, *Journal of a Residence on a Georgian Plantation in 1838–1839* (Athens: University of Georgia Press, 1984: originally published New York, 1863), 55.

[50] Anne Simon Deas, *Two Years of Plantation Life, Part 1* (1910), 48, 121, SCL.

[51] Emily Catharine Pierson, *Jamie Parker, the Fugitive* (Hartford: Brockett, Fuller and Co., 1851), 36.

[52] Ball, *Fifty Years in Chains*, 120–1.

folks. She tend ter all of 'em when dey was brought down."[53] Elders were still often prioritized for general health concerns. Thomas Edward Cox instructed the "managers" on his Virginia plantation to ensure that "an intelligent and otherwise suitable woman will be appointed as a nurse upon each plantation, who will administer medicine and otherwise attend upon the sick."[54] Often, experience was synonymous with advanced age. In Alonzo White's sale lists, we have "Kate old nurse 75 yrs old," "Grace nurse 75 yrs old," and "Luna nurse 59 yrs old."[55]

Former slaves commonly acknowledged that using elders in caring positions spoke to enslavers' utilitarian calculations around productivity and profit. Cyrus Bellus twice emphasized to his WPA interviewer that this transition occurred *after* more exploitative labor had sapped the elder's strength: nurses were "old folks that weren't able to work any longer . . . They wasn't able to work, you know."[56] Others highlighted the limits to enslaved healers' autonomy and the willingness of enslavers to discount their counsel when it suited them. James Boyd stressed that "ef hit was too bad, de white folks had dere doctor come and de Marster doctored us."[57] Elderly healers remained subject to exploitation, even when acknowledged as skilled. In 1817, two South Carolina enslavers argued over the death of an enslaved woman named Catherine, with neither accepting responsibility for her illness and subsequent death from smallpox. Notwithstanding the tragedy of her life and death, the dispute revealed that the use of skilled elderly nurses served the convenience of those who enslaved them. Catherine was initially rejected by the defendant, who "refused to take this negro on hire at any price in consequence of her being old," but he eventually found a use for her. She was unable to work in the fields, but "the defendant expected, and did derive a benefit from [Catherine] . . . for in the character of a cook and a nurse, in which service she was to be employed, it appears that she was considered as useful and valuable." Catherine was not

---

[53] Rawick (Ed.), *AS, Supp., Ser. 1*, 7.2, 373. Enslaved midwives are dealt with extensively in Schwartz, *Birthing a Slave* and Deirdre Cooper Owens, *Medical Bondage: Race, Gender, and the Origins of American Gynecology* (Athens: University of Georgia Press, 2017), 54–66. On general healthcare, see Fett, *Working Cures*; McCandless, *Slavery, Disease, and Suffering*, 177.

[54] J. W. Randolph Plantation Rule Book, in Thomas Edward Cox Books, 1829–54, *Records of Antebellum Southern Plantations*, Series J: *Selections from the Southern Historical Collection*, Part 9, reel 16, 0356–66.

[55] Alonzo White Slave Auction Book, 00014-00016, 00027-00028.

[56] Rawick (Ed.), *AS*, 8.1, 143.

[57] Rawick (Ed.), *AS, Supp., Ser. 2*, 2.1, 366. See, also: Rawick (Ed.), *AS, Supp., Ser. 1*, 10.5, 2192–3.

so "valuable," however, as to warrant protection from an epidemic. Her enslaver was informed on March 12 about "the danger she [was] in, and yet he permitted her to remain exposed to the contagion of this dreadful malady until the 18th of April."[58] Catherine's enslaver received $250 for the loss of his "property."

* * *

Their frequent responsibility for infants meant that many older slaves were tasked with training children for work.[59] Anne Simon Deas, recalling life in antebellum South Carolina, noted that "there are generally one or two younger ones 'learning' in every department of the household, so that as the present incumbents grow too old for active work, their places may be supplied by capable persons."[60] In August 1830, John Nevitt recorded that on his Mississippi plantation the full hands were "hoeing cotton in swamp" but that he had "Set old Nance with 10 r 12 children to Picking cotton in Punch Bowl field."[61] Sometimes elders passed on specific skills, as when Douglas Parish, enslaved in Florida, recalled how he was taught "about the care and grooming of horses from an old slave who had charge of the Parish stables."[62] Some training was more general. Abram Sells of Texas, described how

Us hab a ol' man dat went 'roun' wid us 'n' look atter us, bofe de w'ite 'uns 'n' de black 'uns, 'n' dat ol' man was my great gran'daddy. He was too ol' to do any kin' 'r' wuk 'n' he was jes' 'pinted (appointed) to look atter all de li'l 'uns 'n' teach dem how to wuk. Us all jes' strung 'roun' atter him, w'ite 'n' black, watchin' him potter 'roun' 'n' listenin' to him tell how t'ings ort (ought) to be run 'roun' dat place.[63]

Similar arrangements were in place for domestic service. After listing the domestic "servants" as "de mammy, de butler, de body-servant, de coachman, de ladies-maids, de cook, de gardner," George Glasker of Texas noted how beneath them "wuz de boys an' girls dat wuz in tradin' for de oldest ones place if dey is sold or leave."[64] Both white and Black southerners understood the nature of these arrangements. Mary Esther Huger, whose family enslaved people on a rice plantation in South Carolina, remembered that "When I was a child, our servants were

[58] *De Tollenere v. Fuller*, 8 S.C.L. 117, 1 Mill 117 (1817), 117, 119, 120.
[59] On children's work, see: King, *Stolen Childhood*, 71–106; Pargas, "From the Cradle to the Fields."
[60] Deas, *Two Years of Plantation Life*, 7.   [61] Nevitt, Diary, August 17, 1830, 307.
[62] Rawick (Ed.), *AS*, 17, 258.   [63] Rawick (Ed.), *AS, Supp.*, Ser. 2, 9.8, 3485-6.
[64] Rawick (Ed.), *AS, Supp.*, Ser. 2, 5.4, 1503.

Ketch – an old grey headed Negro, & Johnnie, who he had trained, & when Ketch, was too old & tired of work, Johnnie, then a young man, took his place." Huger noted a similar pattern for those working in the kitchen: "Smarts father was old Smart the cook, & he had an elder son Hampton in the kitchen with him, to do the work, for his health was not strong."[65] Such arrangements sometimes allowed family members to pass on skills or roles to their children. Robert Henry, enslaved in Georgia, recalled that his father, who was "de butler at de big house," was training him to "wait on Marster's table," while Fanny Finney of Mississippi noted her granny, who was "real old and the boss cook on our place . . . learnt all the girls on our place how to cook."[66]

Skilled labor typically placed less emphasis on physicality alone, and elders could hold onto these roles later in life.[67] In *Gantt v. Venning*, 1840, one witness stressed to the City Court of Charleston, South Carolina, that the skills of Phillander, an "old man about 50 years old," outweighed purely chronological assessments of value: "though he was old, yet he might be more valuable on account of being a mechanic."[68] The value placed on skilled elders extended to their ability to train up their replacements and ensure labor continuity. Robert Allston's head carpenter Thomas, his "old and faithful man," had four younger men working under him, while Abner Griffin of Virginia described his own intergenerational apprenticeship: "Old Uncle Jesse Shank taught me to shoemake."[69] One enslaver outlined how this generational apprenticeship system extended across plantations, "generously" offering to lend an "old man for this year" to serve as blacksmith for his friend. Noting "that as he is quite old tho very active I must beg that his work may not be distrutioned [disproportionate]," this writer emphasized that the "old" man's skills lay in training the next generation: "By offering him some trifling present I have no doubt he will teach your boy to do very good work this year if he be apt to learn."[70]

---

[65] Mary Esther Huger Reminiscences, MS vol. bd., 1890–1892, 23, SCL.

[66] Rawick (Ed.), *AS*, *12.2*, 195–6; Rawick (Ed.), *AS*, 8.2, 297.

[67] Morgan, *Slave Counterpoint*, 212–24. See: Rawick (Ed.), *AS*, 2.2, 8.

[68] Testimony of Thomas N. Gadsden, *Gantt v. Venning*, City Ct. of Charleston, Box 34, Jan 1840, S.C., Sup. Ct. Records, South Carolina Department of Archives and History (hereafter SCDAH). Appeal reported in *Venning v. Gantt*, 25 S.C.L. 87 1 Chev. 87 (1840).

[69] James L. Petigur to Robert F. W. Allston, Charleston, April 3, 1855, in Easterby and Littlefield (Eds.), *The South Carolina Rice Plantation*, 122. See also Last will and estate of Alexander C. Wylly, June 30, 1834, Glynn County Court of Ordinary, Estate Records, Wills, Inventories, and Appraisements, book D, GSA.

[70] Letter dated March 13, 1851, Edmonia Cabell Wilkins Papers, 1782–1949, Series 1, Subseries 1.1., Folder 5, January 1851–March 1851, #2364, SHC.

The formal request to not overtax the aged man suggests that overwork might usually be considered par for the course. One former slave even claimed that an enslaver would specifically "buy up de old men that w'd er sold in dey prime fur thousands of dollars, blacksmiths an' men wid er trade an' nen he'd put um to wurk." This was not benevolence but good business: "Sometimes he gittum fur ten dollars or twenty, when they master SURE they bout gone, fur as work went, but Mr. M –, he could keep um alive an' wurkin fur years an' years."[71] Here, longevity meant continued exploitation in order to further the enslaver's profit margins.

For good or ill, skilled workers might hold on to roles as they aged, but time came for all and accordingly affected the dynamics of labor. In 1853, Louis Manigault recorded his annoyance that the carpenter Amos – the "Old Fool" – had "put almost every post down Crooked." Manigault was delighted to hear that the younger man Jack would replace Amos for a short while, as only this would allow him to "get every thing ship shape."[72] In a trial over the fraudulent sale of two enslaved people, multiple witnesses derided the skills of sixty-year-old George on account of his age. George and Clarissa, who had been listed as fifty and forty respectively, were charged as being at least ten years older than this, with "the vigour and activity of both so much impaired by age as to render them of little value." George was said to have lost his skills as a blacksmith and cobbler, with specific claims as to age-related decline. One witness claimed that "George is quite a feeble old negro," and stressed that, in this, "he is like all old men of his age." John Cunningham, who had known George for some time, acknowledged that once "he was a good smith," but believed that now "from age and want of sight he lacks right smart of being a good Blacksmith." James Fish assessed George less sentimentally: "he might do to work in the garden, to how corn and such as that – I did not value him as a mechanic. I think his eye sight is so bad that he is not capable of working at his trade."[73] Despite serving his enslavers well for a nearly half a century, George's talents were dismissed on account of his age; if once finding some personal validation in his skills and specialization, he could expect to do so no more. Nonetheless, he would still be put to work elsewhere.

Enslaved men in trustee positions also saw changes to work roles as they aged. Some enslavers preferred experienced men in charge and valued

---

[71] Perdue et al., *Weevils in the Wheat*, 7.   [72] Clifton (Ed.), *Life and Labor*, 141.
[73] Petition of Mordacai Offutt, November 14, 1852; Depositions of Simeon Griffie, James Fish, and John Cunningham, August 19, 1853, Scott County, Kentucky, #20785209, Series 2, RSPP.

the "good Judgment about Plantation work" and the assumed respect from peers that they had gathered over the years.[74] Lindsey Faucette of North Carolina explained that her enslaver made "Uncle Whitted de overseer kase he wuz one of de oldest slaves he had an' a good n***r."[75] However, enslavers also acknowledged the inevitability of declining force, and its impact on the ability to wield physical and psychological authority over the coerced workforce. As Jeptha Choice recalled, the driver "had to be good with his fists to make the boys who got bad in the field, walk the line."[76]

Inability – perceived or real – to make bad ones "walk the line" sometimes necessitated a change. In Jamie Parker's fugitive narrative, the author noted that on Virginian plantations, "one of the most trusty, strong, and 'likely' of the slaves" was selected as foreman. These men were ostensibly "permitted to keep the situation for life," but in reality it was "rather till worn out." At this point they were "laid aside, like an old garment, labeled in the inventory 'old and useless.'"[77] Such deliberations clearly took place on plantations and farms. Charles Manigault provides insight into how some enslavers viewed these transitions: "Driver Isaac is most old & feeble & crabbed," and so Manigault had already lined up his replacement: "Should he fail one named Will, is best to make driver."[78] William Pettigrew, a North Carolina enslaver, reported more sympathetically on managing the transition between drivers, but shared Manigault's understanding of the inevitable impact of aging on work. Upon the death of Moses, Pettigrew expected Glasgow to take the role as driver, but only for as long as he could maintain the "vigor" required:

[Glasgow] is but thirty two years of age. His comparative youth may militate against him for a short while – but only for a short while, if he prove to be in possession of the abilities requisite for his station. The man of 32 will, in ten years' time, find in any company of persons a far greater number behind him than are in advance of him. It will be many years before those disqualifications for command that usually characterize old persons will overtake the man of 30; While he who has attained 50 must soon expect the inexorable hand of time to soften that vigour which is all important in a ruler and without which he soon permits some stronger spirit than his own to assume the mastery over him.[79]

[74] Plantation Diary, April 21, 1858, Robert Ruffin Barrow Papers #2407-z, 231, SHC.
[75] Rawick (Ed.), *AS*, *14.1*, 303. On authority and age for drivers, see Anthony Kaye, *Joining Places: Slave Neighborhoods in the Old South* (Chapel Hill: University of North Carolina Press, 2007), 143–4.
[76] Rawick (Ed.), *AS*, *Supp., Ser.* 2, 3.2, 708–9.   [77] Pierson, *Jamie Parker, the Fugitive*, 31.
[78] Clifton (Ed.) *Life and Labor*, 11.   [79] Starobin (Ed.), *Blacks in Bondage*, 35.

The suggestion that some "stronger spirit" would "assume the mastery over him" shows that aging was assessed comparatively, and indicates antebellum southerners recognition that age-related decline did not always inspire social support among the enslaved, but could be seized upon by rivals looking to assert themselves.

Whether in field work, domestic spaces, or skilled and managerial positions, enslavers realized that aging negatively affected the laboring qualities of enslaved people. Reduced skill, endurance, or ability, however, did not lead to leisurely retirement. Enslavers creatively exploited elders and enslaved people were forced to work upon pain of punishment, neglect, or abuse.

* * *

White southerners proudly claimed that "many of our slaves, when sixty years of age, imagine and declare that they are eighty or ninety, and are accordingly indulged with an exemption from further compulsory labor."[80] Former slaves, abolitionists, and Black activists rejected this characterization of indulgences for the elderly. Alice Cole, enslaved in Louisiana, told her WPA interviewer: "Believe me son they sure did work the slaves, they did'nt have very much mercy on the poor old slaves in that way." Cole compared the treatment of enslaved people to "poor old mules" whipped "every time they would slow down or stop."[81] Minerva Bratcher likewise informed her interviewer: "Laud Miss, you don't know how much folks had to do them days, and everybody worked, the old slave women who were too old to work in the field cooked, took care of the little n***rs and helped spin and weave cloth."[82] Liza McGhee was reluctant to speak with her WPA interviewer, explaining that she "remember some things about old slave days," but didn't "want to say nothing that will get me in bandage [sic] again." Aged ninety, McGhee explained: "I am too old now to be a slave. I couldn't stand it."[83]

Enslaved elders could neither refuse nor deny the power of their enslavers to force them to continue their labors. Work, even if reduced, still had to be done upon pain of punishment.[84] Lewis Clarke was adamant that advanced age did not protect elders from the expectations of productivity and that antebellum enslavers contrived "all ways to keep

---

[80] Anon, "Editorial," *Southern Medical and Surgical Journal*, 12 (February, 1856), 128.

[81] Rawick (Ed.), *AS, Supp.*, Ser. 2, 3.2, 753.

[82] Rawick (Ed.), *AS, Supp.*, Ser. 2, 2.1, 420.

[83] Rawick (Ed.), *AS, Supp.*, Ser.1, 9.4, 1402.   [84] Rosenthal, *Accounting for Slavery*, 115.

them at work till the last hour of life." Reeves Tucker of Alabama and
Susan Smith of Louisiana separately recalled that while their enslavers
"didn' put de ol' men and women in de fiel' wid de other n***rs," labor
remained compulsory. Smith noted that "dey *put* de ol' n***rs to wuk
shuckin' co'n and pickin' seed co'n" while Tucker noted the "bosses ...
made the old wimmen what was too old to work, tend to the chil'ren while
the slaves worked."[85] These former slaves applied a language of compulsion – of *make* and *put* – that clearly rejected proslavery propagandists'
promises of leisurely retirement. These ex-slaves understood that desire
for profit drove American enslavers and stressed the harm this wreaked on
enslaved people. As Clarke acidly recorded, "they hunt and drive them as
long as there is any life in them."[86]

James Matthews, enslaved in South Carolina, emphasized enslavers'
adaptability when exploiting their slaves. A reduced task rarely provided
real respite: "The old and young always have to work alike. Each one is
made to do as much as he can. I have seen old men and women so bent
down that they have to lean on a stick with one hand, while they hoed with
the other."[87] The emphasis on doing "as much as they can" speaks to
enslavers' creativity in monitoring and measuring their workers from
cradle to grave. "Uncle" Gabe Lance of South Carolina recalled the
violence inherent to enslavers' measurement systems. Whether tasks
were reduced or not, they were not optional: if any slave hadn't "done
task," the "least cut they give 'em (with lash) been twenty-five to fifty.
Simply cause them weak and couldn't done task – couldn't done task!
Give 'em less rations to boot!"[88]

Elders and enslavers held different understandings of peoples' capabilities and the level of task still appropriate, but only one side had the
power to determine how work was allocated. Ellen Cragin described her
elderly aunt's punishment after claiming inability to work on account of
age and infirmity; because she wouldn't do any work, they made her sit
on an ant-infested log and "let the ants bite her."[89] Elizabeth Sparks
recalled how work enslavers framed or recorded as "light" was understood very differently by those forced to perform it. Her "mistress" made
"Aunt Caroline" knit all day and all night. This was neither light nor

[85] Rawick (Ed.), *AS, Supp.,* Ser. 2, 9.8, 3367; Rawick (Ed.), *AS, Supp.,* Ser. 2, *10.9,* 3892.
   Italics mine.
[86] Clarke and Clarke, *Narratives of the Sufferings,* 112.
[87] James Matthews, "Recollections of Slavery by a Runaway Slave," *The Emancipator,*
   August 23, September 13, September 20, October 11, October 18, 1838.
[88] Rawick (Ed.), *AS,* 3.3, 92.   [89] Rawick (Ed.), *AS,* 8.2, 45.

leisurely, instead combining her enslaver's concern for productivity and desire for dominance: "when she git so tired aftah dark that she'd git sleepy, she'd make 'er stan' up an knit. She work her so hard that she'd go to sleep standin' up an' every time her haid nod an' her knees sag, the lady'd come down across her haid with a switch." Sparks was adamant this abuse was not unusual, but was unwilling to tell the unvarnished truth about enslavement: "Well I'll tell yer some to put in yer book, but I ain'ta goin' tell yer the worse."[90]

White contemporaries likewise offered counternarratives to the proslavery claims of old age as a leisurely retirement. Frederick Law Olmsted noted that when residing in Washington, DC, an "aged negro" was tasked with providing fires for the hotel guests. This man was "very much bent, seemingly with infirmity," and had an "expression of impotent anger in his face, and a look of weakness, like a drunkard's." Olmsted's emphasis on impotence suggests he believed the man had little capacity for resistance, despite his obvious resentment at his situation. This was not, as proslavery writers proclaimed, a world where enslaved elders became a "family pensioner, secure from want."[91] Despite his obvious infirmities, the man insisted he was forced to work at a blistering pace:

Don't you tink I'se too ole a man for to be knock roun at dis kind of work, massa? – hundred gemmen all want dair fires made de same minute, and caus de old n***r can't do it all de same minute, ebbery one tinks dey's boun to scold him all de time; nebber no rest for him, no time.

This elder's attempt to gain sympathy because of his advanced age failed; Olmsted brusquely informed the man that his workload was "not my business; Mr. Dexter should have more servants."[92] Olmsted at least did not inform on or abuse the man himself. Others received punishment if they voiced concern or failed to keep up with their work. One WPA respondent described the tragic end for an elder who had been tasked with keeping the fires on the place. Her mistress lost patience with her slow pace: "[she] went out to see what the trouble was, and there was the old lady bending down just like she was making the fire and old lady ___ cut her a lick with the cowhide." This punishment, however, was unnecessary. The woman "was [already] dead," her body stuck in rigor mortis and providing a tragic

[90] FWP, 17 (Virginia), 1936, 51–2, 50.   [91] Hundley, *Social Relations*, 67–8.
[92] Frederick Law Olmsted, *Journeys and Explorations in the Cotton Kingdom of America: A Traveller's Observations on Cotton and Slavery in the American Slave States. Based Upon Three Former Volumes of Journeys and Observations* (London: Sampson, Low, Son & Co., 1862), 30–1.

tableau vivant of a life enslaved.[93] Frances Kemble recalled the exploitation of older slaves on her plantation, indicating that this was endemic to a system that stressed productivity and profits. Kemble described how she was "accosted by poor old Teresa, the wretched Negress who had complained to me so grievously of her back being broken by hard work and childbearing." Teresa begged for help on account of her age and infirmity, but she was "flogged for having complained to me as she did."[94]

Enslaved elders unable to complete their tasks risked punishment. Jacob Green described how Uncle Reuben, "an old negro in the family," was forced to work despite severe sickness. Green described how "the poor old man worked until he fell," but the overseer "came over and told him to get up, and that he was only playing the old soldier ... when the old man did not move to get up Mr. Cobb gave him a few kicks with his heavy boots and told Reuben, sick as he was, that he would cure him."[95] Cobb beat the already unconscious Reuben with his hickory cane, and he died hours later. Likewise, Moses Roper recalled how Phil, aged seventy, "was so feeble that he could not accomplish his tasks." Despite this debility, "his master used to chain him round the neck, and run him down a steep hill; this treatment he never relinquished to the time of his death."[96] William Green similarly emphasized how "reduced" labor was no protection for the elders on the nearby plantation of Harry Holliday, who made an old woman on his plantation "tend the sheep and cows," come rain or shine. One "very cold day in Winter," the woman failed to find the missing sheep and, despite pleading respite on account of the harsh weather, was forced to continue. This "old woman who was almost past work," still "had to try to do all she could" to profit her enslaver. Holliday was adamant she was not doing "all she could": "She told him she was almost frozen with the cold; he told her to be gone or he would make her; – she went, and the next morning she was found frozen to death under the fence."[97]

* * *

Recollections often suggest that the punishment of enslaved elders was particularly harrowing. This assessment spoke to common assumptions

[93] Rawick (Ed.), *AS, 18,* 6.   [94] Kemble, *Journal of a Residence,* 154.

[95] Jacob D. Green, *Narrative of the Life of J. D. Green, A Runaway Slave, from Kentucky, Containing an Account of His Three Escapes, in 1839, 1846, and 1848* (Huddersfield: Henry Fielding, 1864), 10–11.

[96] Moses Roper, *A Narrative of the Adventures and Escape of Moses Roper, from American Slavery* (Philadelphia: Merrihew & Gunn, 1838), 21.

[97] Green, *Narrative of Events,* 7–8.

that the strong should not abuse the weak. These claims were used to emphasize the demeaning nature of slavery and to attack the claims of southern honor. Abolitionist William Armistead explained that, "if the strong attack the weak, if the well armed assail the defenceless ... we turn from the scene with indignation and abhorrence."[98] Henry Watson, who served the gamblers at a Vicksburg hotel, described one such callous scene to his readers. While serving two of the establishment's guests, an "old slave" named Jim dropped down with a fit of apoplexy. This became a new game of chance: "'He is dead!' exclaimed one. 'He'll come to,' replied the other. 'Dead, for five hundred!' 'Done!' retorted the other." These gamblers' cruel treatment of this elder highlighted to Watson "the brutish manner in which a slave is treated," and the degrading influence of slavery itself.[99]

A lifetime of service provided no protection from abuse and harm. Joseph Sanford explained how recognition of the lies in regards to paternalism precipitated his escape: "The whipping he gave me did not hurt me so much as the scandal of it, – to whip so old a man as I was, and who had been so faithful a servant as I had been: I thought it unsufferable."[100] Sanford's testimony reveals how little faith enslaved people could put in the rhetoric of enslavers or their defenders, and antislavery activists commonly used the abuse of elders to underscore this point. Frederick Douglass recoiled from the whipping of "Old Barney" for failing to achieve the "unreasonable and exacting tasks" Colonel Lloyd set for him. Douglass described this event as one of "the most heart-suddening and humiliating scenes I ever witnessed": "the spectacle of an aged man – a husband and a father – humbly kneeling before his fellowman, shocked me at the time; and since I have grown older, few of the features of slavery have impressed me with a deeper sense of its injustice and barbarity than did this existing scene."[101]

---

[98] Wilson Armistead, *A Tribute for the Negro: Being a Vindication of the Moral, Intellectual, and Religious Capabilities of the Colored Portion of Mankind; with Particular Reference to the African Race* (Manchester and London: W. Irwin, 1848), 29.

[99] Henry Watson, *Narrative of Henry Watson, A Fugitive Slave. Written by Himself* (Boston: Bela Marsh, 1848), 27–8.

[100] Benjamin Drew, *A North-Side View of Slavery. The Refugee: or the Narratives of Fugitive Slaves in Canada. Related by Themselves, with an Account of the History and Condition of the Colored Population of Upper Canada* (Boston: J. P. Jewett and Company, 1856), 361.

[101] Douglass, *Life and Times of Frederick Douglass*, 68–72.

WHIPPING OF OLD BARNEY.

FIGURE 1.2 "Whipping of Old Barney," in Frederick Douglass, *Life and Times of Frederick Douglass, Written by Himself. His Early Life as a Slave, His Escape from Bondage, and His Complete History to the Present Time* ... (Boston: De Wolfe & Fiske Co., 1892), 71. Courtesy of The New York Public Library: https:// digitalcollections.nypl.org/items/510d47df-ac26-a3d9-e040-e00a18064a99.

Former slaves and their antislavery allies were thus adamant that claims of leisurely retirement for enslaved elders were far from the truth. Dianah Watson, interviewed some seventy years past emancipation, brought up the image of "old women half-bent from beatin's goin' to the field" to demonstrate the cruelties of slavery. Noting that "I'se seed them take them ole half bent wimmen and beat them till they couldn't walk for three days," Watson recoiled from such hideous memories: "if n***rs of these days done see what I seed in slavery time they'd pray and thank they Gawd every day."[102] John Jackson, enslaved in South Carolina, described the ubiquitous violence toward older slaves and stressed that for most elders, escape came only in death. James English, a violent enslaver, "commenced quarrelling with a slave named Old George, on the plea that he did not pick cotton fast enough." English insisted the man's age warranted neither respect nor reduced punishment: "Never mind, you old rascal, when I get better I'll give you sixty lashes, – never mind, you old rascal you." English died before he could punish George, and this turn of affairs greatly amused the enslaved population. The joy did not last long; English's brother took his place and continued to punish the elderly: "Mack English tied down a slave named Old Prince, and gave him one hundred lashes with the whip, and fifty blows with the paddle, because he could not work fast enough to please him."[103]

Some former slaves recalled that elders were mistreated on account of their reduced productivity. Charles Ball described one of his workmates on a cotton plantation in South Carolina as "quite crooked with years and labor," and stressed his inability to keep up: "The old man whom I have alluded to before, was in the field with the others, though he was not able to keep up with his row. He had no clothes on him except the remains of an old shirt, which hung in tatters from his neck and arms." This man's ragged clothing was likely no coincidence, speaking instead to the reduced value enslavers placed on elders. Ball later noted how shoes were only "given to all those who were able to go to the field to pick cotton." This deprived "the children, and several old persons, whose eye-sight was not sufficiently clear to enable them to pick cotton."[104]

Enslavers clearly made distinctions in material rewards on account of age and utility, with Stephen Duncan Jnr of Mississippi noting that "those who do not work out but stay about the quarter yard, do not receive spring shoes, & do not receive overcoats."[105] Historian David Silkenat notes that on Jefferson's Monticello plantation, "laboring men and women received one pair of leather shoes per year, while enslaved children went barefoot and elderly slaves shod themselves with the remnants of

---

[102] Rawick (Ed.), *AS*, *5.4*, 145; Rawick (Ed.), *AS*, *Supp.*, Ser. 2, *10.9*, 3994.

[103] John Andrew Jackson, *The Experience of a Slave in South Carolina* (London: Passmore & Alabaster, 1862), 12.

[104] Ball, *Fifty Years in Chains*, 55, 78, 201.

[105] Duncan (Stephen Jr.) papers, Z/1980.000/F/Folder 1, Mississippi Department of Archives and History, Jackson, Mississippi (hereafter MDAH). Similar reductions in clothing can be found in Rosengarten (Ed.), *Tombee: Portrait of a Cotton Planter*, 381–2.

previous years." Compared to his neighbors, Jefferson "provided a relatively generous enslaved clothing allowance."[106] Thomas Clay of Mississippi wrote disapprovingly of "the present economy of the slave system," which was "to get all you can from the slave, and give him in return as little as will barely support him in a working condition," but his "plan for improvement" remained a pipe dream for most enslaved people.[107] Those deemed less valuable as workers received less, and these reductions had harmful effects. Philemon Bliss of Florida claimed that worsened material conditions of life meant "the aged and feeble often *suffer from cold.*"[108] Bliss's reporting suggests how the expectations of decline associated with age, or even genuine reductions in capacity, meant that enslavers were less concerned about their fate. They were on the way out, after all, and there were new workers to feed instead.

In the 1970s and 1980s, Richard Steckel's work set-off extended inter-disciplinary research on health and mortality in slavery that demonstrated how enslavers malnourished enslaved children in order to prioritize feeding more productive adult workers.[109] No quantitative study has been under-taken specifically with regards to old age, but both enslaver and enslaved spoke of reductions for the elderly on account of their reduced productivity. Thomas Chaplin recorded in his journal that he "gave out 1st allowance of corn to full hands," but only "potatoes to little Negroes & olde ones." Even this was to be circumscribed on account of fiscal concerns: "I want to try and save what I have left of potatoes, & if they keep, sell them later."[110] Harriet Jacobs stressed that reductions of this sort were a rational choice for

---

[106] David Silkenat, *Scars on the Land: An Environmental History of Slavery in the American South* (New York: Oxford University Press, 2022), 119.

[107] Thomas Clay, *Detail of a Plan for the Moral Improvement of Negroes on Plantations* (Printed at the request of the Presbytery, Georgia, 1833), 20; James Williams, *Narrative of James Williams, an American Slave, Who Was for Several Years a Driver on a Cotton Plantation in Alabama* (New York: American Anti-Slavery Society; Boston: Isaac Knapp, 1838), viii.

[108] Theodore Dwight Weld, *American Slavery As It Is: Testimony of a Thousand Witnesses* (New York: American Anti-Slavery Office, 1839), 41.

[109] See, for example, Richard H. Steckel, "A Dreadful Childhood: The Excess Mortality of American Slaves," *Social Science History*, 10.4 (Winter, 1986), 427–65; Richard H. Steckel, "A Peculiar Population: The Nutrition, Health, and Mortality of American Slaves from Childhood to Maturity," *Journal of Economic History*, 46.3 (Sep., 1986), 721–41; Richard H. Steckel, "Biological Measures of the Standard of Living," *Journal of Economic Perspectives*, 22.1 (Winter 2008), 129–52; Eric B. Schneider, "Children's Growth in an Adaptive Framework: Explaining the Growth Patterns of American Slaves and Other Historical Populations," *Economic History Review*, 70.1 (2017), 3–29.

[110] Rosengarten (Ed.), *Tombee: Portrait of a Cotton Planter*, 598.

enslavers who prioritized profit over people. One man, who "had faithfully served the Flint family through three generations ... hobbled up to get his bit of meat" during the rationing period. Mrs. Flint, however, "said he was too old to have any allowance; that when n***rs were too old to work, they ought to be fed on grass. Poor old man! He suffered much before he found rest in the grave."[111] August Smith, enslaved in Missouri, noted how resistance to reductions could end tragically. A woman of "about seventy years old," suffering from meager rations, stole a chicken to feed herself. Her enslaver caught her "while she had it on boiling" and "was so mad, he told her to get a spoon and eat every bite before she stopped. It was scalding hot but he made her do it. She died right away, her insides burned."[112] The violence of this punishment suggests it mattered little whether the woman now lived or died; her death more usefully reminded the wider community of the futility of resistance.[113]

* * *

Former slaves and antislavery activists believed that the traumas of slavery exacerbated physical and mental ailments associated with the natural aging process, and their references to prematurely stooped backs, grey hairs, or broken bodies demonstrated the violence of slavery.[114] William Brown, interviewed in Canada after escaping from Virginia, was described as "apparently eighty years of age, nearly bald," and "what little hair he had was grey." Brown informed his interviewer that he was mistaken over the chronology, but not the substance of his decrepitude: "I am not eighty – only sixty-three – but I am worked down, and worn out with hard work."[115] Jonathon Thomas, enslaved in Kentucky, insisted that the violence of slavery worsened physical ailments associated with aging. An enslaved man might be "fifty-two years old, if measured by Time's hourglass." However, "if computed by labor done, and the wear and tear of excessive over-work, incited by the hope of freedom, we think he would have found the infirmities of seventy pressing upon his shattered frame."[116]

---

[111] Harriet Jacobs, *Incidents in the Life of a Slave Girl. Written by Herself* (Boston: Published for the author, 1861), 142.
[112] Rawick (Ed.), *AS, Supp., Ser. 1*, 2, 243.
[113] Douglass, *My Bondage and My Freedom*, 112–14.
[114] On cross-cultural physical ailments associated with aging, see Ottaway, "Medicine and Old Age," 342–5.
[115] Drew, *A North-Side View of Slavery*, 280.
[116] John Blassingame (Ed.), *Slave Testimony: Two Centuries of Letters, Speeches, Interviews, and Autobiographies* (Baton Rouge: Louisiana State University Press, 1977), 251.

The physical effects of aging clearly worsened experiences of bondage. John Brown noted that on tobacco plantations the period of transplanting was particularly hard on "the old slaves, some of whom I have seen, who, from constant stooping, could not stand straight up to save their lives."[117] James Reeves explained to his WPA interviewer that ill-treatment while enslaved had sped up the deterioration of his mother's eyesight, which was so bad "before she died that she could hardly see to go nowhere." Reeve's mother "insisted" this loss of sight was "due to bad treatment in slavery time."[118] George P. Ripley, a white traveler from Connecticut, noted the damaging effect of hearing loss for "one aged slave." This man "was remarkable for his industry and fidelity," but was whipped after failing to hear the commands of his overseer. The overseer had no sympathy for his reduced circumstances: "damn you, if you cannot hear I'll see if you can feel."[119] Such testimony is borne out in the words (and deeds) of Louisiana enslaver Bennet H. Barrow, who recorded that "Old Demps" had "been doing nothing since Last November" on account of "loss of his eye sight." Barrow prescribed Demps "25 cuts" and "ordered him to work blind or not, to show the scoundrel."[120]

The elderly also commonly suffered from excessive tiredness, a complaint with devasting effects for those who were forced to continue laboring in old age.[121] Sylvester Sostan Wickliffe described how an "ol' lady name Aunt Jane" was unable to keep up with the ferocious pace of the sugar harvest on their plantation: "One day she was jes' a-cuttin' cane down de row and she fall fas' asleep." Wickliffe claimed that superstitious power (or perhaps muscle memory built up over a lifetime of labor) meant that even though "she ain' woke up 'till she git to de en' of de row," she "fin' she done cut de row jes' right. She ain' miss a stalk. Dat in her sleep, too." Wickliffe noted how lucky this was. Notwithstanding her advanced age, "dey would have wored her out wid de rawhide."[122] Henry H. Buttler, enslaved in

---

[117] John Brown, *Slave Life in Georgia: A Narrative of the Life, Sufferings, and Escape of John Brown, A Fugitive Slave, Now in England* (London: L. A.Chaemerovzow, 1855), 182–3.

[118] Rawick (Ed.), *AS*, *10.6*, 27.   [119] Weld, *American Slavery As It Is*, 85.

[120] June 12, 1844, Bennet H. Barrow Diary, Mss. 2978, Louisiana and Lower Mississippi Valley Collections, LSU Libraries, Baton Rouge, Louisiana. Italics mine. (Hereafter LLMVC.) Demps was described as an "old negro" on June 21, 1842.

[121] On fatigue in old age, see Stanford, *Aged Christian's Companion*, 6, 8, 67–8; Benjamin Rush, "An Account of the State of the Body and Mind in Old Age and Observations upon Its Diseases and Their Remedies," in Rush, *Medical Inquiries and Observations* (Philadelphia: Thomas Dobson, 1797), 310–11.

[122] Rawick (Ed.), *AS, Supp.*, Ser. 2, *10.9*, 4043.

Virginia, described a less fortunate result for "Old Pete." Pete, "the ox driver, had been engaged in hauling rails and then assisting us with the log rolling, became so exhausted that by the time we had finished, that he fell asleep without unyoking the oxen. For that infraction of a rule, he was given 100 lashes."[123]

Outside of punishment, excessive tiredness might simply lead to accidents, as in the death of a fifty-year-old enslaved man from Georgia who fell asleep on a railroad track and was run over by the train. His fatigue meant he slept through the "noise of a running train" and the driver's whistle.[124] Fatigue also apparently led to the death of "Old Pye," recorded by Natchez enslaver John Nevitt as having fallen in the fire and "Burnt his head and face very much."[125] In his slave narrative, William Anderson specifically linked the advanced age of an enslaved man to his tragic death. This "old slave" was the fireman in a Louisiana sugar plantation and was forced to stay awake "every night" during the firing season. The "constant taxing of the old slave's faculties, finally used up his powers of keeping awake, and one night the old man fell asleep and tumbled into the kettle of boiling hot sugar. When found he was cooked through and through – emphatically 'done brown.'"[126] In these cases, enslaved elders were quite literally worked to death.

* * *

Antebellum enslavers claimed the mantle of paternalism to defend their institution, but, in Thomas Jefferson's phrase, the "boisterous passions" of slavery could run roughshod over such self-serving assertions.[127] John Thompson even claimed that the abuse of elders served an ideological purpose in proving the dominance of enslavers. Thompson's enslaver "would not employ an overseer who did not practice whipping one or more slaves at least once a day; if not a man, then some weak or gray-headed woman. Any overseer who would not agree to these terms, could

---

[123] Rawick (Ed.), *AS, Supp.*, Ser. 2, 3.2, 554.

[124] *Sims. v. Railroad Co.* 28 Ga. 93, March, 1859.

[125] Nevitt, diary, January 18–20, 1827.

[126] William J. Anderson, *Life and Narrative of William J. Anderson, Twenty-Four Years a Slave; Sold Eight Times! In Jail Sixty Times!! Whipped Three Hundred Times!!! or The Dark Deeds of American Slavery Revealed* ... (Chicago: Daily Tribune Book and Job Printing Office, 1857), 49. On the fatigue associated with sugar cultivation, see Richard Follett, "Heat, Sex, and Sugar: Pregnancy and Childbearing in the Slave Quarters," *Journal of Family History*, 28.4 (2003), 510–39, 511, 522.

[127] Jefferson, *Notes on the State of Virginia*, 172.

find no employment on Mr. Thomas's farm."[128] When moved onto a new plantation, Thompson found that cruelty to elders was the norm, not an exception: "My old grey-headed mother, now cook, was the first victim to the uncontrollable, hellish passions of her new Mistress." She was unable to please this woman despite her previous experience, and her enslaver beat her "with shovel, tongs, or whatever other weapon lay within her reach, until exhausted herself; then, upon her husband's return, she would complain to him, and cause him to strip and whip the victim until she was unable longer to stand."[129]

Some contemporaries suggested that overseers and hired "masters" were the most culpable for elder abuse, with Thomas Edward Cox of Virginia believing it necessary to instruct his managers to "be kind and attentive to [slaves] in sickness and in old age."[130] Advice manuals specifically noted the dangers of relying on an overseer as "to him it is of no consequence that the old hands are worked down, or the young ones overstrained."[131] Matilda Mumford recounted a case where the overseer asserted his authority over nonproductive elders: "I 'member dere wuz two old women, dey couldn't work much. De overseer so mean, he tie 'em to a buggy, stark mother nekked, put a belly band on 'em, and driv' 'em down de road like dey wuz mules, whippin' 'em till dey drap down in de road." This was too extreme for some observers, who "reported him and prosecuted him, and he got run out of de county," but it was too late to help the women.[132] Laura Clark described how her enslaver similarly let two overseers "go" after returning from the Civil War to find they had abused an elderly woman. This was too little, too late, and this enslaved elder never got to see freedom: "dey done whupped dat ole 'oman what come wid us to deaf."[133]

One Florida enslaver claimed that "divided mastery" ended the life of a "rather old" man he had hired to the Macon Railroad Company. Having discovered the enslaved man "had not the strength" to handle the rails on account of pneumonia, the Company set him to work "ramming dirt under

[128] John Thompson, *The Life of John Thompson, a Fugitive Slave; Containing His History of 25 Years in Bondage, and His Providential Escape. Written by Himself* (Worcester: John Thompson, 1856), 34.

[129] Thompson, *Life of John Thompson*, 48–9.

[130] J. W. Randolph Plantation Rule Book, in Thomas Edward Cox Books, 1829–54, *Records of Antebellum Southern Plantations*, Series J: *Selections from the Southern Historical Collection*, Part 9, reel 16, 0356–66.

[131] Franklin, "Overseers," *The Southern Cultivator* II (1847), 107.

[132] Rawick (Ed.), *AS, Supp.*, Ser. 1, 4.2, 464.   [133] Rawick (Ed.), *AS*, 6, 73.

the cross ties." The man was described by one witness as "between forty and forty five," and another as "between fifty and sixty years old," but there was general agreement he was elderly. As one witness put it, "he showed his age in his grey hairs." As he grew sicker, and accordingly less productive, he was isolated in a railroad car with limited or even "no opening for the air to enter," and he "had not the necessary conveniences." He died not long after his enslaver sent a doctor to check in on him. This dispute speaks less to a kindly paternalist protecting his esteemed elder than to the financial concerns occasioned by his death. The enslaver was awarded six hundred dollars for "his" loss.[134]

Claims that overzealous overseers or hiring "masters," rather than the "masterful" owners, were to blame for mistreatment sometimes masked the everyday abuse of elders. These claims offered up a scapegoat in much the same way as that of a hiring "master" or the "trader," who could be blamed for poor treatment, sale, and separation.[135] Some contemporaries insisted that apparent abhorrence at the poor treatment of elders was self-serving and hypocritical. Abolitionist Richard Hildreth sarcastically noted that "The young lady who dines heartily on lamb, has a sentimental horror of the butcher who killed it; and the slave owner who lives luxuriously on the forced labor of his slaves, has a like sentimental abhorrence of the man who holds the whip and compels the labor."[136] Some former slaves rejected the idea that their enslavers had even pretended to be concerned with overzealous overseers. Essex Henry of North Carolina recalled the cruel treatment his grandmother faced from both overseer and enslaver: "De oberseer tried ter whup her an' he can't, so he hollers fer Mr. Jake. Mr. Jake comes an' he can't, so he hauls off an' kicks granny, mashin' her stomick in. He has her carried ter her cabin an' three days atterward she dies wid nothin' done fer her an' nobody wid her."[137] Wes Brady, enslaved in Texas, likewise noted that the desire for productivity and a concern for

---

[134] *Tallahassee Railroad Co. v. Macon*, 8 Fla. 299 (1859), 300, 299, 300, 302–3; Jonathan D. Martin, *Divided Mastery: Slave Hiring in the American South* (Cambridge, Mass.: Harvard University Press, 2004).

[135] See Michael Tadman, "The Reputation of the Slave Trader in Southern History and the Social Memory of the South," *American Nineteenth Century History*, 8.3 (2007), 247–71; Martin, *Divided Mastery*, 73, 106; William E. Wiethoff, *Crafting the Overseers Image* (Columbia: University of South Carolina Press, 2006), 32–54; Laura Sandy, *The Overseers of Early American Slavery: Supervisors, Enslaved Labourers, and the Plantation Enterprise* (London: Routledge, 2020), 350.

[136] Richard Hildreth, *The White Slave; or, Memoirs of a Fugitive* (Boston: Tappan and Whittemore, 1852), 24–5.

[137] Rawick (Ed.), *AS*, *14.1*, 395.

FIGURE 1.3 *Wes Brady, ex-slave, Marshall.* United States Marshall Texas, 1937. Dec. 4. Photograph. Courtesy of the Library of Congress, Washington, DC.

profit underpinned slavery and legitimized the exploitation or abuse of those incapable of working at such pace. After the stock were set loose in the field, the overseer on Brady's plantation blamed an old man, and broke his neck while punishing him. The slaver kept the overseer on and casually recorded a false cause of death: "the old man jus' got overhet and died."[138]

Brady's testimony illustrates the difficulties historians face when looking for elder abuse or other forms of violence in the records kept by white enslavers.[139] Peter Neilson's account of the life of Zamba, enslaved in

---

[138] Rawick (Ed.), *AS*, 4.1, 135.

[139] On the politics surrounding archival records relating to slavery's violence see Michel-Rolph Trouillot, *Silencing the Past: Power and the Production of History* (Boston: Beacon Press, 1995); Marisa J. Fuentes, *Dispossessed Lives: Enslaved Women, Violence, and the Archive* (Philadelphia: University of Pennsylvania Press, 2016); Raquel Kennon, "Slavery and the Cultural Turn," in David Stefan Doddington and

South Carolina, emphasized how power dynamics shaped the experiences of enslaved people and their historical afterlife: "To say that by law the negro is entitled to this or to that is all a mere mockery; for who is there to see these laws put in execution? or to whom is the aggrieved negro to make his complaint?"[140] Despite the difficulties Neilson identified, some white contemporaries recorded their actions and experiences with older slaves. Priscilla Munnikhuysen Bond of Mississippi noted her anguish at witnessing her father-in-law's casual punishment of elders: "I feel sad – more whipping going on. One poor old man the sufferer of man's passion. Thank God my husband is not so heartless. It is indeed hard to bear, to be compelled to stay where such is carried on *daily*."[141] Frances Kemble likewise emphasized the ubiquity of elder abuse in her critical response to proslavery claims that older slaves "ended their lives among all the comforts of home, with kindred and friends around them, in a condition which he contrasts, at least by implication, very favorably with the workhouse." Kemble recalled instead that elders were exploited until the end. Such was the case with Charity, "a miserable, decrepit old Negress," who Kemble felt must be close to death. Charity, however, was all too aware that her labors had not ended:

She did not think her work was over, much as she looked unfit for farther work on the earth; but with feeble voice and beseeching hands implored me to have her work lightened when she was sent back to it from the hospital. She is one of the oldest slaves on the plantation, and has to walk to her field labor, and back again at night, a distance of nearly four miles.[142]

Plantation journals and diaries reveal enslavers' lack of sympathy with elderly slaves and their use of physical violence to compel work or obedience. After noting his annoyance that "Old Will" had been sick and would thus "not do much work for me soon," David Golightly Harris recorded his need to punish two elderly slaves who were struggling to complete their tasks: "Yesterday I went to old Esthers. When I got there I found her & old Luke hauling her corn. The mule was stauled and would not pull. They whipped him unmercifully." Harris responded in kind: "I got some

Enrico Dal Lago (Eds.), *Writing the History of Slavery* (London: Bloomsbury Academic, 2022), 399–416.
[140] Peter Neilson, *The Life and Adventures of Zamba, an African Negro King; and His Experience of Slavery in South Carolina. Written by Himself. Corrected and Arranged by Peter Neilson* (London: Smith, Elder, 1847), 167.
[141] Priscilla Munnikhuysen Bond Papers, Typewritten transcription, Diary, 27 August 1861, Mss. 2155, LLMVC. Italics mine.
[142] Kemble, *Journal of a Residence*, 359, 288–9.

hickorys and gave them a good whipping."[143] John Nevitt punished older slaves for running away, and the repeated truancy of "Old Edmund" and "Old Sam" in 1828 suggests these men did not consider their life to be one of leisurely retirement. Sam, who was caught while stocking up with supplies from home, was whipped by Nevitt and immediately "put to work."[144] Washington Skinner, Manigault's overseer on the Hermitage plantation, described how he was "forced" to whip Carpenter Jack and Amos, aged thirty-five and fifty-three respectively, to get them to complete their work. The punishments were seen to be proportionate to their age, but the effects were clearly worse for the older man: "I had Ishmael to whip Jack well, and then Amos slightly. Jack has did [*sic*] well since. Amos had been laying up of his old complaint since Sunday night last (Asthma)."[145]

Some enslavers claimed that elders deserved protection, but theoretical reservations meant little. Enslavers wielded extraordinary power over their "property," while there were many practical difficulties standing in the way of flight for the elderly. Laura Cornish described how her own enslaver intervened to protect two elders who sought refuge from violence, but they had been forced to run away to escape violence elsewhere: "Dey takes him round de knees and begs him do he not tell dere massa where dey at, 'cause dey maybe git kilt. Dey say dey am old Lodge and Baldo and dey run 'way 'cause dare massa whips dem, 'cause dey so old day can't work no more." Cornish's enslaver bought these men and allowed them to stay on his plantation, but such escapes were the exception, not the norm.[146]

Everard Green Baker, an enslaver from Mississippi, recounted a case where a woman "between 50 & 60 years of age" was found "hanging in the calf lot, to a sapling & from the evidence it appeared her master had whipped her for 2 nights before because she would not attend to the chickens &c." Green did not seem sympathetic over the woman's choice to kill herself and implied that her response was shaped less by the physical violence than its import. He claimed the woman had been engaged in "immoral conduct" with her enslaver, and this violent punishment showed that she was no longer wanted: "my opinion is that <u>feeling</u> herself slighted, & as she supposed set aside & imposed upon she preferred to die than live thence the rash act."[147] Abolitionists commonly presented

[143] Racine (Ed.), *Piedmont Farmer*, 47, 98.
[144] Nevitt, diary, February 17, 1828 and May 20, 1828.
[145] Clifton (Ed.), *Life and Labor*, 122.   [146] Rawick (Ed.), *AS*, 4.1, 255.
[147] Everard Green Baker Papers, 1848–76, Diary, June 15, 1861, #41, SHC.

images of "concubines" abandoned as they grew older, with the tragic story of Cassie, who was sexually abused, "sold, and passed from hand to hand, till [she] grew faded and wrinkled," underscoring the degrading nature of antebellum slavery in Harriet Beecher Stowe's *Uncle Tom's Cabin*.[148] We must be cautious in using the words of a dismissive enslaver, and even white abolitionists, to uncover how these women felt about, and dealt with, sexually exploitative relations. Brenda Stevenson's assessment of the complex position of enslaved concubines, who frequently met tragic ends, offers insight here. Stevenson shows that "many concubines did not benefit from special support or privileges even when the men were alive," and "slaveholding men could abandon them and their children whenever they desired."[149] The fate of the unnamed woman described by Green aligns with Stevenson's poignant conclusion; her actions speak perhaps to the realization that, as she grew older, abuse of the kind practiced in the chicken house was only likely to worsen.

As they grew older and weaker, some elders concluded that self-destruction was their only escape from continued abuse. T. W. Cotton recalled in her WPA interview that a woman known by the age-related epithet of "Aunt Adeline" "hung herself to keep from getting a whooping," with a sense that such punishments would likely only worsen over time.[150] Adline Marshall bluntly assessed how little advanced age protected elders from the rapacious pursuit of profit, and brought home the tragic implications of this for the enslaved. Marshall told her interviewer that "Old Cap'n was jes' hard on his n***rs," and this punishing pace was felt most by Beans, a Black elder "so old he can't work good no more." Yet work he must, and when he failed to fulfill his task Beans was viciously flogged. The next morning "dey finds him hanging from a tree back of de quarters." Some historians posit suicide as a complex form of resistance for enslaved people, but Diane Miller Sommerville reminds us that such acts must also be seen as "powerful testimony to the brutal conditions under which they lived and worked."[151] This conclusion is brought home in Marshall's

---

[148] Harriet Beecher Stowe, *Uncle Tom's Cabin or, Life Among the Lowly, with an Introduction by David Bromwich* (Cambridge, Mass.: Harvard University Press, 2009; originally published Boston: John P. Jewett, 1852), 459–60, 470–9.

[149] Brenda Stevenson, "'What's love got to do with it': Concubinage and Enslaved Women and Girls in the Antebellum South," *Journal of African American History*, 98.1 (2013), 99–125, 121.

[150] Rawick (Ed.), *AS*, 8.2, 40.

[151] Diane Miller Sommerville, *Aberration of Mind: Suicide and Suffering in the Civil War-Era South* (Chapel Hill: University of North Carolina Press, 2018), 106. On suicide,

interpretation of Bean's actions. Beans was responding to his immediate punishment, but he also understood there was pain yet to come as he grew older and weaker still: Beans "hung hisself to 'scape his misery."[152]

Expectations of control and the essentially unrestrained power of enslavers on farms and plantations was a horrifying mix for some elders. Martha Griffith Browne's antislavery autobiography, based on her "firsthand experiences" as a slaver before turning abolitionist, emphasized the violence practiced on older slaves deemed useless by those who enslaved them. Polly, an elderly woman on a Kentucky plantation, lost her mind after a horrific beating and was simply left to suffer. Her enslaver Mr. Peterkin specifically fought against providing medical treatment "on that old n***r, unless you cure her, and make her able to work and pay fur the money that's bin laid out fur her." The doctor was clear this was unlikely and shared the utilitarian understanding of enslaved peoples' value: "the old thing was of but little value; she was old and worn-out." Polly died from her injuries, and the abuse predicated on economic self-interest continued after death: "Coffin! hoity-toity! Father's not going to give her a coffin, an old store-box is good enough to put her old carcass in." In the end, even this small comfort was not provided: "Good and faithful servant, even in death thou wast not allowed a bed!"[153]

Select cases bring home the horrors of violence in slavery. In Gates County, North Carolina, 1858, "Old Lamb" was beaten by two white men who held an unexplained grudge against him. They "kicked his eye out and beat him over the head with a stick" before putting him on a barrel, "bucking" him, and continuing the abuse. They only stopped "after perceiving that life was nearly extinct," but insisted that "he was deceitful and not dead," carrying him back to his cabin and dumping him on his bed. To continue with the subterfuge, they dressed him and left him there to die.[154] In 1855, in Wilkes County, North Carolina, Jim, aged sixty, suffered hideous abuse for his failure to satisfactorily complete his

---

resistance, and agency, see also Terri L. Snyder, *The Power to Die: Slavery and Suicide in British North America* (Chicago: Chicago University Press, 2015).

[152] Rawick (Ed.), *AS, Supp.,* Ser. 2, 7.6, 2577–8.

[153] Martha Griffith Browne, *Autobiography of a Female Slave* (New York: Redfield, 1857), 128–9, 140–3, 165–9. On posthumous violence, see: Berry *Price for Their Pound of Flesh,* chp 6.

[154] Coroner's Inquest over Slaves, August 29, 1858, Gates County, Slaves Records, 1783–1867, Box CR.041.928.002, NCDAH.

tasks in the stable. Over the course of an evening, Jim's enslaver Christopher Robbins tortured him to death:

After the deceased fell, the prisoner jumped on him, and stamped him for more than ten minutes; that he stamped him upon the head, shoulders, back and sides; indeed, all over; that the prisoner then called for his wagon-whip, and with the butt of it beat the deceased a long time, to wit, for half an hour, upon the head, back and sides; that he would beat until he became exhausted, and then rest and commence again; that he then called for scalding water, and there being none, had water heated, and poured it on the head, back and sides of the deceased; that he then took salt, and putting it on the back of the deceased, whipped it into the flesh with the wagon-whip ... he heated water four or five times, and poured it on the deceased; that this stamping, whipping with the wagon-whip, and pouring of the scalding water, continued without cessation until 9 or 10 o'clock at night.

The coroner's report made clear that Jim was old and comparatively weak, and later reports of the murder emphasized how "Old Jim" was "practically helpless from too much work already done that day."[155] Robbins, however, had the power to determine the levels of work expected of his aged bondsman and used sadistic levels of force to demonstrate this.

Robbins was found guilty and hung, but the court's deliberations revolved on the severity of force and perceived predetermination to kill, rather than the principle of violent punishment. Indeed, the court charged the jury "that if the master chastise his slave for the purpose of correction and amendment, and unfortunately kill him, without any intention of so doing, and without a weapon calculated to kill, he is not guilty of any offense."[156] On occasion southern whites would condemn their own, but in reality enslaved people could not use the law for their own defense, and violence that took place on the plantation was hidden from public view. As Andrew Fede argues, "the recorded antebellum US slave master capital convictions enforcing these laws were among the most brutal, sadistic, and wanton killings." In practice, enslavers who "legally enforced their power ... [could] 'rest assured that no one would interfere with their dominion over their slaves.'"[157] Jim's case was exceptional, but the trial

---

[155] Evidence docket, *State* v. *Robbins* (1855), Wilkes County, Slave papers, 1830–60, Box CR.104.928.006, NCDAH; *State* v. *Robbins*, 48. N.C. 249 (1855), 250–1; "Slave Driver Killed Negro by Hot Lead Poured in Ear," *The Charlotte Observer*, Sunday July 26, 1925 (Charlotte, North Carolina).

[156] *State* v. *Robbins*, 48. N.C. 249 (1855), 253.

[157] Andrew Fede, *Homicide Justified: The Legality of Killing Slaves in the United States and the Atlantic World* (Athens: University of Georgia Press, 2017), 223; Robert Young,

revealed expectations of dominance and of elders continuation in their labors that were simply par for the course.

* * *

Enslavers and their defenders, both during and after slavery, claimed paternalistic protection for elders. The cases listed here, however, reveal the tenuous grasp of an ideological defense of slavery when confronted with white southerners' practical concerns for profit and dominance. As Theodore Dwight Weld noted, theoretical claims over the protections of slavery all too easily melted away in the face of day-to-day tensions and the dialectics inherent to the enslaver/enslaved relationship: "Even if it were for the interest of masters to treat their slaves well, he must be a novice who thinks *that* a proof that the slaves *are* well treated. The whole history of man is a record of real interests sacrificed to present gratification."[158] Other proslavery writers were less romantic when assessing the possibility of violence but used the material interest of the master to reject claims of ill-treatment. One white WPA interviewer discounted their interviewee's recollections of mistreatment because, "irrespective of the moral turpitude involved, common sense – an ordinary regard for valuable personal property, should have restrained them from driving Negroes to the point of exhaustion, thus endangering their lives and depreciating their sales value."[159]

Those who argued that economic concerns protected enslaved people from mistreatment often neglected the inconvenient truth that, when applied to elders, such concerns simply did not hold up. As Weld went on to say: "in respect to large classes of slaves, it is for the *interest* of their masters to treat them with barbarous inhumanity." The first group listed here were "Old slaves," of whom Weld argued "It would be for the interest of the masters to shorten their days."[160] Even proslavery writers such as Josiah Clark Nott raised similar points, when discussing the practical concerns with the life insurance market in enslaved people:

As long as the negro is sound, and worth more than the amount insured, self-interest will prompt the owner to preserve the life of the slave; but if the slave become unsound and there is little prospect of perfect recovery, the underwriters

---

Domesticating Slavery: The Master Class in Georgia and South Carolina, 1670–1837 (Chapel Hill: University of North Carolina Press, 1997), 132–3.

[158] Weld, *American Slavery As It Is*, 132. Italics in original.
[159] Rawick (Ed.), *AS, Supp., Ser 1. 3.1*, 10–11.
[160] Weld, *American Slavery As It Is*, 133. Italics in original.

cannot expect fair play – the insurance money is worth more than the slave, and the latter is regarded rather in the light of a superannuated horse.[161]

The application of this logic is shown in the correspondence of James Bruce, a Virginian master who advised his nephew how best to spread out rations during the Civil War: "put your wife and children on the smallest amount of food, kill dogs, and old negroes if necessary."[162] The callousness of the remark is chilling, and indicates both the dehumanization of enslaved people by their enslavers and the brutally functionalist way elders were perceived in light of their presumed uselessness.

Former slaves certainly believed that elders were viewed as surplus to requirement, and that nakedly functional assessments placed them in danger. Jake Terriell, enslaved in North Carolina, noted that doctors were called when laboring slaves got sick, but deemed unnecessary for those with no hope of recovery: "Sometimes a slave git leg broke and massa say he no more 'count and finish him up with de club."[163] Jim Threat of Alabama claimed that two enslavers had planned on taking such measures with Black elders on account of their reduced financial circumstances, and with reference to the wider dismissal of the aged enslaved by their enslaving peers: "Gum and Alex decided they would kill off their old n***rs so they wouldn't have to take care of them any longer as they couldn't sell them and nobody wanted old n***rs." The plan was only foiled on account of their incompetence, with Alex accidently shooting Gum instead.[164]

John Hawkins Simpson's account of the life of Dinah, a Virginian slave, recorded enslaved people's fears of financially motivated murder. On one plantation, the enslaved people believed the overseer would "give to slaves who were too old to work and required attendance a dose of black juice which sent them to sleep, and that for ever." Simpson counseled skepticism regarding these claims and, outside of the Bruce letter, there is little evidence that enslavers practiced or proposed euthanasia on elderly slaves in the US South. In some respects, however, the "truth" is less important than the meaning imparted by such beliefs. Enslaved people were clearly worried about how they would be treated as they grew older and either

---

[161] Josiah Clark Nott, "Statistics of Southern Slave Population," *De Bow's Review*, 4.3 (1847), 275–89, 286. On life insurance and slavery, see Sharon Ann Murphy, "Securing Human Property: Slavery, Life Insurance and Industrialization in the Upper South," *Journal of the Early Republic*, 25.4 (2005) 615–52; Berry, *Price for Their Pound of Flesh*, 55, 88, 117, 142.

[162] Cited from Barclay, *The Mark of Slavery*, 30.   [163] Rawick (Ed.), *AS*, 5.4, 79.

[164] Rawick (Ed.), *AS, Supp.*, Ser. 1. 12, 331.

became or were perceived as being less productive. Such beliefs that enslavers would casually murder them demonstrates how far enslaved people rejected proslavery claims that enslaved elders were considered "the heir-looms of the house" who would "enjoy the evening of life and repose upon the fruits of labor past."[165] Old age, the enslaved knew, brought with it continued abuse, exploitation, and fear.

Simpson's skepticism was not in defense of enslavers. He did not dispute the rationale of enslavers' efforts to dispose of the elderly, merely the methods applied. The tragic story of Dinah's life demonstrated the range of alternatives available to enslavers seeking to divest themselves of their older slaves: "Mr. Hope determined to sell Di; for, said he, 'You are now of no service; my children are grown up, and you won't marry Jones, so there is no use my keeping you; you will be sold to-night to a trader.'"[166] Josephine Howard, enslaved in Texas, explained to her interviewer that she was glad to be growing old in freedom, not slavery, for these very reasons. According to Howard, "iffen it was slave times, I'd be dead long ago, 'cause white folks den didn't have no use for black folks when dey gets too old to work good, an' dey gets shet of 'em one way or t'other." Her interviewer clearly tried to challenge her on this point, with the transcript only recording Howard's defiant response here: "Yes suh, I's tellin' de truth, white folks sure give us bad treatment."[167] It is to enslavers' efforts to "gets shet of" elders, whether through sale, abandonment, or neglect, that we now turn.

---

[165] "Master and Servant, by the Rev. H.N McTyeire, of New Orleans," in Holland Nimmons McTyeire (Ed.), *Duties of Masters to Servants: Three Premium Essays* (Charleston: Southern Baptist Publication Society, 1851), 34.

[166] John Hawkins Simpson, *Horrors of the Virginian Slave Trade and of the Slave-Rearing Plantations. The True Story of Dinah, an Escaped Virginian Slave ...* (London: A. W. Bennett, 1863), 50.

[167] Rawick (Ed.), *AS, Supp.*, Ser. 2, 5.4, 1810.

2

"Old and broken now; no tongue can tell how much I suffer"

Sale, Abandonment, and Neglect

Some enslavers pushed and punished elders in order to continue to profit from, or simply maintain dominance over, their "property." Others chose the less physical – but no less cruel – route of abandoning (whether through cynical manumission or moving elsewhere), selling, or simply neglecting enslaved people once they had become "old and broken."[1] Manumission can, of course, be considered as evidence of antislavery impulses, but it also can be understood as a form of control designed to reinforce the power of the enslaver. Alongside this, manumission was sometimes understood as a deliberate effort of those seeking to divest themselves of useless "property."[2] Thomas Newby of Perquimans County, North Carolina, said the quiet part out loud when explaining his desire to manumit an enslaved woman named Hannah in 1797. Hannah was being set free, Newby baldly stated, because "she being grown auld, and can be very little service to me, as to any Hard Work or Drudgery."[3]

In theory, laws passed across colonies then states, both North and South, were designed to prevent such actions. Many of these explicitly addressed efforts to manumit older slaves as a form of abandonment,

---

[1] Kemble, *Journal of a Residence*, 268.

[2] On manumission regulations, see note 56 of introduction. On manumission in general, see Orlando Patterson, *Slavery and Social Death: A Comparative Study* (Cambridge, Mass.: Harvard University Press, 1982), 209–40; Marc Kleijwegt (Ed.), *The Faces of Freedom: The Manumission and Emancipation of Slaves in Old World and New World Slavery* (Boston: Leiden University Press, 2006).

[3] Petition to manumit Hannah, February 1797, Perquimans County, Slave records, 1759–1864, Petitions for Emancipation, 1776–1825, CR.077.928.002, NCDAH.

rather than evidence of benevolence, and sanctioned them accordingly.[4] Auld's request, in fact, was denied. The very prevalence of such acts, however, indicates a concern that enslavers would look to take this option without risk of punishment. During the 1790s, for example, Kentucky legislators passed resolutions designed to prevent the manumission without bond of enslaved people who "may be aged or infirm, either of body or mind." This was not out of any sense of kindness, but "to prevent their becoming chargeable to the county." Maryland legislators, building on codes from the mid-eighteenth century, similarly passed "An act to prevent disabled and superannuated slaves being set free" in 1790. This act at least spoke to the presumptions of paternalism, with the lawmakers insisting that "the faithful services of slaves should not be forgotten after they are grown old or incapable of labour." That civil action had to be threatened against those who refused "to provide necessary and sufficient food, cloathing [*sic*], covering or dwelling, for such old or disabled slave or slaves," or to those who suffered, perhaps forced, "any such slave or slaves to depart from their respective habitation or quarter, and wander or remain at large, begging or becoming burthensome" suggests the white community knew that protection promised was not protection guaranteed.[5]

Other statutes insisted that it was the responsibility of "owners of old or infirm slaves to maintain them," or fined any "master or owner of a slave of unsound mind, or aged or infirm, who shall permit such slave to go at large, without adequate provision for his or her support."[6]

---

[4] See Klebaner, "American Manumission Laws."

[5] Maryland. General Assembly, "An Act to Repeal Certain Parts of an Act, Entitled, An Act to Prevent Disabled and Superannuated Slaves Being Set Free, or the Manumission of Slaves by Any Last Will and Testament," in *Laws of Maryland, Made and Passed at a Session of Assembly* ... (Annapolis: Frederick Green, 1790). Maryland passed a revised version of this law in 1796, in which the previous cut-off date for manumission was lowered from fifty to forty-five, indicating that this was considered a marker of old age. Maryland. General Assembly, "An Act Relating to Negroes, and to Repeal the Acts of Assembly Therein Mentioned," *Laws of Maryland, Made and Passed at a Session of Assembly* (Annapolis: Frederick Green, 1796), 67, 251.

[6] Georgia. General Assembly, "An Act To Compel Owners of Old or Infirm Slaves to Maintain Them," in *Acts of the General Assembly of the State of Georgia ... 1815* [Vol. 1], 34–5; Virginia. General Assembly, "An Act to Amend an Act, Entitled 'An Act to Reduce Into One Act, The Several Acts Concerning Slaves, Free Negroes, and Mulattoes,' and For Other Purposes," March 5, 1824, in *Acts Passed at a General Assembly of the Commonwealth of Virginia ...* (Richmond: Thomas Ritchie, 1824), 34.3 (37). That additional protection was required was evidenced by the Georgia General Assembly passing "An Act to Establish an Infirmary for the Relief and Protection of Aged

In *Inhabitants of Winchendon* v. *Inhabitants of Hatfield*, 1808, Chief
Justice Parsons of Massachusetts plainly articulated the rationale for
these types of laws. Referring specifically to Statute 2 Anne, where "a
master of a manumitted slave must indemnify the town where he lives,"
Parsons noted the need to guard against unscrupulous enslavers: "A
practice was prevailing to manumit aged or infirm slaves, to relieve the
master from the charge of supporting them. To prevent this practice,
the act was passed."[7] The judgment in the US Supreme Court on
Wallingsford v. *Allen*, 1836, which built on this earlier legislation,
was likewise clear as to the economic rationale behind these restrictions: "the terms of the Maryland act, and the policy intended by it,
were meant to prevent the manumission of slaves, who, from infancy,
age, or decrepitude, would become burdensome to the community."[8]
The framing of this legislation underscores how old age was understood
as a period of inevitable decline, with the idea that elderly ex-slaves
would, by necessity, be incapable of self-care. It demonstrates, moreover, that the wider white community wished to absolve themselves of
responsibility for the collective harms of slavery, as personified in the
bodies of the aged enslaved.

Despite legal restrictions, ex-slaves such as Harriet Jacobs insisted
that enslavers looked to get "rid of old slaves, whose lives have been
worn out in their service," and described her anguish at witnessing such
treatment of an "old woman, who for seventy years faithfully served her
master," but who had now "become almost helpless, from hard labor
and disease." To absolve themselves of responsibilities and cost, "her
owners moved to Alabama, and the old black woman was left to be sold
to any body who would give twenty dollars for her."[9] One antislavery
"eyewitness to slavery" recalled a similar episode when encountering an
eighty-year-old man in Richmond. This man, whose labor had helped
"to bring up three generations of white people," was now "nearly eighty,
and unable to do much." As a result, his owners had "turned him out to
knock about for himself." The northern author was shocked, claiming
that the numerous laws that "bind the slaveholder to provide for his old
and infirm slaves" should have prevented this. The free Black man who

---

and Afflicted Negroes, in the State of Georgia," *Acts of the General Assembly of the State
of Georgia; Passed in November and December, 1832* [Vol. 1], 176–7.

[7] *Inhabitants of Winchendon* v. *Inhabitants of Hatfield*, 4 Mass. 123 (1808), 129.

[8] *Wallingsford* v. *Allen*, 35 U.S. 10 Pet. 583 (1836), 583.

[9] Jacobs, *Incidents in the Life*, 27.

was guiding him around the city, however, was attuned to the practical workings of power:

"I know not," said he, "whether there are such laws or not; but if there were they would not enforce themselves; and who would take the part of that poor old man against a popular and wealthy family? They turn them out all over to die like old horses when they can work them no longer."[10]

Cases of abandonment occurred in northern states as well as southern, speaking to the institutional violence of slavery and the centrality of economic self-interest for enslavers. In an 1860 editorial celebrating the anniversary of the Colored Home in New York, the *Weekly Anglo-African* noted how this support was needed because "from time immemorial there have been a large number of colored persons in the city, who from age and sickness, were unable to take care of themselves." These individuals had lost the best years of their lives to slavery, having "served with faithfulness for many years the aristocracy of the city, but who had been left by them destitute in their declining years." Indeed, "these were the persons originally selected for inmates of the asylum."[11]

Abandoned elders might find support from the Black community, but local whites were often less than impressed at having to step in for the absent "master." In 1802, the Selectmen of Windsor, Vermont, brought a case charging Stephen Jacob of having abandoned Dinah, who he had enslaved from 1783 until 1800, "when she became infirm, sick, and blind." Dinah was then "discarded by the defendant." The charges were brought to recover monies expended in providing her with healthcare and support, but the plaintiffs addressed the assumed responsibilities of enslavers to elders. Dinah, who had expended "the vigour of her life in his service," should have "presumed to have earned for the master sufficient to maintain her in the decrepitude of old age." Jacob, however, cruelly twisted the logic of emancipation in the postrevolutionary North to absolve himself of any lasting responsibility here. His attorney asked a "simple point": "Is the defendant obligated to refund moneys advanced by others for medicine and attendance, and in support of a woman who had formerly been in his service? We contend that it cannot be upon any other principle than that she is his slave; which cannot be admitted under our constitution of government." Jacob was successful in making his case that, as slavery no longer existed, neither did his responsibility toward

[10] "Slavery by an Eye-Witness," *Provincial Freeman* (July 29, 1854).
[11] "Anniversary of the Colored Home," *Weekly Anglo-African* (June 16, 1860).

Dinah. We hear nothing from Dinah herself as she was left to her decrepitude.[12]

Moving from North to South, the Chancery Court of Prince Edward County, Virginia, heard a callous tale of abandonment and neglect when Richard K. Randolph left Virginia for Rhode Island in 1810, leaving behind property and people. One of these was Betty, who was "old and infirm & helpless." Thompson Craghead claimed to have taken responsibility for Betty's care on the condition that Randolph's agent, William Berkeley, would pay him "a sum of money, for & in consideration of services rendered by your Orator to said Betty." Out of sight, however, was out of mind. Craghead claimed to have fulfilled his end of the bargain, having "gone on to clothe and support, lodge and nurse said helpless & infirm old & decreped negro woman," but Randolph had not. Craghead now wanted relief from this burden. Randolph's defense to the suit shows the expected exploitation of elders, with his lawyers claiming that when he left, and despite her advanced years, Betty was still "capable of rendering important services on a plantation in the superintendance & care of negro children."[13] Randolph rejected the idea that Craghead had taken Betty out of benevolence and instead emphasized that he had expected her to continue laboring long after he had left her. The case was ultimately unresolved, but Randolph appears to have avoided any financial culpability and, in doing so, left evidence of the continued exploitation enslaved elders faced.

In 1836, in Kentucky, one Black elder found himself abandoned not once but twice, by enslavers who sought to avoid supporting him in old age. The Justices of Harrison County, who were "bound by law to provide for the support and maintenance of the poor," sued Jonathon Neal for $400. Neal had moved to Missouri and left behind "a negro slave named James who is about 70 years of age and who is entirely a cripple & cannot work." James had since been residing with the family of George Cleveland, but Cleveland had now moved to Mississippi. The Justices stressed the paternalistic ethos behind their complaint, noting "that it is the moral and legal duty of said Neal to provide for his aged and infirm slave," but also underscored the financial implications of elder abandonment. James would otherwise "become chargeable to your Orators as Justices aforesaid." With no result recorded, it appears unlikely that

---

[12] *Selectmen v. Jacob*, 2 Tyler 192 (Vt. 1802), 193, 194, 198.

[13] Petition of Thompson Craghead, c. July 1831; Answer, Richard K. Randolph, September 18, 1833, Prince Edward County, Virginia, #21683103, Series 2, RSPP.

James received support from his former "masters."[14] The care he received from the Justices is unclear, but the treatment recorded by James Redpath of an abandoned elder in New Orleans does not provide much hope. Redpath encountered a man whose "wool was silvery; his face was deeply furrowed; his eyes were filmy with disease and age," and explained that he had been sold, but the purchaser refused to honor the sale on account of his infirmity: "Alone – sick – a member of an outcast race – without money – without family – and without a home in his tottering old age! Where could the wretched invalid go?" The elder applied to the police for protection, whose care extended to taking "him to the jail," where they "confined him in that putrid cell!"[15]

In Spartanburg District, South Carolina, 1847, a ninety-year-old woman named Tenor was abandoned by her enslaver when she was no longer regarded as productive: "her owner finding she was of no value left the State & left the negro upon the public Charity." This support had dwindled over the years and eventually dried up entirely, leaving Tenor alone and in distress: "she was found in the Road near the house of your petitioners' father in a helpless state." The parents of A. Foster had supported her for some years in this condition, but upon their death she was left helpless once more. The son was unwilling to continue this arrangement and applied "to the commissioners of the poor with a strong presentation of her case to them, while she was actually delivered to the Keeper of the paupers." No one, however, was willing to accept responsibility for a woman who had been enslaved for ninety years: "The Commissioners have rejected her case & turned her off – to perish unless some friendly hand will care for her & feed her." In this instance, the court granted the request and the Commissioners of the Poor were forced to take her on as a pauper. The language with which the decision was framed suggests the court's "generosity" was shaped by their expectation (and hope) such support would be short-lived: "She is now upwards of ninety years of age, as it is supposed & will probably not live long."[16] In 1855 the

---

[14] Petition of Justices of Harrison County Court, September 17, 1836, #20783623, Series 2, RSPP.

[15] James Redpath, *The Roving Editor: Or, Talks with Slaves in the Southern States* (New York: Negro Universities Press, 1968; originally published in 1859 by A. B. Burdick), 179.

[16] Petition of A. Foster, June 7, 1847; Notice from Commissioners of the Poor, James Ezell Clark, April 10, 1847; Order, June 7, 1847; Affidavits, Benjamin Wofford, Calvin Foster, June 5, 1847; Orders, ca. June 7, 1847, June 8, 1847, Spartanburg District, South Carolina, #21384706, Series 2, RSPP.

New Orleans Delta recorded a similar case where an abandoned elder had, in fact, not "lived long": "It appeared from the evidence, that the negro was too old to work any more, being near seventy; and so they drove him forth into the woods to die." Olmsted, who remarked on this case in his travel writing, suggested that such activities were likely widespread but easily hidden from public view: "other papers omit to notice it – as they usually do facts which it may be feared will do discredit to Slavery."[17]

Southern whites were correct to fear the reporting of such actions. Black activists and their allies framed manumission of older slaves as a deliberately abusive and deeply cynical process shaped by financial considerations. Austin Steward recalled the abandonment of his grandparents after "old age deprived them of farther exertion." At this point "they were turned out, like an old horse, to die; and did die destitute and uncared for, in their aged infirmity, after a long life of unrequited toil."[18] Ex-slaves insisted that enslavers' claims of paternalism were paper thin and easily torn when set against economic self-interest. James Watkins stressed that "if a slave, having lived and worked hard for sixty or seventy years, until he can work no longer, requires a shelter for his head in his old age, the workhouse door – open to the most debased and degraded – is closed against him, and he is left to die in the street like a dog."[19] The *North Star* recounted the tale of Sarah Crumwell, who had been set free by her Baltimore enslaver after ninety years of service. This was no act of benevolence, but instead because her age-related infirmities had "depreciated her value as a piece of property." Crumwell responded furiously to the jailor's offer of the fare to Philadelphia if she would accept manumission and attacked the injustice of enslavement: "'No!' was her indignant reply, and her eyes flashed fire as she spoke, 'I told Master, that he had worn all the flesh off my bones, and he should not throw the worthless bones upon any other hands.'" Sadly, however, "she was a slave, and her will was powerless." Crumwell was "turned out homeless, friendless, and

---

[17] Frederick Law Olmsted, *A Journey in the Seaboard Slave States; With Remarks on Their Economy* (New York; London: Dix and Edwards; Sampson & Low, 1856), 710–11.

[18] Austin Steward, *Twenty-Two Years a Slave, and Forty Years a Freeman; Embracing a Correspondence of Several Years, While President of Wilberforce Colony, London, Canada West* (Rochester: William Alling, 1857), 336–7.

[19] James Watkins, *Struggles for Freedom; or the Life of James Watkins, Formerly a Slave in Maryland, US; in Which Is Detailed a Graphic Account of His Extraordinary Escape from Slavery, Notices of the Fugitive Slave Law, the Sentiments of American Divines on the Subject of Slavery, etc., etc.* (Manchester: A. Heywood, Oldham Street, 1860), 70.

almost pennyless" before receiving support from the abolitionist community in Philadelphia.[20]

Sojourner Truth equally stressed the self-interest that shaped enslavers' actions toward elderly slaves and the tragic consequences that stemmed from this, describing how her parents, Bomefree and Mau-mau Bennett, were granted a nominal form of freedom after no one was willing to buy them on account of their age. Mau-mau died shortly after being placed in an isolated cabin with the "support" of her former enslaver, but Bomefree lingered on and suffered. Eventually, "this faithful slave, this deserted wreck of humanity, was found on his miserable pallet, frozen and stiff in death." Truth stressed the lack of support provided to elders and the cynicism of these manumissions: "Yes, he had died, chilled and starved, with none to speak a kindly word, or do a kindly deed for him, in that last dread hour of need!" It was only upon his death that his enslavers rediscovered their commitment to paternalism, as they insisted that "Bomefree, who had ever been a kind and faithful slave, should now have a good funeral." Truth bluntly assessed how little this counted for now: "What a compensation for a life of toil, of patient submission to repeated robberies of the most aggravated kind, and, also, far more than murderous neglect!!"[21]

* * *

Abandonment in such a way was theoretically illegal, but there were few explicit limitations to the sale of elders save that of the logic of the marketplace.[22] Michael Tadman has demonstrated that interregional slave trade was "markedly age-selective, concentrating most heavily on those of about fifteen to twenty-five years of age," while others have

---

[20] "Slaveholding Humanity – Turning Loose," *The North Star*, November 16, 1849.

[21] Sojourner Truth and Olive Gilbert, *Narrative of Sojourner Truth, a Northern Slave, Emancipated from Bodily Servitude by the State of New York, in 1828* (Boston: The Author, 1850), 18–26.

[22] On regulations and the internal slave trade, see Rosenthal, *Accounting for Slavery*, 141–51; Andrew Fede, "Legal Protection for Slave Buyers in the US South: A Caveat Concerning Caveat Emptor," *American Journal of Legal History*, 31.4 (1987), 322–58; Morris, *Southern Slavery and the Law*, 102–32; Gross, *Double Character*, 123–7; Deyle, *Carry Me Back*, 162–6. In Louisiana's Black Code of 1806, reinforced in 1829, some provisions were that "if at a public sale of slaves, there happen to be some who be disabled through old age or otherwise, and who have children, such slaves shall not be sold but with such of his children whom he or she may think proper to go with." See Charles W. Calomoris and Jonathan B. Pritchett, "Preserving Slave Families for Profit: Traders' Incentives and Pricing in the New Orleans Slave Market," *Journal of Economic History*, 69.4 (2009), 986–1011.

shown that "interregional traders preferred to traffic in higher-valued slaves."[23] However, Thomas Jefferson's claim that American slavers were better than the Romans because, unlike in antiquity, they did not sell their "sick and superannuated slaves" was simply untrue.[24] Antebellum southerners saw "human forms, from infancy to grey hairs, sold under the hammer."[25] For sellers, the logic of getting rid of unproductive workers was clear. Hannah Jones, enslaved in Missouri, claimed that it was "de old ones was de ones dey was anxious to get shet of," and Clara Allen of Virginia argued with her interviewer over the frequency of such sales.[26] Allen insisted that "when de sla – '(she corrects herself)' colored folks got ter be old an' couldn't work much longer, their masters would sell um to keep from buryin' um." It "cost ten dollars to bury um" if buying the coffin or the carpenter could be made to take on this job. However, as Allen put it, "de master don't wanner lose de time from other work," so "soon as one got real old you hear talk of sellen him."[27]

Prospective buyers were typically less enthused by the prospect of purchasing elderly slaves. Charles Manigault noted how, after having seen one auction list comprised "more than half old," he "would not even attend the sale," while Mittie Freeman recalled how her elderly father was on the auction block but left unwanted on account of age: "Every auction sale, all the young n***rs be sold; everybody pass old pappy by."[28] Abolitionist Richard Hildreth explained at one estate sale that the younger slaves, including children, were very quickly purchased. "It was very difficult to get a bid for several of the old people," however, and "some of the old and decrepid slaves could not be sold at all. They were not worth purchasing, and nobody would bid." Hildreth did "not know what became of them."[29] Neither do we.

Advanced age was a limiting factor for sale, but this did not stop industrious enslavers from making money from Black elders. Contemporaries recorded, in fact, the layers of deceit enslavers employed when selling those

---

[23] Tadman, *Speculators and Slaves*, 25–31, 25. Further appendices and information on age-related structures to the trade can be found on 241–7; Jonathan B. Pritchett and Herman Freudenberger, "A Peculiar Sample: A Reply to Steckel and Ziebarth," *Journal of Economic History*, 76.1 (2016), 139–62.

[24] Jefferson, *Notes on the State of Virginia*, 151.

[25] Aaron, *The Light and Truth of Slavery: Aaron's History* (Worcester: The Author, 1845), 16.

[26] *FWP, 10* (Missouri), 215.   [27] Perdue et al., *Weevils in the Wheat*, 7.

[28] Clifton (Ed.), *Life and Labor*, 239; Rawick (Ed.), *AS*, 8.2, 347.

[29] Richard Hildreth, *The Slave: or Memoirs of Archy Moore. Vol. I* (Boston: John H. Eastburn, Printer, 1836), 127–8.

considered old. Mark Discus was asked by the seemingly incredulous WPA interviewer whether it was true "that they greased the bodies of the older ones before they sold them," and he simply replied "Yes Suh, they did."[30] Rose Williams explained other methods applied to achieve similar effects, noting that "if one was getting ole and a few gray hairs growin out, dey would have em pulled out cause dat would ruin de sale of em."[31] Lewis Clarke emphasized the efforts traders made to hide visible markers of the aging process: "The old master ordered the waiter or coachman to take Paris into the back room, pluck out all his grey hairs, rub his face with a greasy towel, and then had him brought forward and sold for a young man."[32]

William Wells Brown claimed to have had personal responsibility for managing the physical appearance of slaves to be sold, making clear the significance accorded to – and the connections enslavers drew between – age and ability: "I was ordered to have the old men's whiskers shaved off, and the grey hairs plucked out, where they were not too numerous, in which case he had a preparation of blacking to color it, and with a blacking-brush we would put it on." According to Wells Brown, such deception was often successful: "after going through the blacking process, they looked ten or fifteen years younger … and I am sure that some of those who purchased slaves of Mr. Walker, were dreadfully cheated, especially in the ages of the slaves which they bought."[33] Alongside physical deception, enslaved people were sometimes told to present themselves as being of a certain age, with Wells Brown claiming the "slaves were also taught how old they were by Mr. Walker" and expected to repeat this accordingly. John Brown likewise recalled how enslaved people at auction were told to "conceal any defects they may have, and especially not to tell their age when they are getting past the active period of life." The references to *especially* suggests how significant age was considered in assessing laboring ability, while an emphasis on *getting past* the active period of life underscores how aging was seen as a process of inexorable decline with no way back. Brown reiterated this was not a request: "he must say he is just as old as his master chooses to bid him do, or he will have to take the consequences."[34]

[30] Rawick (Ed.), *AS, Supp.*, Ser. 1, 2, 172.

[31] Rawick (Ed.), *AS, Supp.*, Ser. 2, 10.9, 4127.

[32] Lewis Garrard Clarke, *Narratives of the Sufferings of Lewis Clarke, During a Captivity of More Than Twenty-Five Years Among the Algerines of Kentucky, One of the So Called Christian States of America. Dictated by Himself* (Boston: David H. Ela, Printer, 1845), 70–1.

[33] William Wells Brown, *Narrative of Williams Wells Brown, A Fugitive Slave Written by Himself* (Boston: The Anti-Slavery Office, 1847), 42–3.

[34] Brown, *Slave Life in Georgia*, 115–16.

Prospective purchasers attempted to work around such deception, with physical examinations common, crude, and cruel.[35] Some enslavers claimed to have specific skills in determining age through inspection of the body. Louis Hughes recalled that "sometimes the slave would be required to open his mouth that the purchaser might examine the teeth and form some opinion as to his age and physical soundness."[36] Prospective buyers still had to grapple here with the tensions in assessing chronological or functional age, with Virginia Hayes Shepard recalling how her "mother while she was only thirty or thereabout had lost the use of all her teeth, which practically cut her value in half."[37] James Martin, enslaved in Virginia and Texas, similarly emphasized the significance of teeth when assessing age and ability and recalled how at the auction block a prospective buyer challenged the listings: "one bidder takes a pair of white gloves they have and rubs his fingers over a man's teeth, and he says, 'You say this buck's 20 years old, but there's cups worn to his teeth. He's 40 years if he's a day.'"[38] The enslaved man's price was knocked down, but he was sold regardless. Other enslavers instead lauded their ability to tell age from the condition of enslaved people's skin. James Brown claimed his "Marster could tells de sound n***r soons he looks at dem," with his method entailing assessing the elasticity of the skin: "Ise see hims tak de pinch ob skin on top 'ob de hand and lift it up, den lets it drap. If dat skin goes back quick, de Marster sez, 'dat n***r am still young.'"[39] Henry Bibb similarly recalled how enslavers would "prick up the skin on the back of their hands," as "if the person is very far advanced in life, when the skin is pricked up, the pucker will stand so many seconds on the back of the hand." Bibb noted, however, that despite enslavers' confidence and self-regard, this would always be an imprecise science: it was simply "hard to tell the ages of slaves."[40]

Buyers had recourse to the law in cases of fraud or deceit over the condition of slaves sold, but the doctrine of caveat emptor (buyer

---

[35] See Deyle, *Carry Me Back*, 135–58; Walter Johnson, *Soul by Soul: Life Inside the Antebellum Slave Market* (Cambridge, Mass.: Harvard University Press, 2001), 135–61.

[36] Louis Hughes, *Thirty Years a Slave: From Bondage to Freedom. The Institution of Slavery as Seen on the Plantation and in the Home of the Planter* (Milwaukee: South Side Printing Co., 1897), 8. Enslaved women were routinely sexually assaulted during such "examinations." See Brown, *Slave Life in Georgia*, 117–18; "Slavery by an Eye-Witness," *Provincial Freeman* (July 29, 1854); Perdue et al., *Weevils in the Wheat*, 166; Berry, *Price for Their Pound of Flesh*, 12–13, 72.

[37] Perdue et al., *Weevils in the Wheat*, 261.   [38] Rawick (Ed.), *AS*, 5.3, 63.

[39] Rawick (Ed.), *AS*, *Supp.*, Ser. 2, 3.2, 476.

[40] Henry Bibb, *Narrative of the Life and Adventures of Henry Bibb, An American Slave Written by Himself* (New York: Published for the Author, 1849), 101.

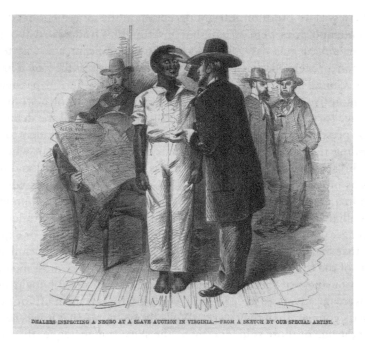

DEALERS INSPECTING A NEGRO AT A SLAVE AUCTION IN VIRGINIA.—FROM A SKETCH BY OUR SPECIAL ARTIST.

FIGURE 2.1 "Slave Sale, Richmond, Virginia, 1861," *The Illustrated London News* (Feb. 16, 1861), 138. Courtesy of *Slavery Images: A Visual Record of the African Slave Trade and Slave Life in the Early African Diaspora*, www .slaveryimages.org/s/slaveryimages/page/welcome.

beware) left some enslavers out of pocket.[41] In one contested sale in Alabama, 1846, Walker Reynolds stressed that he had made clear to John Woodward that he was interested in Dane, aged about thirty, "large and likely," but that he would not buy the forty to fifty-year-old Governor "at any price." Governor was simply "older than he wished to purchase."[42] In the melee of the auction room, however, Reynolds accidently bid for, and successfully "won," Governor. The court dismissed his efforts to back out of the sale, as, without deception or fraud, they determined that Reynolds had no one to blame but himself for his lack of care.

[41] See footnote 22 for laws on sale.
[42] Petition of Walker Reynolds, November 17, 1846; Affidavit, Walker Reynolds, November 17, 1845; Injunction, November 19, 1845; Decree, July 1846, Talladega County, Alabama, #20184517, Series 2, RSPP.

There was no proof of outright deception in the aforementioned case, but contemporaries were certain that unscrupulous traders lied about age and, in making this case, underscored how significant age was to the valuation process. Richard Hildreth recorded the "skills" of a trader named Gouge here: "very few persons could outdo him in passing off a consumptive or scrofulous hand as every way sound, or a woman of forty-five for a woman of thirty." John Brown highlighted the dehumanization present in the "soul" trade by noting the pride some traders took in offloading their useless "stock" through deception: "the man who succeeds in 'shoving off a used up n***r,' as one sound in wind and limb, takes as much pride in boasting of it, as the horse dealer does who has taken in a green-horn with a wall-eyed pony."[43] In his postbellum memoir, William Wells Brown went into great detail about how traders lied about age, with such efforts underscoring the broader culture of exploitation that shaped interactions in the Slave South. Wells Brown detailed the efforts of the trader James Walker, and recalled that "like most men who make a business of speculating in human beings, he often bought many who were far advanced in years, and would try to pass them off for five or six years younger than they were." Wells Brown noted that it was hard to prove the age of those sold, and thus "the slave-trader frequently carried out the deception with perfect impunity." Enslaved people were forced into complicity here, with the contest between buyer and seller revealing the significance attached to age in the context of sale, work, and exploitation. Brown recalled one such episode at length:

Pompey would pick out the older portion and say, "I is de chap dat is to get you ready for de Orleans market, so dat you will bring marser a good price. How old is you?" addressing himself to a man that showed some age.

"Ef I live to see next corn-plantin' time, I'll be forty."

"Dat may be," replied Pompey, "but now you is only thirty years old; dat's what marser says you is to be."

"I know I is mo' dan dat," responded the man.

"I can't help nuffin' 'bout dat," returned Pompey; "but when you get in de market, an' any one ax you how old you is, an' you tell um you is forty, massa will tie yon up, an' when he is done whippin' you, you'll be glad to say you's only thirty."

"Well den, I reckon I is only thirty," said the slave.

"What is your name?" asked Pompey of another man in the group.

"Jeems," was the response.

"Oh! Uncle Jim, is it?"

---

[43] Hildreth, *The White Slave*, 328–30; Brown, *Slave Life in Georgia*, 116.

"Yes."

"Den you muss' hab all dem gray whiskers shaved off, and dem gray hairs plucked out of your head. De fack is, you's got ole too quick." This was all said by Pompey in a manner which showed that he knew his business.

The difficulties in assessing age and ability – and the importance accorded to these categories – are brought to light in complaints raised by enslavers over the "soundness" of enslaved people they had purchased. Wells Brown, in fact, provided a lengthy description of the back-and-forth between the different actors at an auction that showcased the suspicion toward (and significance accorded) age at point of sale:

"What's your name?" asked a man, in a straw hat, of a tall negro, who stood with his arms folded across his breast, leaning against the wall.

"My name is Aaron, sar."

"How old are you?"

"Twenty-five."

"Where were you raised?"

"In ole Virginny, sar."

"How many men have owned you?"

"Four."

"Do you enjoy good health?"

"Yes, sar."

"How long did you live with your first owner?"

"Twenty years."

"Did you ever run away?"

"No, sar."

"Did you ever strike your master?"

"No sar."

"Were you ever whipped much?"

"No, sar; I spose I didn't desarve it, sar."

"How long did you live with your second master?"

"Ten years, sar."

"Have you a good appetite?"

"Yes, sar."

"Can you eat your allowance?"

"Yes, sar,–when I can get it."

"Where were you employed in Virginia?"

"I worked in de tobacker fiel'."

"In the tobacco field, eh?"

"Yes, sar."

"How old did you say you was?"

"Twenty-five, sar, nex' sweet-'tater-diggin' time."

"I am a cotton-planter, and if I buy you, you will have to work in the cotton field. My men pick one hundred and fifty pounds a day, and the women one hundred and forty pounds; and those who fail to perform their task receive five stripes for each pound that is wanting. Now do you think you could keep up with the rest of the hands?"

"I don't know, sar, but I reckon I'd have to."

"How long did you live with your third master?"

"Three years, sar," replied the slave.

"Why, that makes you thirty-three; I thought you told me you were only twenty-five."

Aaron now looked first at the planter, then at the trader, and seemed perfectly bewildered. He had forgotten the lesson given him by Pompey, relative to his age; and the planter's circuitous questions – doubtless to find out the slave's real age – had thrown the negro off his guard.

Pompey stepped in at this point to try and smooth things over and Aaron was eventually "pronounced sound." He was not purchased, however, because "the conflicting statement about his age was not satisfactory."[44] We hear nothing about the consequence of Aaron's failure to keep up the pretense, but this was no minor fault. Overseer-turned-abolitionist John Roles described how one man's unwillingness to lie about his age in the auction house led to abuse and tragedy. After "Preacher George's" aborted sale he was whipped and sold to a known abuser of slaves. George attempted to run away from this horror, but he was instead "found, by a neighbor, a few days afterwards, lying dead in the swamp."[45]

* * *

The legal efforts enslavers made to recover monies from disputed sales speak to the associations of advanced age with declining productivity and the significance of economic self-interest in shaping enslavers' behaviors. After purchasing Ann with an assurance she was twenty-eight and healthy, Georgia enslaver Bennet Dooly was shocked to find Ann was "at least Fifty years of age ... was not firm & Healthy but on the contrary ... afflicted with Divers Diseases & Mallodies." Dooly requested $1,000 in damages because he believed that Ann was "of little value to your petitioner" and that he would need to replace her with someone younger.[46] In *Peers v. Davis*, 1860, the Supreme Court of Missouri heard the complaints of one enslaver's family that he had

---

[44] William Wells Brown, *My Southern Home: Or, The South and Its People* (Boston: A. G. Brown & Co., Publishers, 1880), 113–15.

[45] John Roles, *Inside Views of Slavery on Southern Plantations* (New York: John A Gray & Green, Printers and Stereotypes, 1864), 43.

[46] Petition of Bennet Dooly, c. 1818, Elbert County, Superior Court Minutes & Records, 1819, Box 92, Reel 3, 164–6, GSA.

been "deluded" into purchasing an elderly woman named Katy. Katy had been listed as around fifty but "was in fact worthless, diseased and many years older than represented." The dispute raged on, with some witnesses claiming that the purchaser, Luke Davis, had known Katy's reduced capabilities and thus his estate was not privy to damages. One witness even claimed that Davis was willing to further the deceit if it suited him: "he told Sebastian, at the time the bill of sale was being written, to put the age of the negro at about fifty or fifty-five years, and not to make her too damned old, as he might want to sell her again." Judge Ewing concluded that there was little evidence of deliberate manipulation, with the initial seller deliberately vague on Katy's age and providing a hint that purchasing her came with no little risk: "As to her age there is simply a representation, and that is made in such guarded and cautious terms and with such qualification as clearly to show the vendor's intention to incur no liability on that score."[47] Enslavers and traders daily played games with enslaved peoples' past, present, and future experiences; these contests over age at sale speak to the disregard white southerners had to those whom they enslaved.

In *Scott* v. *Clarkson*, 1808, the Kentucky Court of Appeals heard the complaints of an executrix that her elderly husband had been tricked into buying a woman listed as "twenty-five years of age, and as sound and healthy," but who was, in fact, "unsound, and nearly forty years of age or upward." Scott claimed that the defendants had knowingly misrepresented the woman in their efforts to offload her in her declining years, and now refused to take her back.[48] *Lawrence* v. *McFarlane*, 1829, saw two Louisiana enslavers disagree over the abilities of an enslaved woman described as "old and decrepid," but who was sold for $250 once the seller guaranteed the woman was still exploitable. Indeed, she was still "able to do the house work." Various prior owners derided her as being "more lazy than sick," but the plaintiff insisted that she had been a poor purchase on account of her age and infirmities, which were worse than described. He had even "been compelled to hire another person to do the work he expected from her." The dispute reveals the continued economic exploitation of elders through the sale itself, but also the disdain with which they were treated if they failed to work productively. The plaintiff's charges were dismissed in part because he was deemed to have deliberately

[47] *Peers* v. *Davis' Administrators*, 29 Mo. 184 (1859), 185, 186, 185, 188.
[48] *Scott* v. *Clarkson*, 4 Ky. 277, 1 Bibb 277 (1808), 277.

neglected the woman upon realizing she was useless to him. Justice Martin explained:

It is not extraordinary that a decrepit old woman, sold for $250, whose owner contented himself with a few external applications, while the physician he had called recommended a course of medicine that would cure her, should be disabled by her disease, long left to itself, from labor, and smart severely under the late epidemic.[49]

The financial implications of elder care, not paternalistic obligations following a lifetime of labor, were central to the dispute here. The "decrepit old woman," who was forced to "labor, and smart severely" in her illness, was not even named.

Concerns over the cost and soundness of enslaved people on account of their age reveal the limits to paternalism when the bottom line was under threat. In 1806, Kentucky enslaver William Dougherty claimed he had been tricked into buying Nanny for $150, having been told she was fifty but "was a good one." Upon arrival, however, he was informed she was at least seventy and suffering badly from rheumatism. This elicited no sympathy from the man who had hoped to exploit her: "she was a burthen to him, and not worth her maintenance." Indeed, Dougherty was abundantly clear on how little value he placed on Nanny on account of her age: "had he have known her infirmities and advanced age at the time of the purchase aforesaid he would not have given one dollar for her and would not now give one cent for her." He would, in fact, "thank anyone to take her off his hands and free him from her maintenance & taxes."[50] It is not clear that anyone took him up on this offer. Dougherty's disgust at having to provide for "a burthen" considered "not worth her maintenance" was unlikely to lead to a happy life for Nanny.

The dispute over the value and health of Lucia, sold in South Carolina in 1842, provides insight into the self-interest and economic impulses that influenced some enslavers' treatment of elderly and ailing slaves. Lucia was purchased by William Caldwell at $350, which one witness thought too much "because she is at least forty-seven years of age." Lucia was also suffering from cancer. Despite her plaintive statements on the auction block that she was "unsound," Lucia was purchased at full price. After discovering that Lucia had told the truth, her enslaver sought to return her or recover his money on account of her illness. He had, however, failed to

---

[49] *Lawrence v. McFarlane*, 7 Mart. (n.s) 558 (1829), 559, 560, 563.
[50] Petition of William Dougherty, May 15, 1810, Jefferson County, Kentucky, #20781006, Series 2, RSPP.

take out a written warranty and so lost his case. In the course of testifying about Lucia's condition, the expert witnesses agreed that she could still be put to work, but mainly disagreed over for how long. Dr. Waring declared that "she may live fifteen years; but her sufferings will increase, and her ability to bear them will decrease." Dr. North felt that she was exploitable regardless: "She might live fifteen years, but in increasing pains; she is looking very well now." Perhaps more importantly, "she is capable of service."[51]

* * *

Few planters claimed they went to market with the express intention of buying elderly slaves, and those who had been tricked into buying older than they wished fought hard to recover monies lost. Despite making up a small proportion of interstate and regional sales, however, elders were openly bought and sold across the south and advanced age promised no protection from the horrors of the auction block.[52] As John S. Jacobs recalled in his narrative, "even my grandmother's grey hairs and many years' hard service in the public-house did not save her from the auctioneer's hammer."[53] Many records of sale for older slaves speak to the concerns of small-scale enslavers who were worried about their financial status. Enslavers with large, demographically mixed plantations found it easier to utilize elders in the auxiliary roles discussed earlier, but those with relatively few slaves were less able to adapt. Enslavers who hoped to rise among their peers needed *all* their forced laborers to be productive, and their efforts at disposing of elderly slaves were often shaped by claims to this effect.

To focus on failure and economic concerns here is not to discount the enormous profits created by slavery writ large, nor is it to legitimize the rationale of necessity that these indigent enslavers pled when seeking sale. It is instead to reveal in more detail how slavery was a system of economic exploitation, and that, when hard times came, enslaved people had it hardest. In 1853, John Guilmartin complained to the Court of Equity in Chatham County, Georgia, that he had been entrusted with three slaves to provide for Mary Brown and her heirs. Guilmartin noted, however, that alongside children, "many of them are old Sickly and infirm" and "instead of being a source of income are an absolute Expense to the trust Estate."

---

[51] *Caldwell v. Porcher*, 27 S.C.L. 138, 2 McMullan 329 (1842), 329, 331, 330.

[52] Tadman, *Speculators and Slaves*, 25–31, 241–7.

[53] John S. Jacobs, "A True Tale of Slavery," *The Leisure Hour: A Family Journal of Instruction and Recreation*, 476 (February 7, 1861), 86.

Guilmartin sought to sell the enslaved people and invest in other "property," and he was granted permission to do so by the court.[54] In 1837, sixteen-year-old Thomas Morris applied to the Chancery Court in Henrico County, Virginia to sell two slaves following the death from smallpox of the only valuable one, Jane. Morris wanted to sell Beverly who, "though of a middle age, is so bad a character addicted to running away, to Drunkenness, and a habit of life and vices which bring upon him loathsome and deadly diseases, and on this account [t]he infrequent and fruitful source of expense to your orators estate." That Morris had contracted "the venereal disease" himself suggests the extent of his exploitation of Beverly. Morris also stressed the need to rid his estate of Paul on account of his limited means: "the man Paul is very old and must very shortly become a serious and burdensome charge upon his little estate."[55]

Trading and court records reveal how little faith enslaved people could put in the promise of proslavery propagandists that "in old age," they would become "a family pensioner secure from want."[56] James McDaniel, acting guardian for his two children, explained to the Orphans Court of Baltimore, Maryland, in 1860, that he needed to sell the life interest in two slaves because "the value of the said slaves are constantly diminishing in value by age while the expenses of said infants constantly increases, as they grow older."[57] Time's onward march was counted in dollars lost and dollars gained. As William Adcock wrote when seeking to justify the sale of Anna, an elderly slave, from his young trustee's estate: "this woman is in infirm health & of no profit to the said John McRae, on the contrary is an expense to him."[58] Roberson M. Holladay of Mississippi provided similar motives when explaining his desire to sell Jim, aged sixty-three, rather than hire him out. Holladay argued that "Jim, in consequence of his great age, hires only for $38 per annum, and, of course, becomes less valuable, as time advances." Jim was subsequently sold at public auction.[59] The actions of enslavers like Holladay and

---

[54] Petition of John Guilmartin, February 8, 1853, Chatham County, Georgia, #20685312, Series 2, RSPP.

[55] Petition of Thomas Morris, April 3, 1837, Henrico County, Virginia, #21683702, Series 2, RSPP.

[56] Hundley, *Social Relations*, 67–8.

[57] Petition of James McDaniel, August 10, 1860, Baltimore-Cit. Maryland, #20986027, Series 2, RSPP.

[58] Petition of William Adcock, January 7, 1834, Henrico County, Virginia, #21683431, Series 2, RSPP.

[59] Petition of Roberson Holladay, May 3, 1852, Hinds County, Mississippi, #21085218, Series 2, RSPP.

McDaniel exemplify the economic imperatives of American slavery and reveal further how the cold logic of the marketplace determined the material conditions of life for enslaved people.

The language of utility in justifying these sales highlights the disregard of enslavers toward those whom they enslaved, and the wider willingness of white southerners to accept functionalist assessments of the value of Black peoples' lives. In the Pasquotank County Court of Common Pleas assessment of the estate of Rachel and Emily Harvey, two enslavers from North Carolina, "Old Tom" and Pleasants, who was "seriously afflicted with fits," were simply listed as "damages."[60] Enslaved elders who were put up for sale were often described purely in terms of their declining value. They were "getting old" and from "that cause, become infirm and useless"; others were labeled as "old infirm & valueless."[61] Irrespective of prior service – irrespective of the claims of paternalism – enslavers were more than willing to put up for sale those elders who no longer served their interests and to openly state as much to the wider white community. Such disregard was evident in a petition submitted to the Laurens County Court of Equity, South Carolina, 1851, by the grandchildren of the late William Lowe. Lowe had devised to his heirs an enslaved man named Adolphus, as well as a "feather bed." The bed constituted an heirloom that might stand the test of time, but Adolphus did not. The petitioners felt that the inevitability of aging necessitated a speedy sale: "said slave is now in the prime of life and according to the course of nature will soon be decreasing in value." As a result, it was "deemed most advantageous for the interest of your petitioners that said slave should be sold."[62] Their request was granted, and Adolphus was sold. They appear to have kept the bed.

When A. B. Howard, administrator of the estate of H. B. Howard, sought to sell "an old negro man belonging to the said Estate," he emphasized the crushing pressures of time. The man had been appraised at $350 just two years previous, but Howard claimed it was necessary to now accept $150 for him, as this was "the only offer he has had." Being "upwards of 60 years old" and crippled with rheumatism, Howard had only limited time to make money from him: "if suffered to remain as a part of the Estate [he] will

[60] Petition of Rachel Harvey et al; Commissioners' Report, c. December 1857, Pasquotank County, North Carolina, #212857091, Series 2, RSPP.
[61] Petition of M. C. Stokes, June 9, 1858, Montgomery County, Alabama, #20185825, Series 2, RSPP; Petition of Anthony Debrell et al., February 14, 1848, Chesterfield County, Virginia, #21684816, Series 2, RSPP.
[62] Petition of Isaac Lowe et al., March 8, 1851, Laurens District, South Carolina, #21385124 Series 2, RSPP.

in all probability in twelve months from this be totally unfit for sale or hire and therefore must be a dead expense for the remainder of his life to the widow and children." Howard's request was granted and the unnamed rheumatic sixty-year-old was sold.[63] In Wilkinson County, Mississippi, 1857, Rachel Jane Boland, guardian of two white minors, likewise sought permission to sell an enslaved woman who was "old and of very little value to said Rebecca." She wanted to replace her with a younger woman "whose labor & increase will greatly promote their interest."[64] The combination of (re)productive labor in assessing the value of enslaved women demonstrates the double burden they faced and underscores the brutality of antebellum slavery. Deirdre Cooper Owens has argued that "elderly black women were deemed worthless in a society that prized black females for their presumed hypersexuality and reproductive abilities," and such considerations were obvious to the enslaved themselves.[65] Maria Sutton Clemments described how her mother had been threatened with such a sale and was only saved by the outbreak of the Civil War. Clemments noted that how her enslaver's sons "wanter sell her cause she too old to bear children. Sell her and buy young woman raise mo children to sell."[66]

A concern with reproductive value led to a contextual and comparative framing of age and value. Henry Banner of Arkansas recalled how, regardless of chronological age, "if a woman didn't breed well, she was put in a gang and sold."[67] In 1852, Florida enslaver John Keen justified his sale of Eliza accordingly. Keen noted that Eliza, who was childless despite several years of marriage, "will, therefore constantly diminish in value during the lives of your Orator and Oratrix, and may at the termination of said life estate be of little or no value to the remainderman, the child of your orator & oratrix." Keen also stressed that he was "feeble" and that his infirmities hindered his ability to profit from slavery. Such framing suggests how concerns with age impacted upon enslavers' identities, which will be the subject of Part II of this book. Banner's self-pity in justifying the sale also demonstrates how, while time came for all, its burdens were not shared equally.[68] Indeed, Eliza was sold.

---

[63] Petition of A. B. Howard, October 12, 1858, Anne Arundel County, Maryland, #20985835, Series 2, RSPP.

[64] Petition of Rachel Jane Boland, December 7, 1857, Wilkinson County, Maryland, #21085706, Series 2, RSPP.

[65] Cooper Owens, *Medical Bondage*, 56.   [66] Rawick (Ed.), *AS*, 8.2, 15.

[67] Rawick (Ed.), *AS*, 8.1, 105–6.

[68] Petition of John Keen, March 30, 1852, Leon County, Florida, #20585209, Series 2, RSPP.

Heirs and executors who hoped to sell elderly slaves sometimes challenged the wishes of the deceased in favor of the economic self-interest of the living. The arguments made here reveal further how any claims to protection were contingent and that enslaved people knew better than to put faith in the promises of those who enslaved them. Lewis Clarke noted how his elderly father, upon the death of his enslaver, remonstrated at the public sale of his family but to no avail: "what were the entreaties of a quivering old man, in the sight of eight or ten hungry heirs?"[69] In 1859, two "hungry heirs" in South Carolina made and profited from one such case. Lewis and John Featherston had been left in charge of 32 slaves and 110 acres of land. Their father's will directed them to sell Drucilla, Sarah, and Ceely to pay off existing debts and to "fairly" distribute the remaining slaves without separating existing families. Within the year, however, Lewis and John petitioned for a complete sale of the enslaved property as "a goodly number of the above named slaves are already far enough advanced in years to effect, to a considerable extent, their value, and that value must still continue to decrease as years are added, and most of the females are barren and unproductive." They were adamant that economic self-interest outweighed any ideological concerns and even cast aspersions on their patriarch's plans: "the said property cannot be kept together and so managed as to carry out the *peculiar* and benevolent wishes of the testator and at the same time issue to the benefit of his children which must have been the paramount object which he had in view."[70] With "benevolence" weighed against "benefit," the court sanctioned the sale.

In Henrico County, Virginia, 1826, Francis R. Price sought to offload enslaved people from the estate he was executor of, and to divide the profits among the heirs. Two of the slaves would sell for a profit but Phoebe was "aged and infirm and of no value." He thus petitioned the court to allow him to "sell the two slaves that are of value – and put up the one that is infirm to the lowest bidder, for her support during her life." There was a performance of paternalism here, with Price requesting that any monies left over from the sale of the two productive people (after suitable deduction) would go to the "person who shall undertake to support the said infirm negro."[71] In Tennessee, 1851, John B. McEwen

---

[69] Clarke and Clarke, *Narratives of the Sufferings*, 69–70.

[70] Petition of Lewis and John Featherston, June 9, 1859, Anderson District, South Carolina, #21385964, Series 2, RSPP. Italics mine.

[71] Petition of Francis Price, December 5, 1826, Henrico County, Virginia, #21682603, Series 2, RSPP.

was likewise clear when he stated that as no one wanted to buy Dolly, who was "upwards of sixty years," she should "be put up and sold to the person who will agree and obligate himself to support and take care of her [for] the least sum of money."[72] Both of these requests were granted, but the dispute recorded in *State* v. *Duckworth*, 1864, does not provide much confidence the elders received adequate support. The court heard that Alexander Duckworth had been given $50 by an enslaver who wanted to move away "in consideration that he would take the slave [Peggy] and her husband, both old negroes, and take care of them the rest of their lives." Duckworth had apparently done so for one or two years, but "for several years last past he had done nothing for the woman, the man being dead." The State complained that Duckworth had allowed Peggy to act as a free person, but this was not evidence of antislavery activism. Peggy had been left "to support herself as she could, by begging and what little work she could do."[73] All of the white parties' principal concern – publicly stated and ferociously fought over – was to avoid financial responsibility. Peggy had spent a lifetime enslaved but, now that she had nothing left to give, her enslavers wanted nothing more to do with her.

* * *

The sale of elders might be packaged as a form of "protection," in that they were being passed on to those who had the means to support them, but this was clearly contingent rather than constant. One such account comes from the (admittedly apocryphal) story of the life of the "nurse of George Washington," Joice Heth, who reached the unlikely age of 161. Aged fifty-four, Heth was sold to the woman who owned her husband for a low price as reflection of her long service: "This was not done so much on account of the value of the services which she might render, as to accommodate her in the enjoyment of the constant company of her helpmate, (Peter,) who was also at this time something in years, and a favorite domestic servant." The claims of benevolence here – both in circumstances of sale and reduced work – chime with the accounts of enslavers listed earlier. Once the elderly enslaver died, Heth found herself, and the responsibility for her support, being passed down through the branches of the family, to worse and worse effect. After being "kindly provided for" by one of the heirs, the support dried up. Ever since, "she

---

[72] Petition of John McEwen, May 5, 1851, Williamson County, Tennessee, #21485121, Series 2, RSPP.

[73] *State* v. *Duckworth*, 60 N.C. 240, 1 Winston 243 (1864), 241.

has been very much neglected, laying for years in an outer building, upon the naked floor."[74]

The tale of Joice Heth is obviously apocryphal, but legal disputes show the underlying message of neglect was not. In 1867, one ex-slave took the executors of their former owner to court on account of their failure to support him in old age. In his will, Maxwell Chambers had sought to "make ample provision for my poor old friendless woman Lucy, as well as my old man Peter," and thought he could "rely on the humanity and tender feelings of my executors to have them well taken care of, and kindly treated, during the short time they will probably want it." The emotive language and mantle of paternalism that animated such actions, however, was challenged by his heirs, who sought to clarify if this was an imperative or simply precatory, and thus not legally binding on them. In this instance, however, the Reconstruction-era court decreed that "the plaintiff is entitled to whatever sum may be found necessary as an annual support during life."[75]

In Tennessee, 1852, Henry Ward was forced to sue the heirs of the estate he was executor for because they had failed to fulfill the request of their mother, who had directed that her "two old servants," named Molly and Lydia, would "have the privilege of living with any of her children or any where that might convenience them best." Ward feared that he would be "at a loss to know what to do with these old negroes in the event none of the children will receive them," and recounted that this had sadly come to pass. Molly had been hired for a nominal fee of fifty cents and had "such liberty as was contemplated in the will." Lydia, however, was in a worse condition and was encumbered with a sickly child: "No one would propose to take Lydia and she now remains a charge upon the Estate." Ward successfully sued the heirs, but the fact they fought against taking this responsibility all the way up to the Supreme Court indicates the limited care elders might receive over time.[76]

In *Mooney v. Evans*, 1849, John Kelly's will was likewise contested over who was responsible for two aged slaves. Tibby, "stricken with palsy," was regarded as a poor legacy: "she is old; there is no longer hope of her recovery; and she is now and will be for the rest of her life

[74] P. T. Barnum, *The Life of Joice Heth, the Nurse of Gen. George Washington, (the Father of Our Country,) Now Living at the Astonishing Age of 161 Years and Weighs Only 46 Pounds* (New York: Printed for the Publisher, 1835), 3–5.
[75] *Chambers v. Davis*, 62. N.C.152 (1867), 113–14.
[76] Petition of Henry Ward, April 6, 1852, Wilson County, Tennessee, #21485219, Series 2, RSPP.

a charge." Evans, who acted as trustee, simply "decline[d] accepting" her, and there was a dispute over who was responsible for her care. The court eventually found that "the slave Tibby is a proper charge upon the fund remaining in the hands of the executor undisposed of," but the lack of interest does not suggest any real concern for her well-being after a lifetime of labor.[77] In New Jersey, 1808, Hannah Potter, widow of Caleb Potter, sought to recover money from her late husband's heirs for the support she had provided to Jin, "an old and infirm black woman, who was the property of the said Caleb Potter at the time of his death." Potter claimed that the laws of New Jersey meant the heirs were supposed to support and maintain Jin but that they had "refused to do so." The Court, however, explicitly denied this was a legal obligation and seemingly chided Potter for having taken on this support herself: "the plaintiff below could not take upon herself to maintain the slave, and then bring an action for such maintenance, and reversed the judgment."[78] The heirs in the cases above were happy to take on the inheritances built on slavery. They did not want sight of the physical reminders of how this wealth was made.

Court records typically provide little information as to how enslaved people felt about sale, abandonment, or neglect. Former slaves, however, recounted the sadness of elders who found themselves "wrenched from . . . friends and family, where the tenderest associations clustered."[79] Henry "Box" Brown believed that the separation of elders from kith and kin was a tragedy that was difficult to recover from:

And there is no doubt but they under the weighty infirmities of declining life, and the increasing force and vividness with which the mind retains the memoranda of the agonies of former years – which form so great a part of memory's possessions in the minds of most slaves – hurry thousands annually from off the stage of life.[80]

Lewis Clarke intimated that the sale of "old slaves, who are past labor" was, in fact, a deliberate strategy to help "hurry" them off the stage. Clarke recalled how "one man, on moving to Missouri, sold an old slave for one dollar, to a man not worth a cent," which resembles earlier cases where enslaved people were sold to "the lowest bidder, for . . . support during her life."[81] Clarke's understanding was that these situations rarely

---

[77] *Mooney v. Evans*, 6 Ired. Eq. 363 (N.C. 1849), 364, 365, 368.
[78] *Heirs of Potter v. Potter's Widow*, 3 N.J.L. 415 (1808), 416.
[79] Isaac D. Williams, *Sunshines and Shadow of Slave Life: Reminiscences as Told by Isaac D. Williams to "Tege"* (Evening News Printing and Binding House: Michigan, 1885), 67–9.
[80] Brown, *Narrative of the Life*, 16–17.   [81] Fn 72 of this chapter.

ended well for the enslaved elders. In this particular case, the purchaser had neither the means nor morality to care for the elderly man, who was simply "turned out to do the best he could." According to Clarke, "he fought with age and starvation awhile, but was soon found, one morning, starved to death, out of doors, and half eaten up by animals."[82]

Andrew Jackson of Kentucky described the heart-rending sale of "an old slave and his wife, who had become so infirm they could not work": "their master wished to get rid of them, so he put them up to the lowest bidder to be taken care of." The language, as in the cases noted earlier, indicates the presumption of support. The new owner, however, "did not care what became of them so that he got his pay" and simply "put them in a small hut, and fed them the refuse of his table where he fed his dogs." The end result of this was tragedy: "One night the old man fell into the fire in a fit and died, his wife being unable to get him out; and the only remarks made about it were – 'Well, poor old man, he is out of trouble and suffering.'"[83] One Richmond slave who had "become old and a little unwilling to work" found himself handed over to a cruel man who cared little for his survival. This man forced "old Peter" to earn three dollars a week or suffer floggings, and Peter took to the woods to escape such violence. He was shot as a runaway. The "old man" was "found dead two or three days afterwards in such an awful state of decomposition that it could scarcely be determined whether it was old Peter or not."[84]

* * *

Enslavers, of course, did not need to be so proactive as to sell or even force out their enslaved people. They could simply neglect elders under their care, and the power dynamics of slavery meant there was little recourse for those who suffered in such a way. Frances Kemble recounted how "old house Molly" told her "of the special directions left by her old master for the comfort and well-being of her old age," but stressed that there was no one willing to ensure this support materialized: "his charge has been but little heeded by his heirs, for the poor faithful old slave is most miserably

---

[82] Clarke and Clarke, *Narratives of the Sufferings*, 112.

[83] Andrew Jackson, *Narrative and Writings of Andrew Jackson, of Kentucky; Containing an Account of His Birth, and Twenty-Six Years of His Life While a Slave; His Escape; Five Years of Freedom, Together with Anecdotes Relating to Slavery; Journal of One Year's Travels; Sketches, etc. Narrated by Himself; Written by a Friend* (Syracuse: Daily and Weekly Star Office, 1847), 24–5.

[84] "Slavery by an Eye-Witness," *Provincial Freeman* (July 29, 1854), 2.

off in her infirm years."[85] Rev. Horace Moulton, who resided in Georgia before moving North and becoming an abolitionist, believed this type of abuse was endemic: one particular "dark side of slavery is the neglect of the aged and sick."[86]

Ex-slaves were adamant this was true. Lewis Clarke claimed to have "known several cases where slaves were left to starve to death in old age."[87] Bill Simms of Missouri explained that "when a slave got too old to work they would give him a small cabin on the plantation and have the other slaves wait on him. They would furnish him with victuals, and clothes until he died."[88] The onus for support, according to Sims, was firmly on the slave community. Sims believed that support would be forthcoming, but others understood that the hardships of slavery left elders vulnerable here. Moses Grandy recalled how, "when my mother became old, she was sent to live in a little lonely log-hut in the woods," and described this as the norm: "Aged and worn out slaves, whether men or women, are commonly so treated." Support was meant to be provided by family members, but this was inevitably restricted on account of their own excessive workload. Grandy painted a pitiful portrait of life for "the aged inmate of the hut [who] is often found crying, on account of sufferings from disease or extreme weakness, or from want of food and water in the course of the day." This was the norm, not the exception: "she was not treated worse than others: it is the general practice."[89]

This type of neglect as "standard practice" was directly addressed in the abolitionist account of Jamie Parker's flight. On Parker's plantation were two elderly slaves, Agga and her husband Scipio, who were sixty-eight and seventy respectively. Scipio was kept as hog-minder "since he was too infirm for field-work," while Agga, who was "old and useless," was "to be employed in any way to be kept from idleness." These two elders were kept apart from the field workers, and this broader isolation and sense of uselessness rendered Agga miserable. With her only children "sent to the sugar plantations of the far southwest," Agga was left "not only 'useless,' but in a measure helpless." She would simply "knit mechanically" with no real purpose or care. As Pierson noted, "In the inventory she was labeled 'old and useless;' justly, for the light of hope was all extinct

---

[85] Kemble, *Journal of a Residence*, 254.   [86] Weld, *American Slavery As It Is*, 45.
[87] Clarke and Clarke, *Narratives of the Sufferings*, 112.   [88] Rawick (Ed.), *AS*, *16*, 9.
[89] Moses Grandy, *Narrative of the Life of Moses Grandy; Late a Slave in the United States of America* (London: C. Gilpin, 5, Bishopsgate-street, 1843), 51–2.

within her."[90] This type of arrangement resembles the proslavery claim of a "retirement" of sorts: the elders had a cabin to themselves and did not work. Their accumulated suffering, personal loss, and the misery of having given their best years to slavers, however, meant that surface claims of care counted for little. Such testimony underscores the necessity of caution when taking into account slavers' repeated references to limited work regimes or to the "support" systems in place for elders.

Frederick Douglass famously wrote of the suffering of his grandmother once she had outlived her usefulness to her enslavers. As in the description of "Old Barney," ill-treatment toward those who had given the "best years and the best strength of [their] life" to enslavers represented, to Douglass, the very worst of bondage.[91] Douglass wrote that if anything had "served to deepen my conviction of the infernal character of slavery and fill me with unutterable loathing of slaveholders," it was the treatment of his grandmother, Betsey. Despite having "served [Douglass's] old master faithfully from youth to old age" and "been the source of all his wealth" through her (re)productive labor, her past efforts counted for naught. Douglass furiously recounted her fate:

Finding that she was of but little value; that her frame was already racked with the pains of old age and that complete helplessness was fast stealing over her once active limbs – [her enslaver] took her to the woods, built her a little hut with a mud chimney and then gave her the bounteous privilege of there supporting herself in utter loneliness; thus virtually turning her out to die.[92]

Douglass condemned the individuals who had exploited his grandmother and attacked slavery itself, asserting that such treatment was a logical consequence in a society built on exploitation. It is a poignant scene conjured up by Douglass, where he acknowledged that aging was a period of natural decline, but insisted that the suffering of the aged was exacerbated by the systemic violence of slavers:

All is gloom. The grave is at the door; and now, weighed down by the pains and aches of old age, when the head inclines to the feet, when the beginning and ending of human existence meet, and helpless infancy, and painful old age combine together, at this time, – this most needed time for the exercise of that tenderness and affection which children only can bestow on a declining parent, – my poor old

[90] Pierson, *Jamie Parker, The Fugitive*, 13–15.
[91] Douglass, *My Bondage and My Freedom*, 112–14.
[92] Frederick Douglass, *Life and Times of Frederick Douglass, Written by Himself. His Early Life as a Slave, His Escape from Bondage, and His Complete History to the Present Time* ... (Boston: De Wolfe & Fiske Co., 1892), 121–3.

grandmother, the devoted mother of twelve children, is left all alone, in yonder little hut, before a few dim cinders.

Having furiously recounted the treatment of his grandmother in his antebellum narratives, Douglass's postbellum writings contained a correction to this story.[93] By this point Douglass had discovered that Betsey had been saved from this fate by his former enslaver, who recovered her from the neglect of his grandson and "took care of her as long as she lived." Douglass even apologized to Capt. Auld and stressed he "had at no time any wish to do him injustice" with this testimony. Notwithstanding Douglass's apologies, it is worth reiterating that Betsey *was* abandoned by Auld's grandson and it was only because of Douglass's righteous condemnation of this treatment that she had been saved from this fate: "The fact is, that, after writing my narrative describing the condition of my grandmother, Capt. Auld's attention being thus called to it, he rescued her from her destitution."[94] The neglect of Betsey reveals the broader systemic violence practiced on those who were surplus to labor requirements. Douglass could not save every elder.

Theodore Dwight Weld's antislavery work included vivid testimony from white southerners about the neglect of elders who were no longer profitable or productive. Mr. Caulkins of North Carolina recalled the horrible ways "in which old and worn-out slaves are sometimes treated" by noting the neglect of a sick man aged around seventy. He lay in his hut for "four or five days, groaning in great distress, without any attention being paid him by his master, until death ended his miseries." He "was then taken out and buried with as little ceremony and respect as would be paid to a brute." Horace Moulton of Georgia likewise stressed how the relative weakness of elders marked them out for neglect: "God alone knows how much the poor slaves suffer for the want of convenient houses to secure them from the piercing winds and howling storms of winter, especially the aged, sick and dying." In North Carolina, Moulton encountered an enslaved man, "whose head was white with age," suffering from cancer. This man, "who had been worn out" in slavery, was left "shockingly neglected." Such abuse was not unique, with "a similar case of

[93] Frederick Douglass, *Narrative of the Life of Frederick Douglass, an American Slave. Written by Himself* (Boston: Anti-Slavery Office, 1845), 47–9; Douglass, *My Bondage and My Freedom* ... (1892), 180–2; Douglass, *Life and Times* ... (1881), 448–9.

[94] Douglass, *Life and Times of Frederick Douglass* (1892), 121–3, 536–8. In *My Bondage and My Freedom* (1855), 427, Douglass published the letter he sent to Auld while residing in England, within which he castigated Auld for his treatment of his grandmother and asked for her freedom.

suffering" witnessed in South Carolina: "an aged woman suffering under an incurable disease [was] in the same miserably neglected situation." Moulton emphasized that this was emphatically not evidence only of a "bad" enslaver: "the 'owner' of this slave was proverbially kind to her negroes; so much so, that the planters in the neighborhood said she spoiled them."[95] According to Moulton, mistreatment of the aged was the norm in a system that prioritized the extraction of maximum profits from people.

J. W. Lindsey, who escaped from slavery in Tennessee, was heart-broken by memories of the neglect of unproductive elders. Despite acknowledging proslavery claims of support, the elders Lindsey encountered were left at the end of their lives with nothing but "dirt, poverty & distress." Lindsey was adamant that such poor treatment was inseparable from the cruelty of a system that connected value to productivity:

When a man hardens his heart & stiffens his neck against all human feelings, what can you expect of him? the old slaves are generally left to sit round in rags and direct, and take care of the children; and when they cannot do that, they just lie round and suffer, until they die, & there is no great account taken of them, any way.[96]

Mrs. Hood, a white woman interviewed by the WPA, and whose family had lived among enslavers in Kentucky, corroborated Lindsey's traumatic memories. Hood recalled elders suffering neglect on account of their relative lack of productivity. On a nearby farm lived "several slaves and among them was one old man-servant who was very old and had served out his usefulness." This prior service was forgotten in favor of maintaining the active workers, with the hunt for profit outweighing benefits earned: "the younger and stronger slaves got most of the food, and old Tom was always hungry." Hood's mother, in fact, provided food for Tom while his "master" would not.[97] Those without such intervention simply suffered, with Roberta Manson of North Carolina claiming that "de ole men an women dat wus unable to work wus neglected till dey died or wus killed by beatin' or burnin'," and provided an example where Col. Skipper "did dat thing." Manson noted that Skipper, "one of the richest men in the South," deliberately set apart a group of sickly old men and women from his main workers and put them on an island. The river rose while they were there "an dey parished to death." The framing of such a tragedy with

---

[95] Weld, *American Slavery As It Is*, 12, 19, 23–4.
[96] Blassingame (Ed.), *Slave Testimony*, 401.   [97] FWP, 7 (Kentucky), 87.

reference to Skipper's wealth – "over two hundred slaves … one of the richest men in the South" – aimed to undercut any appeal that this outcome was simply evidence of a "bad apple."[98] Skipper's actions revealed the logic of exploitation and utility which structured life and death in slavery.

* * *

Frances Kemble's recollections of slavery in Georgia serve to highlight how exploitation from cradle to grave underpinned the experiences of enslaved people and the structures of slavery. Kemble insisted that enslaved people were seen purely as "tools, to be mended only if they can be made available again; if not, to be flung by as useless, without further expense of money, time, or trouble." Kemble explained the practical dimensions to such logic, with the removal of unproductive workers to a separate location representing their reduced status. Out of sight was out of mind, with Woodville, a settlement on the mainland, consisting only of "a few deplorably miserable hovels, which appeared to me to be chiefly occupied by the most decrepit and infirm samples of humanity it was ever my melancholy lot to behold." This was a place where the unproductive could be thrown out of sight, with Kemble recalling that "here some of the oldest slaves who will not die yet, and cannot work any more, are sent, to go, as it were, out of the way."

The enslaved people situated here, who had the temerity to yet live, were aware of the cruelty of casting them aside after having "worked as long as [their] strength had lasted," but had little recourse beyond pleading for support when Kemble visited.[99] St. Simon and St. Annie's Islands also operated as a dumping ground for the "old, young, and feeble." Kemble acknowledged that the slaves had little to do, but this was not cause for celebration. The enslaved people "turned out to grass here" suffered from neglect and lived in "deplorable homes," particularly when compared to the residences of working slaves. The connection between productivity and support was evident to Kemble, who noted that "all the slaves' huts on St. Simons are far less solid, comfortable, and habitable than those at the rice island." Kemble was distraught at the suffering she witnessed, but also recoiled from the physical evidence of exploitation.

---

[98] Rawick (Ed.), *AS*, 15.2, 102.

[99] Kemble, *Journal of a Residence*, 72, 125–8. On healthcare arrangements in the Lowcountry, including plantation arrangements, see McCandless, *Slavery, Disease, and Suffering*; Dusinberre, *Them Dark Days*, esp chs. 7 and 8.

She recounted her horror at encountering the "old crone" Hannah and "old House Molly, whose face and figure, seamed with wrinkles, and bowed and twisted with age and infirmity, really hardly retained the semblance of those of a human creature."[100]

Kemble was ashamed of, but unable to hide, her disgust at the condition of these elders. Writing to her sister, Kemble recorded the small measure of respite she provided to Dorcas, "one of the most decrepit, rheumatic, and miserable old Negresses from the farther end of the plantation," by allowing her to ride in the wagon to get back home. Kemble acknowledged "it was not otherwise than slightly meritorious in me, my dear E[lizabeth], to take her up in the wagon and endure her abominable dirt and foulness in the closest proximity, rather than let her drag her poor old limbs all that way back," and stressed her relief "when we gained her abode and lost her company." Kemble was adamant that such abuse was not an anomaly but instead inevitable in an institution that prioritized profit above all. In a letter to *The Times* challenging proslavery reports, Kemble used the death of Friday to puncture the self-serving slaver myths of care from cradle to grave. Kemble was adamant that this man received no reciprocity, respect, or even remembrance despite a lifetime of labor. Friday suffered and died alone:

Like a worn-out hound, with no creature to comfort or relieve his last agony, with neither Christian solace or human succor near him, with neither wife, nor child, nor even friendly fellow being to lift his head from the knotty sticks on which he had rested it, or drive away the insects that buzzed round his lips and nostrils like those of a fallen beast, died this poor old slave, whose life had been exhausted in unrequited labor, the fruits of which had gone to pamper the pride and feed the luxury of those who knew and cared neither for his life or death, and to whom, if they had heard of the latter, it would have been a matter of absolute though small gain, the saving of a daily pittance of meal, which served to prolong a life no longer available to them.[101]

Slavery, as Kemble saw it, was a system of economic exploitation and a contested site of personal domination, and enslaved people suffered tremendously on account of these dual pressures as they grew older and had comparatively less to "give." Concerns with age, productivity, and power fundamentally structured the dynamics of slavery and influenced interactions between enslaver and enslaved alike. Proslavery claims of "retirement" or of cradle-to-grave care were no match for the economic

[100] Kemble, *Journal of a Residence*, 202–7, 219, 228.
[101] Kemble, *Journal of a Residence*, 302, 288, 359.

self-interest of enslavers, small and large, and the driving force of slavery revolved around taking the "best years and the best strength" from enslaved people.[102] As one ex-slave explained, "Master has all my strength, and I have these old bones."[103] Enslaved people understood this exploitative dynamic all too well, with "old" Nancy's statement to Kemble serving an appropriate conclusion here: "I have worked every day through dew and damp, and sand and heat, and done good work; but oh, missis, me old and broken now; no tongue can tell how much I suffer."[104]

[102] Douglass, *My Bondage and My Freedom*, 112–14.
[103] Aaron, *The Light and Truth of Slavery*, 41.   [104] Kemble, *Journal of a Residence*, 268.

3

"Young people think that old people are fools but old people know that young people are fools"

Intergenerational Conflict Among the Enslaved

Enslaved people commonly claimed they sought to protect the aged from the excesses of their abusers, and that they were "raised to respect old age."[1] Most scholarship on the topic reinforces this position. As Daina Ramey Berry argues, whatever the dismissal of the aged by enslavers, Black elders' "internal values were elevated and celebrated within their communities."[2] Corinne T. Field emphasizes how enslavers who defined "old in terms of uselessness and disposability" inverted "West African value systems that venerated elders as spiritual and political leaders – values that many enslaved people tried to reproduce on New World plantations and in free Black communities."[3] This chapter, however, considers the consequences when enslaved people appropriated, internalized, or perhaps simply shared a belief that old age equated to diminished value and declining powers. It suggests how "respect" predicated on agedness was not always meant seriously, nor received positively by the recipient. The transition to "elder" could be taken instead as emblematic of reduced status within the community and seen as an enforced relegation from the people one had once imagined as peers. The "aged" party sometimes resented and even resisted the imposition of such a label and

---

[1] Robert Anderson, *The Anderson Surpriser: Written after He Was Seventy-Five Years of Age. An Account of His Florida and Northern Trip* (Macon: Printed for the Author, 1895), 76.

[2] Berry, *Price for Their Pound of Flesh*, 134. See introduction for general work emphasizing positive portrayals of elders in the community.

[3] Corinne T. Field, "Antifeminism, Anti-Blackness, and Anti-Oldness: The Intersectional Aesthetics of Aging in the Nineteenth-Century United States," *Signs*, 47.4 (2022) 843–83, 848.

its associated narrative, with such tension reflecting the broader complexities of age serving as a chronological, functional, and relational category and identity. People who were *seen* as elderly but struggled with this categorization of themselves were forced to make choices – to accept, adapt, or to resist – and this could come at no little cost.

Black southerners commonly agreed enslavers devalued and exploited elderly slaves but insisted the slave community stepped in at this point. George Pretty of Florida told his interviewer that "in older times people taught their children to respect older persons."[4] Morgan Ray, aged eighty-three, relayed a similar tale and unfavorably compared the situation with his own treatment by the Black youth of the 1930s:

My mothah allus told me to be polite and respectful to folks older dan me. Chillun nowadays ain't brought up dat way. I got grandchillun and I hear how dey talk and act. Cullud chillun today are better learned dan de wuz. But de kids are sassy and impudent. And as for de younger generation, I declare a lot of dem seem headed for de electric chair.[5]

Claims of elder care in slavery, with a comparative sense of diminished respect for elders from the younger generation of Black southerners, was a near article of faith for WPA respondents.[6] Dina Beard of Arkansas positioned the enslaved and newly freed generation as representatives of a different mentality entirely: "we did not go necked like these folks do now. Folk did not know how we was made. We did not show our shape, we did not disgrace ourself back in 1800." Beard wistfully recalled the reverence for the aged among her peers: "We chaps called everybody old that married. We respected them because they was considered as being old. Time has made a change."[7] Silas Dothrum of Arkansas, aged eighty-two, put it more bluntly: "The young people today ain't worth a shit."[8]

The frequency with which these assertions of elder care were made by the formerly enslaved highlights a powerful collective memory of the support offered within slave communities.[9] That so many who professed personal reverence for elders explicitly compared these attitudes with disregard from the rising generation, however, speaks to one of the most enduring cross-cultural themes in histories of aging: a "golden age" for the

---

[4] Rawick (Ed.), *AS, 17*, 268.   [5] Rawick (Ed.), *AS, Supp.,* Ser. *1, 5,* 427–8.

[6] Intergenerational relations are briefly addressed in Stephanie Shaw, "Using the WPA Ex-Slave Narratives to Study the Great Depression," *Journal of Southern History,* 69.3 (2003), 623–58, 657.

[7] Rawick (Ed.), *AS, 8.1,* 129–30.   [8] Rawick (Ed.), *AS, 8.1,* 188.

[9] On the broader issues surrounding collective and vernacular histories in WPA testimonies, see Baptist, "Stol' and Fetched Here," 245.

aged. The proposition that elders believe themselves to be uniquely living in a period of disrespect for the aged, as compared to the unquestioned respect they proffered to the elderly when they were young, is a staggeringly ubiquitous refrain in world history. Beard's comments in 1937, for example, would not look out of place next to the Greek poet Horace's exhortation in Odes 3.6 (c. 23 BCE):

> What has not cankering Time made worse?
> Viler than grandsires, sires beget
> Ourselves, yet baser, soon to curse
> The world with offspring baser yet.

The very ubiquity of such a claim, however, requires us to approach it with caution.[10]

These narrators likely truly believed they had been respectful to their elders, with cultural conventions and shared oppression undoubtedly encouraging these types of attitudes. We should look carefully, nonetheless, at retrospective claims of respect for the aged from ex-slaves who were not old in slavery themselves, and acknowledge the self-serving nature of such testimony. Dina Beard's comments indicate some of the problems here. Beard professed to remember – and seemingly longed for – the respect that existed for the aged enslaved. She was, however, born in 1862, and the image of unquestioned respect for enslaved elders was one she had not experienced herself.

Similar problems bedevil the fugitive slave narratives, within which authors – predominantly men under forty – regularly stressed their reverence for Black elders.[11] Despite these protestations, fugitives frequently depicted aged people as reduced in capacity, often using an elder's descent into decrepitude to best assert the horrors of slavery. The political impetus for making such a case was clear, and often tragically accurate. This

---

[10] Horace. *The Odes and Carmen Saeculare of Horace.* John Conington. trans. (London: George Bell and Sons, 1882) 3.6. Consulted at http://data.perseus.org/citations/urn:cts:l atinLit:phio893.phio01.perseus-eng1:1.1. On the wider prevalence of such perceptions, see John Protzko and Jonathan W. Schooler, "Kids These Days: Why the Youth of Today Seem Lacking," *Science Advances*, 5.10 (2019); George Abosede, Clive Glaser, Margaret D. Jacobs, et al., "*AHR* Conversation: Each Generation Writes Its Own History of Generations," *American Historical Review*, 123.5 (December 2018), 1504–46. On "golden age" narratives, see, for example, Susannah Ottaway, *The Decline of Life: Old Age in Eighteenth-Century England* (Oxford: Oxford University Press, 2004), 1–2; Paul Johnson, "Historical Readings of Old Age and Ageing," in Paul Johnson and Pat Thane (Eds.), *Old Age from Antiquity to Post-Modernity* (London: Routledge, 1998), 1–18.

[11] Blassingame, "Using the Testimony of Ex-Slaves," 480.

nonetheless required portraying real people as diminished and even degraded as they grew older, with implicit or explicit comparisons between the active (young) protagonist and the passive (elderly) foil character. Solomon Northup, as noted earlier, described "Old Abram," an enslaved man around the age of sixty, as "a sort of patriarch" on the plantation. Title of respect notwithstanding, Northup also portrayed Abram as almost always a step behind the other members of the community. Alongside punishment from his enslaver for his mistakes, Abram was ribbed by his peers about his state of mind. Northup's description of Abram getting so wrapped up in telling stories that he forgot he was married, for example, seems lighthearted, but it clearly contains a joke at the expense of the elder:

He had permission to visit [his wife] once a fortnight, but he was growing old, as has been said, and truth to say, had latterly well nigh forgotten her. Uncle Abram had no time to spare from his meditations on General Jackson – connubial dalliance being well enough for the young and thoughtless, but unbecoming a grave and solemn philosopher like himself.[12]

Northup's comments about Abram's failing memory may have been accurate. The discursive structure of this passage, however, suggests both author and reader were expected to share a smile at the unrestrained wanderings of the aged mind, and of Abram's dismissal of the young as "thoughtless" while forgetting his own marriage. We simply cannot know if Abram truly appreciated or shared in the joke.

Enslaved people who recorded their veneration for the aged in the fashion of Northup may have presumed their respect was received gratefully. Elders sometimes recorded less positive perceptions of their status, treatment, and understanding of their younger peers. We might also – with caution – read backwards from the testimonies of WPA respondents who recorded their own sense of hurt and loss as they grew dependent upon others in their old age, and consider whether the typically voiceless aged enslaved shared similar fears. As Jesse Davis of South Carolina explained, "It's mighty hard to be 'pendent on others for your daily rations, even if them others is your own bone and flesh."[13] Others were less generous in their assessments. One formerly enslaved (unnamed) respondent informed the all-Black interviewing team from Fisk University that "young folks think old folks are fools, but old folks know young folks are fools."[14] This aphorism was not new. The short

---

[12] Northup, *Twelve Years a Slave*, 185–7, 221–2.   [13] Rawick (Ed.), *AS*, 2.1, 263.
[14] Rawick (Ed.), *AS*, 18, 46.

account of one ex-slave from Virginia from 1847 hints at the complex solidarities among the enslaved and the cyclical nature of intergenerational tension. Ninety years before the WPA respondent shared his thoughts, this unnamed Black elder equally voiced the opinion "that young people think that old people are fools but old people know that young people are fools. this I have seen varified [*sic*] too often not to know its truth."[15] This man would likely have contested the claims of universal elder respect in slave communities made by Pretty, Ray, and Beard in their WPA interviews, and perhaps also have taken umbrage at Northup's depiction of Abram. The two unnamed ex-slaves, if they ever met, might have taken a minute to consider their shared experiences and the seeming timeless quality to generational strife.

The following chapters thus focus on moments of intergenerational tension in the slave community. I show how far the discourse associating aging with decline affected interactions within the quarters and the ways the choices, identities, and relations enslaved people forged were entangled in the structural violence of slavery. There is a necessary flexibility to my use of the language of "elder," as the label itself was a point of contest between different parties in the community. The chapters underscore, however, the ubiquity of a belief that the process of aging involved some measure of decline, the importance of age to enslaved peoples' identities, and how concerns over the effects of aging – real or imagined – shaped social conflict among the enslaved.

* * *

Enslavers with the means to do so frequently employed enslaved elders in auxiliary roles that allowed them to maximize the productivity of their "prime hands."[16] Historians have extensively documented and stressed the reverence with which these figures were held in the Black community, and noted the support elders gave to children under their care, both practical and moral.[17] Wilma King has shown that enslaved children frequently "became attached to

---

[15] Fields Cook and Mary Jo Jackson Bratton, "Fields's Observations: The Slave Narrative of a Nineteenth-Century Virginian," *The Virginia Magazine of History and Biography* (1980), 88.

[16] Pargas, "From the Cradle to the Fields," 482.

[17] See, for example, Schwartz, *Born in Bondage*, 86; Stevenson, *Life in Black and White*, 227; Stevenson, "Gender Conventions," 174–5; King, "Suffer with them till death," 145–68; King, *Stolen Childhood*, 64; Morgan, *Slave Counterpoint*, 474; White, *Ar'n't I A Woman?*, 114.

caregivers and entered into fictive kin relationships," and "older slaves often showed kindness to children" in an emotionally and psychologically supportive intergenerational arrangement.[18] Daina Ramey Berry has similarly argued that caring relationships with elders "were not only important, but also primary" for enslaved children on account of the labor dynamics of slavery.[19]

Close supervisory relationships, and the intensity of intergenerational contact associated with them, also came with the potential for conflict. Carers sometimes found themselves – or believed they were – disrespected by the younger slaves, while some elders appeared to have resented their position and taken this out on their charges. Sometimes tension arose because children under the charge of elders misbehaved. This is not exactly revelatory nor indicative of anything sinister. It is worth flagging, nonetheless, because it underlines the need to consider positionality and who gets to speak for whom when we consider issues of respect for the aged. George Henry, enslaved in Virginia, fondly recalled how he used to trick the old nurse who cared for the children, including when he took her claim that babies were born in the "pulsey bed" literally: "I set about digging, and uprooted the whole bed without finding one, and when the old lady found me out, she was much enraged at the damage I had done, and drove me away."[20] The anecdote is obviously framed as a joke. However, if we consider how the nurse risked punishment given the damage to property under her care, as well as how often WPA elders framed similar antics from the "youth" as evidence of disrespect, interpreting children's actions might require a more nuanced assessment of the complexity to generational dynamics.[21]

Seemingly small-scale battles, and struggles for control between carer and caree, were frequently discussed by WPA respondents. Orris Harris noted on his plantation how "'Old Cisley wus too old to wurk an' she look afte' de chaps," and that his elder waged a constant campaign to maintain control. As Harris remembered, "de chaps wud git 'way frum

---

[18] King, *Stolen Childhood*, 64.   [19] Berry, *Price for Their Pound of Flesh*, 131.

[20] George Henry, *Life of George Henry. Together with a Brief History of the Colored People in America* (Providence: The Author; H. I. Gould, 1894), 7, 9.

[21] Maria Jenkins Schwartz notes how small misbehaviors could cause familial tension as mothers, in particular, faced possible abuse or additional labor for damaged clothes or dirty living quarters. Brenda Stevenson poignantly addressed how the pressures enslaved people faced could see internal traumas and violence. See Schwartz, *Born in Bondage*, 83, 111; Brenda Stevenson, "Distress and Discord in Virginian Slave Families," in Carol Bleser (Ed.) *In Joy and Sorrow: Women, Family, and Marriage in the Victorian South, 1830–1900* (New York: Oxford University Press, 1991), 103–25, 116.

her."[22] Hattie Jefferson recalled how the "old and cripple[d]" lady who looked after the children took a different route to try and maintain control, and "wud knock us round wid her crutch an' make us mind." Jefferson remembered her as continually scolding and smacking the children for ignoring her commands, and her insistence that "we [children] wus all bad an' wud neber low de babies to sleep long as we made too much fuss."[23] Barney Alford of Mississippi provided further insight into the complexity of intergenerational relationships when noting his positive memories of "Ole Mammy 'Lit." Lit, who cared for the children while their parents worked, was described by Alford as being "good to all de chilluns," but he also indicated the pleasure he took in subverting her authority by stealing her pipe and hiding it from her. This led to a constant battle between the two: Alford "would hide dat pipe, en she would slap me fur it, den sum times I would run way en go ter de kitchen whar my mammy wus at wurk en mammy Lit would hafter cum fur me en den she would whip me er gin. She sed I wus bad."

We have no access to Mammy Lit's words but, if we take seriously the complaints of the WPA generation, we can surely appreciate how such interactions might have been felt as evidence of disrespect by the elder in this dynamic. Marilda Pethy, for example, was described in 1937 as living with her daughter and grandchildren, "whom she tries to rule with an iron hand." According to the interviewer, her efforts were ridiculed rather than respected: the "younger generation … largely disregards the irate old woman" and this lent "quite an air of belligerency to the tumble-down building that houses them."[24] Louella Williams told her WPA interviewer that "Chillun ain't like day used to be years ago … all dey does now is give you big talk, an' put on airs," and that her own daughter fostered such disrespect: "Dere's Cora, my daughter, don't make dem chillun of hers min's an' respect me in my old age … Things is sho' different, when I was a child we knowed what it was to mind."[25] WPA respondents who recalled their own childhood japes with fondness had no little cognitive dissonance when describing their resentment of young people's disregard on account of their own advanced age. Alford himself claimed disappointment at how the youth of the 1930s stacked up to their elders and expressed sadness that times had changed for the worse.

---

[22] Rawick (Ed.), *AS, Supp.*, Ser. *1*, 8.3, 929. The children clearly cared for Cisley, and when she caught fire after smoking her pipe, they got water to put it out. The injuries were severe, however: "[Cisley] burnt her leg mighty bad."
[23] Rawick (Ed.), *AS, Supp.*, Ser. *1*, 8.3, 1132.   [24] *FWP, 10* (Missouri), 277.
[25] Rawick (Ed.), *AS, Supp.*, Ser. *1*, *1*, 455.

Alford sagely told his interviewer that "de young folks don't know how to work like de old folks," and bemoaned his abandonment by his own children, who "left home an' went up north an' dun fur git us ... dat is de way chaps treat deir parents dis day an' time." Lit, who described Alford "as bad" and perpetually struggled to uphold authority among her charges, might not have agreed times had truly changed for the worse.[26]

None of these examples are particularly egregious, but they indicate how enslaved youth might perceive their "old folks [as] fools" they could trick, deceive, and ignore when they wanted to, as well as the varied efforts elders employed to try and assert control.[27] A dismissal or devaluation from the enslaver might be expected on account of the asymmetries of power and understandings of slavery's exploitation, but to be diminished within the community was hurtful. We must be cautious in using enslaver management material, but claims that "children should be *required* to be respectful to those who are grown, more especially to the old, and the strong should never *be allowed* to impose on the weak" – with an emphasis on the necessity of an enslaver's oversight here – were not entirely fictional.[28] Philip Morgan, while generally stressing the respect in which elder carers were held, noted that on one South Carolinian plantation "Jack Lubbar, so old that he was almost blind, asked to be removed from overlooking Fork quarter because his great-grandchildren abused him."[29] Elders might try and maintain power, but for some this meant ever-diminishing returns. One postbellum writer recalled how Jacques was dismayed by the lack of respect accorded to him by the younger slaves and, "still retaining a feeling of authority," sought to enforce respect. The children, however, simply paid lip service to any notion of control. They "tried to look busy or grave when his eye was on them, long after his corporeal and mental powers had ceased their activity," but changed tack as soon as he stopped watching.[30] Elders who hoped for respect from within the community could find themselves disabused of this; this realization could occasion sadness, tension, and even violence.

Some of the recollections of aged carers focused on physical weaknesses or the general limitations of the aged, indicating how the deprivations of age were understood by Black southerners as shaping elderly carers' attitudes and status. Jim Threat of Alabama described the childminder as "an old

---

[26] All testimony from Barney Alford: Rawick (Ed.), *AS, Supp.*, Ser. *1, 6.1*, 25, 27, 45.
[27] Cook and Bratton, "Fields's Observation," 88.
[28] Agricola, "Management of Negroes," *Southern Cultivator* 13 (1855), 173. Italics mine.
[29] Morgan, *Slave Counterpoint*, 473–4.
[30] Caroline Gilman, *Recollections of a Southern Matron* (New York: Harper & Brothers, 1838), 80.

decrepit woman," while another ex-slave simply viewed the woman in charge of childcare as being "one that had broke down."[31] Brenda Stevenson has argued that "obedience and reverence of slave elders" was a lesson the community took to heart, and elderly carers have been noted as "primary" figures in the lives of enslaved children. Some enslaved children instead framed elderly carers as marginal figures, even a hindrance, in their day-to-day lives, on account of their debilities.[32] The fugitive author James Watkins was under the charge of "an old female slave whom they called Aunt Comfort," but the woman's name was not well given, in Watkins's telling: "I lived with this old woman till about five or six years old, rolling in the dirt like a pig, and little better cared for."[33] Watkins understood the woman's aged debility impacted on her actions but his suffering, and her neglect, were foregrounded here, with a limited appreciation of how far her extended suffering might have shaped her inaction.

Childcare was constant and taxing on those who held these roles and, as Watkins intimated, sometimes this was just too much for the elderly. Louis Hughes recorded in his postbellum memoir the hard work expected of elders in nursing or caring roles, explaining how on their plantation "a woman who was too old to do much of anything was assigned to the charge of these babies." Hughes painted a troubling picture of the difficulties carer and caree faced: "It was rare that she had any one to help her. The cries of these little ones, who were cut off almost entirely from motherly care and protection, were heart-rending." This laboring role was, contrary to proslavery claims, no leisurely retirement; it was hard work that negatively impacted upon the relations between young and old: "The children ranging in age from one to seven years were numerous, and the old woman had them to look after as well as the babies. This was indeed a task, and might well have taxed the strength of a younger woman."[34] Hughes had little to say about the aged woman's feelings, but R. C. Smith of Oklahoma suggested how this overwork led to tension between carer and caree. Smith recalled how his aunt struggled to cope with the requirements expected of her and indicated that she took this out on her charges: "My auntie hated being a slave. She had to take care of the babies on the farm while their

---

[31] Rawick (Ed.), *AS, Supp.*, Ser. *1, 12,* 335; Rawick (Ed.), *AS, 18,* 255–6.

[32] Stevenson, "Gender Conventions," 174–5; Berry, *Price for Their Pound of Flesh*, 131.

[33] James Watkins, *Narrative of the Life of James Watkins, Formerly a "Chattel" in Maryland, US; Containing an Account of His Escape from Slavery, Together with an Appeal on Behalf of Three Millions of Such "Pieces of Property," Still Held Under the Standard of the Eagle* (Bolton: Kenyon & Abbot, 1852), 7.

[34] Hughes, *Thirty Years a Slave*, 43–5.

mothers worked in the field. Sometimes she would git cranky and wouldn't speak to any body for a week."[35]

Reduced ability, or perhaps "crankiness," could thus affect the levels of care provided and undermine intergenerational networks of support. Jennie Webb explained to her WPA interviewer that her Aunt Adelene was in charge of the children and that Adelene was unwilling to wash their food bowls and simply made the children eat off dirty plates. Webb recalled how "after we got through eatin' in 'em de flys swarmed over 'em an' de dogs licked 'um an' dey sho' did smell bad."[36] As Webb grew older she refused to eat off the plates, looked after the children herself, and informed her enslaver of the woman's neglect. This woman was perhaps too tired, physically and emotionally, to do this labor but her actions negatively affected her response to, and relationship with, the enslaved youth in her community. The children under this elder's care, led by Webb, saw not a supportive figure but instead someone whose (in)action harmed them, and they were willing to perhaps see her disciplined to protect themselves. Enslaved people were forced to make choices over loyalties in such circumstances and, in the instance noted earlier, the lack of support given to the children outweighed any sense of generalized respect for elders. Structural violence here was personified in the individual failings of the aged nurse, and Webb's decision to inform on her shows the hegemonic power of enslavers and their ability to affect solidarities in the slave community.

* * *

If some formerly enslaved people viewed their carers as frail or felt comfortable ignoring them, others viewed the power dynamics as heavily skewed in the other direction. Some ex-slaves viewed their elderly carers as tyrannical and exploitative, and as having sought control – or enforced respect – through violence or coercion. Dora Franks explained to her WPA interviewer that the "old black woman" who was the cook believed that, as a mixed-race child, Franks was a "favorite" of their enslaver – Franks's father – and expected unearned privileges.[37] Aunt Caroline sought to put Franks in her place:

[35] Rawick (Ed.), *AS, Supp., Ser. 1, 12,* 281.

[36] Rawick (Ed.), *AS, Supp., Ser. 1, 10.5,* 2250.

[37] On the complexities of these dynamics, see Fay Yarbrough, "Power, Perception, and Interracial Sex: Former Slaves Recall a Multiracial South," *Journal of Southern History,* 71.3 (2005), 559–98; Andrea Livesey, "Conceived in Violence: Enslaved Mothers and Children Born of Rape in Nineteenth-Century Louisiana," *Slavery & Abolition,* 38.2 (2017), 373–91; Stevenson, "What's love got to do with it."

I 'members one time when dey all went off an' lef' me wid a old black woman called Aunt Ca'line what done de cookin' 'round de place some o' de time. When dey lef' de house I went in de kitchen a' asked her for a piece o' white bread lak de white folks eat. She haul off an' slap me down an' call me all kin' o' names dat I didn' know what dey meant. My nose bled an' ruint de nice clean dress I had on.

Franks did not accept this treatment from her elder and informed upon Aunt Caroline, and the consequences for the old woman were severe: "I hear tell dat dey whup her so hard dat she couldn't walk no mo."[38]

Rosa Washington of Louisiana also struggled with her elder in the kitchen, noting how "Ole Aunt Clarissie cooked for us" but stressing that she neither cared for nor protected her. Instead, "she was mean to me" and would tell "lies on me to white overseer."[39] Washington was entirely unsympathetic to Clarissie, but the longer testimony provides some sense of motive for the elderly woman's actions. Indeed, the "lie" came when Clarissie was confronted by the overseer about the poor state of the cutlery in the kitchen and she blamed her young apprentice. This led to the overseer stabbing Washington in the head with the offending item.[40] Washington suffered tremendously here, but we must acknowledge the fear of personal punishment that possibly animated her elder's actions. This was a woman looking to secure her own position, no doubt acting selfishly, but such selfishness is entirely compatible with seeking to survive slavery.

At times the dynamics were reversed. When Israel Campbell was captured after his first abortive flight, his enslaver tried to make Campbell blame the old woman who looked after the children. Campbell initially resisted, but the lash worked to tragic effect and he cast blame accordingly: "He then stopped whipping me, and commenced at poor old Aunt Fanny." Fanny, according to Campbell's telling, bore her punishment "patiently," and such a message fits with the wider abolitionist desire to stress enslaved solidarity in the face of enslaver brutality.[41] Such cases undoubtedly existed, but we must also question Campbell's ability to speak for Fanny, and to consider whether he truly knew how she felt about his (tortured) acquiescence to her punishment. Campbell eventually escaped, but we hear no more of Fanny; perhaps she resented Campbell, or perhaps she simply came to believe that her best option the next time

---

[38] *FWP*, 9 (Mississippi), 50.   [39] Rawick (Ed.), *AS, Supp.*, Ser. 2, *10.9*, 3979.

[40] Rawick (Ed.), *AS*, *5.4*, 135.

[41] Israel Campbell, *An Autobiography. Bond and Free: Or, Yearnings for Freedom, from my Green Brier House. Being the Story of My Life in Freedom. By Israel Campbell. Minister of the Gospel* (Philadelphia, Published by the Author, 1861), 19–21.

around would be to look out for herself. This would appear to have been Clarrissie's response and, while less overtly "heroic," her actions are understandable given the violence enslavers wielded. Both instances reveal how the desire for survival in the face of oppression might lead to strife between young and old, as well as underscore the tragic choices enslaved people had to make surrounding solidarities in bondage.

Enslaved people sometimes positioned childcare arrangements as a space where tensions arose between the young and the old. These tensions could be conditioned by contests for respect or suspicions over mixed loyalties, but also shaped by wider sufferings in slavery that led to division as opposed to mutual support. Anna Baker of Mississippi noted how "old" Aunt Emmaline looked after all of the orphans and children of women in "de breedin' quarters," but stressed how this care was not shared evenly: "She was sho' mean to me. I think it was 'cause de marster laked me an' was always a-pettin' me. She was jealous." Baker noted how this power struggle rippled out of the quarters and that the abuse received was returned in kind. After Baker burnt the meal she was meant to be parching Emmaline hit her over the head with "a iron miggin" and left her with a visible wound. Fearing punishment herself, Emmaline "made me promise to tell de marster dat I hurt my head when I fell out o' de door" and clearly hoped that respect, or perhaps even fear, would occasion compliance. Emmaline found out to her cost the limits of her control: "He took Aunt Emmaline down to de gear house an' wore her out. He wouldn' tell off on me."[42] Baker believed Emmaline's actions related to jealousy, but she might simply have hoped to avoid personal punishment for the burnt meal and been willing to cast blame on another to achieve this. Caring relations could become spaces where individual strategies for survival might lead to tension, and where the use of elders to hold supervisory roles over children saw intergenerational strife develop almost by design.

These examples provide no fond memories of elder care and instead suggest the complex power dynamics that might erupt between young and old, carer and caree, and the complex networks of solidarity in slave communities. These dynamics could be shaped by the structures of slavery itself, with the desire of the aged carer to show they were fulfilling their role leading them to punish or inform upon the children. Isaac Martin of Texas noted how "back in slav'ry dey allus had a ol' darky to train de young ones and teach 'em right from wrong. And dey'd whip you for doin'

---

[42] *FWP*, 9 (Mississippi), 14.

wrong. Dey'd repo't to de overseer." Martin believed this allowed some elders to settle scores with those under their care: "Some of 'em was mean and repo't somebody dey ain't like jis' to git 'em in trouble."[43] These actions and perceived loyalties to enslavers were often recalled negatively by the child so affected, but the aged carer was walking a tightrope where their own failure may have led to personal punishment. Mary Reynolds, enslaved in Louisiana, recalled the ferocious pace set by the "old woman" who was instructed to teach the children labor skills. This was no carefree creche:

That old woman would be in a frantic. She'd show me and then turn 'bout to show some other li'l n***r, and I'd have the young corn cut clean as the grass. She say, "For the love of Gawd, you better larn it right, or Solomon will beat the breath out of you body."[44]

Reynolds saw the panic in the old woman's actions and held no resentment for the pace she kept, referring instead to slavery being "the worst days was ever seed in the world." Others were less willing to recognize the structural constraints placed on aged carers. Irrella Battle Walker and Monroe Franklin Jamison both saw Black elders as the drivers of their own personal misery in slavery. Walker explained how "Old man Jonas watched us chillen and kept us divin' for dat cotton all de day long. Us wish him dead many a time."[45] Jamison depicted Aunt Harrietta Best, who oversaw the children, as "the most cruel creature in the form of a human being that I had ever seen. She would cut and slay right and left. During each day she would lay it on to some of us." According to Jamison, "we children took her for the devil untied, and we were not much mistaken."[46] WPA respondents sometimes blamed Black trustees to avoid risking the wrath of white southerners amidst "Jim Crow," but Black authority figures could and did use force to establish their position and assert themselves over others.[47] For elders with childcare responsibilities, the desire to perform to the standard expected of them and to maintain control over their charges could lead to tension. One former slave recalled how "Old Aunt Fanny," who supervised the children, informed their

---

[43] Rawick (Ed.), *AS*, 5.3, 59.   [44] Rawick (Ed.), *AS*, 5.3, 238.

[45] Rawick (Ed.), *AS*, 5.4, 123.

[46] Monroe Franklin Jamison, *Autobiography and Work of Bishop M. F. Jamison, D.D. ("Uncle Joe") Editor, Publisher, and Church Extension Secretary; a Narration of His Whole Career from the Cradle to the Bishopric of the Colored M. E. Church in America* (Nashville: Published for the Author by the Publishing House of the M. E. Church, 1912), 22.

[47] See Doddington, *Contesting Slave Masculinity*, ch. 2.

enslaver that "that my sister wouldn't keep her dress klean" and she was whipped as punishment. This led to a furious response from their mother, who "throwed Aunt Fan out the kitchen door." The respondent was clearly upset about Fan's actions and described how this type of behavior was par for the course: "You see, she would tell things on the others, trying to keep from getting whipped herself."[48] The respondent was entirely unsympathetic, but Fan's actions clearly indicate how the invidious divide-and-rule policies employed by enslavers filtered into, and shaped, intergenerational dynamics in childcare arrangements. This sometimes led to conflict between those expected to keep order and those under the control of elders.

Tension arose occasionally when an aged carer was perceived to be playing favorites, deliberately supporting only some at the expense of others. Lula Jackson recalled how the "old lady named 'Aunt' Charlotte" used to look after the children "when the hands were working" but stressed her care came with caveats: "If she liked you she would treat your children well. If she didn't like you, she wouldn't treat them so good . . . if she didn't like the people, she would leave the babies' napkins on all day long, wet and filthy."[49] Rather than reflecting broader support networks within slave communities or being viewed as supportive and kind, then, some elders were positioned by ex-slaves as having used their position to prioritize chosen favorites or to punish people they disliked. James Williams, who fled slavery as a child, explained that his flight was precipitated by an old woman, considered by most to be a "good old aunty," becoming "affronted" with him and lying to their enslaver so to as cause his punishment. Williams claimed to forgive the old woman by blaming her "ignorance" for her actions, noting that "Slaves, at times, did things which worked directly against each other, ignorantly." In framing her actions in such a way, however, Williams was negating the troubling possibility (for Black activists) that this woman simply sought to protect herself even at the expense of others.[50] Claims of forgiveness aside, Williams's recollections show how loyalty was conditional among the enslaved and that the brute force of slavery challenged intergenerational support networks.

Frederick Douglass was insistent about the significance of elder respect among the enslaved, but also described his suffering at the hands of elders in

[48] Rawick (Ed.), *AS*, *18*, 116–17.   [49] Rawick (Ed.), *AS*, 9.3, 18.

[50] James Williams, *Life and Adventures of James Williams, a Fugitive Slave, with a Full Description of the Underground Railroad* (San Francisco: Women's Union Print, 424 Montgomery Street, 1873), 13.

positions of authority. Douglass recalled how the older woman tasked with childcare on the plantation protected her own family members but punished others, including Douglass himself. Douglass's comments at being left "to the tender mercies of Aunt Katy" underscored the power relations embedded in childcare and the conditional loyalties among the enslaved. Douglass believed Aunt Katy to be "ill-tempered and cruel by nature," but also indicated that her management was firm because she was "ambitious of old master's favor." Douglass framed this negatively, and, when set against the heroism of his own fugitivity, it is hard not to share Douglass's perception of Katy as a problematic figure. Katy's "ambition," however, plausibly related to a survival strategy of her own, where her success in gaining the enslaver's favor allowed her to provide for her family members. That this came to the detriment of the children who lacked her favor was a sacrifice she was willing for them to bear: "in her instinct to satisfy their demands for food she was often guilty of starving me and the other children." Douglass further stressed that "Aunt Katy could beat as well as starve me," and that, despite his mother's intervention, he was constantly forced to navigate "the virago in my master's kitchen, whose fiery wrath was my constant dread."[51] Douglass's experiences suggest the need to view the dynamics between children and aged carers as a site of power relations, where the structural force enslavers wielded, and their use of elders as authority figures, created divisions among the enslaved. It also suggests how far some elders made decisions about how to navigate and employ any authority left to them to support themselves, family, and friends. This type of support could lead to, or even require, the neglect of those on the "outside."

Douglass's travails did not end with Aunt Katy, and he went on to recall his vexed experiences under the tutelage of "Uncle Isaac Copper." Douglass spoke of Copper in terms of ostensible respect, noting the veneration which allowed him to be granted his "title" as "both our Doctor of Medicine and our Doctor of Divinity," and scholars such as Jenifer Barclay have used these words to emphasize how Copper "was a respected figure in an important social role."[52] Nonetheless, Douglass subtly cast shade on Copper's abilities and clearly resented his style of management: "Where he took his degree I am unable to say, but he was too well established in his profession to permit question as to his native skill or attainments." Copper's care, in Douglass's telling, was sorely lacking, and Douglass's framing to his readers gently mocked his elder's

---

[51] Douglass, *Life and Times of Frederick Douglass* (1892), 34–6.
[52] Barclay, *The Mark of Slavery*, 43.

pretensions to knowledge: "His remedial prescriptions embraced four articles. For diseases of the body, epsom salts and castor oil; for those of the soul, the 'Lord's prayer,' and a few stout hickory switches." Douglass recalled how the children faced punishment if they failed to please Copper or if they were perceived as acting impudently, and underlined how this reflected the structural violence of the Slave South. According to Douglass, "everybody in the South seemed to want the privilege of whipping somebody else. Uncle Isaac, though a good old man, shared the common passion of his time and country." Notwithstanding his claims of respect, Douglass resented these punishments and took aim at his elder's claims of piety in justifying his actions. He implied that, even while a child, he perceived himself as superior to his elder: "there was in my mind, even at that time, something a little inconsistent and laughable in the blending of prayer with punishment."[53] We cannot know, but it is plausible that Copper's actions were shaped by his dismay at the idea of the young Douglass finding his elder's actions and belief system "laughable."

On occasion, disputes shaped by concerns with authority and status between elders and the wider slave community escalated and children became pawns in these wider quarrels. Damian Alan Pargas has noted that "enslaved parents' dependency on others to raise their children was for many a hard pill to swallow," and this was worsened if elders took out their frustrations or anger at the parent on the child under their care.[54] Frederick Douglass's mother was able to intervene for a short while with "Aunt Katy," if not with "Uncle Copper," but others had not even this limited support. George Conrad, born in Kentucky, believed that his brothers were murdered by Aunt Sarah, who "took care of the children" while her mother "cooked and took care of the house." Becoming convinced that Conrad's mother received favorable treatment from their enslaver at her own expense, Sarah "got jealous, and killed both of the babies."[55] Intergenerational power struggles embedded in caring relations could come at a tremendous cost, and solidarity between the young and old was neither universal nor immune from the wider violence of enslavement. One former slave, whose mother fled from bondage and left her children, lived to survive the care she received from "Charlotte – the old woman we was living with." Not all of her charges were so lucky. The ill-treatment went beyond neglect and was creatively cruel, with the respondent recalling how Charlotte "would take nettle weeds and whip us with them" and force

---

[53] Douglass, *Life and Times of Frederick Douglass* (1892), 46–7.
[54] Pargas, "From the Cradle to the Fields," 481.   [55] *FWP, 13* (Oklahoma), 40.

"the little one (Tobe) get up and go outdoors to do his business" irrespective of the cold. The respondent noted how the children were forced to fend for themselves and that she personally "would dip my hand in the gravy and rub it on his toes when his feet was cold." Tobe's sufferings did not abate and his neglect, and the general poor conditions in the quarters, saw him suffer lockjaw. It was the young respondent, not Charlotte, who discovered Tobe was unable to eat, but it was too late to help him: "the next night he died." The memories here were far removed from the positive perception of aged carers described elsewhere, and this respondent could neither forgive nor forget her elder's mistreatment of her family.[56] Intergenerational caring relationships were sites of complex power dynamics that could involve tension and abuse, both physical and verbal. These conflicts were conditioned by the structures of slavery, but also by the actions, choices, and identities of enslaved people who took different routes in navigating, and seeking to survive, slavery.

* * *

Enslaved people who held skilled or technical roles, both in domestic settings and outside of it, could find themselves in the position of having to train up their own replacements before transitioning away from this work. Historians have typically viewed these types of intergenerational transitions as relatively unproblematic. The image of elders teaching and training their younger peers has been viewed as important in developing supportive communities and in forging positive links between young and old. Sergio Lussana has noted how enslaved men who had skills "took pride in their work and passed on their prized skills to younger men, creating an intergenerational male network."[57] Levi Branham, enslaved in Georgia, explained how this type of process worked: "While I was still a little boy I was very fond of plowing. There was an old black man who plowed for my master. Sometimes I would give him a dime or a nickel to let me plow a round. That's the way I learned how to plow."[58]

---

[56] Rawick (Ed.), *AS, 18,* 272.

[57] Sergio Lussana, *My Brother Slaves: Friendship, Masculinity, and Resistance in the Antebellum South* (Lexington: University Press of Kentucky, 2016), 35. See also White, *Ar'n't I A Woman?*, 119–20; Erica L. Ball, "To Train Them for the Work: Manhood, Morality, and Free Black Conduct Discourse in Antebellum New York," in Timothy R. Buckner and Peter Caster (Eds.), *Fathers, Preachers, Rebels, Men: Black Masculinity in US History and Literature, 1820–1945* (Columbus: Ohio State University Press, 2011), 60–80.

[58] Levi Branham, *My Life and Travels* (Dalton: A. J. Showalter Co. Printers and Publishers, 1929), 4.

This type of transition, however, involved a very real confrontation with the public perception of one person's decline, whether physical or mental. Historian Stacey Close acknowledged the possibility that enslaved elders "lost a great amount of self-esteem because they were displaced by younger, stronger, and talented slaves," while Deborah Gray White posited that elder craftsmen might struggle if "replaced by younger, more energetic, and nimble slave artisans."[59] Both scholars identified, but did not explore further, the possibility of conflict here. And yet such examples can clearly be found. Aunt Juda described to her WPA interviewer how the public perception of her father's growing frailty forced his relegation from a valued role as the ferry boat captain: "Pa ran the ferry boat for [enslaver] until he was so old and weak until he was afraid that he would fall in the river so had him to quit."[60] In Juda's telling, the decision was taken out of her father's hands, with the conflation of old age with weakness – and the public affirmation of his reduced capacity – leading to a forced withdrawal. Juda did not share how her father felt about this, but some enslaved people refused to accept work-related transitions, relegations, or age-related snubs from their enslavers or peers – whether real or perceived. Rather than openly direct anger at the enslaver, these elders might externalize and take aim at the person marked as their replacement. Age in this context was a vector of power and a space through which social hierarchies in slave communities might develop and shift.

When Puritan minister Joseph Lathrop described the travails of age to his audience in 1805, he described how where "once our advice was sought and regarded; now we are passed by with neglect, and younger men take our place." Those replacements, moreover, risked becoming the object of spite: "And if we are, now and then, consulted, perhaps our jealousy whispers, that it is done merely to flatter our aged vanity and keep us in good humor."[61] Lathrop was speaking to a mostly white audience, but the themes and patterns he identified were clearly understood by Black contemporaries. In some instances, elders resented the idea they should hand over their knowledge and skills to the young, with such a role serving only to remind them of their inexorable decline. Ed Jackson, who earned the nickname "ol' Cow King" in his prime as a rancher, was asked to provide guidance to trainees but refused on account of his reduced

---

[59] Close, *Elderly Slaves*, 102; White, *Ar'n't I A Woman?*, 114.

[60] Rawick (Ed.), *AS, Supp.*, Ser. 1, 7.2, 557.

[61] Joseph Lathrop, *The Infirmities and Comforts of Old Age: A Sermon to Aged People* (Springfield: Henry Brewer, 1805), 6–7.

capacity. Jackson informed his admirers that he was "no good. Cain't scas'ley look after myself" and that he was not going to "goin' down there and make no fool outen myself." The recruiters sought to placate him by explaining that he only had to "sit around and whittle and tell the chillun stories 'bout you'self," but this only disturbed his pride. As Jackson put it: "No, I'm not goin' to be no nursemaid for the brats iffen I can't bus' hosses like I use to, then I don' wan' to sit around seein' these young ikes tryin' to. They can't stay on!"[62] Jackson's sadness at his own decline was manifest in an unwillingness to guide the young, as well as open disdain at the rising generations' abilities compared to his own.

Given the limits of antebellum testimony identified earlier, we mostly hear about these transitions from the apprentice rather than the "master." Calvin Moye explained to his WPA interviewer how he took over the role of blacksmith on the plantation and described the supportive apprentice-ship he had with the elder statesman, Zeke. Their enslaver put Moye to work under his elder after noting that "Uncle Zeke is getting ole and I's going to needs a new blacksmith before long." Moye was delighted to be appointed to the smithy, with a clear sense this role would provide greater benefits than field work, and appeared to have a positive relationship with Zeke. After arriving early on his first day, Moye recalled how "Uncle Zeke comes walkin slow to de blacksmith shop and when he sees me he begins laughing at me and says 'I see de new blacksmith is down early to go to work.'" Moye was proud of his natural ability and claimed that Zeke recognized this, with the elder claiming "I was about as good as he was, already doing this." Whether Zeke genuinely meant this, or simply wanted to bolster his apprentice's confidence, Moye clearly believed it. Moye had earlier explained that his enslaver deliberately fostered compe-tition in work to better manage the plantation, and Moye had clearly internalized at least some of this logic. The language of competition suffused his recollections of his transition into the leading blacksmith above Zeke, with Moye proudly claiming that "in about 4 years Maser Ingram and Uncle Zeke says I could beat Uncle Zeke."[63]

Moye depicted the relationship between him and Zeke positively, and their interactions could easily fit the mentoring relationship scholars have used to discuss age-related transitions. We do not have access to Zeke's words to question this. We might, however, use Moyes's annoyance at his own age-related work decline to suggest this relationship, and the shifting

[62] Rawick (Ed.), *AS, Supp.*, Ser. 2, 5.4, 1889.
[63] Rawick (Ed.), *AS, Supp.*, Ser. 2, 7.6, 2826–7, 2832, 2837.

hierarchies associated with it, might have occasioned at least some reflective sadness for his elder. The idea of being "beaten" by your replacement was not always graciously accepted by the one on the way out. Moye eventually lost his own job as blacksmith due to the march of time and he was bitter at this turn of events: "I was gitten ter be an ole man, dat is everbody says I was. Dey says I could'nt do some jobs it was too heavy fer me." Moye disputed these allegations and insisted he was still better than the "young men cause I had been a blacksmith all my life and I was stouter den dey thought I was." He could not fight time forever: "I got older and older and dey finally got to where dey would'nt lets me work at all unless it was water boy or some light job."[64] If Zeke were to tell his version of this transition away from the role of blacksmith, we might surely see a similar tale of regret at the comparative loss of status and authority, or perhaps simply at the diminished perceptions of his skill and status from others in the community. Moye's personal experiences of these transitions – both his positive memories of supplanting an elder and then disappointment at the onward march of time himself – suggest some of the complexities in thinking about generational dynamics, and the tensions aging presented for enslaved people at work.

Reduced powers on account of age could be taken poorly by enslaved people who valued their prowess or skills and had connected this to their sense of self. John Matthews, who forthrightly insisted to his WPA interviewer "dey tells me I is old, but I aint. I plow right now jes' as good as I did twenty years ago . . . an' I can step 'round as good as any young man," would have understood the anger of John Brown of Georgia, who, eighty years earlier, recorded his resentment at being told by his enslaver that he "was old and hard-looking."[65] Brown acknowledged he was "worn down by fatigue and poor living." He "was not, however, very well pleased to hear myself run down."[66] This may have related to a desire to avoid being deemed useless but also to an identity connected to physical strength and laboring skills. Indeed, notwithstanding the horrors of slavery, enslaved people clearly found some measure of pride in their abilities – whether technical, mental, or physical. William Dusinberre has emphasized how the "opportunity to develop one's skills" in certain roles provided a "limited independence" that was worth something given the hardships of day-to-day life.[67]

[64] Rawick (Ed.), *AS, Supp.,* Ser. 2, 7.6, 2868.
[65] Rawick (Ed.), *AS, Supp.,* Ser. 1, 9.4, 1458–9; Brown, *Slave Life in Georgia,* 20–21.
[66] Brown, *Slave Life in Georgia,* 20–1.
[67] William Dusinberre, "Power and Agency in Antebellum Slavery," *American Nineteenth Century History,* 12. 2 (June 2011), 139–48, 144. See also Johnson, *River of Dark Dreams,* 164.

Black activist James Pennington accepted as much himself, acknowledging that his "blacksmith's pride and taste was one thing that had reconciled me so long to remain a slave."[68]

William Dusinberre came closest to exploring the damaging conse-quences if enslaved people *lost* valued roles, noting the suicide of a driver who was returned to field work as a punishment by his enslaver.[69] To be relegated from a skilled role on account of perceptions of age-related decline, as opposed to a calculated punishment, might necessitate a degree of reflective thinking about one's position among peers, or even resistance to those who sought (or were made) to replace you in an effort to refute the claims of reduced power and capacity. Tom Morris explained to his WPA interviewer how this realization was a tough pill to swallow and revealed his personal anguish at community disregard on account of age: "I cud wurk now, but ebery body tells me I am too old."[70] The tension between sense of self and public perception of age could manifest differently, but it was clearly a struggle for some enslaved people to accept that others viewed them as old. The commonality with which this transition was framed through a language of weakness or frailty underscores how antebellum Americans, Black and white, under-stood age was a vector of power.

Some ex-slaves explained how they or others tried to address this decline. West Turner described to his WPA interviewer the difficulties he faced in maintaining laboring strength as he grew older and wistfully compared this to his earlier prowess: "Was strong as an ox when I was a boy. Could' h'ist up on en' a hogshead of tobacoo, an' spec' I could carry it if someone put it on my back. Cain't do it now. Old age got me good."[71] Turner accepted his reduced capacity, but others struggled with this realization and even fought against it. Mike Lawrence recalled how "Old John Drayton" refused to accept reduced labor capabilities because of his desire to showcase his abilities to his peers but also to his enslaver. As Lawrence put it, "he wuk so haa'd some time dat Maussa jest got to stop him, or he kill heself." Drayton sought to prove the doubters wrong and "W'en [enslaver] go back in de wood dat evening he check up and find dat Old John done cut five hundred rail." Lawrence, for one, was

---

[68] James W. C. Pennington, *The Fugitive Blacksmith; Or, Events in the History of James W. C. Pennington, Pastor of a Presbyterian Church, New York, Formerly a Slave in the State of Maryland, United States* (London: Charles Gilpin, 1849), 8–9.

[69] Dusinberre, "Power and Agency," 142–3.

[70] Rawick (Ed.), *AS, Supp.*, Ser. *1*, 9.4, 1588.

[71] Perdue et al., *Weevils in the Wheat*, 289.

impressed at this rejection of time's relentless march, exclaiming "Oh, dem been man in dose day, I tell you."[72] Drayton's efforts seemed connected to pride in his prowess and a desire to maintain his positive personal identity. Given the connection enslavers drew between productivity and value, as well as the real material consequences of such connections outlined in Chapter 1, such efforts also plausibly reflected Drayton's desire to avoid being cast aside.

A similar motive appeared to shape the actions of Ben, described by a WPA respondent from Indiana as a man who in his prime "stood six feet four inches tall, was raw boned with little fat and weighted three hundred sixteen pounds." Ben struggled to reconcile his pride in his physical prowess with the hardships of aging and sought to impress upon others his fortitude even as he grew older. This, the narrator insisted, came at a cost: "Late in life, he lifted a clay mixer from a wagon to the ground; a job for several men with skids. He succeeded, but the effort was fatal to the old fellow and he died soon after." The respondent was entirely unsympathetic to the "old fellow's" plight, and depicted this as evidence of the dangers of ego: "Ben's vanity was his undoing."[73] Enslaved people understood time's onward march could be fought, but there was only ever one winner here. The lack of sympathy, moreover, indicates how such activities and stories might serve a discursive purpose, with the WPA respondent using Ben's fate to highlight the necessity of humility in the face of time's relentless march. The tale hints at the problems enslaved people who refused to reconcile their sense of self with the transitions associated with aging might face.

Sometimes a movement toward being replaced occasioned sadness and a need to grapple with one's identity. In other instances a feared decline – or the perception of inferiority that aging was understood as representing – led to public protestations and conflict. Jerry Boykins told his WPA interviewer that his mother struggled with jealousy from her peers, to the extent "one of them she-devils poison her one day to git her cookin' job in the house." According to Boykin, this related to the woman's hope that in replacing his mother, the poisoner "wouldn't have to do the hard field work."[74] Workplace transitions could be tied into internal power dynamics among the enslaved; the ferocious discipline one enslaved cook wielded over her young charges to reassert her supremacy when challenged, and her rejection of assistance as she grew older, indicates a fear

---

[72] Rawick (Ed.), *AS*, 3.3, 99.   [73] Rawick (Ed.), *AS, Supp.*, Ser. 1, 5, 139.
[74] Rawick (Ed.), *AS, Supp.*, Ser. 2, 2.1, 373.

that being "replaced" meant losing important authority and status: "An' I bin manage my own affa'rs, an' I gwine manage my own affa'rs long is I got breff."[75] The same author also intimated at conflict between the elderly blacksmith and his young apprentice when describing how "'Uncle Joe,' the blacksmith, burned his nephew's face with a hot iron," which led to the younger man's removal from the smithy entirely: "The man carries the scar to this day, and in speaking of it always says: 'Soon as my marster fin' out how Uncle Joe treated me, he wouldn't let me work no mo' in his shop.'"[76] Both instances suggest how contemporaries understood that one person's descent down the steps of life allowed for the ascent of another, and this sometimes led to trouble.

* * *

Work-related conflict between "apprentice/masters" could be understood as intergenerational contests over authority, with the fear of replacement and attendant loss of status looming in the background of such encounters. Historian Timothy R. Buckner has used the diaries of William Johnson, the free Black barber of Natchez, to note how these hierarchical arrangements could see conflict develop, with the elder expecting, even demanding, deference from those they believed to be working "under" them.[77] Enslaved people who had held positions of authority might be particularly anxious to avoid a loss of power in the eyes of others, with Pettigrew's insistence that older trustees must "soon expect the inexorable hand of time to soften that vigour which is all important in a ruler," followed by the realization that "without which he soon permits some stronger spirit than his own to assume the mastery over him."[78] To be mastered by another was to be made dependent, to be denigrated in the eyes of others, and suggests that decline associated with age, and challenges to working authority, could lead to contests over identity and status. One such encounter developed among two enslaved people near Rutherfordton, North Carolina, in 1829, where "old negro Bob" was threatened with execution after murdering Silva, a woman he worked alongside. Bob and Silva had oversight of the children on the plantation

[75] Letitia Burwell, *A Girl's Life in Virginia Before the War* (New York: Frederick A. Stokes, 1895), 7.

[76] Burwell, *A Girl's Life in Virginia*, 29–30.

[77] Timothy R Buckner, "A Crucible of Masculinity: William Johnson's Barbershop and the Making of Free Black Men in the Antebellum South," in Buckner and Caster (Eds.), *Fathers, Preachers, Rebels, Men*, 41–60.

[78] Starobin (Ed.), *Blacks in Bondage*, 34–5.

and publicly disagreed over how best to plant the potatoes, with Silva
denigrating Bob's suggestion and denying him deference. Enslaved men
could position authority in work as vital to their sense of self, and Silva's
refusal to accede to his view and threat to "take the children away" clearly
infuriated Bob: "I was then so mad that I raised the hoe and struck her
over the head." Bob sought to blame the demon drink, but he also insisted
this "provocation" was no small matter: "I had been drinking the night
before & I 'spose' it was the remains of the whisky that put me in such
a sudden passion when she provoked me."[79] To have his authority questioned publicly in front of the children appeared to set Bob off and Silva
was the victim of his rage. Elders who hoped to maintain authority might
struggle when this was publicly repudiated by others, and, especially if this
undercut previously established gendered norms, this might lead to tension in the community.[80]

Historian Dea Boster has noted that enslavers deliberately used
enslaved elders as drivers in the hope of capitalizing "on the slave community's respect for its older members," and Philip Morgan has noted that
aged drivers' authority tended to have "waxed rather than waned."[81]
When assumed authority was put to the test, however, older trustees
might struggle to answer satisfactorily. W. E. Hobbs, whose father was
an enslaver in Tennessee, recalled the consequences of another such
conflict. Hobbs recalled the time a driver struggled to subjugate a group
of young men, described as "seven or eight young, well muscled bucks,"
whom his master had placed under his authority. From the first, the young
men "wouldn't do anything he told them to do." The man's failure to
maintain control revolved around his comparative lack of physical ability:
"He couldn't make them do anything, because any one of them could
whip him in a fight." The reference to the youth and physical vitality of
these men suggests some perception of age difference as part of their
dominance over the driver. The younger men's' actions could be seen as
resistance to their enslavement, but the results of their defiance for the
driver was devastating: he was mocked, beaten, and humiliated by the
younger men, and then whipped by his enslaver and sold on.

William Grimes of Virginia outlined his violent response to the
demands of the aged driver and used his victory to cement his identity as
a powerful resistor and to disrupt the existing plantation hierarchy. After

---

[79] Roswell Elmer Diary, 1829–30, November 25, 1829, #4670-z, SHC.
[80] This is acknowledged but quickly moved on from, in Close, *Elderly Slaves*, 69.
[81] Boster, *African American Slavery and Disability*, 58; Morgan, *Slave Counterpoint*, 223.

being told to work while injured, Grimes simply ignored the "old negro driver" and a conflict ensued. The driver had assumed his authority would be respected, but he was soon taught a lesson about how dominance was embodied instead of innate. Grimes "heard him coming back, and when he burst open the door, I let him have it in old Virginia stile, (which generally consists in gouging, biting and butting)." The driver was left cringing on the floor and forced to relinquish his stick – which served as both a weapon but also a visual symbol of his authority – and the image of Grimes pacing up and down the room with the staff provides a visual signifier of his usurpation of the man's authority. The driver was not viewed as excessively cruel by those under his charge, with the men who gathered around, led by "the stoutest of them," simply asking him "why I had treated the driver so." Grimes clearly saw physical force as a means of overawing the community and continued his campaign in the quarters: "I then seized him by the shoulders, and said to him, I will show you. So I served him in the same way I had the driver, and almost as severe."[82]

When defending his actions to his enslaver, Grimes portrayed the driver as "an ignorant old African, or Guinea negro," with "not judgment sufficient to superintend any one in my present situation." Through utilizing the discourse equating old age with mental and physical decline, Grimes convinced his enslaver that the driver was in the wrong and the man was, in fact, dealt with "severely" by their enslaver.[83] We do not have to sympathize with the driver, who was willing to punish Grimes, to recognize the personal costs of this conflict. Trustees were in a difficult position but these roles came with the potential for material and monetary reward, and offered a space to develop an identity based on authority and control. To have this publicly repudiated through force and to be humiliated in the eyes of those nominally under their "control" was no small issue. The conflict identified here shows how far age factored into work rivalries, as well as how older authority figures might become the objects of scorn, if not physical violence, once the community understood they were no longer capable of enforcing respect or obedience.

Conflict between elderly trustees and those under their control could relate to a perceived need to prove one was still capable of maintaining dominance, but also because of a desire to respond to a public challenge that undercut their sense of self. Such concerns appeared relevant to the

[82] William Grimes, *The Life of William Grimes, the Runaway Slave, Written by Himself* (New York: W. Grimes, 1825), 37.
[83] Grimes, *Life of William Grimes*, 38.

fight between George and James in Fluvanna, Virginia, in 1858. George, "about 55 years of age," was a wagoner and clearly believed himself to be in a position of authority over others in the community. When arriving at the plantation with meal and shoats he directed his fellow slaves with precise instructions about who should take which bag, but Jim deliberately ignored his "commands" and, according to one witness, chose the lighter bag. This denial of his authority appeared to infuriate George, who told all and sundry he could back up his words with action: "if Jim came back and done the like again he would knock him down." The witness promptly informed Jim of the threat, but the younger man was not cowed. As he returned and saw that "George had a bag setting up for him," Jim provocatively "reached by George" to get a different one and all hell broke loose. If George, who witnesses stressed was Jim's elder, had thought to assume deference by virtue of age and authority as the wagoner, he was sorely mistaken. As one witness put it, "licks were seemingly in anger [. Jim] hit George as hard as he could ... George had no chance, the way Jim was coming on him." George had assumed superiority over those he perceived under him, and clearly believed he still had the physical prowess to back up his position of dominance. He was mistaken, and the community understood his reduced capacity, even if George was unable to accept it. As one witness put it, "George was larger but a good deal older than Jim."[84]

Intergenerational work rivalries can be found in the writings of James Stewart McGehee, whose family were enslavers in Mississippi and Louisiana. In his extended portrait of the Veals – a "remarkable slave family" – McGehee gave sustained attention to Hector, "the serious member of the family." All of the children in this family were granted the option of "house" work, with domestic labor considered emblematic of their more privileged position, but Hector conspicuously rejected this path. Of his "own accord he chose the vocation of 'field hand.'" This was no random decision, but instead spoke to his belief (and desire to fulfill the edict) that "field hands were all supposed to be manly."[85] As time went on the Stewarts moved west, forcing their coerced workers to relocate to a sugar plantation in Louisiana. Hector continued to stand out, first becoming a foreman, and then the fireman in the sugar house. Hector had proven himself to be a powerful and skilled worker. He was respected,

---

[84] Executive Papers, Henry A Wise, Misc. reel 4211, Box 15, Folder 5, 220–5, LVA.
[85] All quotes here from James Stewart Mcgehee, "A Remarkable Slave Family, 1775–1903," 123–36, James Stewart McGehee Collection, Mss. 326, LLMVC.

perhaps even feared, by other enslaved people, and able to uphold a position of authority. He could not do so forever. After noting Hector's successes as fireman, as well as his general sense of independence and autonomy, McGehee indicated that problems occurred in the sugar house when Hector "became old." This was not a neutral observation: McGehee claimed that this aging was noticeable because Hector had less strength or stamina (or at least that others felt so).

Hector's work had apparently been central to his personal identity and standing in the community, but his age was now a source of concern to his enslavers, who resolved to bring in support. A "stout 'man-hand'" was directed to assist with the physical labor so that "Hector would have naught to do but attend to the firing." The use of the words "stout man-hand," juxtaposed with the image of an old man deemed unable to work as hard as he once did, indicates how gendered identities and the perceived abilities of men to perform masculine roles could be based on comparative assessments. These changes plausibly resemble the beginning of Hector's transition to the role of respected elder, or some form of training model. Hector did not share the positive view of these shifts commonly identified by historians.[86] After having been asked to offer assistance, the "stout 'man-hand'" soon reported back and asked for a new task. When challenged over why he did not stick to his job, the man's reply suggests that Hector was not willing to be replaced:

When reproached for having left the one already allotted he [the "man-hand"] said he was willing to work but was not hunting the grave; that "Unc Hec" had a pocket-knife with a long blade and had threatened to disembowel him if he did not leave. Hector therefore continued to fire the boilers until the place was finally turned to cotton cultivation.

The image of a "loyal slave" refusing to stop working plausibly reveals only the proslavery sentiment of the author. However, the anecdote also speaks to identified tensions surrounding aging and identity. For enslaved people, to be perceived of as in decline could mean losing security and status in the community, as well as a hard-earned identity. Samuel Williams, who published his 1929 memoir of slave life to support himself against the troubling "prospects of a blind and helpless old age," recorded one such encounter where the elderly cook, "Uncle Renty," refused assistance and forthrightly declared that it was "my kitchen."[87] Mattie

---

[86] Lussana, *My Brother Slaves*, 35; Close, *Elderly Slaves*, 39.
[87] Sam, Aleckson, *Before the War, and after the Union* (Boston: Gold Mind, 1929), 39–41.

Mooreman, interviewed in 1937, suggested some of the tensions inherent in being *forced* to move away from work and her fears this would hasten her descent to decrepitude. Mooreman's daughter wanted her to quit work, but the older woman bluntly refused: "You put that over on Mrs. Murphy – you made her quit work and took care of her. What happened to her? She died. You're not going to make me old."[88]

These connections between age, productivity, and value – and a fear that a loss in status would hasten a physical, psychological, but also social decline – seemed to cross generations and gender boundaries, with these concerns informing Hector's actions in the nineteenth century but also Mooreman's response in 1937. The directing of threats to the younger man, and the ferocious response to the daughter, underscores how perceptions of age-based decline – and the implications of helplessness – were solidified or intensified by comparison to others in the community. Some enslaved people might have appreciated taking on supervisory positions or having reduced labor, but others clearly resented the implication that they were unable to perform in the fashion they previously had and were hence inferior to their replacement. Rather than coming on account of old age, a transition away from certain roles and responsibilities would, in fact, serve to "make" them old in the eyes of their peers, and there was no coming back from such a decline in status.

Deborah Gray White argued that Black women's "status in the slave community seems to have increased with old age," but women with authority might also struggle in the face of a challenge.[89] "Aunt Sally," enslaved in Louisiana, explained how a fear of the personal and psychological consequences of being "replaced" led to strife in her community. On the plantation of Mr. and Mrs. Cone, Aunt Eve "had quite a fame in the kitchen in her younger days, and in consequence had grown very vain and tenacious of her position." Eve struggled, however, to maintain these standards over time: "She was now getting old and incompetent. Her mistress was much dissatisfied, and hardly a meal passed without complaints on her part." In a similar fashion to Hector, Cone decided to place Sally in the kitchen alongside Eve to train up as a replacement. Eve seemingly shared Hector's view on the matter, and did not positively accept her position as tutor to her eventual replacement. Eve took this as a deliberate slight and "revenged

[88] Rawick (Ed.), *AS*, *10.5*, 134.   [89] White, *Ar'n't I A Woman*, 114.

herself by treating Sally in the most capricious and provoking manner." This extended to deliberately seeking the punishment of her rival:

Sometimes she would refuse to tell her what [Cone] asked–sometimes she would give her wrong measures, and so it came to pass that Sally's cooking was even less satisfactory than Eve's. "Dis made missis angry," said Sally, "an' she'd come in de kitch'en an' scold me, an' crack me over de head, an' den Eve would be glad, an' wouldn't tell me nothin', an' 'peared like I did worse all de time. Oh, how I cried every night, an' wished I could die 'fore de next mornin'."

Rather than find support from an enslaved elder in the workspace, Sally was subject to her wrath on account of a fear of being replaced. The conflict escalated so that Sally went to her enslaver to explain why she was struggling (and to plausibly scare Eve through punishment), but she was told to simply ignore her tormentor. The willingness of both Sally and Eve to use their enslaver to punish one another to better protect themselves underscores how enslaved peoples' responses to the traumas of enslavement, to their enslavers, and to one another do not neatly correspond with notions of solidarity based on shared oppression. It suggests how age factored into the complex social dynamics and hierarchies in slave communities, as well as the negotiations and conflicts between enslaver and enslaved.

The battle for supremacy in the kitchen continued, but it was clear to all that Eve's powers – both physical and psychological – were waning. Sally described the seeming inevitability to this transition and the anger this occasioned in Eve: "De next mornin' while I was gettin' de breakfast, Aunt Eve come in, an' begun to order me about, an' says I, 'Missis said I was to lay down your rules, an' pick up mine.'" Although Eve continually tried to get their enslaver to punish Sally, she found out that "her rules" – and perhaps even her – were on the way out. Eve was not willing to go without a fight, and she eventually framed Sally for theft and watched her punishment with glee. Sally depicted Eve as being "full of vexation," of a "naturally violent temper," and being controlled by her envy and hatred of "her new rival," and there is a distinct lack of sympathy. This, of course, reflects the subjective nature of the source material and the narrator's personal suffering on account of her "rival." It is worth grappling, however, with the logic of Eve's actions insofar as they were shaped by the structural violence of slavery and to take seriously how her removal from the kitchen by the protagonist – through no fault of her own – was likely the occasion of very real personal loss. The author hinted at Eve's already meager existence when noting how, after a lifetime of service, "she had hardly clothes enough to make herself decent."

Eve caused great harm to Sally: she stole her family heirloom, abused her, and was the cause of a whipping on account of her lies. And yet, it is hard not to see the pain and misery manifest in Eve having "to see Sally promoted and herself set aside as useless, where once she had been supreme." After a lifetime in bondage, all Eve had to call her own was the respect she had garnered on account of her work: "All her life had been spent on an isolated plantation ... the only instruction she had ever received had been in relation to her cooking."[90] The narrative is shaped around the subjective life story of Sally and we are meant to sympathize with the protagonist. Eve's abuse is but one element of the horrors Sally experienced on her long march to freedom. Yet, if we move our perspective to Eve, we can surely appreciate how the direct association of advancing age with uselessness left her isolated and publicly pushed off a pedestal she had valued for reasons both material and psychological. We do not hear from Eve, but George Bollinger's WPA interview from the 1930s provides insight into how the inexorable march of time included displacement by the young, and the sadness and even fear this entailed: "If I goes down de walk and a bunch young folks is coming along, I knows I's got to step out of de way – 'cause dey won't give any."[91] The choices Eve made – her understanding of Sally as the visible manifestation of her own decline and the person forcing her to "step out of de way" – can be connected to the sense of loss Bollinger described as inherent to the process of aging, but also to the structural violence of slavery. After twenty years of servitude, Sally found "the way of freedom." We hear no more about Eve once she had been "set aside as useless."[92]

* * *

When Mariah Robinson informed her WPA interviewer of the positive identity she had crafted through her skills as a cook, washer, ironer, and midwife, she candidly explained how a loss of prowess here hurt: "But physically dis-ability an' old age had to come, I am now old an' disabled, feel stunted, an' poverty stricken. If I could see, I would like to wurk now but I'm worn out, I had rather wurk den to beg."[93] We rarely hear from the elders "retired" in slavery, but the conflicts identified in this chapter

---

[90] Sally and Eve's battle is found in Isaac Williams, *Aunt Sally: Or, The Cross the Way of Freedom. A Narrative of the Slave-Life and Purchase of the Mother of Rev. Isaac Williams of Detroit, Michigan* (Cincinnati: American Reform Tract and Book Society, 1858), 145–50.
[91] *FWP, 10* (Missouri), 39.   [92] Williams, *Aunt Sally.*
[93] Rawick (Ed.), *AS, Supp., Ser.* 2, 8.7, 3358.

suggest how these feelings of loss materialized in antebellum slave communities. Enslaved people could come to realize that they were considered "old" on account of shifting work patterns and through invidious comparisons to others in the community. For some, this meant being replaced in skilled roles that had provided a measure of respite, whether material or psychological, while for others it simply meant isolation and removal from your peers. This involved confrontation with wider public perceptions of a loss of power, whether physical or mental, and this came at no little cost. Intergenerational relationships forged in childcare arrangements were no doubt positive for many enslaved people, but these spaces also saw tension erupt on account of contested authority and in relation to the dynamics of resistance and survival in the face of enslavers' demands for control. Age was a vital factor in shaping enslaved working environments, which in turn meant age became a vital factor in shaping the contested social hierarchies which developed in enslaved communities.

4

"Don't kill such an old creature as I"

Old Age and Community Tension

Leisure activities have long been understood by historians to have provided enslaved people with the chance to gain material benefits, showcase valued abilities, and gain the approval, respect, and affection of their peers.[1] Amidst a life of violence and abuse, enslaved people cared deeply about how they were perceived by the community in these activities and in public spaces. Pharaoah Jackson Chesney of Tennessee explained how log-rolling was a "favorite occasion for the showing off of strength and general physical manhood," while Irving E. Lowery of South Carolina stressed how much success in physical competition mattered to the men directly involved.[2] The competitors "took great pride in the development

---

[1] This scholarship is vast, but prominent examples include John Blassingame, *The Slave Community: Plantation Life in the Antebellum South* (New York: Oxford University Press, 1972); George P. Rawick, *The American Slave: A Composite Autobiography. From Sundown to Sunup: The Making of the Black Community* (Westport: Greenwood Press, 1972); Leslie Howard Owens, *This Species of Property: Slave Life and Culture in the Old South* (Oxford: Oxford University Press, 1976); Stephanie M. H. Camp, *Closer to Freedom: Enslaved Women and Everyday Resistance in the Plantation South* (Chapel Hill: University of North Carolina Press,2004), ch. 3; Daina Ramey Berry, *"Swing the Sickle for the Harvest is Ripe": Gender and Slavery in Antebellum Georgia* (Urbana: The University of Illinois Press, 2007), chapter 3; T. J. Desch Obi, *Fighting for Honor: The History of African Martial Arts in the Atlantic World* (Columbia: University of South Carolina Press, 2008); Sergio Lussana, "To See who was Best on the Plantation: Enslaved Fighting Contests and Masculinity in the Antebellum Plantation South," *Journal of Southern History* 76.4 (2010), 901–22; Emily West, *Chains of Love: Slave Couples in Antebellum South Carolina* (Urbana: University of Illinois Press, 2004), 19–43; Rebecca Griffin, "'Goin' Back Over There to See That Girl': Competing Social Spaces in the Lives of the Enslaved in Antebellum North Carolina," *Slavery and Abolition*, 25.1 (2004), 94–113.

[2] Pharaoh Jackson Chesney and John Coram Webster, *Last of the Pioneers: Or, Old Times in East Tenn., Being the Life and Reminiscences of Pharaoh Jackson Chesney (Aged 120 Years)* (Knoxville: S. B. Newman & Co., Printers & Book Binders, 1902), 51.

of their muscles" and "took delight in rolling up their shirt sleeves, and displaying the largeness of their arms." Beyond the sense of self-esteem and personal validation, the comparative demonstration of physical prowess was of keen interest to the watching crowd of women, all of whom "wanted their husbands and sweethearts to be considered the best men of the community."[3] The public nature of leisure and pleasure was vitally important for the construction of communal hierarchies; enslaved people learnt about their relative strength, mental aptitude, physical prowess, and more besides in the social activities they undertook together. Social spaces were thus places where reputations could be made; they were environments where enslaved people could develop self-esteem and forge the personal relationships necessary to survive enslavement.

The very importance of social affairs, however, meant that they were also spaces where rivalries developed and where people fell out. Competitive pursuits invariably entailed a winner and a loser, and leisure time could turn into an arena in which people publicly fought over status, respect, and their relative position among their peers. Elsie Payne recalled with pleasure how "us all went to de corn-shuckings, and all de mens went to de log-rollings and had one more big time, trying to see which could pull de udder down."[4] The pleasure came, in part, from seeing who was able to publicly supplant another, and to lose or fail in these types of physical activities was not consequence free. Returning to Lowery, he acknowledged as such when discussing log-rollings, recalling that "if one fails to lift his part, he is said to have been 'pulled down,' and therefore becomes the butt of ridicule for the balance of the day. When the women folks learn of his misfortune, they forever scorn him as a weakling."[5] Historians who emphasize how social affairs provided a space for positive personal and communal identities risk prioritizing the perspective of the winners, and not those publicly "scorned" as weaklings. Scholars still struggle to conceptualize interactions between the enslaved that complicate notions of solidarity in the face of oppression and instead reflect internal division and strife. In a chapter addressing social stigma toward disabled enslaved people – a category which elsewhere in the book included elders – Jenifer Barclay ultimately concluded that "this was not a commonplace experience" and that "a distinctive ethos – characterized by a collective, community-centered worldview and a sense of solidarity forged from shared

[3] Irving E. Lowery, *Life on the Old Plantation in Ante-Bellum Days, or, A Story Based on Facts* (Columbia: The State Co., Printers, 1911), 90.
[4] Rawick (Ed.), *AS, Supp.*, Ser. 1, *1.1*, 293. [5] Lowery, *Life on the Old Plantation*, 91.

experiences of oppression and adversity – guided enslaved people's interactions."[6] This chapter, however, demonstrates the limits to solidarity in social spaces, and the impact of intergenerational tension in the community life of enslaved people.

Lowery did not explicitly frame a comparative loss of physical power (and attendant public humiliation) on account of age. The connection between advanced age and comparative weakness, however, was a frequent observation among antebellum Americans, Black and white, and as people grew older they needed to consider how such a decline – real or imagined – would affect their actions or placement in the social affairs of their peers. How did those who had prided themselves on the "largeness of their arms," for example, deal with the inevitable onset of what is known now as sarcopenia but was described by contemporaries such as Benjamin Rush as the natural "declension of the strength of the body by age"?[7] In the remainder of this chapter, I show how aging shaped the structure of social activities and the difficulties that arose when enslaved people found themselves cast as incapable of taking the "part" they had once prized on account of advanced (or advancing) age. The chapter predominantly focuses on conflict between men, with the available source material generally supporting the contention of scholars such as Sergio Lussana that physical competitions in slave communities were largely homosocial affairs, and which perhaps underlines Deborah Gray White's contention that for many men "old age . . . was marked by decreased status" on account of the connections contemporaries drew between masculinity, stamina, and strength.[8] This chapter reveals the significant impact of this loss of status for enslaved men, but the next chapter complicates White's related argument that elderly women's status "seems to have increased"

---

[6] Barclay, *The Mark of Slavery*, 62, 47.

[7] Rush, "An Account of the State of the Body and Mind in Old Age," 314. See also Barnard van Oven, MD, *On the Decline of Life in Health and Disease, Being An Attempt to Investigate the Causes of Longevity; And the Best Means of Attaining a Healthful Old Age* (London: John Churchill, 1853), 38–9. For an overview of current socio-medical discourse on muscle-loss associated with aging, see Miles D. Witham and Avan Ahie Sayer (Eds.), "Introduction to the Age and Ageing sarcopenia collection," *Age and Ageing*, 45.6 (2016).

[8] Lussana, *My Brother Slaves*, 56–7; White, *Ar'n't I A Woman*, 114. Enslaved women asserted themselves against rivals but activities associated with enslaved femininity appear less directly confrontational; Doddington, *Contesting Slave Masculinity*, 175. On violent women, see Stephanie M. H. Camp, "Pleasures of Resistance: Enslaved Women and Body Politics in the Plantation South, 1830–1861," *Journal of Southern History*, 68.3 (Aug., 2002), 533–72, 558; Forret, *Slave Against Slave*, ch. 8.

" *The Sabbath among Slaves.*"

FIGURE 4.1 "The Sabbath among Slaves," in Henry Bibb, *Narrative of the Life and Adventures of Henry Bibb, an American Slave* (New York: Published by the Author; 5 Spruce Street, 1849), 22. Courtesy of Library of Congress, Prints and Photographs Division, LC-USZ62-107750.

through consideration of the treatment of elderly conjurers, men and women.[9]

* * *

Social gatherings have generally been depicted by historians as having provided a vital space for enslaved elders to assert their autonomy and to create – and have affirmed by others – a positive personal identity.[10] The aged enslaved may have been dismissed by whites who looked at them purely for profit, but elders held court in social gatherings in the quarters; among their peers, their age-old experience and hard-won wisdom was cherished and elevated. Ned Chaney of Mississippi powerfully expressed this sentiment when explaining the respect his great grandmother had held in the community: "Her head was as white as a piece of cotton, an' ever'body set a heap of sto' by her. I reckon, because she done 'cumeillated

---

[9] White, *Ar'n't I A Woman*, 114.

[10] See, for example, Sterling Stuckey, *Slave Culture: Nationalist Theory and the Foundations of Black America* (Oxford: Oxford University Press, 2013 [1987]), 33, 84, 86, 97; Pollard, "Aging and Slavery," 232; Close, *Elderly Slaves*, 14, 26, 97–9; Stevenson, "Gender Conventions," 175; Desch Obi, *Fighting for Honor*, 106–7; Berry, *Price for Their Pound of Flesh*, 131.

so much knowledge an' because her head was so white."[11] The connection drawn between wisdom and visible identifiers of old age indicates the broader sense of reverence toward elders among ex-slaves.

Black contemporaries made frequent reference to the importance of elders in their social affairs, whether as orators, conveyers of culture, or religious leaders. Henry "Box" Brown recorded how the enslaved on his plantation organized their own illicit religious services and that it was regulated by "an old slave, whom they called Uncle John." John, and not their "master," had the power to adjudicate "upon their piety, and would baptize them during the silent watches of the night."[12] Johnson Thompson, enslaved in Texas, connected age with oratory force and cultural responsibility, noting how the rest of the community "learned something about religion from an old colored preacher named Tom Vann."[13] Brenda Stevenson has argued that "elderly enslaved women also wielded some social power, derived from the African tradition of reverence for the elderly and ancestral," but also on account of their "obvious spiritual enlightenment and moral superiority."[14] In one account of enslaved spirituals, the white observer noted how the community was led by "an old woman on the outskirts of the meeting" in singing "'Nobody knows the trouble I've had,' and the whole audience joined in."[15] In these accounts the elders' responsibilities – and the respect accorded to them – speak eloquently to the "soul values" Daina Ramey Berry has emphasized as shaping generational relationships among the antebellum enslaved.[16]

Alongside religious responsibilities, enslaved elders were commonly recorded as both the entertainers and the educators of the Black community. John Sneed, enslaved near Austin, Texas, recalled how "Ole man Jim Piper was de fiddler on our plantation. He played de fiddle for dances fer black an white on nearby places"; Lewis Jones, also of Texas, noted how "weuns cullud fo'ks have a big time at de pahties. Ol' Tom am de preachahman an' de musician."[17] Nettie Rocket emphasized to her WPA

---

[11] Rawick (Ed.), *AS, Supp.,* Ser. *1,* 7.2, 369.

[12] Henry Brown, *Narrative of the Life of Henry Box Brown, Written by Himself* (Manchester: Published by the Author, 1851), 23.

[13] Rawick (Ed.), *AS, Supp.,* Ser. *1, 12,* 311.

[14] Brenda Stevenson, "Marsa never sot Aunt Rebecca down": Enslaved Women, Religion, and Social Power in the Antebellum South," *Journal of African American History,* 90.4 (2005), 345–67, 346.

[15] William Francis Allen, Charles Pickard Ware, and Lucy McKim Garrison, *Slave Songs of the United States* (New York: Timpson & Co., 1867), 55–6.

[16] Berry, *Price for Their Pound of Flesh.*

[17] Rawick (Ed.), *AS, Supp.,* Ser. *2,* 9.8, 3702; Rawick (Ed.), *AS, Supp.,* Ser. *2,* 6.5, 2111.

interviewer how these activities – and even individuals – crossed farm and plantation borders and insisted on the affective ties the enslaved held for their elders: "The n***rs visited around among each other and some would sing around the fires and sometimes listen at the ole ones tell tales." The postbellum figure of "Uncle Remus" was shaped by white racial myths, but Black contemporaries who recorded fond memories of elders as having entertained (and educated) the slave community with the trickster tales of Brer Rabbit, among others, insisted as to the vital role elders played in community life.[18] George Glasker of Texas explained to his WPA interviewer that "it wuz from de ole plantation mammies dat we learned de stories of 'Uncle Remus an' Brer Fox," while Rose Thomas of Mississippi similarly explained how "at night we used to sit on the steps and Uncle Ben would tell us stories, mostly about animals that acted like folks."[19] She recalled these stories – and their inversions of expected power dynamics – with some pleasure: "Mr. Fox was always so smart, but Brudder Rabbit usually came out best."[20] The broader significance of elders in the social affairs of the enslaved is neatly summarized in Charles Ball's narrative, where he recounted the pleasures of leisure and the close generational relationships among the enslaved:

Our quarter knew but little quiet this night; singing, playing on the banjo, and dancing, occupied nearly the whole community, until the break of day. Those who were too old to take any part in our active pleasures, beat time with their hands, or recited stories of former times. Most of these stories referred to affairs that had been transacted in Africa, and were sufficiently fraught with demons, miracles, and murders, to fix the attention of many hearers.[21]

It is abundantly clear that elders played a significant role in the social world of slave communities and, as a result, historians have explored this in great depth. The point Ball makes about people being "too old" to take part in "active pleasures," however, is something that requires greater depth of analysis as it has typically been underexamined in research. In Ball's rendering there was a natural transition wherein as people grew older they understood their social role would change accordingly. Rather than engage in "active" pleasure, enslaved elders willingly stood back and

[18] On Remus, see, for example: Alice Walker, "Uncle Remus, No Friend of Mine," *The Georgia Review*, 66.3 (2012), 635–37; Jennifer Ritterhouse, "Reading, Intimacy, and the Role of Uncle Remus in White Southern Social Memory," *Journal of Southern History*, 69.3 (2003), 585–622; Cheryl Thompson, *Uncle: Race, Nostalgia, and the Politics of Loyalty* (Toronto: Coach House Books, 2021).
[19] Rawick (Ed.), *AS, Supp.*, Ser. 2, 5.4, 1504; Rawick (Ed.), *AS, Supp.*, Ser. 2, 9.8, 3825.
[20] Rawick (Ed.), *AS, Supp.*, Ser. 2, 9.8, 3825.   [21] Ball, *Fifty Years in Chains*, 140.

enjoyed the activities of the young vicariously; by guiding and supporting
the rising youth the older parties gained respect and support. There is no
indication in Ball's account, however, nor in much of the extant historiography, about how and when people came to realize they were no longer
capable of "active pleasures," or, perhaps, when others viewed them as
such. I want to suggest that a transition away from treasured activities
based on perceptions of age-related decline – whether real or imagined –
was not so simple and instead became a site of sadness and conflict, both
physical and psychological.

Age-related transitions could occasion a rupture in existing community
hierarchies where the young supplanted the old, with a sense of superiority and dominance made visible. Daniel Peterson, who escaped slavery as
a child and moved to New York City, indicated just some of the complexity to, and the fluid nature of, these social hierarchies. According to
Peterson, "old age is honorable, and should be respected at all times and
upon all occasions." There was, however, a "but"; Patterson insisted, all
honor and respect aside, "*but* there is a fitness to be observed in the
administration of public affairs; and when a man is far advanced in life,
he is generally incompetent to govern a great body of men." Peterson
insisted that, "therefore, there is a change required in this respect."[22]
Respectful comments on the social position of the aged, followed by an
assertion that they must step down and be replaced on account of assumed
incompetence, indicates just some of the tensions and dissonance involved
in age-related transitions that shall be outlined in this chapter.

* * *

In their discussions on leisure and pleasure, ex-slaves commonly explained
that social dynamics were shaped by, and in turn helped to shape, understandings of the rhythms of the life cycle. Josiah Henson explained his
ability in – even enjoyment of – brawls with white men during his
enslavers' social affairs by reference to the energy of youth: he "was
young, remarkably athletic and self-relying."[23] Similar significance was
accorded to age and physicality in competitive activities, such as log-
rolling, boxing, dancing, and wrestling. Jane Smith Hill Harmon wistfully

---

[22] Daniel H. Peterson, *The Looking-Glass: Being a True Report and Narrative of the Life,
    Travels, and Labors of the Rev. Daniel H. Peterson, a Colored Clergyman; Embracing
    a Period of Time from the Year 1812 to 1854, and Including His Visit to Western Africa*
    (New York: Wright, 1854), 44–5. Italics mine.
[23] Henson, "*Uncle Tom's Story of His Life*," 35.

recalled how "one night when I was young, I danced down seben big strong mens." Now in her late eighties, this triumph still brought joy to Harmon: "dey thought dey wuz sumpin'! Huh, I danced eb'ry one down!"[24]

These activities were commonly understood as the preserve of the young because of their emphasis on physical strength and stamina; outside of dancing and racing, physical competitions such as boxing, wrestling, and log-rolling were also typically gendered masculine. Jermain Wesley Loguen recalled how when he was "verging on manhood, with a fine person and social temperament, he begun to feel the pride of youth." It was at this point that he determined to "indulge his social propensities with young companions, of both sexes, in the neighborhood."[25] Lougen's intimation that social activities were structured according to age and gender was reiterated in Allen Parker's postbellum memoirs. Parker explained how at Christmas "the young people were dancing," while "the old ones would be holding a prayer meetin'."[26] Returning to Lowery's recollections, we see a clear divide articulated between the old and young in how they chose to use their "free" time. Youth, it seemed, was a time for competition and pleasure, whereas the passage of time entailed increased responsibilities to others and a gradual withdrawal from these less "serious" affairs:

Sunday was always a welcome day on the old plantation, not only by the slaves, but also by the white folks. It came in all right to break the monotony of plantation life. The older and more serious ones went to 'meetin'" or visited the sick, or made social calls, while the youngsters met other youngsters from the adjoining plantations and spent the day in wrestling, jumping, boxing, running foot races and sometimes fighting.[27]

The specific reference to "youngsters" meeting other "youngsters" implies that these temporal categories were well understood. And yet, as has already been noted, age was a fluid and relational category; those who had valued their skills as fighters, dancers, racers, and more might struggle to accept that they were no longer welcome in the parties of the young. Minnie Davis of Georgia recalled how "on Saturday nights the young

[24] Rawick (Ed.), *AS*, *12.2*, 99.
[25] Jermain Wesley Loguen, *The Rev. J. W. Loguen, as a Slave and as a Freeman. A Narrative of Real Life* (Syracuse: J. G. K. Truair & Co., 1859), 138–9.
[26] Allen Parker, *Recollections of Slavery Times* (Worchester: Chas. W. Burbank & Co., 1895), 67–8.
[27] Lowery, *Life on the Old Plantation*, 69.

folks and *a few* of the older folks danced."²⁸ There was no judgment in Davis's recollections, but Lowery's reference to the "more serious ones" going to meetings or caring for the sick suggests he believed there were *less* serious ones who struggled to find their place between the "young" and the "old" in social affairs.

One postbellum white author asserted the joys of corn shucking were enough to turn back time – "No rheumatism here this evening; no stiffness of joints, no aches, no pains" – but contemporaries frequently depicted physical depletion associated with aging as affecting social interactions and the dynamics of leisure.²⁹ Some ex-slaves believed that elders understood and accepted the different social roles expected of them as they aged. Aunt Dice of Tennessee explained that in corn shuckings and similar affairs, the older slaves enjoyed the fact that their role was now to assist the "strong hands" of the youth: "Old men passed the compliments of the day or related their experiences, replete with wisdom. Young men 'swapped' their jokes, or bantered for shucking races in braggadocio-like tones." Louis Hughes, enslaved in Virginia, explained that parties planned for the 4th of July occasioned happiness for the entire slave community. Where the youth looked forward to "congregating" and having the chance to "sing and dance," however, the elders simply took vicarious pleasure from the affairs of the young: "The older slaves were not less happy, but would only say: 'Ah! God has blessed us in permitting us to see another feast day.'"³⁰ Ball, Lowery, Dice, and Hughes clearly perceived a natural and normal division between the pastimes of the young and the old, where, even if elders were no longer physically capable of participating in the same fashion, they remained respected and were still able to engage in social activities as advisors or adjudicates.

For some enslaved people, however, the realization that youth had gone and they were expected to withdraw from "active pleasures" elicited sadness and wistfulness for their earlier prowess. Exploring these dynamics can further reveal the intricacy of social relations among the enslaved and underline the complex and fluid identities people created in slavery. Allen Parker recalled in his postbellum memoir how these dynamics might play out at a group level, noting that one popular song sung on the plantation

---

²⁸ Rawick (Ed.), *AS*, 12.1, 259. Italics mine.
²⁹ James Battle Avirett, *The Old Plantation: How We Lived in Great House and Cabin Before the War* (New York; Chicago; London, 1901), 140–1.
³⁰ Hughes, *Thirty Years a Slave*, 46–7.

addressed the inexorability of, and comparative element to, the aging process:

> When I was a little pickanninny, playin' around de cabin door,
> I was de happiest little darkey in de land,
> Now I'm getting ole and feeble and my hair is turnin' gray,
> And I am goin' back to Georgia, if I can.
> Good ole Georgie, happy land!
> Gwine to live and die in good ole Georgie land.

The song provided "much enjoyment," according to Parker, but there are clear references to loss – both real and symbolic – embedded in the lyrics. The singer wistfully compares the freedom of physical movement in youth to their feebleness in old age; given the frequency of forced separation in the antebellum internal slave trade, the reference to "goin' back" is likely to be elegiac as opposed to anything tangible. For the more than one million enslaved people forcibly moved during the nineteenth century, the chance to "go back … if I can," was simply not an option and so this "ole and feeble" person was simply left with memories of youth and of accumulated loss.[31]

In none of the preceding comments are ex-slaves clear about when the participants became "old," or how they knew or came to understand that they had moved from one camp to the other. In some instances the transition away from "active pleasures" was a choice made for them. James Bolton of Georgia explained to his WPA interviewer that "we never did no wuk on Sundays on our plantation," and were instead allowed to attend cross-plantation church services. This gave the wider slave community a chance to socialize with a degree of independence, and this mixing was clearly appreciated in Bolton's telling. The church was nearly nine miles away, however, and Bolton understood this imposed a separation of the strong from the weak, and the old from the young: "Anybuddy too ole an' feeble to walk the nine miles jes' stayed home, kyazen Marster diden' 'low his mules used none on Sunday."[32] In this instance, the "old" and the "feeble" were simply unable to attend social activities and this separation was accepted as natural and normative; the

---

[31] Parker, *Recollections of Slavery Times*, 69–70. On the scale of the internal slave trade, see Tadman, *Speculators and Slaves*; Johnson, *Soul by Soul*; Deyle, *Carry Me Back*; Heather A. Williams, *Help Me To Find My People: The African American Search for Family Lost in Slavery* (Chapel Hill: University of North Carolina Press, 2012); Damian Alan Pargas, *Slavery and Forced Migration in the Antebellum South* (New York: Cambridge University Press, 2015).

[32] Rawick (Ed.), *AS, Supp.*, Ser. *1*, 3.1, 85.

conflation of old with feeble underscores how commonly the aging process was framed in a language of decline by enslaver and enslaved alike.
Rather than take pleasure vicariously or receive support, these elders were
left alone and isolated.

Enforced isolation of elders was equally apparent on the rice and cotton
plantations of Pierce Butler. Frances Kemble made frequent reference to the
abuse of elders and also underscored their physical isolation from the wider
community too. Kemble described a tripartite system where the strongest
workers were based on the rice plantations of Butler Island, the "old,
young, and feeble," were situated on St. Simon's island to work on the
less valuable cotton farms, and the mainland settlement of Woodville was
"occupied by the most decrepit and infirm samples of humanity it was ever
my melancholy lot to behold." The physical distance, pace of work, and
treacherous geography meant that these communities were mostly self-
contained, and thus both work and community activity was shaped by
age. The enslaved people on St. Simon's island, according to Kemble, had
time for leisure among themselves, but this mostly entailed talking about
memories of the past, and their physical separation from the wider slave
community was near entire. To be "turned out to grass" here was compared
by Kemble to being "flung by like an old rag, crippled with age and disease,
living, or rather dying by slow degrees in a miserable hovel." This was still
an improvement from the deplorable conditions of the truly decrepit based
at Woodville. This was the space where "some of the oldest slaves who will
not die yet, and cannot work any more, are sent, to go, as it were, out of the
way." Their social isolation was complete, and it worked to utterly devas-
tate these elders: "Remote recollections of former dealings with civilized
human beings in the shape of masters and overseers seemed to me to be the
only idea not purely idiotic in the minds of the poor old tottering creatures
that gathered to stare with dim and blear eyes at me and my children."[33]
This age-related isolation was dictated by the institutional violence of
slavery. Nonetheless, we are able to see how far social isolation for the
elderly could be a vicious cycle. Once removed from the wider community
on account of advanced age, it was difficult to recover.

* * *

A transition away from certain activities or isolation from social affairs
was often said to revolve around the type of physical decline described by

---

[33] Kemble, *Journal of a Residence*, 202, 126, 203, 207, 203.

Bolton and Kemble. The "old" and "feeble" slaves were mostly voiceless here, and gaining access to their experiences and interior world is incredibly difficult. We might reflect on the sadness of aged individuals interviewed in the 1930s, however, to consider the range of emotions connected to these types of transition. Mary Myhand, who experienced slavery in Tennessee and Missouri, explained to her WPA interviewer that she did not have much contact with the "young generation" because she was "old and crippled and don't go out none."[34] The intimation was that they did not come to see her, either. Lewis Brown, enslaved in Mississippi, described a similar sense of regret at being neglected. Brown regretfully insisted that "when you get old and stricken, nobody cares, children nor nobody else."[35] These respondents understood their isolation related to a vision of aged decline shared by both Black and white, and they were both reflective and resentful of this perception and the seemingly self-fulfilling prophecy.

For some, isolation was self-imposed. Charles Ball explained that his eighty-year-old grandfather "had always expressed great contempt for his fellow slaves" and preferred to keep his own company away from the wider community.[36] It is hard not to imagine that for those who did not make this choice, to be left behind – to be assumed decrepit or invisible – hurt. A comparative loss of power on account of age brought to light by one's peers in a social setting – whether physical or mental – likely occasioned reflection, if not some sadness. Solomon Northup conjured up the ghosts of "old" Abram's youth by recalling that he once "had been athletic," but insisted that time's inevitable march had weakened him, with effects in work, but also in social affairs where his "wisdom" was seemingly taken with a wink and a nod:

Very often, indeed, while discussing the best method of baking the hoe-cake, or expatiating at large upon the glory of [Andrew] Jackson, he would forget where he left his hat, or his hoe, or his basket; and then would the old man be laughed at, if Epps was absent, and whipped if he was present.

The abusive treatment clearly came from the enslaver, but the image of the young laughing at the forgetfulness of their elder, however lighthearted in intent, requires caution when assessing its impact. An inability to recall events, words, or deeds was often frustrating and frightening, with WPA

---

[34] Rawick (Ed.), *AS*, *10.5*, 178.   [35] Rawick (Ed.), *AS*, *8.1*, 297.
[36] Charles Ball, *Slavery in the United States: A Narrative of the Life and Adventures of Charles Ball, a Black Man* ... (New York: John S. Taylor, 1837), 21–2.

respondent Lizzy Davis explaining her dismay at being unable to remember a song for her interviewer: "I studied so hard bout dem songs de other night, I beg de Massa to show me de light en he hope me to recollect dis one for you. See, when you gets to de age I is, you is foolish."[37] Dismay at memory loss was clearly true of Abram. As Northup recalled, "so was he perplexed continually, and sighed to think that he was growing aged and going to decay."[38] Abram's reflective recognition of personal decay was exacerbated by the abuse of his enslaver. It was surely reinforced, too, by the laughter of people he had once assumed, and had perhaps still hoped, were his peers and equals.

* * *

Information provided by WPA respondents offers further insight into how the "decay" associated with old age, whether physical or mental, might come to light in the context of leisure and pleasure. Some of these memories relate to activities in the postbellum era but speak to enduring themes surrounding aging, identity, and the dynamic nature of Black social hierarchies, and can be used to think critically about life in slavery. The WPA interviewer of "Old Isaac" of Alabama, for example, recorded how this elder was perceived by his community as a weak link. Young Black men in his neighborhood exploited Isaac's desire to participate in their social activities and manipulated him accordingly. As the interviewer explained, "Old Isaac once was enticed into a crap game by some of the younger members of his race, when they knew he had a five dollar bill. Not knowing much about the game, he lost as they were sure he would."[39] These events happened after slavery, but the implication that youth might look to their elders and see an easy mark, as opposed to a respected patriarch, undercuts the normative myth of veneration for the aged and allows for speculative readings of motive and meaning in these situations. "Old Isaac" may have desired to play the game to demonstrate he was still part of the group, but the younger mens' actions reveal they no longer considered him their equal nor worthy of their respect. There was possibly a tragic element to such behavior, as the interviewer tried to understand why Isaac, who relied on "hand outs" and did not work, continued with his daily "round of the plantation" despite the "'misery' in his knee." When asked why he would put himself through this, Isaac explained: "he 'neber wants ter to be forgotten. Forgotten folks die quick.'" The young

---

[37] Rawick (Ed.), *AS*, 2.1, 281.   [38] Northup, *Twelve Years a Slave*, 186–7.
[39] Rawick (Ed.), *AS, Supp.*, Ser. *1, 1*, 424.

men "kept tormenting him to pay his 'hones' dets,'" and Isaac recalled that in this game he "loss all I haid, and mor'n I haid." Perhaps, however, financial loss was better than being "forgotten."[40]

When speaking about postbellum life, ex-slaves who recalled their transition away from active pursuits or movement out of group activities commonly suggested this occasioned reflection and even some measure of sadness, particularly if it was accompanied or caused by a broader reduction in physical capacity and disability. These respondents came to realize that they were "old" because they were no longer able to physically compete in the fashion they once had. There was an inevitability to this decline, but also an indication that their loss of prowess occasioned indifference, at best, among the youth who supplanted them; what was a traumatic downward step for the aged was simply brushed past by those ascending the steps of life. Ambus Gray, enslaved in Alabama, understood, but seemingly resented, the rationale for such indifference. As Gray put it, "mighty hard to make young folks think they ever get old."[41] Memories of physical prowess in youth could bring pleasure but also wistfulness among those who had prided themselves on competitive pleasures and had refused to believe time would come for them, too.

One such case was evident in the recollections of Henry Coleman of South Carolina. Coleman was clearly proud of his physical capacity in youth, informing his interviewer of his superiority to all others while a young man in slavery: "when I wuz a young fellow I used to race wid de horses. I wuz de swifes runner on de plantation." He acknowledged, however, that this came at a heavy physical cost, recalling how "after I got through, my legs used to jus shake like a leaf." Coleman shook this off with the idealism of youth, disregarding his wife's warning that if he continued to race he "was gwine to give out in my legs," but he came to realize that time came for all: "now, I is gib plum out in dem [legs] and I tributes it to dat." Coleman was clearly nostalgic for his physical prowess, but he was, of course, no longer in his prime. Coleman's interviewer concluded their meeting by noting the truth to his wife's warning: "'Uncle' Henry says that his legs have given out in the bone."[42]

Frederick Shelton of Arkansas was similarly nostalgic for past glories, telling his interviewer that he had "a willful mind but a weak body" and implying that his desire to maintain physical activity was one that his body refused to fulfill. Shelton, who poignantly described himself as "just like

[40] Rawick (Ed.), *AS, Supp.*, Ser. *1, 1*, 424.   [41] Rawick (Ed.), *AS, 9.3,* 89, 79.
[42] Rawick (Ed.), *AS, 2.1,* 215.

an old tree – de limbs are withered and almost dead," explicitly compared his current frailty with his youthful strength, proudly recalling how as a young man in slavery he would always triumph in log-rolling contests: "Log rollings wuz lots ob fun to me as I wuz strong den, an' I could 'show off' befo' de odder n***rs." The competitive element of socializing was integral to Shelton's enjoyment of the affairs and his identity. Shelton was proud of how much stronger he was than his competitors, remembering "de time when I lifted de end ob a log, an' four men tried at different times to lift de odder, but dey couldn't do it." As with Coleman, however, Shelton acknowledged how physical debts incurred while young eventually had to be paid. He also indicated that the price of competition for the men desperate to match his prowess was high: "three of dese men went to an early grave from trying to lift dis log – all tore up inside." Shelton was left to ponder whether he was suffering similarly now that it was he who was old: "Maybe dat's whut ails me."[43] Both Coleman and Shelton were men who struggled to accept it was time to step away from "active pleasures," wistfully holding onto memories of their prowess and hoping for respect on account of physicality long since lost. This longing for recognition of their triumphs indicates the significance of social activities in (and out of) slavery for the development of social hierarchies but also personal identities. For these men, the loss of power and the desire to maintain respect were expressed merely in the language of reflection and nostalgia. Others, however, indicated that a perceived decline and loss over time led to sadness or strife, and this was particularly true if one person's ascent on the steps of life hastened another's descent.

The importance accorded to identities based on strength and vigor is reinforced by the fact that some enslaved men viewed by their peers as "old" would demand to compete even when outmatched, unable or unwilling to take the suggestion they were past their prime. This reinforces earlier arguments about the fluid nature to masculine identities in slave communities, and the necessity of publicly proving manhood through competition and conflict.[44] One unnamed WPA respondent provided clear insight into this competitive masculine mentality when noting that "in my younger days I used to be a hell-cat" and proudly recalling how "all the bad fellows around Nashville stood back when I came around." The man believed, moreover, that he still had juice in the tank: "Even now though I am 84 years old, my arms and chest are active and I don't believe many boxers today could make a punching bag out my head." This

---

[43] Rawick (Ed.), *AS, 10.6*, 146.   [44] Doddington, *Contesting Slave Masculinity*, 175–9.

confidence was almost certainly misplaced, given he belatedly acknowledged to being "sorter down in my knees and thighs, though," but his
identity was still predicated on hopes of physical superiority.[45] Some
elders would not accept the plantation proverb that "de proudness un
a man don't count w'en his head's cold" and refused to step away from
active pleasures.[46] Clarissa Scales of Texas recalled how "old Hamlet"
drowned when attempting to "show off" his swimming skills. He had
built up a reputation for physical strength and stamina and "wanted to
show-off and show a lot ob de boys dat he could swim 'cause he had
always told 'em dat he had swum in a big ocean." Hamlet valued the name
he had built up for himself based on earlier prowess, but his skills were not
what they had once been. Hamlet was found drowned the next day; "his
body was all scratched up, and his clothes was all tore off." Scales believed
the old man's demise related to his desire to impress the young boys, but
she had no sympathy for her elder's plight: "Old Hamlet, he sure oughta
never went into dat water to show off. He was always good at showin'
off."[47]

* * *

For enslaved men who had built their identities on physical competition,
knowing when or how to bow out of competitive pursuits was a difficult
process. This tension was clearly represented in folk tales recorded by
enslaved people across the Americas. These materials have been used
fruitfully by scholars to consider community dynamics among the
enslaved, with Sergio Lussana recently insisting that folktales best exemplify the "friendship" and "altruism" present in enslaved communities.[48]
These tales also address moments of tension and can be used to explore the
complex relationships and contested hierarchies present in slave communities, including those related to generational power dynamics. Select
stories address the "passing of the torch" from one figure to the next
and reveal the conflict and strife this might entail.[49]

---

[45] Rawick (Ed.), *AS*, *19*, 125–6.
[46] John Mason Brewer (Ed.), *American Negro Folklore* (Chicago: Quadrangle Books, 1968),
313–14.
[47] Rawick (Ed.), *AS*, *Supp.*, Ser. 2, 9.8, 3462.
[48] Sergio Lussana, "Reassessing Brer Rabbit: Friendship, Altruism, and Community in the
Folklore of Enslaved African-Americans," *Slavery & Abolition* 39.1 (2018), 1–24.
[49] On tension, see Sterling Stuckey, "Through the Prism of Folklore: The Black Ethos in
Slavery," *Massachusetts Review* 9 (1968); Lawrence Levine, *Black Culture and Black
Consciousness: Afro-American Folk Thought From Slavery to Freedom* (New York:
Oxford University Press, 1977), 110–16; Rebecca J. Griffin, "Courtship Contests and

FIGURE 4.2 *Clarissa Scales, Age 79.* United States Texas, 1936. Between 1936 and 1938. Photograph. Courtesy of the Library of Congress, Manuscript Division.

In "What Makes Brer Wasp Has a Short Patience," Brer Wasp mocked his rival Brer Mosquito's comparative physical weakness but was warned not to laugh too hard in case he had a downfall of his own. The phrasing resembles complaints raised by antebellum writers that the young should not mock the frailty of the aged as the "decay of nature" would eventually come for them too.[50] Indeed, Wasp was left to rue his hubris and, after laughing too long, and too hard, at his fallen foe, he found himself shrunk and shriveled: "he looked again and he saw what all that shaking, and pushing, and squeezing had done to him." Wasp's reduced stature and

the Meaning of Conflict in the Folklore of Slaves,"*Journal of Southern History* 71 (November, 2005), 769–802; Charles Joyner, *Remember Me: Slave Life in Coastal Georgia* (Athens: University of Georgia Press, 2011), 52.

[50] Van Oven, *On the Decline of Life,* 42; [Anon], "Growing Old," 277.

physical decline left him fearful for his status among his peers, with the narrator sagely explaining that "he thought about how now the others were going to have their turn to laugh at that little waist he had now" and "that he couldn't get that shameful thing out of his mind."[51] It was this fear of mockery, in fact, that meant all wasps were ornery.

There is no specific reference to age in the tale, but the similarity to the familiar antebellum discourse that outlined the "shrivelled look of age and infirmity," alongside the emphasis on the dangers of hubris for those who reveled in physical prowess, makes it plausible this could be understood by contemporaries in the context of age and generational strife.[52] Similar concerns were found in "The Lion in the Well." In this story Brer Rabbit manipulated "ole Mister Lion," who was known as "the Boss of the Woods," by playing up his fear of a nascent challenge to his supremacy. Lion, who had made the other animals provide him victuals (and eaten a significant number who brought him them), was informed when it was Brer Rabbit's turn that the meat was at the bottom of the well. Lion looked and saw his reflection, but believed it was another Lion come to take his place. This challenge could not be accepted and he responded with ferocity:

Old Brer Lion began to get mad and he hollered down the well again, 'WHO ARE YOU, I SAY?' And the voice came back up out of the well, 'WHO ARE YOU, I SAY?'
Then Brer Rabbit nudged the old lion in his side and said, 'You heard him, didn't you, Brer Lion? Didn't you hear him mocking you like that? Are you going to take that from him?'

Old Lion was not going to "take" it: "'STAND BACK BRER RABBIT, HE'S MY MEAT!' and in he jumped." After Lion jumped into the well to meet his imagined foe, Brer Rabbit "slammed the cover shut and locked it," leaving the "old mangy-hided Brer Lion," as Rabbit had earlier derided his rival, to die. Brer Rabbit sauntered back home and proudly informed his fellow animals that he had triumphed over his rival: "when he tried to get rough with me, I beat the scoundrel half to death and threw him in my well and drowned him." After showing the skeptical crowd the "big old fool" Lion's body, Rabbit found himself acclaimed "king," with rewards accordingly.[53] Lion was clearly understood as the most dominant

---

[51] Roger D. Abrahams (Ed.), *African American Folktales: Stories from Black Traditions in the New World* (New York: Pantheon Books, 1985), folk tale 34, 119–20, 120.

[52] [anon], "Premature Old Age," *The Magazine of Domestic Economy*, 1 (London: W. S. Orr and Co., Paternoster Row, September 1842), 127.

[53] Abrahams (Ed.), *African American Folktales*, folk tale 61, 185–91, 190–1, 186.

animal in the community on account of his physical prowess. Rabbit understood, however, that the "King's" only real fear was of the rival he could not beat. The sense of insecurity among even the strongest animals suggests how supremacy based on physicality was understood as ephemeral; the constant disparaging references to the Lion as "old" indicate how far this type of supplanting related to concerns over aging and physical supremacy.

If there is a degree of ambiguity over the generational element in the previous tales, the folktale entitled "The Old Bull and the Young One" – recorded as coming from St. Vincent – outlines this plainly. In the anthropomorphist tale, the father tells his son not to be rude to his elders, but the son shakes off the mantle of assumed authority and rebels against paternal rule. The tale outlines how authority, power, and status were dynamic and subject to contest through the temporal rhythms of the life cycle and the rise and fall of individuals accordingly. After being warned "not to be rude to his elders," the son told his father: "We will fight. And if I kill you, I reign, and if you kill me, you reign."[54] The young bull won, and the mantle of power was publicly and violently seized from the elder.

The cross-cultural resonance of tales of intergenerational rivalry and conflict are clear, with similar tales recorded in the US South. In "Meeting the King of the World," social hierarchies based on physical strength were entwined with concerns over age, identity, and status. The tale relays how a bear sought to challenge a man named "John" over the title "King of the World." Bear claimed that John was "going around telling everybody that you are the King of the World," but that he needed to earn this title the hard way: "No, you aren't King of anything. Not until you whip me. Get down here and fight it out with me." Bear and John fought, but the bear was grievously wounded by his foe and went to lick his wounds. As Bear consoled himself over his reduced status, Lion entered the fray. He viewed Bear's loss with scorn and threatened to eat his now pitifully reduced foe. However, after hearing the bear admit "the King of the World" had "cut me all up," Lion became determined to prove himself as the one true King. Lion sat and waited for his rival and, as he waited, he encountered people at different parts of the life-course. He first met an "old man" labelled as "Uncle Yistiddy, he's used-to-be," and then a small boy described as "little tomorrow, he's going-to-be." His foe, who was next to arrive, was clearly positioned as being in the prime of life.

54 Abrahams (Ed.), *African American Folktales*, folk tale 82, 244–51, 247.

The temporal language applied throughout the tale indicates how enslaved people understood the passage of time as affecting social hierarchies and status; the ferocity of the conflict that erupted shows how difficult it was to accept a loss of power, whether perceived or real. Lion confronted John and pointedly took aim at his supposed place atop the social hierarchy: "They tell me you call yourself King of the World!!" John's steely response indicates how contemporaries understood that status built on physicality and force was the inevitable subject of challenge: "John looked him dead in his eye and told him, 'Yeah, I'm King. If you don't like it, you don't have to take it from me.'" Words turned to actions and, after a bitter fight, Lion was forced to confront the fact that he, too, was no match for the "King." After conceding defeat, "old Lion gave John the back of his tail" as trophy. Lion then slunk off to lie down in ignominious shame alongside Bear; both were symbolically emasculated and defeated, and these fierce animals were now like "Uncle Yistiddy" and "used-to-be." Antebellum Americans, Black and white, understood that identities built on physical strength could not last forever. Lion's final statement on the matter reveals this shared understanding that social hierarchies were subject to the inexorable hand of time. Those who once stood atop of the mound had only one place left to go. As Lion sadly noted, "I have met the King of the World and he has ruined me."[55]

* * *

Fables and folktales have long been identified as providing insights into broader social and cultural dynamics among the enslaved, and the messages imparted in the aforementioned tales clearly speak to a perception that intergenerational conflict could arise to no little strife. T. J. Desch Obi has noted that enslaved men valued competitive conflict "to such an extent that they would walk miles, risk severe beatings, and sacrifice sleep despite an abusive work routine because their participation was a badge of honor."[56] Enslaved men who had built their identities on physical prowess, strength, and endurance – as much as the aforementioned anthropomorphized creatures – would be devastated to find out they no longer had power or were held in high regard by their peers. Emily Liles Harris of Tennessee recorded in her plantation journal just some of the possible consequences when violence interrupted existing hierarchies. Harris noted that an enslaved man known as "Old Will" asked to leave

---

[55] Abrahams (Ed.), *African American Folktales*, folk tale 22, 85–6.
[56] Desch Obi, *Fighting for Honor*, 112.

the plantation entirely and find a new home. "Old Will" had been badly beaten by an enslaved peer, and his humiliation led him to seek a new start elsewhere: "Old Will came to me and asked me to give him 'a paper' and let him go and hunt him a home. York has given him a whipping and he wishes to leave the place." Will's decision to leave suggests his defeat did not lead to sympathy from his peers, and that he feared any such violence or abuse was only just beginning.[57] Enslaved people sometimes looked at their elders and saw weakness to exploit; those who had previously been atop social hierarchies were forced to confront the dynamic nature of authority and the inevitable rhythms of the life cycle. This was a hard lesson to learn.

Desch Obi has argued that victory in public combat was less important than participation, noting that "even the vanquished retained their sense of status and validated anew their claims to honor by boldly entering into such conflicts," while Sergio Lussana similarly claims that fighting allowed enslaved men to "assert and display distinctly gendered identities, which were judged, recognized and validated by their peers."[58] Both scholars emphasize the affirming and supportive nature of combative leisure activities, but evidence shown here suggests that a loss of force associated with aging could see a loss of respect, and that any such decline could be seized upon – and highlighted to all – by rivals in the community. One enslaver suggested the possibility of conflict as social hierarchies shifted in slave communities, insisting that caution was required to ensure "the strong should never be allowed to impose on the weak," and violent contests for dominance certainly did erupt among the enslaved.[59] This dynamic appeared to play out in one violent encounter in Muscogee County, Georgia, 1855. Bill and Caesar, two enslaved men of noticeably different ages and stature had a "scuffle, or *tussle*, as they called it," one morning, and the younger man won. This physical loss appeared to depress Caesar, while Bill publicly celebrated his victory and elevation over another. Indeed, one triumph was not enough; Bill reveled in, and seemed determined to reveal to the entire community, that even though he was "just grown and smaller than Caesar," he was now the bigger man.

After this first conflict Caesar appeared to have realized he was no match for Bill and wanted to put the episode behind them. The court heard

---

[57] Racine (Ed.), *Piedmont Farmer*, 355–58.

[58] Desch Obi, *Fighting for Honor*, 216; Lussana, "To see who was best on the plantation," 918.

[59] Agricola, "Management of Negroes," *Southern Cultivator* 13 (1855), 173.

that he "begged [Bill] to let him alone." Bill, however, sought to cement his superiority and secure his mastery over Caesar: "Bill had his hand in his pocket on his knife – dared Caesar 'to make a riffle towards him, and he would cut his heart out of him.' Caesar would not hit him, and then Bill said he would give him first lick, and see if Caesar would '*mash him up*.'" The reference to "mash him up" indicates that Caesar had used these words to assert his supremacy prior to their first scuffle. Bill was flaunting his foe's failure to live up to his promise and Caesar appeared deflated, but submission alone was not enough: "Bill left his horse, and went around and slapped Caesar, with his hand, on the shoulder. Caesar showed no fight. Bill then stabbed him." There was a noted "disparity in age, size, and manhood of the parties," and suggestions that Bill had been bullied by the elder parties at the stable, but the court gave short shrift to this. Justice Lumpkin opined for the court that Bill had not only started, but also finished the contest. He had, they determined, deliberately picked a fight with an older man and sought to establish his supremacy for all to see: "from the commencement to the fatal termination of this unfortunate affair, Bill, by words as well as by acts, was the aggressor."[60]

Youth did not always triumph in violent encounters. During one gathering on a boat in Rockbridge County, Virginia, an enslaved man named Jim Gooch killed the man who insulted him. The conflict began as a dispute over cheating during a card game, but it escalated when one of the men involved in the fracas brought age into the equation. Gooch was quarreling with one man before Sam, who was known to be "overbearing" and an intimidating presence, stepped in. Sam felt that Gooch should be grateful to even be at the event rather than cause such a scene, and dismissively told his rival to "go sit down and behave yourself." When Gooch responded with force, Sam derisorily told him "I don't like to see an old man like you going about and meddling with things of no account." This was clearly no small insult; it was a contemptuous retort designed to inform Gooch that he was not wanted in the social space and that he should not consider himself the group's peer. His presence might be tolerated, but it was not wanted. This was, to return to Ball, a more pointed suggestion that the aged should retire from "active pleasures," and it was not taken well by Gooch, who instead informed Sam "he was a better man than he was." To punctuate his message, Gooch stabbed his rival to death.

As the gravity of the situation sunk in an enslaved man named Charles lamented the outcome, reiterating his (ignored) advice that Gooch should

[60] *William (a slave)* v. *State*, 18 Ga. 356 (1855), 358, 356, 358.

never have attended: "Jim did I not advise you not to play."[61] Gooch's
desire to join in the affair even when challenged, and his emphasis on using
words and then deeds to assert himself, suggests how age was a vector of
power in leisure and pleasure and the ferocity with which elders might
resist their relegation – in words or deeds – from social activities. Stacey
Close argues that "African American slaves believed that these old persons
existed in a state somewhere between heaven and earth" and "thus, it
would be an insult to the ancestors and a possible detriment to the afterlife
if a young person mocked an elder."[62] In this case, Sam's insult of his elder
precipitated his passage to the afterlife.

The white satirist Henry Deedes witnessed a fight between two enslaved
men in Montgomery, Alabama, where age shaped the dynamics of the
conflict. Deedes described how an older man working as ferryman witnessed another enslaved man stealing his food and his efforts to prevent this
by publicly calling out the thief. The man responded by taking aim at his
rival's advanced age: "I'll tell you, ole man, I'll smash your wool skull in if
you call me tief." To be labeled a thief was a direct attack on a man's honor,
and the deliberate (and repeated) use of "old" in the man's response
suggests he knew this was a way of diminishing his opponent's status and
asserting himself over him. As one antebellum writer claimed: "The young
are fond of the distinction between them and the old; and though the old
cannot deny the distinction, yet they generally regret it."[63] After the aged
ferryman stated he would "kill you where you stand if you not take that
gourd back to where you found it," the alleged thief demonstrated his
"fondness" with their age difference with his disdainful reply: "Like to
see you do it; come on, ole man." This was designed to denigrate, and it
worked to effect. The "ole man" was "quite game" for the fight, at least
until he saw the large stick the man was wielding. At this point he cried foul
play and managed to use the threat of the law to regain his property. It was
clear, however, that the young man did not respect his elder, and that he
added insult to injury by using age-related epithets to escalate the conflict.[64]

In some cases, weapons allowed older men to even the scales if they felt
outmatched by younger rivals. On December 5, 1850, South Carolina

---

[61] Rockbridge County Minute Book, Reel 43, November 1853, 189–202, LVA.

[62] Close, *Elderly Slaves*, 101.

[63] Emmons, "Piety, a Peculiar Ornament to the Aged," 493.

[64] Henry Deedes, *Sketches of the South and West or Ten Month's Residence in the United States* (William Blackwood & Sons: Edinburgh and London, 1869), 142–6. The episode is discussed in the context of community – but not intergenerational – strife in Penningroth, *The Claims of Kinfolk*, 99.

enslaver Thomas Bennett successfully sought a pardon for Peter Blacklock who, despite being "considerably advanced in years," had broken the skull of another slave with a wooden board during their altercation. Blacklock was apparently "prostrate mentally and physically" in his advanced age but was able to overcome his rival with the aid of weaponry.[65] More detail was provided in a case from January 1861, in Warwick County, Virginia, where Caesar Old was found guilty of the murder of George, a free Black man who worked alongside him. Caesar's enslaver sought to mitigate his sentence by painting an image of an older man being bullied by his younger, with one witness insisting that George was known for "Quarrelling & disputing over trivial things & would fight but for my interference." The conflict arose following a dispute over rations, and George appeared to assume mastery over Caesar by taking his meat and dismissively stating "he meant to keep it." He was believed to have escalated the conflict even after Caesar "asked George to excuse him" and tried to retreat. George was mistaken if he thought his rival was an easy mark: Caesar beat him to death with a stave billet.

The prisoners' counsel used the discourse that associated advanced age with weakness and played up the distinctions between the combatants. Caesar, aged fifty, was "a small & slender man much smaller & weaker than George," while George, aged thirty-two, was described as "a strong young negro." Although the attorney for the Commonwealth insisted that Caesar was "healthy, strong & vigorous," they were forced to concede that this was "not in proportion to George." In this deadly conflict, enslaver and enslaved alike believed that age-based discrepancies in power might manifest in tension, and a fear of declining status and loss of respect possibly animated Caesar in his violent response. One witness recalled how, the day after the murder, they confronted an entirely unrepentant Caesar: "Caesar said next day if it were to do over again, he would kill him, and would knock anybody down before they should take the stick from him."[66] The seizing of the stick was, of course, in one sense literal in its reference to the murder weapon. It is not hard to imagine, however, and linking back to William Grimes's seizure of his aged driver's staff, that this was a symbolic reference to Caesar's unwillingness to allow another to assume mastery over him.[67]

[65] Petition of Thomas Bennett, December 5, 1850, Charleston District/Parish, #11385006, Series 1, RSPP.

[66] Executive Papers, John Letcher, Misc. Reel 4722, Box 7, Folder 8, 308–16, LVA.

[67] Grimes, *Life of William Grimes*, 37.

Similar fears appear evident in Lula Jackson's recollections of how her "mama's first husband," a man named Myers, "was killed in a rasslin' (wrestling) match" with another slave. The conflict seemed exacerbated by concerns over age and status, and the fear that to be thought of as "old" meant no longer being respected – or even included – as part of the social community. Jackson highlighted the comparison and the insult that marked out physical competition and male combat, noting how "it used to be that one man would walk up to another and say, 'You ain't no good.' And the other one would say, 'All right, le's see.' And they would rassle." The sense of having to prove reputation and abilities to other men, rather than simply have this claim respected, speaks to the contested nature of masculine identity in slave communities. Jackson also brought up age-related concerns, noting that Myers was "pretty old." This detail was clearly important to the conflict. According to Jackson, "a young man come up to [Myers] one Sunday morning when they were gettin' commodities" and a conversation was struck up. Given what then ensued, it is likely that there was the customary trade of insults which Jackson suggested sparked most matches.

The frequent references to age in Jackson's testimony, with Myer's "old age" and the youth of the other man shaping the contours of the story, suggest that this distinction between the combatants was a factor in exacerbating the conflict. Myers spent some time attempting to make the young man "rassle with him," but the younger man refused, stating that "Myers was too old."[68] This rebuttal might have been an attempt to show respect to his elder. It is possible, however, that this was a deliberate attempt to antagonize Myers. Folklore recorded in the twentieth century suggests that this language was a deliberate means of stoking conflict, with a respondent for the Louisiana WPA describing how "a young man will gibe at an older one, saying, 'Old man, you is like a linen suit, out of season.'"[69] Regardless of motive, the younger man's comment only antagonized Myers. As Black activist Robert Sears sardonically noted, "We really forget how old we are, until some kind-hearted friend, of more *knowledge* or *observation* than ourselves, begins to count the number of our grey hairs."[70] Whether intended or not, the connotation that he was past his prime and therefore unworthy of fighting was an insult that Myers

---

[68] Rawick (Ed.), *AS*, 9.3, 12.
[69] Lyle Saxon, Edward Dreyer, Robert Tallant (Eds.), *Gumbo-Ya-Ya: A Collection of Louisiana Folk Tales* (Baton Rouge; Louisiana State University Press, 1945), 373.
[70] Robert Sears, "Desultory Reflections," *Weekly Advocate*, February 18, 1837.

desired to disprove. If positive personal identities could be demonstrated through physical competition among peers, to be refused access to this activity as an equal was a public denial of one's status in the community. Myers eventually badgered the young man into combat, but quickly lost and was thrown to the ground. This first taste of defeat was not enough: "Myers wasn't satisfied with that. He wanted to rassle again."

Whether content with his first victory or aware of the dangers of the conflict escalating, the young man refused. Myers, however, "made him" fight once more. On this occasion the consequences were more severe: "the second time, the young man threw him so hard that he broke his collar-bone ... He lived about a week after that." Despite the frequent use of "old" to describe Myers and the emphasis on the relative youth of his opponent, he was clearly not decrepit. Indeed, Myers had a wife, and she was "in a family way at the time." Myers's insistence on fighting, how-ever, meant that he died "before the baby was born."[71] Myers may simply have enjoyed wrestling, but evidence presented in this chapter underscores how enslaved men worried about a loss of power and prestige as they grew older, that they felt sadness at the passing of time and the passing of the torch, and that they could direct anger toward those who they felt disres-pected them on account of advancing age. In light of this, it is worth emphasizing that Myers likely responded with force – and even escalated the action – to avoid coming to terms with the idea that he was no longer considered by his peers as their equal or as deserving of respect.

When older men faced insult and abuse in social spaces, they were forced to confront the realization they were not welcome or were now seen as too weak to remain atop social hierarchies. Some were able to defend themselves against the charge, but others clearly struggled when matched against younger, more physically able men. In Blandford, Virginia, 1848, an older man named John was murdered by Billy after they traded insults with one another on a Sunday night, when it was "in the habit of the negroes to collect and drink" together. John, described by numerous witnesses as "an old man," was clearly hoping to join in the merriment but did not have the money to pay for a drink. He perhaps believed he could make use of his status as elder to lean on others and sought to borrow money from those gathered there, including the afore-mentioned Billy, but found his request rebuffed. In frustration John lashed out and insulted Billy, stating that "it was not worth while to tell a damned lie about money; if you have none I can't keep it," and made his exit.

[71] Rawick (Ed.), *AS*, 9.3, 12.

Whether Billy was lying or not, John's public insult worked him "up into a passion," and he chased after his elder, saying "what is my money to you," before he "overtook [him] and knocked him down." An enslaved man named Knight tried to pull Billy away from this assault, noting "it was a damned shame to strike such an old man," but the damage had been done. John was clearly no threat to the "much younger" Billy and he "made no resistance" after being struck, but the elder's insult to the younger man's honor could not be shrugged off.[72] John had perhaps expected to join in the fun, to be accorded respect, or simply to be granted leniency for the insult, on account of his age and standing. He was wrong, and died within minutes of receiving the blows.

* * *

Leisure time and social affairs were of paramount importance for enslaved people; in these spaces they developed positive personal identities and meaningful relationships with others. The significance of competition in leisure activities, however, with its attendant emphasis on contest, even conflict, meant the identities forged in these spaces were never static, nor fixed in time. Competition involves putting your reputation on the line and, regardless of any sense of shared honor through participation, to lose is to be publicly revealed as having been mastered by another. Enslaved people who had valued their physical prowess, or mental aptitude, as allowing them to demonstrate themselves as the best in the community might struggle in the face of challenges from younger rivals or simply from time itself. Younger members of the community might see in their elders a rival to supplant, and, in doing so, a hierarchy they might stand atop. Such conflicts demonstrate the necessity of intersectional analysis when exploring enslaved social dynamics and identities, wherein age must be incorporated as much as the well-studied categories of gender, class, and race.

By way of conclusion, I return to King's murder of Moses, a "feeble old man," in Richmond, Virginia, 1848. While gathered in a shop with numerous white and Black people, Moses claimed that King's son had stolen a herring and cast doubt on his parental control. This infuriated King to the point of trying to hit his elder, but he was prevented from striking Moses by the shopkeeper. The matter was not closed, however, and King insisted he would have revenge. King waited for Moses outside

---

[72] Executive Papers, William Smith, Box 7, Folder 4, February 18, 1848, LVA.

the house, and, once he left, knocked his elder to the ground and violently beat him. After dropping the old man with a stick, King "jinked him down in a hole of water and began to kick him and choke him, and hold him down in the water." All this time Moses was "hallowing murder and said King please don't kill me." He pled for his life by offering "every cent of money I have got." The scale of the abuse did not seem equivalent to the insult, and the violence was being used to publicly reinforce King's standing above Moses and, indeed, above all others in the community. Throughout the beating King gloatingly asserted supremacy, asking his rival to tell him "how come his name was King"? He did not really expect an answer: "every time [Moses] went to get up he dabbed him down in the water and kicked him and choked him and held his knees on him to keep him from getting up." With utter despair and almost unbearable sadness, Moses begged for his life: "King I aint fit to die. I don't want to go to Hell King, don't kill such an old creature as I." His begging was in vain. Aged sixty, and described by the coroner as a "feeble old man," Moses died face down in a muddy puddle.[73] In this instance, and to cement his dominance, the "King of the world" killed "uncle yistiday."[74]

[73] Executive Papers, William Smith, Box 7, Folder 4, March 18, 1848, LVA.
[74] Abrahams (Ed.), *African Americans Folktales*, folk tale 22.

5

"You wont notice me now but you'll wish you had"

Conjure, Community, and Intergenerational Conflict

Enslaved men who were no longer deemed worthy of participating in "active pleasures" on account of old age struggled to accept, mitigate, or resist these changes. This chapter turns the tables to examine those who took alternative routes toward enforcing the respect they believed was owed to them in old age. Rather than rely on physical force, some elders wielded the cultural and spiritual force associated with conjuration, hoodoo, and root-work to solicit respect, even fear, from others in the community.[1] This was a route available to enslaved women and men, and this chapter moves beyond some of the heavily gendered dimensions of earlier discussions on physical competition to address wider concerns over generational power dynamics in community life. Conflict presented in the context of conjure offers another window into – and reveals the significance of – intergenerational strife among the enslaved, and shows how age operated as a contested relation of power that ran alongside, but sometimes superseded, gendered beliefs relating to power and authority. The chapter shows the existence of multiple, occasionally conflicting belief systems that were understood as marked by generational differences, as well as the impact of this for notions of solidarity among the enslaved.

---

[1] Yvonne P. Chireau defines conjure as "a magical tradition in which spiritual power is invoked for various purposes, such as healing, protection, and self defense." Chireau acknowledges different labels for supernatural traditions and figures, but notes that "'conjurer' eventually became the most commonly used term for African American supernatural practitioners" and predominantly uses this nomenclature, while always remaining conscious of the diverse labels that are within this label. See Chireau, *Black Magic: Religion and the African American Conjuring Tradition* (Berkeley: University of California Press, 2003), 12, 20–2.

Scholars have long addressed the social and cultural power of conjure in slave communities and acknowledged that these roles were often associated by enslaved people with advanced age. Ex-slaves frequently noted generational differences and perceived distinctions between those who retained "African" knowledge – or had this specifically passed down to them – and those who were born in the United States. Louis Hughes recorded in his postbellum narrative that knowledge of conjuration "was handed down from generation to generation."[2] Specific references to conjuration as the preserve of the elderly were prominent in Black testimony on the matter, including cultural tropes and folklore. Rias Body of Georgia explained to his WPA interviewer that "among the very old slaves whom he knew as a boy were quite a few whom the Negroes looked up to, respected, and feared as witches, wizards, and magic-workers. These either brought their 'learnin' with them from Africa or absorbed it from the immediate African forebears."[3] Marrinda Jane Singleton sagely informed her WPA interviewer that knowledge of conjuration "was handed down from the wilds of Africa."[4] Physical prowess might lessen over time, but the powers associated with conjure were understood as predominantly the preserve of the aged. These powers could serve to secure and reinforce older people's status in the community.

Historians have often noted how aged conjurers were held in high esteem by their peers and assessed how their activities, and relationships with others, provide evidence of enslaved cultural resistance and connected to broader networks of solidarity. Conjurers cared for enslaved people, in ways both mental and physical; they advised and adjudicated on relationships within slave communities; and they supported resistance to slavery. Many of these same scholars have noted, too, that conjurers "possessed the ability both to harm and to heal."[5] Conjuring conflicts,

---

[2] Hughes, *Thirty Years a Slave*, 108. This emphasis on African knowledge is addressed in Albert J. Raboteau, *Slave Religion: The Invisible Institution in the Antebellum South* (Oxford: Oxford University Press, 2004 [1978]), 284–6.

[3] Rawick (Ed.), *AS*, *12.1*, 89.   [4] Perdue et al. (Eds.), *Weevils in the Wheat*, 267.

[5] Quote from Fett, *Working Cures*, 41. For discussions on respect and harm, see, for example, Blassingame, "Status and Social Structure," 151; Blassingame, *The Slave Community*, 110; Raboteau, *Slave Religion*, 236, 275–88; Theophus Harold Smith, *Conjuring Culture: Biblical Formations of Black America* (Oxford: Oxford University Press, 1994), 4; Close, *Elderly Slaves*, 23–4; Yvonne P. Chireau, "The Uses of the Supernatural: Toward a History of Black Women's Magical Practices," in Susan Juster and Lisa MacFarlane (Eds.), *Religion and American Culture* (Ithaca: Cornell University Press, 1996), 171–88; Morgan, *Slave Counterpoint*, 612; Walter Rucker, "Conjure, Magic, and Power: The Influence of Afro-Atlantic Religious Practices on Slave Resistance and Rebellion," *Journal of Black Studies*, 32.1 (2001), 84–103; Chireau, *Black Magic*, 15–16,

however, have rarely been explored through the lens of age. This chapter seeks to build on the conflict-driven dimension of the historiography by focusing on intergenerational strife relating to conjure beliefs and practices. Aged conjurers, both women and men, attempted to use spiritual powers to try and enforce the respect they believed was owed to them by younger members of the community, with conflict often arising when elders found themselves cast aside or neglected by those who refused to accede to or acknowledge their supremacy. The aged party was sometimes successful in reinforcing their status, but younger members of the community did not inevitably accept these powers as real and were instead willing to undermine or actively usurp their aged antagonist. The first half of the chapter shows how aged conjurers sought to use their powers to enforce respect, emphasizing how Black elders' position in social hierarchies was contestable rather than inevitably secure. The latter half will further underscore the limits to veneration for aged conjurers, and the consequences of this, by noting challenges to spiritual authority both physical and psychological. In so doing I reveal the fissures that developed in slave communities, the contested social hierarchies among the enslaved, and the broader significance of age as a vector of power in the American South.

* * *

White southerners frequently saw conjure as playing a major role in enslaved conflict. Although enslavers typically rejected the "magical" element of conjure power, and portrayed these figures as either deluded or remnants of a "primitive" Africanity, they certainly believed that enslaved elders might use belief in spiritual powers or selective knowledge of herbs, roots, and poisons to enforce respect, wield power, or gain revenge for slights real and imagined. They understood that these episodes of conflict and violence sometimes occurred as a result of jealousy and intergenerational strife, as when proslavery author Daniel Hundley

---

ch. 3; Jeffrey E. Anderson, *Conjure in African American Society* (Baton Rouge: Louisiana State University Press, 2005), 79–81, 83–6, 89; Fett, *Working Cures*, ch. 4; Schwartz, *Birthing a Slave*, 59–65; Rebecca Fraser, *Courtship and Love among the Enslaved in North Carolina* (Jackson: University Press of Mississippi, 2007), 49–51; William Dusinberre, *Strategies for Survival: Recollections of Bondage in Antebellum Virginia* (Charlottesville: University of Virginia Press, 2011), 121–41; Forret, *Slave Against Slave*, 64, 66, 87, 176, 239, 255, 298; Alexis S. Wells-Oghoghomeh, *The Souls of Womenfolk: The Religious Cultures of Enslaved Women in the Lower South* (Chapel Hill: University of North Carolina Press, 2022), 189–90, 195, 217, 221.

described poisoning as being the preserve of the "old toothless hag" on the plantation. Hundley conjured a viciously racist and misogynistic image of an old woman, isolated and ignored, seeking revenge on those who neglected her so. In Hundley's view, this spoke to internal tension between the enslaved, where a loss of status with age effected a more general relegation from ones' peers: "being superannuated, [she] sits all day long in her cabin-door like a great black spider, the while with busy brain and a leer that would shame the devil himself, either laying new schemes for murder or gloating over the murders with which her skinny hands are already stained."[6] A. P. Merrill, a southern physician, insisted on the significance of conjuration among the enslaved. He believed the respect for elders so commonly identified by antebellum southerners, Black and white, was conditioned by fear. According to Merrill, the enslaved person "venerates age, but mingles with his veneration a superstitious dread of the control, which the aged are supposed to possess, over spiritual and ghostly influences; often assigning disease and misfortune solely to these agencies."[7]

The image of diminished elders using conjure practices to enforce respect they believed deserved was not simply the preserve of white racists. Formerly enslaved people articulated similar tropes when recalling conjure and emphasized their uneasiness at the power of select aged individuals in their communities. Bessie Royal claimed that her father was "conjured by a [woman] that was said to be a hag," causing a psychological affliction that ultimately led to his demise.[8] Alexis S. Wells-Oghoghomeh has argued that enslaved people "distinguished categories of power through semantic decisions," and the use of terms such as "hag" and "witch," which connected to nineteenth-century negative tropes of old age, to describe conjurers indicate the multifarious views on Black elders that go beyond notions of unquestioned respect.[9] The fusion of terror, derision, and respect that was subsumed within these labels underscores how far "respect" for aged conjurers might be

---

[6] Hundley, *Social Relations*, 331, 337, 332.

[7] A. P. Merrill, MD, "An Essay on some of the Distinctive Peculiarities of the Negro Race," *Southern Medical and Surgical Journal*, 12 (1856), 21–36, 35. See, also, Thomas Bangs Thorpe, *The Master's House; A Tale of Southern Life, by Logan* (New York: T. L. McElrath, 1854), 241–2.

[8] Georgia Writers' Project, *Drums and Shadows: Survival Studies among the Georgia Coastal Negroes* (Athens: University of Georgia Press, 1986), 79–80.

[9] Alexis S. Wells-Oghoghomeh, "'She Come Like a Nightmare': Hags, Witches and the Gendered Trans-Sense among the Enslaved in the Lower South," *Journal of African Religions*, 5.2 (2017), 239–74, 249.

conditioned by fear and could lead to mistrust. One WPA respondent noted that enslaved people would "shuts the door if we sees [the hag] coming," with this suspicion leading to the forced exclusion of elders, as opposed to their integration or even elevation in the social world of the enslaved.

This exclusion occasionally arose after direct encounters with the aged conjurer. Anna Marie Coffee told her WPA interviewer that tales of spirits frightened her as a child, and that her terror of witchcraft was personified by an isolated old woman. According to Coffee, "Dar wuz er ole 'oman living way back en er woods en folks done say that she wuz er witch," and she held nefarious powers over others. As a child Coffee avoided contact with this elder, and she was not alone; the woman was marginalized by her peers on account of the harm she apparently wrought on others.[10] A connection of witchcraft to old age was commonplace among the enslaved, with Jacob Stroyer recording in his postbellum memoir that "the witches among slaves" were almost uniformly old and using negative stereotypes associated with the aging process to describe those individuals: "both men and women, who, when they grew old looked odd, were supposed to be witches." Stroyer explained how these elders were known as "old hags or jack lanterns," and professed to be able to identify particular elders on account of exaggerated physical features and oddities:

When they would see a light at a great distance and saw it open and shut they would say "there is an old hag," and if it came from a certain direction where those lived whom they called witches, one would say "dat looks like old Aunt Susan," another said "no, dat look like man hag," still another "I tink dat look like ole Uncle Renty."

Dismissive names aside, the aged witches wielded very real power in the community. The fear of supernatural harm, although tempered with adult knowledge, lingered in Stroyer's imagination: "I was very much troubled with witches when a little boy and am now sometimes, but it is only when I eat a hearty supper and then go to bed."[11]

Stroyer's belief that elders might use spiritual powers to settle grudges was, in fact, commonly shared by ex-slaves. A Georgia interviewer for the WPA project recorded, with seeming incredulity, a respondent's claim that "in the olden days ... the 'ole witches' got on the darkies' chests while they were asleep. If the witches wanted to kill them they died right

[10] Rawick (Ed.), *AS, Supp.*, Ser. *1*, *5*, 287.
[11] Jacob Stroyer, *Sketches of My Life in the South: Part I* (Salem: Salem Press, 1879), 42–5.

there in the bed, but if not, they just 'rode 'em.'"[12] Sam Rawls of South
Carolina insisted he had personally suffered on account of "one old
woman [who] was a witch." Rawls explained that she had abused him
for some unknown insult and told his interviewer of his fear at being
unable to breathe while "she rode me one night."[13] William Grimes
outlined his own struggle with an old woman named Frankee. Having
recently been moved to Savannah, Grimes struggled to fit in; Frankee, who
Grimes "always believed ... to be a witch," was one of his principal
tormentors.

Rather than a situation in which young and old joined forces to survive
the miseries of forced dislocation, Grimes's experience suggests the difficulties in integrating newcomers and the generational divides present in
some communities. Indeed, Frankee appeared to have some measure of
supervisory authority on the farm, as the two fell out on account of the
elder informing their enslaver that Grimes had stolen an umbrella. Grimes
did not know whether Frankee did so erroneously or out of spite, but he
sought revenge after she caused him to be whipped. Grimes fought back
by informing his enslaver that Frankee had contraband rum; Frankee
protested her innocence, but she was caught dead to rights. As their
enslaver put it, "hey, you old bitch I have caught you in a lie." In this
instance, old and young appeared to have little sense of solidarity with one
another; they refused to see in one another a kindred spirit attempting to
survive bondage and instead became rivals. Grimes understood his "victory" was short-lived, noting that "On this same account she appeared to
be determined to kill me, by some means or other," and he believed that
her powers as a witch allowed her to do harm:

I have heretofore stated that I was convinced that this creature was a witch, and
would turn herself into almost any different shape she chose. I have at different
times of the night felt a singular sensation, such as people generally call the nightmare: I would feel her coming towards me, and endeavouring to make a noise,
which I could quite plainly at first; but the nearer she approached me the more
faintly I would cry out. I called to her, aunt Frankee, aunt Frankee, as plain as
I could, until she got upon me and began to exercise her enchantments on me. I was
then entirely speechless; making a noise like one apparently choking, or strangling.

Grimes's plaintive cries of "aunt" when under attack perhaps speak to
a belief that he needed to show respect, or to plead for relief, through the
appellation of age. The damage had been done, however. Frankee continually abused him while successfully playing on her enslaver's disbelief

---

[12] Rawick (Ed.), *AS, Supp.*, Ser. 1, 4.2, 495.   [13] Rawick (Ed.), *AS*, 3.4, 6.

in witchcraft to plead innocence. Grimes used labels of respect during the attacks, but he was more pointed in the light of day and insisted that "some old witch rode me, and that old witch, is no other than old Frankee," when seeking her punishment. This bravado did not last through the night, and he continued to believe he was suffering nightly abuse from the old woman. Grimes found no comfort from the wider community and it was only through tricking his enslaver into selling him that he found himself freed from the clutches of his aged rival. Grimes's resistance, and strategical escape from the plantation, was as much about removing himself from the harm of his elder as it was his abusive enslaver.[14]

Supernatural violence could be used against people of any age, but some ex-slaves specifically framed these practices as reflecting tension between young and old.[15] John Moore remembered an aged woman violently abusing a younger rival, informing his WPA interviewer that "an old slave woman borrowed a poker from another slave woman and was cruel to the poker," and stressed that this was a deliberate hex on a rival: "the other woman became bent nearly double from rheumatic pain."[16] The reference to rheumatic pain suggests the "old" woman was forcing her rival to experience the pains of aging herself.[17]

Elders with conjure power used their prowess to assert themselves over enemies and rivals, and were willing to do harm to others to ensure that they remained figures of fear in their communities. Anna Grant believed her mother was murdered by an "old lady we called Aunt Gracie." Gracie sought revenge for some slight and "buried a bottle under our fire chimney and my ma nebber could eat anything that wuz cooked from that chimney. Ma lingered and lingered until she died." Grant did not understand the motive but understood that conjure typically took place "cause somebody didn't like 'em" or "when a person would git mad with annuder one." Unsurprisingly, Grant was left terrified of her elder: "I wuz always fraid of her and when she came to our house I would run away and hide." Grant's traumatic memories disturb the notion that "younger generations venerated and cherished" elderly bondspeople and insist instead as to the

---

[14] Grimes, *Life of William Grimes*, 23–7.
[15] Rawick (Ed.), *AS, Supp.*, Ser. 2, 6.5, 2205–6.
[16] Rawick (Ed.), *AS, Supp.*, Ser. 1, 5, 144.
[17] On rheumatism and age, see Rush, "An Account of the State of the Body and Mind in Old Age," 314; James C Williams, "Rheumatism," 1848, Box 151, Part II, Joseph Meredith Toner Collection of Manuscripts, LOC; Carole Haber, *Beyond Sixty-Five: The Dilemma of Old Age in America's Past* (Cambridge: Cambridge University Press, 1983), 50.

complex power struggles that erupted among the enslaved.[18] That neither
Grant nor Moore seemed to know exactly *what* had motivated the violence plausibly speaks to a heightened sense of insult among the aged party
on account of a fear of growing old and invisible, but also their willingness
to use extreme force to resist slights, whether real or imagined. Grant
vividly remembered, and could not forgive, the violence proffered by her
elder: "Chile thats der trufe dat 'oman killed my folks."[19]

Beyond generic revenge, a concern with respect and status appeared of
paramount importance. In his postbellum memoir, William Wells Brown
recounted the tale of Dinkie, the so-called "Goopher King," and explained
this man's use of conjure to cement his status among his peers. Dinkie, "a
full-blooded African, large in frame, coarse featured" was aged around
fifty and was known as "the oracle on the 'Poplar Farm.'" His powers
were understood as enabling him to avoid work, with Wells Brown
emphasizing that "he was not sick, yet he never worked," and that the
wider community simply took the slack out of appreciation of his powers:
"No one interfered with him ... everybody treated him with respect."
Wells Brown was personally dismissive of Dinkie's prowess but he understood that on Poplar Farm the man held court and insisted that this was
conditioned by fear:

The negroes, everywhere, stood in mortal fear of "Uncle Dinkie." The blacks who
saw him every day, were always thrown upon their good behaviour, when in his
presence. I once asked a negro why they appeared to be afraid of Dinkie. He
looked at me, shrugged his shoulders, smiled, shook his head and said, – "I ain't
afraid of de debble, but I ain't ready to go to him jess yet."[20]

Wells Brown intimated that Dinkie worked in tandem with his cabin-
mate, Uncle Ned, another elder on the plantation. As "the old, superannuated slave knew more about the affairs of the conjurer, than anyone else,"
he was the narrator of (and perhaps embellisher to) Dinkie's escapades.
Ned received gifts from the community as payment for this knowledge,
and his story-telling meant that he played an important role in social
gatherings. On one occasion, the community was amazed to hear that
Dinkie had avoided a planned punishment, with the rumor that this
related to his conjuring of the overseer eliciting furious gossip. Of course,
"no one dared to ask Dinkie," but "there was, however, one faint chance
of getting an inkling of what had occurred in the barn, and that was

[18] Barclay, *The Mark of Slavery*, 164.   [19] Rawick (Ed.), *AS, Supp.*, Ser. *1, 3.1*, 265–6.
[20] Wells Brown, *My Southern Home*, 70–7.

through Uncle Ned." According to Wells Brown, "this fact made the old, superannuated slave the hero and centre of attraction, for several days. Many were the applications made to Ned for information, but the old man did not know, or wished to exaggerate the importance of what he had learned." It was only after receiving payment in the form of additional food that Uncle Ned let loose the tale to his awestruck audience. Wells Brown was entirely dismissive of Dinkie's supernatural powers and, while he did not directly cast aspersions on Ned, it is hard not to see insinuation that the two elderly cabin-mates worked in tandem to further the legend of "the Goopher King" and to uphold their own social status in the community.[21] The tale reveals, nonetheless, the degree to which respect for aged conjurers related to the possibility they would harm those who went against them.

Wells Brown's postbellum narrative was part of a body of literature that sought to "uplift" African Americans and emphasize spiritual and moral development through Christianity.[22] His references to those who believed in Dinkie's powers as "ignorant" reveals his personal disdain for such beliefs, with this dimension of generational conflict addressed in the second part of the chapter. Those who *did* believe, however, insisted on the power elders wielded and their willingness to use this strategically to uphold their status among their peers. Ellen Crowley of Arkansas, known as "'Old Aunt Ellen' to both white and colored people," was "much feared and also respected by the colored race owing to the fact that she could foretell the future and cast a spell on those she didn't like." The conflation of fear and respect was important, and Ellen made examples of those who failed to pay her deference. After being "teased by a small negro boy," Ellen "promptly put the 'curse' on" and the boy immediately took sick. As noted in earlier chapters, to be abused, ignored, or neglected by one's peers, or, in the case of elders, by the children who were supposed to venerate you, clearly hurt some Black elders. Conjuration provided a means to strike back, and Ellen did so with ferocity. The seeming disproportionality of the response – with the less-than-threatening language of "teasing" and references to the diminutive size of the boy – showing the intensity of intergenerational strife, all

---

[21] Wells Brown, *My Southern Home*, 70–7.
[22] On racial uplift, see, for example, Albert G. Miller, *Elevating the Race: Theophilus G. Steward, Black Theology, and the Making of an African American Civil Society, 1865–1924* (Knoxville: University of Tennessee Press, 2003); Kevin K. Gaines, *Uplifting the Race: Black Leadership, Politics, and Culture in the Twentieth Century* (Chapel Hill: University of North Carolina Press, 1996).

underscored by the longevity of this punishment. The boy was subject to fits throughout his life, all, at least as the community believed it, on account of his mockery of old Aunt Ellen.[23]

The willingness of aged conjurers to do serious injury to those who disrespected them reveals the contested social hierarchies among the enslaved and the potential for generational strife to escalate dramatically. Historian William Dusinberre has argued that "to be looked up to and respected carried special meaning for a people normally regarded by whites with disdain," and conjuration allowed some elders to maintain status and power.[24] This was something worth fighting for. Ebenezer Brown told his WPA interviewer that his "grand pappy cud hoodoo eny body" and understood that this made him someone people *had* to respect, even if out of fear: "Ebery body sed he wus a bad n***r."[25] Public status and reputation was no small matter, and this meant that any public disrespect – perceived or real – warranted a severe response. Julius Jones of Mississippi recalled how an elder enacted revenge on the young man who sought to knock them off their pedestal through a public disavowal of their powers. The tale was specifically framed with reference to comparative age, with Jones recalling the time "one young n***r cussed the old conger man on the place." Physical conflict between young and old was rarely positive for the elder, but conjure might even the scales: "The old man reached up and cut off some of his hair, put it in a sack and throwed the sack in the water." The young man's bravado, in deliberately mocking his elder and attempting to assume mastery over him, did not last long. The young man "got scared most to death" after seeing his hair floating downstream and pled for mercy: "He ran all day trying to get that hair back. He most went crazy 'fore he got that spell lifted."[26] In both of these incidents, conjure power was used specifically by elders, women and men, to enforce respect otherwise denied to them by younger members of the community. The tales were explicitly framed as conflict between old and young, with a clear sense that esteem for the aged enslaved was not inevitable, and could instead be reliant on demonstrations of their powers. Those who sought to undercut or supplant the aged conjurer could find themselves being made an example of to all and sundry, with a ferocity that undermines the notion of unquestioned solidarity or reverence for the aged enslaved.

---

[23] Rawick (Ed.), *AS*, 8.1, 61.   [24] Dusinberre, *Strategies for Survival*, 108.

[25] Rawick (Ed.), *AS, Supp.*, Ser. 1, 6.1, 254.

[26] Rawick (Ed.), *AS, Supp.*, Ser. 1, 8.3, 1219.

Some interventions related to more specific sites of intergenerational tension, including rivalries in work roles or in intimate affairs. One WPA respondent believed that a woman had sought to use conjure against her to take her job by noting that this woman sought her out and shook her hand, after which it "began ter swell up jest lak it would bust open." She was forced to seek healing from another aged woman and found out that this had been no accident: "this same 'oman came ter [employer] and tried ter git my job; but they wouldn't have her."[27] On occasion, conjurers sought to use their prowess in intimate spaces. The framing of these recollections suggests a degree of tension and sadness for those perceived to be "past" their prime in matters of lust and love, but also the willingness (if not always ability) of the aged to bend others to their will. Lula Taylor explained that an "old man [who] was a conjurer" gave her "mother a cup of some kind of herbs and made her drink it" to trick her into marriage, but that she fortunately escaped.[28] Ben Chambers of Alabama recalled when an "ol' lady name Liza" tried to dance with him at a party but he refused on account of her age and appearance: "she sho was ugly." This rebuff got Liza "mad" and she resolved to take revenge on the object of her affections: "She git mad and go home and beat up a rattlesnake head and mek dus'. I dunno how she got dat dus' on me but I git a big swellin' under my arm."[29]

Public humiliation, at least in the eyes of the elder, was not simply accepted in these cases, and the aged party planned to use their powers to take revenge on those who slighted them. Emmaline Heard revealed how one elder's humiliation at their public rejection entailed a harsh response, and her testimony underscores how age affected social relations among the enslaved. Heard explained that "Uncle Ned" was a figure of fear in the community, with Heard's father "afraid ter ask old uncle Ned what he did with these bags" because he "heard he conjured folks with 'em." He was right to be fearful, with Heard recalling the time Uncle Ned "conjure a gal 'cause she wouldn't pay him any attention." The woman had publicly snubbed Ned because of his advanced age, making clear that he was no longer her peer, let alone an object of desire. This was too much for Ned to bear:

This gal wuz very young and preferred talking to the younger men, but uncle Ned always tried ter hang around her and help hoe, but she would always tell him to go do his own work 'cause she could do hers. One day he said ter her, "All right madam, I'll see you later, you wont notice me now but you'll wish you had."[30]

---

[27] Rawick (Ed.), *AS, Supp., Ser. 1, 3.1,* 139.   [28] Rawick (Ed.), *AS, 10.5,* 266.
[29] Rawick (Ed.), *AS, Supp., Ser. 2, 3.2,* 674.   [30] Rawick (Ed.), *AS, 13.4,* 259–260.

According to Heard, Uncle Ned conjured the woman's hoe to gain revenge for his public humiliation. When the woman returned and touched the cursed hoe, she died. Age once again was the fulcrum of conflict in this story, with a sense that Ned was absurd to even consider socializing with, much less courting the younger woman. Conjure, in this instance, allowed the "insulted" elder to gain revenge and to unsettle all others who might dismiss them on account of their age. Ned's specific phrasing, that he had not been "noticed," hints at a broader fear of isolation among the aged, as when "Old Isaac" informed his WPA interviewer that he "neber wants ter to be forgotten" because "forgotten folks die quick."[31] Ned's actions here were unlikely to be forgotten, and they speak to the ferocity with which some elders might respond if they felt the respect they had earned was being denied to them.

* * *

Some WPA respondents believed elders used conjure as a tactic to secure respect from children, with a suggestion that these powers were necessary to maintain control over youth. Such accounts further reinforce how childcare arrangements were a site of tension for young and old seeking to cement their place in the social hierarchy. Abram Sells explained how the man placed in charge of childcare on account of being "too ol' to do any kin' 'r' wuk" used conjure powers to elicit good behavior from his charges. In this framing, respect for elders connected to fear of punishment as opposed to something automatic or culturally conditioned: "N' us sho' hab to min' (mind) him, 'sides iffen we didn', we was sho' (sure) to hab bad luck. Sump'n bad was sho' to happen to us." According to Sells, this was no small fear:

He allus hab he pocket full 'r' t'ings to conjure wid; dat ribbit foot, he tek it out 'n'he wuk dat on you 'til you tek de creeps 'n' git to shakin' all ober. Den dere was a pocket full 'r' fish scales. He kinder squeak 'n' rattle dem in he han; right den you wish you was dead 'n' promise to do anyt'ing.

Sells noted the man would occasionally get "all tangle' up 'n' boddered" in his duties, indicating that he struggled with the physical and mental burden of the role, or perhaps simply with slavery itself. This necessitated removing himself from the children and using a charm and ritual to heal himself: "Atter a w'ile he git eb'ryt'ing ontwis' (untwisted) 'n' straighten out, den he come back wid a smile on he face 'n' maybe whistlin."[32] Belief

---

[31] Rawick (Ed.), *AS, Supp.,* Ser. *1, 1,* 424.
[32] Rawick (Ed.), *AS, Supp.,* Ser. 2, *9.8,* 3485–6.

in the powers of conjure, but also a willingness to wield this over his young charges, allowed this elder to maintain his dignity and status in bondage.

Elders clearly resented abuse or disrespect by young members of the community, and using – or playing up to – conjuration was a route by which they might avoid such a fate. Ellen Betts of Texas recalled how one elder made an example of the children who mocked him. The man was clearly struggling with the physical effects of aging, with Betts noting that he would simply "hobble long side de road," but she insisted this manifest decline occasioned no sympathy from the enslaved youth. Betts recalled how "De chillen start to throw rocks and sech and one little squirt 'bout nine year old sock dat old man right in de face." The aged man did not have the physical capacity to secure respect from his youngers, and they took his debility as a sign of weakness to exploit. They had chosen their target poorly, and were soon to find out that power came in different forms: "Den de old man turn 'roun' to dat prissy one and point his finger at him and say, 'Go on, young un, or you'll be whar de dogs can't bark at you tomorrow!'" Betts claimed this scared the majority of the children "but dat little boy don't stop. He jes' pester de old man right on in to de plantation." The old man's revenge was not long in coming: "Next mornin', we was busy in de kitchen cookin' rice and fryin' up meat when all of a sudden dat lil boy jes' crumple up dead on de floor." The wider community understood this as the direct consequence of the boy's mocking of his elder and Betts underscored this was a lesson hard learned: "Nobody ever bother dat old man after dat, for he sho lay de evil finger on you."[33] The old man's use of spiritual violence protected him from mockery and undermined expectations of declining powers in old age; his pointed retort to the "young un" underlined his message about the need for the young to respect the old or else fear the consequences.

Tales of aged conjurers tricking children can suggest an undercurrent of tension between young and old in enslaved communities, where elders believed it necessary to make examples of those who refused to honor them accordingly. Grace Lintner claimed to have been told by an ex-slave about how one elder, "Aunt Dorah," who was "too old to work," deliberately "filled the minds of her young charge with tales of spooks, conjuration and witchcraft," and this had the functional purpose "that they regard her with the greatest fear and veneration."[34] White postbellum elegies to the "Lost Cause" are problematic sources, but claims that elders used conjure powers, or simply their association with supernatural forces, to ensure they

---

[33] Rawick (Ed.), *AS, Supp.,* Ser. 2, 2.1, 273.
[34] Grace Lintner, *Bond and Free: A Tale of the South* (Indianapolis: C. B. Ingraham, 1882), 75–7.

received respect correspond with recollections from the formerly enslaved. Plomer Harshaw told his WPA interviewer that "there was an old slave woman on the place in Arkansas who scared the young folks with her haunts," while Lizzie Norfleet indicated how stories of the supernatural served a purpose for the aged enslaved. According to Norfleet, children weren't "allowed to be sassy and impertinent to old folks," and this expectation was reinforced through fear: "The old folks told them ghost stories that scared them most to death."[35]

Stories of conjure and haunts were sometimes recalled in a lighthearted tone, but underlining this was a sense that elders who faced disrespect would not hesitate to rectify this with force if required. Returning to Harshaw, the elderly woman buttressed her spiritual powers with physical force when disrespected by her peers. Having claimed the thrashing machine to be a "haunt," and the "biggest ghost I ever knowed about," the woman became the subject of mockery from Harshaw after his enslaver informed him of the elderly woman's mistake. This public dismissal of the woman's supernatural powers, however, led to a different type of haunt applied to Harshaw: "That made her so mad she took off her leather belt and most smother me down with it."[36] On other occasions, though, conjure itself was used to extract revenge. Moslie Thompson of Georgia recalled how, as a young woman, her grandmother was put under pressure by an old man to give him milk from her enslaver's cow. Thompson's grandmother refused this request:

Dat ol' n***r have long w'te hair an' whiskers an' de sharp eye. Well, my Grandma goes fo' to do her milkin' an' while she am a milkin' dat ol' n***r comes to de milk shed whar she am an' sez, "Give me a drink of de milk." Grandma am not 'llowed to do dat an' sez, "No Ise can' do dat." Dat ol' n***r sez, "Youse will wish yous had."

The old man assumed supremacy over the younger woman and demanded compliance to his will. Despite knowing she would be contravening her enslaver's orders and that he was placing her in an invidious situation, her refusal occasioned no sympathy. The man insisted she would learn her lesson about who held power here. Thompson's grandmother was soon found "a layin' on de floah. Her eyes am a-rollin' an' her whole body am a quiverment ... dere am foam comin' out her mouth an' she am rigid all ovah." This was understood by all to be punishment from the aged

---

[35] Rawick (Ed.), *AS, Supp.*, Ser. *1*, *12*, 171; Rawick (Ed.), *AS, Supp.*, Ser. *1*, *9.4*, 1646.
[36] Rawick (Ed.), *AS, Supp.*, Ser. *1*, *12*, 171.

conjurer, but after a frantic search they were able to locate him and force him to remove the spell. The old man evinced no regret and clearly resented having his plans foiled: "Dat ol' n***r sneaks off like de egg suckin' dawg."[37] Negative tropes of advanced age were used to paint a portrait of an old man consumed by cruelty and cunning; his threat – "youse will wish yous had" – reveals the force which some elders were willing to use – and the consequences of this for others – to enforce respect for the aged.

Sometimes memories of aged conjuration and violence came from within family units. The intergenerational transfer of conjure knowledge identified earlier could become a site of tension as opposed to solidarity, especially if this practice was rejected by the young. One ex-slave recalled in her WPA interview how such violence came from "Old Aunt Dolly," who ruled the roost on account of her perceived powers. The respondent explained how "ebbey body wuz 'fraid of this 'oman cause she ter boast that if she come ter your house and out down her tricks she would fix you." Respect for one's elder, in this context, was conditioned by the understanding that Aunt Dolly would not hesitate to take action if she felt slighted. Family members were not safe from this form of retribution, with Dolly's nephew William facing punishment on account of his unwillingness to accept his Aunt's teaching. William was expected to follow her ways and learn to "use her tricks," but he refused and even belittled her belief system as "devilment." This insult from young to old was not to be tolerated: "Old Dolly got mad with William and sed 'I'm gwine ter fix you so you won't nebber stop walking.'" This was no idle threat: "The last I heard of him he wuz still walking."[38] William's walk of shame was framed as a deliberate punishment for the contravention of an elder's command and, perhaps more broadly, in response to a generational rejection of an earlier belief system.

On occasion, elders with conjuring powers sought to punish those who abused, ignored, or belittled their skill, with injury seen as a deserved fate for those seduced by the arrogance of youth. Henry Barns of Alabama told his WPA interviewer that an enslaved woman named Penny had been sick for a long time and that a conjurer tried to heal her. Penny, however, would not agree to, or did not believe in, the treatment and her dismissal occasioned a spiteful response: "dere was a cunjer doctor wukkin' on her tryin' cyure her, but her wan't 'greeable, so he let her die."[39] At times this punishment seemed almost a deliberate effort to negate the effects of time

---

[37] Rawick (Ed.), *AS, Supp.*, Ser. 2, 9.8, 3866.
[38] Rawick (Ed.), *AS, Supp.*, Ser. 1, 3.1, 139.   [39] Rawick (Ed.), *AS*, 6, 23.

itself, with conjurers said to be stealing energy from their victims. Peter Ryas told his WPA interviewer that "dey old mens on plantations what they think which mens" and explained their ability to "put bad mouth on you." The language Ryas used indicates a sense of contested temporality, with the "bad mouth" causing the victim to "dry up and die 'fore you time." This loss of "time" entailed a gain for the old men. As Ryas put it, these old men wanted to "take your strength."[40]

A folk tale recorded from Georgia posits a similar situation, where elders were depicted as desperate to reverse the effects of aging, and where conjurers sought to exploit the young to restore their glory days. The language indicates how the aged might be portrayed as diminished and decrepit, how they might need fear to enforce respect, and, more broadly, how the process of aging was understood in negative terms. "The Story of Grumma Growey or Why the Crawfish Goes Backward," was recorded as having been told to an enslaver by his "childhood nurse, Old Mauma," and it begins with a detailed, and uniformly negative, description of an "ole conjure man name Grumma Growy: "He ole tay he all ben' ober. He ent had no teet. He ent hab no hair pon e' haid. He went hab no cloes but ole rags." Growy's obvious physical decline was mitigated by his conjure powers, as "ebery body faid him caus he can witch em," but fear alone was not enough. Growy wanted to regain the powers of youth and he believed the way to do so was by stealing time from another. As the narrator explained, "Well, if he can fool one young gal for married to him, de gal will turn ole and him will tun young again." Growey soon found his target.

The discursive framing of the tale suggests how a belief in physical decline associated with age might entail jealousy on the part of the aged, as well as indicating some of the possible ramifications of this in social encounters and community hierarchies. In his quest to trick the young woman, Growey conjured himself into a respectable looking man by "requesting" shoes, a coat, trousers, and a horse and carriage from other men on pain of conjuration. The exterior markings of desirability were not enough, however, as Growey needed to mask his physical decline:

He staat out and he go to pine tree. He say, "Budder Pine tree, len me yo stiffnin a few days and I will fix so axe can't cut you, but if you don' len em to me I will mek ma'ak on you so tunder will strike you." Pine tree say, "Well, lay down onder me tonight, and in de mawnin I will ben down and you will stan' up straight. He gone dere sleep dat night, next mawnin pine tree all ben down to de groun, Grumma Growey stan up straight."

[40] Rawick (Ed.), *AS*, 5.3, 276.

With his youth returned, and having successfully coerced from others the trappings of respectability, Growey convinced his chosen victim to marry him. She did so despite the concerns of her parents, as well as "de old house man," with the framing here suggesting a cautionary tale for the young to heed the advice of their elders. The young girl, of course, ignored her parents and dismissed their advice before driving off with Growey: "De ma der cry. De nuss der cry, der pa der cuss. All der n***rs der cry; dey ain't like de look ob dat man." They were right to fear "that man."

Having secured his prey, Growey began to let down the mask. He gave back the clothes as they drove along, becoming more disheveled at every turn, but the clearest evidence of his deception came after returning to the pine tree. A loss of material possessions could perhaps be forgiven, but "when e come back e all ben ober," Growey revealed his true self and it was not a pretty sight. The language conjured up a hideous image of aged decline and its attendant jealousy of youth: "At wile e begin for da'k Grumma Growey squinch all up in de cornder; e eye shine lack cat eye. He say 'ent you know who I is? I is Grumma Growey an' ef you try fer ter git way I will mek ole hag carry you right off to de debble'." The girl was eventually saved by an enslaved man who exploited the fact that the aged conjurer could not stay awake to watch over his captive, with the image of an older man falling asleep playing up to wider tropes of aged weakness. Once he realized what had happened Growey took chase but failed to catch them and, in frustration, threw the poison he planned to use on them into the river. Growey's troubles were not yet over: his horse bolted and threw him in the water, where he drowned.

Growey's mortal end was not the finale to the story, however. The poison, which would make anything it touched "hab for go backwards," had apparently worked its magic on the fish and it was this contact with Growey's poison, the narrator sagely concluded, that meant the "crawfish go backwards from dat day till dis." The poison worked literally in the case of the fish, but it is hard not to connect its magic with the theme of challenging time's forwards march. The entire message revolved around Growey's desire to regain his youth, and his willingness to destroy others to achieve this.[41] Such a tale serves as an illuminating example of how age shaped social conflict, and community relations, in the American South.

* * *

[41] "The Story of Grumma Growey or Why the Crawfish Goes Backward," Archibald Smith Family Papers, AC 1988-0012M, Box 19, Folder 3–1–007, GSA.

Aged conjurers were at times able to exploit fear of punishment to assert themselves over the wider community and to maintain status despite the physical decline associated with the aging process. Historians such as Sharla Fett have stressed that aging brought respect for conjurers, given that "spiritual potency increased as the approach to death brought them closer to the ancestors." This has been perceived as part of wider social norms, where "proper respect for one's elders figured powerfully within the behavioral code of enslaved African Americans, and individuals who transgressed that code walked on dangerous ground."[42] This part of the chapter, however, seeks to emphasize the different types of challenges aged conjurers faced in the community. Not all enslaved people were convinced about the claims of supernatural power from their elders and were willing to walk "on dangerous ground" by openly dismissing their pretensions to power. Lorenza Ezell told his WPA interviewer that during slavery conjurers were "'garded as bein' dangerous" but he personally regarded them as "jes mos'ly fake." Ezell claimed that he "could be a conjure doctor and mek plenty money," but this was not to his taste. As Ezell put it, "dat ain' good." Despite personal skepticism of conjure, as well as his cynicism toward its practitioners' motives, Ezell believed that it was a common tactic of the aged to try and enforce respect: "Iffen some de ol' folks p'int dey finger at you, it scare' you to dea'f. You mos' likely go git all de neighbors to go beg dem not put no bad trubble on you."[43] Ezell's claims indicates that elders needed to use a variety of tactics to enforce respect, and that they could not expect to take it as a given.

Ezell was not alone in dismissing supernatural claims, with other respondents highlighting the failure of aged conjurers to make good on their promises of protection from the violence of slavery. Albert J. Raboteau asserted that "slave conjurers kept their credibility and their authority because their power worked," emphasizing the practical and psychological tools they applied to survive skepticism if they failed in specific cases.[44] Stacey Close noted the charms of elderly conjurers "did not always work," but he did not interrogate how such failure was evaluated by members of the community and potentially used to denigrate the aged party. Although Close generally insisted that conjurers "commanded respect in the slave community," this was not a given and the authority of a conjurer could be publicly, even permanently, undone when rhetoric did not match reality.[45] Aunt Silvia Witherspoon expressed the

---

[42] Fett, *Working Cures*, 55, 88.   [43] Rawick (Ed.), *AS, Supp.*, Ser. 2, 4.3, 1329.
[44] Raboteau, *The Invisible Institution*, 281.   [45] Close, *Elderly Slaves*, 23.

incredulity of the community when Monroe King, an "ole" conjurer who
extorted food and provisions from the Black community so that "he
wouldn't conjure dem," was unable to set himself free after being jailed
for theft. As Witherspoon put it:

I ain't never understood it, he got tuk off to jail for stealin' a mule, an' us n***rs
waited 'roun' many a day for him to conjure hisself, out, but he never did. I guess
he jus' didn't have quite enough conjurin' material to git hisself th'ough dat stone
wall. I ain't never understood it, dough.[46]

Witherspoon may have been deliberately obfuscating, but others were less
willing to extend the benefit of the doubt when these failures occurred.
Ben Chambers of Alabama personally suffered when the old woman
whose advances he had rebuffed used a harmful powder on him, but he
was less credulous over the wider claims of conjuration. According to
Chambers, "Dey was a ol' man on de place what was a conjur' man. He
mek out like he could keep de marster from whippin' you. He mek dis and
dat pow'ful toby." Chambers stressed, however, this was an easily proven
falsehood, and that "de trouble was maybe dey git whip' de very fus' day
dey wear dat toby."[47] As Dave Harper told his WPA interviewer when
asked about conjure: "You know dat if he could do any tricks he would
keep dem from whipping him or selling him and dey couldn't do dat or dey
would have done it long time ago." Conjure, and by extension its practitioners, were not worth Harper's time: "I don't pay no 'tention to it."[48]

The consequences of failure were especially serious when aged conjurers made specific claims of protection on account of their powers,
which of course came at a heavy price for the believer. In these instances,
enslaved people sometimes positioned these figures as either deluded or
deceitful. Both scenarios involved a repudiation of the reputation of the
elder in the community and typically ended with their status diminished.
Julia Henderson of Edgefield, Georgia, recalled the time an "old hoodoo
man" provided a root for a young man hoping to avoid physical punishment but that it came to no avail. The young man was nearly beat to death,
and his experiences led to a public dismissal and outright rejection of the
power of the aged conjurer. Henderson intimated the elder was lucky it
remained a rejection in words and not deeds: "Tom thow'ed dat root jus'
as far as he could and when he met de old hoodoo man, he give him a good
cussin', cause de hoodoo wouldn' work!"[49] This was the end of the "old

[46] Rawick (Ed.), *AS*, 6, 431.   [47] Rawick (Ed.), *AS*, *Supp.*, Ser. 2, 3.2, 673–5.
[48] *FWP*, *10* (Missouri), 167.   [49] Rawick (Ed.), *AS*, *Supp.*, Ser. *1*, 3.1, 322.

hoodoo" man's power over Thom; such failure also likely extended into how the wider community perceived him. In another instance of spiritual overreach, Horace Overstreet described to his WPA interviewer the time an old woman bought a bag of sand from a conjurer with the promise this would save her a whipping, but revealed how this was found to be fool's gold: "dat same day she git too uppity and sass de massa, 'cause she feel safe. Dat massa, he whip dat n***r so hard he cut dat bag of sand plumb in two." This led to a wider decline in the power of the conjurer among the enslaved. As Overstreet put it, "dat ruint de conjure man business."[50]

Formerly enslaved people at times insisted that, rather than serve as respected elders who looked out for the community, conjurers only cared for themselves, and this led to tension. Annie Stanton claimed that hoodoo doctors were "agoin' 'round foolin' folks out ob dey money," while Squire Irvin insisted there "aint nothing to none of them Hoo-Doo doctors neither. They is just highway robbers and should be run out of the country."[51] Both respondents claimed a general disbelief in the power of such figures and cast aspersions on their motive – this was not delusion but deceit. Celestia Avery reveled in the comeuppance of an aged conjurer who sought to exploit the needy when discussing the matter with her WPA interviewer. Avery claimed that an old conjurer "told Alec [her cousin] that Anna [his wife] wuz poisoned, but if he would give him $5.00 he would come back Sunday morning and find the conjure." Alec was skeptical and decided to take precautions here. As Avery put it, Alec "wuz wise and bored a hole" in the floor in order to spy on the conjurer. On the Sunday the conjurer came back and the safely hidden Alec found his suspicions well grounded: "as Alec watched im he dug down in the ground a piece, then he took a ground puppy, threw it in the hole and covered it up." The conjurer then began digging, until, lo and behold, he discovered the charm and claimed it had been planted by someone seeking to do Anna harm. The ruse failed, however, and conjure tricks, let alone the man's advanced age, proved to be no protection: "Alec wuz so mad he jumped on that man and beat him most to death." Avery claimed that this was not the first time this Black elder had tried to extort those in need, recalling that "they say he did that all the time and kept a lot of ground puppies."[52] It was, however, likely the last time. Although some ex-slaves believed conjurers had genuinely tried to help (or do harm) but were

---

[50] Rawick (Ed.), *AS*, 5.3, 161.
[51] Rawick (Ed.), *AS*, 6, 355; Rawick (Ed.), *AS, Supp.*, Ser. 1, 8.3, 1087.
[52] Rawick (Ed.), *AS*, 12.1, 30.

simply unable to do so, others viewed these elders as fraudsters willing to trample over others simply to better their own circumstances.

* * *

Those who believed in conjure were sometimes depicted as lacking the "correct" religious faith, or even intelligence. Some of these claims plausibly reflect the dynamics of the WPA interviews, and select interviewees' efforts, or concerns, in presenting an image associated with racial uplift and "civilization," but they can also be used to explore hierarchies and contested status in the Black community. George Washington Miller, for example, explained that "we didn't believe in hants and laughed at others who were superstitious." Miller dismissively reported that "some superstitious negroes wore charms, but we didn't countenance anything like that."[53] Ank Bishop of Alabama claimed that "dis here voodoo an' hoodoo an' sperits ain't nothin' but a lot of folk's outten Christ," while Mandy Jones of Mississippi similarly believed her Christian faith marked her as superior to those who had practiced conjuration: "daddy an' mammy brought us up in the fear of the Lawd." While she had "heered of hoodoos," she "don't believe in 'em."[54]

Some ex-slaves directly stated how belief in conjuration and witchcraft reflected intergenerational divides in slave communities and distinguished the old from the young. This sometimes entailed a negative assessment of the aged party. Fred James told his WPA interviewer that "some of de old folks did believe in spooks, but I don't know much about dem," while Mark Oliver insisted that he refused to believe the elders who sought to scare him: "The old folks told us all sorts of stories about hants and ghosts. They said I was so hardheaded they couldn't scare me."[55] Betty Cofer responded to a WPA interviewer's question on conjure by explaining that she "don't know much about spells an' charms," and indicated this was because of her youth in slavery: "Course most of the old folks believed in 'em."[56] Peter Ryas told his WPA interviewer that "dey was ol' mens on us plantation w'at lots of de peoples t'ink was witch mens" and recalled their claims that "dey t'ink dey could put a mou'f (bad mouth) on you" and do harm. Ryas held such views in short shrift, dismissively recording how "dey t'ink dey say t'ings and tek yo' skin right off and all

[53] Rawick (Ed.), *AS*, *Supp.*, Ser. 1, 9.4, 1492.
[54] Rawick (Ed.), *AS*, 6, 36–7; Rawick (Ed.), *AS*, *Supp.*, Ser. 1, 8.3, 1231–3.
[55] Rawick (Ed.), *AS*, 3.3, 15; Rawick (Ed.), *AS*, *Supp.*, Ser. 1, 9.4, 1667.
[56] Rawick (Ed.), *AS*, 14.1, 170.

sich foolishness" but that this was merely the ranting of old fools. Indeed, belief in conjuration provided evidence of a wider intergenerational divide: "I can't tell you much 'bout dat foolishness 'cause I was too li'l. I neber was 'roun' no very ol' people."[57] In Ryas's telling, conjuration was a foolish belief of a generation whose ways and days were done.

When Aaron Russel of Louisiana explained to his WPA interviewer that it was only "de old n***rs [who were] scart of hants," he similarly relayed how the younger members of the community not only did not share these beliefs but, moreover, used them to embarrass their elders:

Us young'uns takes de long rawhide string and makes de tick-tack on de cabin roof where Tom and Mandy livin'. I climbs de tree 'bout 50 foot high back de cabin and holds de string. It go thump on de roof, 'bout darktime. Tom and Mandy settin' in dere, talkin' with some folks. Us keep thumpin' de tick-tack. Tom say, "What dat on de roof?" Dey stops talkin'. I thumps it 'gain. Mandy say, "Gosh for mighty! What am it?" One n***r say, "De hants, it de hants," and dem cullud folks come 'way from dere right now.

This mockery of the elders caused much mirth for the children, but also for their enslaver, with Russel explaining how he "hears de massa laugh for to split de sides." No physical harm became of Tom and Mandy, and it was clearly a joke to the children, but the elders were evidently stung by the event: "dey wouldn't stay in de cabin dat night, no, sar, dey sleeps in de yard."[58] Russel's comment on the matter – "us young'uns have de fun with de old n***rs" – suggests the need for caution when encountering claims of reverence for elders from those who were young in slavery, as well as the need to recognize how conflict might erupt between young and old on account of disrespect, both perceived and real.

Cornelia Robinson of Alabama recorded how "us had a old quack herb Dr. on de place," but that he offended others on the plantation and they took revenge. This man's tools were eventually used against him, with Robinson noting how some "bad boys went up to his house one night and poured whole lot of his medacine down him and you know dat old man died too next day."[59] The lack of fear over the man's abilities was telling, with a clear sense that this was trickery, not sorcery, and that the physical powers of youth would prevail over his deceit. Those who had once been accorded respect on account of their powers could find themselves pushed off their pedestal by rivals or from those who did not accept their claims of legitimacy. Henry Pyles described how "Old Bab Russ" had held court in

---

[57] Rawick (Ed.), *AS, Supp.*, Ser. 2, 8.7, 3400.   [58] Rawick (Ed.), *AS*, 5.3, 271.
[59] Rawick (Ed.), *AS, Supp.*, Ser. 1, 1, 353–4.

the community on account of his perceived spiritual powers. According to Pyles, "all the young bucks and wenches was mortal 'fraid of him!" This power was soon discovered to be illusory and was brought to light in direct conflict with younger members in the community. Russ "was hoeing in a field and got in a squabble about something with a young gal name Polly," and he sought to make an example of her: "After while he git so mad he reach up with his fingers and wet them on his tongue and point straight up and say, "Now you got a trick on you! Dere's a heavy trick on you now! Iffen you don't change your mind you going pass on before de sun go down!" The references to the age of Russ and the youth of Polly speak to concerns with generational shifts. Notwithstanding his earlier claims that the young were "mortal 'fraid" of Russ, they clearly found the threat amusing. The other elders begged for relief: "All de young n***rs looked like they want to giggle but afraid all, and the old ones start begging old Bab to take the trick off." Polly, however, was neither overawed nor impressed: "She knocked him down, and he jest laid there kicking his feet in the air and trying to keep her from hitting her in the head!" Aging could invert expected gendered power dynamics related to violence and physical confrontations, with elderly men surprised to find they were no longer perceived of as physically capable by all and sundry, and this reveal had significant impact on an elder's standing among their peers. This public humiliation, Pyles acknowledged, "kind of broke up Bab's charm."[60]

On occasion, conflict associated with conjuration, and an apparent tension between the spiritual power of the aged and the physical prowess of their rivals, escalated to tragic effect. Frederic Knight recently argued that antebellum Black Americans commonly acknowledged that "black women elders possessed exceptional spiritual power," and used this to assess the supportive relationships Black people forged in both slavery and freedom.[61] The case heard by the congregation at the Welsh Neck Baptist Church, South Carolina, in the summer of 1826 shows the complex power dynamics relating to spiritual force and social cohesion. The congregation heard a lurid tale of the murder of Rachel, an "aged woman." Rachel was beaten to death by Jim and Plenty, two enslaved men, who were aided and abetted by Jim's wife, Shine. The murderers claimed self-defense, with Mariam, Plenty's wife, testifying that "Plenty had threatened to whip Rachel, for having tricked or injured him; being as he believed a Witch,"

---

[60] *FWP, 13* (Oklahoma), 246, 248–9.
[61] Knight, "Black Women, Eldership, and Communities of Care," 555.

and that she, too, believed "the deceased had slighted her." This sense of injury was not enough of a threat to dissuade them, however, and Jim and Plenty determined to punish the "witch" they believed had crossed them. Jim brought "a Grape Vine to [Mariam's] house, & she understood it was for Plenty to beat the Old Woman with." In this first instance Mariam convinced them to leave Rachel alone, but she was unable to keep them at bay forever. Just days before the murder, the old woman lamented the position she was in and insisted she had done no wrong. Creassy, another witness, explained that she and Rachel "had often talked together about it, & the dec.d lamented her case. She had tried to console her. They had talked together the day before her death; & she then declared herself innocent of the Charge of Witch Craft."[62] We cannot know for certain whether Rachel was telling the truth here, or had practiced conjuration in this instance or prior to this. She was perceived by others in the community as a danger, but this danger was balanced with her obvious physical weakness, as well as her apparent social isolation from the Black community. The threat of conjuration was not enough to prevent her being abused and eventually beaten to death. Aged conjurers were clearly understood as potential threats in the community, with distrust of or disbelief in their powers shaping tension among the enslaved in ways that complicate visions of unquestioned support for elders.

* * *

Aged conjurers sometimes had their beliefs rejected by those who associated personal and political development for Black Americans with the uptake of Christianity and its necessary replacement of the belief systems of old. The focal point of conflict here revolved around the (deemed) necessary replacement of "superstition" with Christianity, and the conflation of one with progress and the other with the past. Religious rivalries have been noted by scholars, but few have explicitly addressed how far this rivalry could be framed as evidence of generational tension in the Black community.[63] Nor, too, have these scholars emphasized how

---

[62] May 21, 1826, Baptist Church, Welsh Neck, Society Hill, Records, 1737–1935, SCL.

[63] Dusinberre, *Strategies for Survival*, 132, 136. See also Raboteau, *Invisible Institution*, 286–88, where he believed the two coexisted and served vital complementary functions. Attention to some of the tensions associated with progress and "civilization" when set against religion/conjure, if not explicitly noting issues surrounding age and generational shifts, can be found in David Murray, *Matter, Magic, and Spirit: Representing Indian and African American Belief* (Philadelphia: University of Pennsylvania Press, 2007), esp. chps 1 and 2, and in Chireau, *Black Magic*, 121–50.

a rejection of conjure – with its clear association with older slaves – complicates any notion of unquestioned respect for Black elders. This type of challenge clearly comes across in fugitive narratives and postbellum accounts influenced by and connected to the program of racial uplift. Henry Clay Bruce's memoir was intimately shaped by his connection to this political and religious platform and, as part of this, he regularly discounted the significance of conjure and "Africanisms." Indeed, Bruce was delighted to be able to report on "the advancement made upon the stronghold of ignorance, superstition and voodooism by the Colored people." Bruce compared this progress with the power conjurers had wielded in slavery, noting with disdain that these "conjurors held whole neighborhoods, as it were in such mortal fear, that they could do unto the Colored people anything they desired, without the least fear of them telling their masters."[64] He was also clear that these individuals used their "powers" for personal advancement at the expense of the credulous, weak, and wicked: "I readily recall many instances wherein they were fleeced out of their little valuables or money by professional humbugs, known as conjurors." Bruce was not one to fall for such tricks, and he recounted the failings of aged conjurers with some pleasure.

One such tale related to the dramatic fall in fortunes of an "old, whiteheaded, crippled man, known as a conjurer," with the specific reference to physical frailties associated with age conjuring up an image of "yesterday's man," whose beliefs and practices stood in the way of progress. This elder had convinced the enslaved people on his original plantation of his powers, "and among those who belonged to his master he was believed and feared." The community was then forcibly relocated to Missouri, where they merged with an existing plantation, and his new audience was distinctly unimpressed: "the Colored people in that vicinity laughed at him, defied his threats, and denounced him as an old humbug." The old man found himself cast from his pedestal and it was not long before everyone came to see that the emperor had no clothes: "when those who believed in him saw him defied and denounced, and his inability to carry out his threats, they took courage and denounced him too." This man's status as a respected elder had relied on fear, and, once this fear had gone, so too had his standing in the community. The man attempted to

---

[64] Henry Clay Bruce, *The New Man: Twenty-Nine Years a Slave. Twenty-Nine Years a Free Man* (York: P. Anstadt & Sons, 1895), 52–3. On uplift and race, see also John B Meachum, *An Address to All the Colored Citizens of the United States* (Philadelphia: King & Baird, 1846), 17–20.

save face by claiming the changed locale impacted upon his powers, but he was left a pitifully reduced figure. This public humiliation of an old crippled man, forcibly removed to a new locale and grappling with this new reality, occasioned no sympathy from Bruce: "The truth of the matter was, that the Colored people in that state were more intelligent than those from whence he came, and therefore could not be easily humbugged."[65] The conjurer had previously frightened his peers, and it is hard not to see why this might be a site of pleasure for his victims. Nonetheless, it is also possible to believe this was a strategy applied by an old man seeking to survive slavery, and to recognize the violence that structured his actions here too. It was clear to Bruce, however, that conflict was necessary for the old to make way for the new, and collective uplift was more important than an individual's pain.

Louis Hughes also presented the rejection of conjure as a necessary repudiation of the old ways, equally personified in the dismissal of an enslaved elder. Hughes noted how belief in "voo-doo bags" was "handed down from generation to generation" and that he received his from an "old slave who claimed that it had power to prevent any one who carried it from being whipped." Hughes personally discovered the limits of such power, and any lingering belief in the "superstitions of a barbarous ancestry" was whipped out of him.[66] As part of his broader message of uplift, similar to that of Bruce, Hughes set out a divide between the beliefs of the young and the old, and clearly elevated the former over the latter. In Hughes's framing, the rising generation would and should reject this "barbarous ancestry" in order to rise in freedom. Irving E. Lowery explained that on antebellum plantations enslaved people "very often connected sickness and death with voodooism or conjuration," and noted that such beliefs were expressed and taught by elders on the plantation: "This belief and practice of voodooism and conjuration originated in Africa, and was brought over to America when the native African was brought here and made a slave." Lowery appeared relieved to be able to approvingly quote the University Encyclopedia, however, in noting that, "as the negroes advance in education[,] the belief is dying away."[67] The temporal language of advancement and progress required a removal of the beliefs of old; the dying away here related to the elders as much as to their ideologies.

Douglass's statement of elder respect is a constant refrain on studies of old age and slavery, but this claim ran into tension in practice. This was

---

[65] Bruce, *The New Man*, 58–9.   [66] Hughes, *Thirty Years a Slave*, 108.
[67] Lowery, *Life on the Old Plantation*, 81.

true of conjuration, as when Douglass portrayed his "old advisor" Sandy's beliefs in root magic as emblematic of his inferiority; the growing dismissal of Sandy's perspectives in subsequent editions of his life story indicate how perceptions of progress could depend on the repudiation of belief systems of old.[68] Yvonne P. Chireau has noted that "according to his famous autobiography Frederick Douglass was once assisted by a Conjure man named Sandy," and that "the assurance that these individuals supplied to persons who accepted the virtue of supernatural actions was often indispensable."[69] This emphasis on acceptance and assistance, however, risks understating the difficulties Douglass faced in assessing his elder's belief system and, indeed, his direct repudiation of it in explaining his success in physical resistance and in finding the confidence necessary to resist further.

According to literary scholar Sarah Elizabeth Ingle, Douglass encountered Sandy "at his lowest point, physically, spiritually, and psychologically."[70] Douglass had been hired out to Mr. Covey, known locally as a "n***r breaker," and this reputation was tragically well earned.[71] At this juncture he met and "fell in with Sandy Jenkins," who then served as an "old advisor." Sandy told Douglass, "with great solemnity," to return to Covey with the defense of "a certain *root*" that would protect him from punishment. In his first narrative Douglass simply explained that he "at first rejected" Sandy's idea (and belief system) as he doubted its efficacy.[72] In *My Bondage and My Freedom* (1855), and repeated in both the 1881 and 1892 versions of *The Life and Times*, however, Douglass was more abrupt in recording his rejection as being animated by his belief that his elder's views were "very absurd and ridiculous, if not positively sinful."[73] Douglass did, eventually, accede to Sandy's

---

[68] Douglass, *Narrative of the Life*, 70. Tensions between Sandy and Douglass have been addressed in, for example, Eric Sundquist, *To Wake the Nations: Race in the Making of American Literature* (Cambridge, Mass.: Harvard University Press, 2003), 130; Sarah Elizabeth Ingle, "Conjured Memories: Race, Place, and Cultural Memory in the American Conjure Tale, 1877–1905" (PhD Dissertation, College of William and Mary, 2004: https://libraetd.lib.virginia.edu/public_view/zw12z565t); Murray, *Matter, Magic, and Spirit*, 36–7; Kameelah L. Martin, *Conjuring Moments in African American Literature: Women, Spirit Work, and Other Such Hoodoo* (New York: Palgrave Macmillan, 2013), 57. These scholars address the tensions over belief systems, but they do not explicitly consider age or generational strife.

[69] Chiraeu, *Black Magic*, 15.   [70] Ingle, "Conjured Memories," 15.

[71] Douglass, *Narrative of the Life*, 57.

[72] Douglass, *Narrative of the Life*, 69–70. Italics in original.

[73] Douglass, *My Bondage and My Freedom*, 239; Douglass, *Life and Times* (1881), 134 (1892), 170–1.

suggestion, with the stated intention of trying "to please" Sandy present in all the narratives.[74] Later versions, however, provided information on Douglass's latent sense of superiority to his elder and his belief that he was merely pandering to superstition: "Sandy was so earnest, and so confident of the good qualities of this weed, that, to please him, rather than from any conviction of its excellence, I was induced to take it." In such a way, Douglass implied he already knew better than the older man; claims of respect for elders did not extend to actually *believing* in Sandy's powers, suggesting some limits to rhetorical claims of respect toward the aged. Sandy, in fact, understood Douglass saw himself as superior, telling the younger man: "'book-learning,' he said, 'had not kept Covey off me' (a powerful argument just then), and he entreated me, with flashing eyes, to try this."[75]

Douglass did eventually triumph over Covey, and his victory was "the turning point in my career as a slave." Ingle claims that the 1845 narrative is ambiguous regarding whether Douglass believed Sandy had helped, with references to the root's possible "virtue" and wonderment over how he managed to find "the spirit" to fight back, but this would appear to miss the clear rejection of Sandy's powers found in the same text.[76] In a later account of Sandy, Douglass described his elder as "'a clever soul,'" but insisted Sandy's root was not the occasion of his triumph: "We used frequently to talk about the fight with Covey, and as often as we did so, he would claim my success as the result of the roots which he gave me." Douglass gave short shrift to the wisdom of his elder: "This superstition is very common among the more ignorant slaves."[77] Douglass did not call Sandy "ignorant" in the postbellum accounts, but references to the conflict with Covey removed the ambiguity of the earlier text. Ingle notes that Douglass's decision to fight back was framed almost as a deliberate rejection of the notion of supernatural assistance, and a wider assertion of supremacy over his elder's worldview: "I now forgot my roots, and remembered my pledge to stand up in my own defense."[78] Douglass no

---

[74] Douglass, *Narrative of the Life*, 70; Douglass, *My Bondage and My Freedom*, 239; Douglass, *Life and Times* (1881), 134 (1892), 170–1.

[75] Douglass, *My Bondage and My Freedom*, 239; Douglass, *Life and Times* (1881), 134 (1892), 170–1.

[76] Ingle, "Conjured Memories," 17. Douglass, *Narrative of the Life*, 71.

[77] Douglass, *Narrative of the Life*, 80; Douglass, My *Bondage and My Freedom*, 238–41, 264.

[78] Ingle, "Conjured Memories," 33–5; Douglass, *My Bondage and My Freedom*, 242; In the 1881 and 1892 *Life and Times*, on 136 and 173 respectively, the encounter is described as

doubt respected Sandy's deep "insight into human nature, with all his superstition," but he refused to accept his elder's views on the world.[79] Douglass's willingness to repeatedly state that Sandy practiced an "absurd" belief system – with reference to the man as "a genuine African" marking out generational distinctions – and to assert the supremacy of his own worldview instead, suggests how generalized claims of respect for elders among the enslaved could minimize generational conflict among Black Americans both in and out of slavery.

When Henry Bibb recalled his use of conjure when courting Malinda, his later wife, he expressed annoyance at his failings here, and in his credulity toward conjurers. Bibb also noted how he was tricked by two enslaved elders into thinking he could avoid whipping and his anger at the deception practiced on him. After the first charm failed Bibb claimed to believe "there was no virtue" in conjuration, but his desire for protection left him open to exploitation and another "old slave" was all too happy to oblige. This elder "told me the first one was only a quack, and if I would only pay him a certain amount in cash, that he would tell me how to prevent any person from striking me." Bibb found no relief here either: "The old man had my money, and I was treated no better for it." Bibb gave voice to intergenerational tension by noting that his credulity related to the expectation of respect for elders. According to Bibb, he only believed in such tales because he "had been taught by the old superstitious slaves, to believe in conjuration." Bibb acknowledged "it was hard for me to give up the notion, for all I had been deceived by them," but he clearly now viewed them as either deceptive or deceived, and positioned himself above the superstitious aged. Historian Rebecca Fraser notes that Bibb continued to have faith in charms "despite their lack of success," but this understates Bibb's emerging sense of superiority over the older generation.[80] Having won his freedom through flight, Bibb positioned himself and the rising generation of Black Christian activists above the superstitious mass of enslaved: "Such is the superstitious notions of the great masses of southern slaves. It is given to them by tradition, and can never be erased, while the doors of education are bolted and barred against them."[81] The rejection of tradition was personified in Bibb's rejection of the aged conjurers he had known and eventually dismissed.

"I now forgot all about my roots, and remembered my pledge to stand up in my own defense."
[79] Douglass, *My Bondage and My Freedom*, 239–40; Douglass, *Life and Times* (1881), 135 (1892), 170.
[80] Fraser, *Courtship and Love*, 50.   [81] Bibb, *Narrative of the Life*, 27–8, 30, 31.

William Wells Brown likewise painted an image of generational divide and potential tension when younger members of the community looked to their elders and saw superstition to be cast aside. Wells Brown described the significance other slaves gave to "Uncle Frank," an old man who told peoples' fortunes. Wells Brown was not overtly disrespectful, but he indicated his own distrust of soothsaying and his disdain for those who believed it: "Whether true or not, he had the name, and that is about half of what one needs in this gullible age." Wells Brown accepted that many of Frank's predictions came true but undercut the claims of superstitious powers by noting how obvious most of these claims were. Wells Brown, for example, was told he was going to be free, but "that in trying to get my liberty, I would meet with many severe trials." Wells Brown was not impressed by his sagacity: "I thought to myself, any fool could tell me that!"[82] Outward expressions of respect for elders therefore sometimes masked dismissive rhetoric or behavior toward individuals who were perceived as foolish, deceitful, or deluded, with a sense that a generational shift, and movement away from conjure beliefs, was the sign of advancement and progress for Black Americans.

Similarly judgmental comments were made in Wells Brown's relaying of the tale of the "Goopher King," Dinkie, discussed earlier in the chapter. Wells Brown understood the mass of enslaved people were frightened of Dinkie's power, but he clearly articulated his own disbelief, conflated Christianity with civilization and progress, and dismissed those who believed in conjure as remnants of the old ways: "forty years ago, in the Southern states, superstition held an exalted place with all classes, but more especially with the blacks and uneducated, or poor, whites." Wells Brown dismissed Dinkie, who "was about fifty years of age, and had lost an eye, and was, to say the least, a very ugly-looking man," but was yet more derisive in describing the Voudou "Queen" of St. Louis, "a short, black, old negress" in the 1840s. Wells Brown witnessed her popular midnight meetings but was distinctly unimpressed by his elder, describing her performance as providing little more than "a certain amount of gibberish and wild gesticulation." Wells Brown cast such beliefs as belonging to "the ignorant days of slavery," and insisted that his own generation were, or at least should be, moving beyond the old ways: "It is not strange that ignorant people should believe in character's of Dinkie's stamp; but it is really marvellous that well-educated men and women should countenance whatever to such delusions as were practiced by the

[82] Wells Brown, *Narrative of William Wells Brown*, 91–3.

oracle of 'Poplar farm [*sic*].'"[83] The structural forces discussed in earlier chapters means we rarely hear from those who believed themselves to be conjurers, but it is hard not to imagine that such mockery and disdain occasioned reflection and sadness on the part of the elders involved. Conjurers, or simply those who believed in conjure, might struggle when their skills were no longer recognized or valued and perceive this as evidence of their general separation from the community. Sarah Felder of Mississippi explained that in slavery "de old peeple uster try ter 'kunjer' sum uf de slaves," and, while insisting she was no conjurer herself, underscored how the passing out of the skills and knowledge of the old was a painfully personal realization: "I am old now an' de young folks doan think we old folks hev eny sense, but dar is er lotter things I culd tell dem iffen I wuld, but when dey git sick dey hev ter buy store bought medicine." Feldner clearly mourned the passing of time, and the passing out, of her generation's skill sets and believed this reflected a wider dismissal of the old on the part of the young.[84]

* * *

Aged conjurers, both women and men, attempted to use spiritual powers to try and enforce the respect they believed was owed to them by younger members of the community. The aged party was sometimes successful in reinforcing their status, and securing their venerated position, but this entailed conflict and even violence toward others in the community. Not all enslaved people, however, accepted the powers of aged conjurers, or respected them uncritically on account of their age. Instead, they were willing to undermine or actively usurp their aged antagonist, to use negative tropes of aging to belittle those who did believe, or to cast conjuration as the "superstition" of an older generation that must be cast aside in the way of progress. These conflicts around conjuration underscore how far respect for some elders needed to be enforced, rather than received uncritically; the dynamic and contestable nature of social hierarchies shaped by intergenerational tension; and the broader significance of age as a vector of power in slave communities of the American South.

---

[83] Wells Brown, *My Southern Home*, 68–71, 77.
[84] Rawick (Ed.), *AS*, *Supp.*, *Ser. 1*, 7.2, 723–4.

6

"The summer of my life was passing away"

Resistance, Old Age, and Surviving Slavery

Solomon Northup, a free Black man from New York State, was lured to Washington, DC, by two white men in 1841 on the pretense of a job. Instead, they drugged him; when he awoke, he was in the pen of the notorious slave trader, William H. Williams.[1] Northup was beaten into accepting a new name and a new life as the enslaved man "Platt," eventually ending up in Louisiana on the plantation of Edwin Epps. Northup sought escape by writing a letter to his friends in the North, trusting a local white man to deliver the news of his condition and seek their aid. He was betrayed, and only avoided punishment by exploiting his enslaver's paranoia that this "poor" white man was attempting to trick him.[2] Despite avoiding a whipping, Northup was left devastated at this turn of events. His dream of escape ended, Northup recalled how hope which "sprang up in my heart" was thus "crushed and blighted." After this failure, Northup feared that he would remain enslaved until death: "The summer of my life was passing away; I felt I was growing prematurely old; that a few years more, and toil, and grief, and the poisonous miasma of the swamps would accomplish their work on me – would consign me to the grave's embrace, to moulder and be forgotten."[3]

In describing his fears of remaining enslaved forever, Northup applied a language of aging and embodied time. He noted how the harsh conditions

---

[1] Further information on Williams can be found in Jeff Forret, *William's Gang: A Notorious Slave Trader and His Cargo of Black Convicts* (New York: Cambridge University Press, 2020).

[2] On class and slavery, see Timothy J. Lockley, *Lines in the Sand: Race and Class in Lowcountry Georgia* (Athens: University of Georgia Press, 2001); Jeff Forret, *Race Relations at the Margins: Slaves and Poor Whites in the Antebellum Southern Countryside* (Baton Rouge: Louisiana State University Press, 2006); Keri Leigh Merritt, *Masterless Men: Poor Whites and Slavery in the Antebellum South* (New York: Cambridge University Press, 2017).

[3] Northup, *Twelve Years a Slave*, 234–5.

of slavery would see him pass prematurely through the "seasons" of life and send him resignedly to the grave. The use of aging in the context of plans for resistance – perhaps the most well-studied and politically charged dimension of enslaved histories – serves as a fitting coda to this reconsideration of the position of enslaved elders and the fluidity to, and contested nature of, solidarity in slave communities. Northup's anguish at the thought of living and dying enslaved revealed his fear of growing old in slavery, but perhaps also his pity for those who had done so. Northup's depiction of old age as a remorseless period of decline was not just applied metaphorically. Northup noted how he lived on the Bayou Boeuf plantation with two older slaves named Phebe and Abram. Phebe was a "sly old creature" who navigated the system in a cunning fashion. "Old" Abram cut a more forlorn figure.[4]

The language of "patriarch" which Northup used to describe Abram perhaps spoke to wider expectations of reverence for elders that historians have typically emphasized when discussing enslaved community norms. Enslavers may have neglected or devalued older slaves, but this scholarship insists enslaved communities did not.[5] As has been shown, however, enslaved elders held complex positions in slave communities. In the context of resistance, intergenerational tension sometimes shaped networks of solidarity and personal relationships among the enslaved; younger slaves could look to their elders and view them as people who had survived, but who had also failed to successfully resist their enslavement. Elders, in contrast, could see and hear of youthful plans of resistance and remember personal failure, trauma, and strife in the wider community. A dichotomy of resistance/ survival is problematic, but these comparative assessments were applied by contemporaries and affected personal and political relationships in and out of slavery. Fugitive authors who utilized the pitiful figure of the aged enslaved to press for immediate action against slavery made implicit or explicit judgments about the actions and identities of those who lived and died enslaved. The complex life stories of the aged were subsumed within a teleological narrative bound by the celebration of fight and flight; the inherent subjectivity of the narratives meant the aged could not speak for themselves. Instead, elders were employed as foil characters whose suffering moved the protagonist to action. Northup, for example, clearly believed the ravages of time had impacted upon Abram and sought to avoid his fate. There was a firm emphasis on decline and loss: Abram "had been athletic,

---

[4] Northup, *Twelve Years a Slave*, 187.
[5] Berry, *Price for Their Pound of Flesh*, 131, 147. Barclay, *The Mark of Slavery*, 41. On generalized claims of respect for elders, see introduction.

and more keen and powerful than the generality of his race, but now his eye had become dim, and his natural force abated." Abram was weakened by a life in chains, and he suffered abuse when he could not work to the pace expected of him: "so was he perplexed continually, and sighed to think that he was growing aged and going to decay."[6] Northup cared about and valued Abram. However, the overwhelming image was of a man to be pitied and a fate to be avoided. When Northup wrote of his concerns of growing old and dying in slavery, it is hard not to imagine he was looking at Abram and fearing a similar end. Northup, famously, did escape his bondage. He acknowledged, however, that he left a community behind, notably naming Patsey and his elders, Phebe and Abram. They were hidden "from [Northup's] eyes forever."[7] They were likewise hidden from ours.

Northup's vision of age-related decline, his horror at the thought of growing old in bondage, and his depiction of Abram as decaying before his eyes suggests that enslaved elders – and the idea of growing old in slavery – could be viewed with a mixture of pity, fear, and perhaps even disdain from within the quarters.[8] Enslaved people and antislavery activists who valorized resistance could look to enslaved elders and see people whose paths were to be avoided, rather than people to be emulated or venerated. A close examination of how elders were portrayed in the context of resistance, focusing particularly on fight or flight, concludes this section of the book and asks us to address the fissures that developed among people navigating an oppressive environment and to understand how the violence of slavery filtered into and influenced enslaved peoples' responses to one another.[9] It reveals how competing strategies of resistance and survival were depicted and understood as being shaped by age and embodied time in slavery.

* * *

[6] Northup, *Twelve Years a Slave*, 187.   [7] Northup, *Twelve Years a Slave*, 308.
[8] Northup, *Twelve Years a Slave*, 187.
[9] While recognizing the significance of more subtle acts of dissidence and cultural survival, fight and flight were clearly understood by contemporaries as resistance, with attendant legal, political, social, and cultural significance. As the Georgia Supreme Court ruled when justifying the murder of a runaway who fought back against his pursuer, "This slave was in a state of revolt, as every slave is when in open and forcible resistance to lawful authority." *Hart* v. *Powell*, 18, Ga. 635 (1855), 641. On debates over what constitutes resistance, as well as the politics of such depictions, see James C. Scott, *Weapons of the Weak: Everyday Forms of Peasant Resistance* (New Haven: Yale University Press, 1985), and *Domination and the Arts of Resistance: Hidden Transcripts* (New Haven: Yale University Press, 1990); Camp, *Closer to Freedom*; Dusinberre, *Strategies for Survival*; Lussana, *My Brother Slaves*; Kellie Carter Jackson, *Force and Freedom: Black Abolitionists and the Politics of Violence* (Philadelphia: University of Pennsylvania Press, 2020).

Statistics from the colonial era through to the 1860s reveal that long-term flight in the American South was overwhelmingly the preserve of "young men in their teens and twenties." In their quantitative analysis of 2,000 runaway adverts between 1790–1816 and 1838–60, John Hope Franklin and Loren Schweninger recorded how 78 percent of runaways in the first period were boys and men between the ages of thirteen and twenty-nine, with only a small drop to 74 percent in the later period. Those forty and older only made up 5 percent in the early period and 6 percent in the later period.[10] Similar demographic trends were evident in the breakdown of enslaved women, where fugitives in their teens and twenties "represented more than two-thirds of the women in both periods." Older slaves – men and women – certainly engaged in truancy, but long-term flight was clearly affected by age.[11] Some contemporaries specifically recalled the failures of older fugitives compared to the successes of others. Sarah Benjamin, of Clavin Parish, Louisiana, noted that while "a few did run away to de north," an older man was memorably unsuccessful: "one ole man run away, he traveled all night den de next mornin he hollered and he was home. Dey put him in stocks, he had been travelin in a circle all night and kem back ter whar he started from."[12] Samuel Ringgold Ward, who escaped slavery in Maryland, clearly outlined how contemporaries understood the dynamics of long-term flight: "fugitives coming to Canada are, the majority of them, young, single men. Many more young than old, many more male than female, come."[13]

These demographic trends can possibly be explained by the shifting responsibilities of enslaved people as they grew older and had families, but also by the practical difficulties and physical hardships which both

---

[10] John Hope Franklin and Loren Schweninger, *Runaway Slaves: Rebels on the Plantation* (New York: Oxford University Press, 1999), 209–13. See also Marvin L. Michael Kay and Lorin Lee Cary, "Slave Runaways in Colonial North Carolina, 1748–1775," in Darlene Clark Hine and Earnestine Jenkins (Eds.), *A Question of Manhood. "Manhood Rights": The Construction of Black Male History and Manhood, 1750–1870* (Bloomington: Indiana University Press, 1999), 130–65, 134–5; Michael P. Johnson, "Runaway Slaves and the Slave Communities in South Carolina, 1799 to 1830," *William and Mary Quarterly*, 38.3 (Jul., 1981), 418–41.

[11] On truancy, see Camp, *Closer to Freedom*.

[12] Rawick (Ed.), *AS, Supp.,* Ser. 2, 2.1, 256.

[13] Samuel Ringgold Ward, *Autobiography of a Fugitive Negro: His Anti-Slavery Labours in the United States, Canada, & England* (London: John Snow, 35 Paternoster Row, 1855), 151.

long-term flight and truancy occasioned on the body and mind.[14] Fugitives such as Andrew Jackson commonly stressed the fortitude – physical and mental – needed to endure flight, asking his reader to:

Imagine yourself on the road, flying for liberty among your enemies, alone, unarmed, trembling at every step with the greatest anxiety and with fear. Sleeping during the day alone in the wilderness, exposed to wild beasts and serpents; hungry, lame, and almost spirit broken – starting up from a disturbed sleep, with frightful dreams of arrest and torture. Hunted and chased during the day by men of no heart, and with ferocious dogs, trained to the pursuit – the faint gleams of freedom now shooting up, and then lost in darkness – hope and despair constantly filling your heart.[15]

Successful flight required stamina and strength, and these were qualities antebellum Americans, Black and white, associated with youth. In contrast, bodily powers were expected to fail as people aged. In Nathanael Emmon's 1842 treatise on piety and old age, he described aging as a process of "sinking under the decays of nature," while Barnard Van Oven noted how "the decline of life begins, and is shown by most unmistakable signs, signs affecting the corporeal frame."[16] Black Americans commonly spoke to and through the same discourse, with William Walker, enslaved in Virginia and Louisiana, positioning old age as a return to the dependency of infancy: "Life begins and ends in dreams, from the sleeping smile in the cradle to the babbling over the death bed as worn out nature sinks into the last sleep of all."[17] Ike McCoy informed his WPA interviewer that "when we get old we get helpless," and offered reflective commentary on his own frailties: "I'm getting feebler every year. I see that. Times goiner be hard ag'in this winter and next spring."[18] A loss of strength and stamina associated with aging – whether premature or "normal" – had serious repercussions for enslaved people hoping to flee bondage.

Limited endurance associated with old age could limit the chances of successful flight. Kittie Stanford noted how "Old Henry run away

[14] Gutman, *The Black Family*, 264–70; Franklin and Schweninger, *Runaway Slaves*, 210; Johnson, "Runaway Slaves," 418–19. Gendered norms associating caring with femininity restricted – but did not inevitably stop – enslaved women seeking flight. See King, "Suffer with them till death"; Morgan, *Laboring Women*, 166–96; Camp, *Closer to Freedom*, 35–60.

[15] Jackson, *Narrative and Writings of Andrew Jackson*, 12–13.

[16] Emmons, "Piety, a Peculiar Ornament to the Aged," 497; van Oven, *On the Decline of Life*, 38; Caldwell, *Thoughts on the Effects of Old Age*, 14.

[17] William Walker, *Buried Alive (Behind Prison Walls) for a Quarter of a Century: Life of William Walker* (Saginaw: Friedman & Hynan, 1892), 36.

[18] Rawick (Ed.), *AS, 10.5*, 13–14.

and hide in the swamp and say he goin' stay till he bones turn white," but underscored that he was unable to stick to this: he "come back when he get hongry and then he run away again."[19] Carey Davenport, who was enslaved in Texas, sadly recalled the fate of one elderly runaway. "Old man Jim" was a regular truant, but his luck eventually ran out: "he run away one time and it was so cold his legs git frozen and they have to cut his legs off."[20] Lula Wilson, born in Kentucky, described her mother's stories of an "old man what the n***r dogs chased and et the legs near off," and compared this with her own power and prowess: "She said she was chased by them bloody hounds and she jus' picked up a club and laid they skull open."[21] This inversion of the commonly masculinized narrative of fight and flight suggests that enslaved people understood age was a relation of power that upended cultural scripts of gendered resistance.

Some enslaved people clearly believed the reduced endurance associated with old age negatively affected the chances of resistance, but also the self-belief required to succeed in these endeavors. Archy Moore explained how he only survived the punishment meted out after a failed runaway effort – and had the desire to try again – on account of this energy: "My youth and the vigor of my constitution had carried me through it."[22] Ambrose Douglas likewise explained to his WPA interviewer how his plans for escape centered around his youthful idealism: "'I was a young man,' he continues, 'and didn't see why I should be anybody's slave.'" The inverse of this statement, and the clear inference, was that time and accumulated suffering risked leading to resignation instead. Douglas, in fact, described how he was "so scared" of his next enslaver that he "didn't ever run away from his place." Thankfully, however, "the war was near over then" and Douglas "was as free as I am now."[23]

Moving to episodes of direct violence, fugitive slave narratives and abolitionist accounts frequently associated violent resistance with youth and manhood in particular.[24] Indeed, a significant number of enslaved

---

[19] Rawick (Ed.), *AS*, *10.6*, 214.   [20] Rawick (Ed.), *AS*, *4.1*, 282.

[21] Rawick (Ed.), *AS*, *5.4*, 191.   [22] Hildreth, *The Slave: or Memoirs of Archy Moore*, 89.

[23] Rawick (Ed.), *AS*, *17*, 102.

[24] On some of the historiographical tensions relating to the gendering of violence, see White, *Ar'n't I A Woman?*, 62–91; James Oliver Horton and Lois E. Horton, "Violence, Protest, and Identity: Black Manhood in Antebellum America," in Hine and Jenkins (Eds.), *A Question of Manhood*, 382–95; Camp, *Closer to Freedom*; Berry, *"Swing the Sickle for the Harvest is Ripe"*; Doddington, *Contesting Slave Masculinity*, ch. 1.

men's narratives portray violence against their oppressors as a transitional moment in their lives. Frederick Douglass famously used violence to demonstrate "how a slave was made a man," but he was not alone.[25] Jourden Banks likewise established how resistance proved masculine identity and strength, as well as a concomitant emasculation of his enemies. In his recollections of heroically beating his overseer and enslaver, he described how he left them "literally crawling about on the ground like a pair of ricketty boys." Banks further established the gendered ramifications of resistance by telling the shocked crowd of enslaved men around him: "Farewell, men. I have done my work. I am going to leave. Look out for yourselves. If you undertake to do anything, do it like men. If I am brought back, it will be when I am dead."[26] The discursive framing of his actions as proof of manhood, while his assailants were instead reduced to "boys," speaks further to the connections drawn between age, identity, and resistance.

* * *

If historians have generally agreed about the connection of youth or "prime" adulthood with both fight and flight, they have been less direct in assessing how enslaved elders could be held up negatively by those who conducted such activities and constructed resistant identities. Scholars have generally argued that, while less likely to flee themselves, elders were guides in planning, offered advice and encouragement (both moral and practical), and generally strengthened the solidarity of the slave community.[27] Such examples are clearly visible in contemporary recollections. Moses Roper described how, after he fled from his plantation, he found "an old slave hut" where he met an "old man" of around seventy or eighty. He informed this man that he "had a very bad master, from whom I had run away; and asked him, if he could give me something to eat." This man "cheerfully" gave him the only food he had.[28] As elders frequently held cooking roles , they were perhaps best placed to provide victuals to

[25] Douglass, *Narrative of the Life of Frederick Douglass*, 65–6.
[26] J. W. C. Pennington, *A Narrative of Events of the Life of J. H. Banks, an Escaped Slave, from the Cotton State, Alabama, in America* (Liverpool: M. Rourke, Printer, 1861), 63.
[27] Franklin and Schweninger, *Runaway Slaves*, 67–71; Camp, *Closer to Freedom*, 47–50; Close, *Elderly Slaves*, 34–6, 99–101; Herbert C. Covey and Paul T. Lockman Jr., "Narrative References to Older African Americans Living in Slavery," *Social Science Journal*, 33.1 (1996), 31–2; Berry, *Price for Their Pound of Flesh*, 147; Lussana, *My Brother Slaves*, 35, 136, 142–3; Ferguson, "The Elder(ly) 'Uncle' in Plantation Fiction," 49–50, 66; Barclay, *The Mark of Slavery*, 119.
[28] Roper, *A Narrative of the Adventures and Escape of Moses Roper*, 65.

runaways.[29] David Holmes, who was interviewed in England after escaping slavery, noted how he was aided by two older slaves who had cared for him after being separated from his family. Their love and compassion extended to aiding him in flight:

> The old woman began to get me ready for a start. She gave me a big corn-loaf she had just got baked, and a little rum and tobacco, and when all was quite still she and the old man set me outside, and told me to run for it. We cried a good deal, but we couldn't stop long about it.[30]

Assistance could extend beyond food and moral support. William Robinson noted how an "old woman eighty years old" showed him the best route to avoid the prowling overseers and told him "how to decoy the blood hounds" by rubbing "onions on the bottoms of my feet and run, and after running a certain distance to stop and apply the onions again, then when I came to a large bushy tree, to rub the trunk as high up as I could reach, then climb the tree."[31] In Jamie Parker's flight from bondage, "a white-headed old man" was instrumental to the success of the young runaways. "Old Archy" took them in, clothed and fed them, before guiding them to a safe passage. Archy even used the expectations that old age equated with infirmity to trick a band of suspicious patrollers, who simply couldn't envision an elderly man as a potential rebel.[32] When one of their party was captured, Archy stressed a willingness to sacrifice his own safety to ensure the young runaways had the chance of freedom: "'I must take your place, for I am an old man, and never expect to get free. If you stay here until you follow the star again, you may be free, but if you turn back' – the old man concluded the sentence by an ominous shake of the head."[33] Archy believed he was unable to escape himself on account of his age and wider responsibilities, but his assistance was vital to the runaways from beginning to end. The heroic framing of such actions in the narrative spoke to broader abolitionist messages relating to the necessity of collective resistance in the face of oppression.

* * *

[29] Close, *Elderly Slaves*, 26. [30] Blassingame (Ed.), *Slave Testimony*, 297–8.

[31] William H. Robinson, *From Log Cabin to the Pulpit, or, Fifteen Years in Slavery* (Eau Clair: James H. Tifft, 1913), 62. On the use of hounds, see Tyler D. Parry and Charlton W. Yingling, "Slave Hounds and Abolition in the Americas," *Past & Present*, 246.1 (2020), 69–108.

[32] Pierson, *Jamie Parker, the Fugitive*, 107–11, 152–7.

[33] Pierson, *Jamie Parker, the Fugitive*, 132–6, 135.

Accounts of support, respect, and even the personal heroism of enslaved elders are commonly addressed or alluded to by historians of slavery. What is less commonly assessed is how older slaves could be portrayed as a hindrance when planning escape – whether through fear, resignation, or weakness – and be positioned as people who had to be left behind in the quest for freedom. In the course of planning the failed Camden uprising in South Carolina, 1816, "old Jack" expressed doubts about the rebels' chances of success but was informed his opinion barely mattered: "they did not want old people to take any part in it."[34] The reports of an abortive insurrection in North Carolina took such disregard further: "they were to kill the White men & old negro women & take the white women for Wives & the young negro Girls."[35] We must recognize that enslaved testimony on insurrection was mostly recorded under duress, and that such information more often than not corresponds with what the torturer wants to hear.[36] While remaining cautious over the truth of such claims, the fact they were recorded as *plausible* highlights a perception of elders as unlikely rebels among both enslaver and enslaved. Charlie Davenport witnessed the consequences of intergenerational insurrectionary disputes, describing to his WPA interviewer how a planned uprising in Natchez failed after encountering resistance from plantation elders. Jupiter, the leader, "harangued de ole folks but dey wouldn't budge," and he was forced to flee after "de sheriff en a passel ob men" arrived on the scene. He did not get far: "My granny tole me next day dat dey kotch him hidin in a bayou en hung him on a limb."[37] The risks of rebellion were revealed here: Davenport's recollections reinforce the rationale behind the exclusion of individuals like "Old Jack" but also validate his skepticism of success. Such examples suggest further how resistance and survival could be framed by enslaved people as separate and even – for those with long memories of failed uprisings – mutually exclusive.

Abolitionist narrators, fugitive slaves, and occasionally the elders themselves asserted that advancing age had diminished people's will or

---

[34] Kershaw District, Court of Magistrates and Freeholders, Trial Papers, L28225, Case 20, L28225, SCDAH. On the conspiracy, see Ford, *Deliver Us From Evil*, 174–9.

[35] North Carolina Slave Collection, 1748–1922, Slavery Papers, Conspiracy, 1802, PC. 1629, NCDAH.

[36] On insurrectionary testimony, see, for example, Michael P. Johnson, "Denmark Vesey and His Co-Conspirators," *William and Mary Quarterly*, 58.4 (October 2001), 915–76; "Forum: The Making of a Slave Conspiracy, Part 2," *William and Mary Quarterly*, 59.1 (January 2002), 135–202.

[37] Rawick (Ed.), *AS, Supp.*, Ser. *1*, 7.2, 569–70.

capacity to resist. During James Redpath's travels in the South, he spoke to men who claimed they were unable to escape due to their age. One man in North Carolina had always hoped to be free, but believed that it was impossible now: "Well, massa, you's a funny man – dat am a fact. I's *would* like to be free; but it's no use, massa – it's no use. I's a slave, and I's been one sixty years, and I 'specs to die in bondage." Another man, aged thirty-seven, explained to Redpath that he no longer even contemplated escape, utilizing a language of embodied time to explain his reluctance: "I wouldn't run the risk now of trying to escape. It's hardly so much an object, sir, when a man's turned the hill. Besides, my family. I might be sold away from them, which I won't be, if I don't try to run away – leastways till I'm old." This man clearly recognized that he was not chronologically "old." However, the language of having "turned the hill" denotes an inexorable decline associated with aging.[38] To return to Northup's phrasing, the "summer" of this man's life had passed away and – in his mind – the possibilities of escape had gone with it.

A degree of fatalism, if not acceptance, of slavery could be understood and articulated through a binary discourse of youth/old age. Frances Kemble recounted how, on her ex-husband's rice plantation in Georgia, a young woman had attempted flight to avoid a punishment. She was captured and badly beaten. The young woman longed for escape, albeit only temporarily, but her grandmother considered such a plan futile. Her long memories and harsh experiences invoked a degree of resignation: "taint no use – what use n***r run away? – de swamp all round; dey get in dar, an' dey starve to def, or de snakes eat 'em up – massas's n***r, dey don't neber run away."[39] Allen Crawford, born in 1835, acknowledged his own grandmother's anguish when confronted with the personal costs of insurrection, claiming that she had attacked Nat Turner following his failed uprising: "Grandma ran out and struck Nat in the mouth, knocking the blood out and asked him, 'why did you take my son away?' [I]n reply Nat said, 'your son was as willing to go as I was.' It was my Uncle Henry dat they was talking about."[40]

Such fatalism was not always received sympathetically by those who yet hoped for freedom. Fugitives such as Jermain Wesley Loguen, who

---

[38] Redpath, *The Roving Editor*, 40–1. [39] Kemble, *Journal of a Residence*, 248.
[40] Perdue et al., *Weevils in the Wheat*, 76. For general information on Turner's rebellion, see Patrick H. Breen, *The Land Shall Be Deluged in Blood: A New History of the Nat Turner Revolt* (New York: Oxford University Press, 2015); Vanessa Holden, *Surviving Southampton: African American Women and Resistance in Nat Turner's Community* (Urbana: University of Illinois Press, 2021).

escaped slavery in Tennessee in his early twenties, would likely have responded to Crawford's mother in a similarly dismissive way. Loguen, who continually stressed the need for outright resistance in his fugitive account, bluntly recorded his resentment at the inaction of the elders he found himself travelling with before sale. Loguen clearly equated "old" here with acquiescence: "the older slaves were habituated to their imprisonment and severe exercise under the lash of the driver, and had looked their wrongs and prospects so long in the face, that they were drilled into a state of sad contentment." Loguen, however, was still capable of flight and, after escaping bondage, marshalled his own experiences into the forceful promotion of direct action in the fight against slavery. Fugitives, himself included, "present[ed] a sample of a strong and hardy and bold race – whose manly qualities the severest tyranny cannot subdue," with the clear steer that these were the people to applaud and elevate over those who had been "drilled into a state of sad contentment." According to Loguen, "slavery can endure no longer than its victims are submissive and servile."[41] In this framing, enslaved people had a personal and collective responsibility to resist rather than "submit" to oppression. They had to do so, moreover, before the march of time robbed them of the vigor required for resistance.

Former slaves who had not escaped bondage also connected resistance with the energy of youth, with John McCoy, enslaved in Texas, noting his enslaver didn't "whip de old folks none, jes' de young bucks, 'cause dey wild and mean."[42] Others stressed the laudable nature of resistance as compared to accommodation and bemoaned what they took to be the limited response of their forebears. Minta Maria Miller, who recounted her experiences of being sold on the auction block, noted how she responded with fury to the abuse she received. When explaining why she – unlike those sold alongside her – was willing to take such a risk, she recalled: "I felt mad. You see I was young then, too young to know better."[43] Miller intimated that she grew to acknowledge the power imbalance that limited the space for resistance, but others were less generous in their assessments. Ryer Emmanuel remembered being scornful about her mother's seeming passivity: "I remember, we chillun used to

---

[41] Loguen, *The Rev. J. W. Loguen*, 72–3, 122, 241–2. On political tensions among abolitionists surrounding the use of violence in fighting slavery, see Sarah Roth, *Gender and Race in Antebellum Popular Culture* (New York: Cambridge University Press, 2014); Carter Jackson, *Force and Freedom*, 15–48.
[42] Rawick (Ed.), *AS*, 5.3, 33.   [43] Rawick (Ed.), *AS*, 5.3, 86.

set down en ax Ma all bout dis end at. Say, 'Ma, yunnah couldn' do nothin?' She say, 'No, white people had us in slavery time.'" Emmanuel confidently asserted that she would not have accepted her mother's fate and instead would have taken the rebel's route in adulthood: "if I had been big enough to get whip in slavery time, I know I would have been dead cause I would have been obliged to fight dem back en dey would kill folks for dat in dem days."[44] Lucretia Alexander, another WPA interviewee, however, revealed how such an attitude might be worn down. Alexander's father "wouldn't take nothin" from his oppressors while in his prime but he could not fight forever. His final overseer – "Bad man" Phipps – took advantage of his declining powers as he aged: "My father was an old man when Phipps was an overseer and wasn't able to fight much then."[45] Alexander understood the impossibility of fighting against time itself and underscored how age and embodied time shaped resistant actions and identities in bondage.

Fugitive authors and ex-slaves could, therefore, associate the effects of aging in slavery with fatalism and use this to explain – but also to cast judgment on – any seeming rejection of resistance from their older peers. After Frederick Douglass and his "band of brothers" were captured following their escape attempt, he was accosted by the elderly mother of one of his group. She did not applaud him in his efforts to gain freedom:

The lady made the following parting address to me, looking and pointing her bony finger at me. "You devil! you yellow devil! It was you that put it into the heads of Henry and John to run away. But for you, you long legged yellow devil, Henry and John would never have thought of running away."

This woman's desire to protect her son indicates the complex coexistence of different support networks within slave communities. To keep a family together – albeit subject to the capricious will of enslavers – might necessitate rejecting fight or flight. This woman clearly felt the runaways made the wrong choice, and her response suggests an understanding of the incompatibility of some elements of resistance with survival, whether at an individual, familial, or communal level. Douglass, however, gave her short shrift: "I gave the lady a look, which called forth a scream of mingled wrath and terror, as she slammed the kitchen door, and went in, leaving me, with the rest, in hands as harsh as her own broken voice." The references to her "bony finger" and "broken voice" speak to common signifiers of old age and underscore how the generalized language of elder

---

[44] Rawick (Ed.), *AS*, *2.1*, 25.   [45] Rawick (Ed.), *AS*, *8.1*, 33, 37–8.

respect employed by enslaved people could hide a multitude of negative views on aging and on individual elders themselves.[46] The earlier framing of Douglass's resistant group as being made up of "five young men, guilty of no crime, save that of preferring liberty to a life of bondage," suggests the connections contemporaries drew between age, resistance, and survival in slavery, as well as a sense of whose actions need be applauded and acted upon.[47]

In some cases, older slaves served as the counterpart to the heroic identity of the young resistor and were relegated to the sidelines of narratives in favor of more active resistance to slavery. The fact that Redpath so vividly applauded enslaved men who rebelled, and denigrated those who refused to as having "that certificate of soulless manhood which the Southrons style, when they refer to the existence of the passive-obedience spirit in a slave, 'a good character,'" indicates the stark comparisons some contemporaries drew between resistance and survival.[48] Louis Hughes, who escaped with his wife and children during the Civil War, explicitly equated old age with fatalism, recalling how, on his plantation, insurgent whites aimed to inspire insurrection but mostly failed: "They would say encouragingly to them: 'Ah! You will be free some day.' But the down-trodden slaves, some of whom were bowed with age, with frosted hair and furrowed cheek, would answer, looking up from their work: 'We don't blieve dat; my grandfather said we was to be free, but we aint free yet.'" Hughes did not blame these people for their resignation. However, he clearly framed their outlook as negative compared to the more heroic rebels, those "who were bright and had looked into the matter, [and] knew it was a curse to be held a slave – they longed to stand out in true manhood – allowed to express their opinions as were white men."[49] Hughes, of course, was one such man.

A lack of support – perceived or real – might cause tension in the community. More problematic, however, were those occasions when enslaved elders were considered by their peers as having so resigned themselves to their condition that they would betray rebels and resistors. George, a runaway from Mississippi, dealt harshly with a man who caught him returning to the plantation for supplies, with his animus suggesting a fear of treachery. George beat "Old Frank ... so severely that tis thought he can't live." Their enslaver was forced to take "5 pieces of

---

[46] See, for example, van Oven, *On the Decline of Life*, 43.
[47] Douglass, *My Bondage and My Freedom*, 294–5.   [48] Redpath, *The Roving Editor*, 10.
[49] Hughes, *Thirty Years a Slave*, 78–9.

bone out of his head," and such an assault had lasting impact. A month later, Eliza Magruder wrote how "poor Old Uncle Frank seems to be rather desponding [sic]."[50] One former slave interviewed by the WPA in the 1930s, named only as Charlie, explained how he and his brother Jeff sought escape during the Civil War but that "an old slave man ... tried to dissuade us from running away." This man had seemingly accommodated himself to his condition, telling the brothers "that Mars' Bill was our friend and that we never had to want for anything." The runaways rejected his arguments and continued on their way, but they feared his acquiescence extended beyond mere words. Charlie, in fact, recommended they pick up the pace in case the "old man ... would tell them which way we went." Charlie did not explain his reasoning to his brother because he feared such betrayal would lead to retribution: "I didn't let on that I was thinking this until we left because Jeff was mighty fiery and he might have got suspicious of the old man and done him dirt with his axe."[51]

Occasionally, runaways and rebels were correct in viewing elders as a danger. In 1792, Toney, an enslaved man "advanced in years," informed on a conspiracy of slaves to run away.[52] Local whites sought to reward Toney with manumission. When Jordan attempted to steal meat from his enslaver's smokehouse in Isle of Wight County, Virginia, it was "the old negro woman" who oversaw the site that first alerted the enslaver, leading to his capture and punishment.[53] Elders were at times deliberately tasked with such surveillance by their enslavers, with an expectation that a separation from the main body of workers – whether real or imagined – might encourage a lack of solidarity. Others believed trusted elders were better able to convince (or coerce) their fellow slaves to remain on the plantation. Sometimes these trustees were praised for their actions by family members. Robert Prout noted that "Daddy was a ole man, and Mawster Barton made him a sort of leader among de slaves" on his plantation, while Lindsey Faucette of North Carolina explained that her enslaver made "Uncle Whitted de overseer kase he wuz one of de oldest

[50] Eliza L. Magruder Diary, June 3, 1857, July 29, 1857, Mss. 654, LLMVC.

[51] Rawick (Ed.), AS, 19, 115.

[52] Petition to free Toney, December 6, 1792, Pasquotank County, Records of Slaves and Free Persons of Color, 1733–1866, 1892, Bonds and Petitions to free slaves, 1778, 1792, 1793–1800, Box CR.075.928.009, NCDAH.

[53] November 2 1819, Auditor of Public Accounts, Condemned Blacks Executed or Transported Records, Condemned Slaves, Court Orders, and Valuations, 1810–22, Misc., Reel 2551, Frame 919, LVA.

slaves he had an' a good n***r."[54] While subject to the caprice of their enslavers, some enslaved elders likely believed holding disciplinary roles provided a degree of security and that this was a safer option to outright resistance.[55]

This strategy for survival was rarely celebrated by rebels and runaways who encountered aged trustees. Charles Ball recorded his annoyance at how, after being recaptured following his escape, he was "put under the charge of an old African negro, who was instructed to give immediate information, if I attempted to leave the field."[56] Peter Smith, who escaped slavery from Tennessee, initially believed that "young slaves were not to be trusted – that they were more apt to betray the wanderer," and thus deliberately "chose the older ones for favors." His views were likely altered after betrayal by "an old colored man" whom he had asked for food. This was presumably not the first time the older man had betrayed runaways, as his enslaver trusted him to guard Smith overnight. It was only by exploiting this old man's inability to keep awake at his post that Smith was able to escape.[57] The positive depiction of Smith's vigor and strength compared with the image of an elderly man falling asleep at his station indicates how age was understood by contemporaries as shaping the dynamics of resistance to slavery.

In a similar fashion, William Grimes noted how his efforts to escape slavery in Virginia were frustrated by older slaves in trustee roles. He was – as in the case of Smith – able to escape on account of their relative debility. When making his plans, Grimes confided in "old George" that he was planning to escape. Rather than applaud his endeavors, George "immediately repaired to the house of the overseer and informed him of my intention to run away in the morning." Grimes was then guarded overnight by "old Daniel." His enslaver's overseer was also known as "old Voluntine," which suggests he believed older slaves could be relied upon to enforce orders on the plantation. Throughout his night in captivity, Grimes pleaded with "Old Daniel" to set him free. He refused, but when Grimes saw an opportunity, he seized it: "I gave a jump, and Daniel after me, but my step was as light as the snow flake." Grimes was young and fleet of foot, but the old man was not: "the last glimpse I had of Daniel

---

[54] Rawick (Ed.), *AS, Supp., Ser.* 2, 8.7, 3193–4; Rawick (Ed.), *AS,* 14.1, 303.
[55] Further information on the complex choices made by trustees can be found in Doddington, *Contesting Slave Masculinity,* ch. 2; Kaye, *Joining Places,* 143–4; Dusinberre, "Power and Agency in Antebellum Slavery," 144; Rosenthal, *Accounting for Slavery,* 36.
[56] Ball, *Slavery in the United States,* 491.   [57] Blassingame (Ed.), *Slave Testimony,* 247–8.

showed him prostrate over a log."[58] As in Smith's account, the serious promotion of resistance over accommodation in the narrative was accompanied with a tragi-comical image of youth triumphing over age. Both accounts suggest that a lack of support from elders, whether on account of resignation or, worse, accommodation to bondage, was a factor that enslaved people considered when planning fight or flight.

On occasion, the end result was less comical. In April 1852, Giles County, Virginia, an enslaved woman named Aunt Sally was murdered by Mahala, aged around fifteen. The "old negro woman" was found "lying in the floor, a handkerchief was over her head and near her was a pool of blood," and the first responders "concluded that [an] axe had been used to kill the old woman." Mahala had sought to hide her actions in plain sight, as one witness recalled she "came to my store room . . . said that someone has murdered Sally. She was crying." The blood on her apron, combined with a number of witnesses recalling her oft-voiced disgust toward her elder, meant this story did not hold up for long. Letitia, an enslaved woman, recalled Mahala informing her "that old Sally was the meanest negro in the world, and that she intended to kill her some of these days," while another witness overheard her saying she could "kill [Sally] as freely as ever she eat a mouthful of bread. That she could cut her up with an axe." Mahala's motives speak to the tensions surrounding solidarity and supervision identified earlier. Mahala simply did not trust her elder; she informed one witness her reason for "hating [the] deceased was that she was in the habit of telling news on her," and told another "that she could kill Aunt Sally as far as eat a piece of bread – that Sally always told on her every thing she did." Mahala was true to her word, and the elderly informant found the costs to conflicting loyalties in the quarters.[59]

* * *

When recounting their efforts at flight, enslaved fugitives noted how they identified allies and established plans for escape in small groups. On occasion, fugitive authors made direct reference to older slaves who refused to leave, bemoaning their choices, or using them as cautionary tales. The abolitionist James W. C. Pennington explicitly compared Jourden Bank's actions in flight to those of his parents. Pennington

---

[58] Grimes, *Life of William Grimes*, 10–12.
[59] Executive Papers, Joseph Johnson, Box 411, April 1852, 228, LVA.

established a clear hierarchy between having survived slavery and actively fighting it:

This young man loved his parents; but at an early age his spirit revolted at the idea of ending his days in the condition of his mother, or in slavery. This aversion to the condition of slavery grew with his growth and strengthened with his strength, until like a giant he broke his chains, and sought and found his way to a free country.[60]

Banks undoubtedly loved his parents. He refused, however, to share their fate and grow old in chains, and this choice was applauded and elevated by his abolitionist allies. Harriet Tubman, the famed rebel and leader of runaway bands *into* the South, eventually rescued her parents from this same outcome. Her initial flight, however, was occasioned by the fear that she would grow resigned to bondage as her parents had: "She saw the hopeless grief of the poor old mother and the silent despair of the aged father, and already she began to revolve in her mind the question, 'Why should such things be?' 'Is there no deliverance for my people?'" Tubman took flight before it was too late and left without informing her parents out of fear their distress would hinder her escape: "the old woman was of a most impulsive disposition, and her cries and lamentations would have made known to all within hearing Harriet's intended escape."[61] In both instances the aged parents – father and mother – were cast as the foil to the hopeful young rebel, where age and accumulated suffering appeared as factors limiting the possibilities of resistance. Such depictions suggest the necessity of considering how age, alongside gender, played a significant role in shaping attitudes toward resistance and in affecting identities and personal relationships for enslaved people navigating slavery.

An emphasis on comparative vigor – even courage – as the province of the young was evident in William O' Neal's representation of his attempted flight from Louisiana. O' Neal explained how, aged only fifteen, to be "free was the ambition of [his] life." He believed, however, that as "he was only a boy," he needed an experienced guide: "he must have a confederate older than himself." O' Neal thought he had identified the ideal coconspirator in Russ, a "tall and square-shouldered" man of thirty-two. Despite initially thinking he needed the wisdom of an older

[60] Pennington, *Narrative of Events of the Life of J. H. Banks*, 5–6.
[61] Sarah H. Bradford, *Harriet, the Moses of Her People* (New York: Geo. R. Lockwood and Son, 1886), 15–16, 29.

confederate, O' Neal took the lead and envisioned himself as the leader. He directly connected his confidence here to his relative youth:

No thought of failure had entered his mind. Does not the poet say: "In the bright lexicon of youth, which Fate reserves for a brighter manhood, there is no such word as fail." He believed that the thought of freedom was as sweet to Russ as it was to him, and never doubted that Saturday night would find him ready to go. Having indomitable courage himself, he was ready to judge Russ by the same standard.

Russ, however, failed to show up the first night they had planned to escape. He repeated this until O' Neal lost confidence in him entirely, with Russ's "failure" to accept the risks of fight and flight occasioning no sympathy from O' Neal: "The last interview was a most stormy one, and ended by William telling Russ that he had played the craven, and that he could have no further confidence in such a man . . . With this comment we will drop Russ into that oblivion which his cowardice so richly deserves."[62] The word "fail" was, apparently, understood by the older man and O' Neal condemned him for it.

Ex-slaves who detailed how elders counselled patience or submission thus crafted a comparative assessment of enslaved peoples' actions in navigating their oppression. James Curry managed to escape from slavery in North Carolina, but, when later explaining his actions in the antislavery paper *The Liberator*, noted that others in his neighborhood had consciously rejected this path. Curry recalled how the enslaved people and the wider community had heard via the "grapevine" that Martin Van Buren, if elected president, would "give all the slaves their freedom," and this led to "great rejoicing." One elderly slave declared that freedom would now be granted: "One old man, who was a Christian, came and told us, that now, all we had got to do, was, as Moses commanded the children of Israel on the shore of the Red Sea, 'to stand still and see the salvation of God.'" Curry was unconvinced by this passive stance and was proven right in his suspicions: "Mr. Van Buren was elected, but he gave no freedom to the slaves." Curry was unwilling to wait for freedom to be granted and stressed the need for agency and activism instead. He expected his readers to understand and applaud his choices: "I firmly resolved that I would no longer be a slave. I would now escape or die in the attempt. They might shoot me down if they chose, but I would not live a slave."[63] In making resistance a choice, and in

---

[62] William O' Neal, *Life and History of William O'Neal, or, The Man Who Sold His Wife* (St. Louis: A. R. Fleming, 1896), 19–26.
[63] James Curry, "Narrative of James Curry, A Fugitive Slave," *The Liberator*, January 10, 1840.

elevating his own actions in taking flight, Curry applied a hierarchal assessment of enslaved peoples' responses to bondage shaped by age and experience.

Curry did not explicitly bemoan the old man's belief in waiting for freedom, but he did not view such a path as being likely to succeed and instead positioned overt resistance as the active choice worthy of applause. Sojourner Truth likewise established resistance as the active choice worthy of applause but flipped the established antebellum script that associated active resistance with masculinity and more passive behaviors with femininity.[64] Truth was desperate to escape from slavery in New York state but her husband, "who was much older ... preferred serving his time out in slavery, to the trouble and dangers of the course she pursued." There were some positives here, in that he remained with the children, but Truth was clear that his decision was unlikely to lead to stability or safety: "it is comparatively little that they can do for each other while they remain in slavery."[65] Truth's account reveals how far age was understood by contemporaries as potentially overturning antebellum masculinized scripts of resistance to slavery.

Some fugitive authors explained how the treatment meted out to elders, and the consequences of growing old in slavery, provided a warning to younger enslaved people about their own possible fates and precipitated their plans to escape. As noted earlier, Douglass's witnessing of Old Barney's whipping, which he took with a "humble and debasing attitude," and to which he "made no resistance," shocked him to the core and motivated his desire for freedom.[66] James Adams, enslaved in Virginia, made similar links when explaining his flight aged only seventeen. Despite claiming to have not been treated badly *yet*, Adams "had seen older men treated worse than a horse or a hog ought to be treated; so, seeing what I was coming to, I wished to get away."[67] Josiah Henson recalled stopping at a Vicksburg plantation on the way to New Orleans, where he faced sale from his conniving enslaver, and made similar observations over the subjective nature of age. Some of his "old companions" now lived there and Henson was devastated at how "four years in an unhealthy climate and under a hard master had done the ordinary work of twenty." These prematurely aged people "looked forward to death as their only

---

[64] On these cultural scripts, see Roth, *Gender and Race*, 211–13.
[65] Truth and Gilbert, *Narrative of Sojourner Truth*, 63.
[66] Douglass, *Life and Times of Frederick Douglass*, 51.
[67] Drew, *A North-Side View of Slavery*, 19.

deliverance" and Henson became convinced of the need to escape after witnessing their suffering:

If this is to be my lot, I cannot survive it long. I am not so young as those whose wretched condition I have but just seen, and if it has brought them to such a condition, it will soon kill me. I am to be taken to a place and a condition where my life is to be shortened, as well as made more wretched.[68]

In such accounts, enslaved elders served not only as evidence of suffering in slavery, but also as part of people's subjective self-fashioning in the context of resistance and in the broader political calculus for abolitionists. The suffering elder was regarded with sympathy but was by necessity left behind. Jourden Banks, for example, noted how his new overseer in Alabama deliberately used "two of the old hands" to demonstrate his power. Banks noted with pity, but perhaps also a degree of disdain, that they did not even need restraining before abuse: "These men were so completely cowed, that they did not need to be tied at all when flogged. The overseer would just take one of them by the back of the neck, bring him down upon his knees, and with the other hand ply the lash to his back." The men's powerlessness was both personal and political: by using their ill-treatment as the precursor to his own triumphant fight and flight, Banks was suggesting to his readers that this fate could, and perhaps should, be avoided by those who would "act like men."[69]

Solomon Northup recalled how the older slaves on the plantation counselled against resistance on account of their prior experiences. The enslaved man Wiley's decision to abscond to visit another plantation went against "the philosophy of Uncle Abram" and set "the counsels of Aunt Phebe utterly at naught." After being punished for his efforts, Wiley never again attempted escape: "The long scars upon his back, which he will carry with him to the grave, perpetually remind him of the dangers of such a step."[70] Enslaved people who looked at elders might see in them a fate they desperately wished to avoid. In Rankin County, Mississippi, 1854, Jack killed his enslaver while fleeing. He explained his need to escape on account of the permanent damage wrought upon two older slaves and his fears of such an end for himself. His enslaver, William Williams, was "very tyrannical [*sic*]" and "had whipped (Jack's) mother's eyes out, he had also whipped old Solomon's eyes out," and Jack "was afraid of some

[68] Henson, "*Uncle Tom's Story of His Life,*" 67–70.
[69] Pennington, *A Narrative of Events of the Life of J. H. Banks,* 58–9.
[70] Northup, *Twelve Years a Slave,* 236–40.

great injury." Black and white witnesses agreed about the severity of Williams's treatment of his slaves, but Jack's claim of self-defense was anathema to the logic of enslavement. The Court of Appeals rejected the plea for a mistrial, the Governor refused clemency, and Jack was executed.[71]

In the account of Peter Wheeler, a free Black man in New York state, former slaves noted how elders were deliberately abused by enslavers as a means of demonstrating dominance. Susan, a free Black woman in Philadelphia, was kidnapped and sold into slavery in Charleston. She eventually escaped but was scarred by her experiences. Susan noted how the abuse of elders was designed to overawe the rest of the population:

> There was an old man there with a gray head, stripped and drawed over a whipping-block his hands tied down, and the big tears a rollin' down his face, and he looked exactly like some old gray headed, sun-burnt revolutioner; and a white man stood over him with a cat-o'-nine-tails in his hand, and he was to give him one hundred lashes.

This was a public punishment designed to reinforce the enslaver's power: "And he says, 'now look on all on ye, and if you git into a scrape you'll have this cat-o'-nine-tails wrapped round you.'" This old man had suffered terribly in chains – "his back and body was all over covered with scars" – and such violence had worked its terrible charms. He spoke "in kind'a broken language," and "groaned like as if he was a dyin." After this he was put back to work. The punishment lingered in the mind of all those around them; the language of having been "broken" underscores the desolation and despair of (and for) an old man whose only escape would be the grave. Susan feared a similar end for herself, noting that "this spectacle affected me so, I could scarcely git about the house" and that it "wore upon me," to the extent of growing sick and weak herself. The language of "worn" reinforces the tropes of premature aging on account of suffering identified earlier, but Susan was fortunately rescued from this fate by the Quaker family she had worked for in New York. Upon her return, the family cried: "Let us rejoice! for the dead is alive, and the lost is found."[72] Of the old man, however, we hear no more.

* * *

[71] *State of Mississippi* v. *Jack, A Slave*, 1854. Box 5835, Case 7094, MDAH.

[72] Peter Wheeler, edited by Charles Edwards Lester, *Chains and Freedom: Or, The Life and Adventures of Peter Wheeler, a Colored Man Yet Living. A Slave in Chains, a Sailor on the Deep, and a Sinner at the Cross* (New York: E. S. Arnold & Co., 1839), 240–5.

Personal and political tensions relating to resistance were thus sometimes framed as generational conflict in slave communities. Some fugitives recalled that elders had explicitly counselled against resistance by offering their knowledge of punishment, betrayal, and defeat for fugitives and rebels. They aimed to convince their loved ones to avoid such a dangerous path, and such arguments were often tragically accurate. The language used by the protagonists, however, frequently implied regret, even shame, over such counsel and elevated resistance over accommodation by associating the former with courage and the latter with weakness. James Watkins, enslaved in Maryland, recalled how his mother continually argued against flight: "she did all she could to dissuade me from it ... she told me that 'she had been a slave all her life, that all my brothers and sisters were slaves, that I had better be satisfied and remain with them.'" Watkins pitied his mother, describing her as a "Poor woman" who "could not bear the thought of parting with me." He still "resolved to try" and did, in fact, manage to escape. His mother was eventually set free as "she was getting into years and not of much marketable value" to her enslaver. Watkins was delighted to hear of her freedom, but he never saw her again.[73]

Accounts of punishment and the improbability of success were realistic, but such counselling could also be held up as emblematic of the submission of such figures and framed negatively. These negative depictions cut across lines of gender and suggest that enslaved people understood the process of aging as something that would unsettle and undercut gendered identities, values, and even family dynamics. Andrew Jackson, who escaped from Kentucky, clearly loved and valued his grandfather. He also explained how his elder (unsuccessfully) counselled Jackson to accept bondage, telling his grandson "you cannot better yourself; you will be taken and killed or sold; you are now in good standing in the church, and to runaway and be taken will ruin you." Jackson acknowledged the brute force of slavery in shaping such a belief, but he rejected his grandfather's view and revealed the pity, rather than respect, he held for his elder: "This is the nature of slavery ... Yea, all self-respect must be thrown away."[74] In the abolitionist narrative describing the attempts of an enslaved woman named Dinah to avoid the sale of her child, the author applauded this woman's spirited resistance in comparison to her elders. Her grandmother was not so firm and assisted the enslaver in separating mother from child.

---

[73] Watkins, *Narrative of the Life of James Watkins*, 14–15, 30–1.
[74] Jackson, *Narrative and Writings*, 40.

In the eyes of the author, such submission was accounted for by her long memories of slavery, the "chilling effects of age," and her attendant resignation:

But the grandmother, who had felt keenly her own sorrows early in life, through the chilling effects of age in part, but still more from long experience of the hopelessness of all resistance, was able now, without having a muscle of her face disturbed, or shedding a single tear, with her withered hands to deck for the auction-block the child who, for ten years, had been like a dancing sunbeam in that lowly household.[75]

In the eyes of these narrators, both ex-slave and abolitionist, the window for successful resistance, already limited by the brute force of enslavers, only narrowed further as the sands of time ran out. The aged had lost their chance, in these renditions, and nothing could turn back time. The personal tragedy of their submission, moreover, was compounded by a refusal or inability to support others in their resistance. In these depictions enslaved elders – claims of respect notwithstanding – were held up as objects of pity and people whose fates could, and even should, be avoided.

The role Harriet Jacobs's grandmother, Molly Horniblow, played in supporting and protecting Jacobs from abuse is well known by historians of slavery. Horniblow had, in fact, gained notoriety by having "once chased a white gentleman with a loaded pistol, because he insulted one of her daughters."[76] She was also depicted by her family members as someone who had reconciled herself to slavery existing, and as having imparted this message to the children. John Jacobs noted Horniblow's "meekness," while Harriet Jacobs recalled her overall message of resignation: "Most earnestly did she strive to make us feel that it was the will of God: that He had seen fit to place us under such circumstances; and though it seemed hard, we ought to pray for contentment." Harriet and John acknowledged their grandmother's beliefs were determined by a "beautiful faith, coming from a mother who could not call her children her own." They were personally unwilling to accept this fate, however, and ultimately "condemned it."[77] When it came to more specific plans for flight, Jacobs's grandmother likewise served as a foil to resistance. Horniblow's memories of her youngest son Benjamin's failed runaway attempt left scars that shaped her repudiation of resistance, notwithstanding his eventual escape from bondage: "she was strongly opposed to her

---

[75] Simpson, *Horrors of the Virginian Slave Trade*, 34.
[76] Jacobs, *Incidents in the Life*, 47.
[77] Jacobs, "A True Tale of Slavery," 85; Jacobs, *Incidents in the Life*, 28.

children's undertaking any such project, and counselled against it . . . She had not forgotten poor Benjamin's sufferings, and she was afraid that if another child tried to escape, he would have a similar or a worse fate." While Jacobs could not think of anything "more dreadful than my present life," her grandmother frequently counselled patience and submission to bondage, if not to specific abuses from enslavers.[78]

WPA interviewees also recounted memories of older family members counselling against resistance. Molly Reynolds, enslaved in Louisiana, noted how the older slaves on the plantation looked only to death on account of their sufferings. Rather than attempt flight, "some the old ones say we have to bear all, 'cause that all we can do. Some say they was glad to the time they's dead, 'cause they'd rather rot in the ground than have the beatin's."[79] Austin Grant revealed that his elderly grandfather's advice was not to run away but, instead to "work, work and work hard. You know how you hate to be whipped, so work hard!"[80] Martin Jackson of Texas recalled how his father went beyond advising acquiescence, and applied moral pressure to keep him from escaping enslavement: "I spent most of my time planning and thinking of running away. I could have done it easy, but my old father used to say, 'No use running from bad to worse, hunting better.'" Jackson explained how such advice ultimately worked on him: "I think I really was afraid to run away, because I thought my conscience would haunt me. My father knew I felt this way and he'd rub my fears in deeper."[81]

In some instances, enslaved men and women who attempted escape believed their responsibilities to older family members or the wider community were too great to escape, noting their fears that to leave would be to abandon these elders to misery or death. Such claims belie the common proslavery refrain that enslaved people received care from cradle to grave, and serve to underline how enslaved people instead believed growing old in slavery led to suffering and misery. Potential runaways were thus put in an invidious position: in staying to protect otherwise neglected or exploited Black elders, they were forced to witness daily their own potential fate. Despite the harrowing personal toll it took, some enslaved people could not countenance sharing their elders' torment and acknowledged this required leaving them to suffer. Francis Fedric piercingly wrote of his trauma at knowing his mother "would be flogged, old as she was, for my

---

[78] Jacobs, *Incidents in the Life*, 66. On Benjamin's tortures, see 35–8.
[79] Rawick (Ed.), *AS*, 5.3, 241.   [80] Rawick (Ed.), *AS*, 4.2, 84.
[81] Rawick (Ed.), *AS*, 4.2, 189–90.

FIGURE 6.1 *Austin Grant, Age about 90.* United States Texas, 1936. Between 1936 and 1938. Photograph. Courtesy of the Library of Congress, Manuscript Division.

escaping," and understood she would struggle to see past her personal pain to understand his need to escape. Fedric mournfully wrote that alongside her torture, his aged parent would "be distressed that I had left her for ever until we should meet hereafter in heaven," but that he needed to take flight while he still could: "At length I walked rapidly away, as if to leave my thoughts behind me."[82]

Historians commonly note how childcare and parental responsibilities hindered fight or flight, particularly for enslaved women, or stress how elders played important roles in providing for and protecting children. It is commonplace, for example, to see Horniblow's admonition to Jacobs – "Nobody respects a mother who forsakes her child" – in work on gender

---

[82] Francis Fedric, *Slave Life in Virginia and Kentucky; or, Fifty Years of Slavery in the Southern States of America* (London: Wertheim, McIntosh, and Hunt, 1863), 103.

and enslaved resistance.[83] Comparatively less attention has been paid to how elders might use their own advanced age to pressure people into remaining enslaved and the intergenerational tension this might occasion. Jacobs recalled her grandmother's sustained efforts here:

"Linda, do you want to kill your old grandmother? Do you mean to leave your little, helpless children? I am old now, and cannot do for your babies as I once did for you . . . If you go, you will make me miserable the short time I have to live. You would be taken and brought back, and your sufferings would be dreadful. Remember poor Benjamin. Do give it up, Linda. Try to bear a little longer. Things may turn out better than we expect."

Such pleadings worked, for some time. Jacobs noted how her "courage failed," on account "of the sorrow I should bring on that faithful, loving old heart. I promised that I would try longer, and that I would take nothing out of her house without her knowledge."[84]

Some elders, of course, took vicarious pleasure in the flight of those who *could* still resist. After seeing Horniblow distraught following the successful escape of her grandson William, and hearing her laments that "it seems as if I shouldn't have any of my children or grandchildren left to hand me a drink when I'm dying, and lay my old body in the ground," Aggie, "an old slave woman," told her she was looking at it all wrong. Instead of sadness, Horniblow should "Git down on your knees and bress de Lord" that even one enslaved person had freed themselves.[85] We have no right, however, to expect such fortitude of all those who suffered in slavery; the divergent views on the matter speak to the complex choices – perhaps even the "choiceless choices" – enslaved people were forced to make when navigating slavery.[86] For every Aggie there were others in Jacobs's narrative who counselled remaining in order to protect others, to prevent punishment, or to avoid personal loss, and they were clearly convincing to Jacobs. A "faithful friend" informed Jacobs, for example: "Don't run away, Linda. Your grandmother is all bowed down wid

---

[83] White, *Ar'n't I A Woman?* 74; King, "Suffer with them till death"; King, *Stolen Childhood*; Julia W. Berner, "'Never be free without trustin' some person': Networking and Buying Freedom in the Nineteenth-Century United States," *Slavery & Abolition*, 40.2 (2018), 341–60, 351; William L. Anderson, *Slavery and Class in the American South: A Generation of Slave Narrative Testimony, 1840–1865* (New York: Oxford University Press, 2019), 310.

[84] Jacobs, *Incidents in the Life*, 139–40.   [85] Jacobs, *Incidents in the Life*, 203–4.

[86] The phrase "choiceless choice" was coined by Lawrence L. Langer in the context of Jewish suffering and how to address notions of agency in the Holocaust. See Gabriel N. Finder, "Introduction: Interrogating Evil," *Journal of Holocaust Research* 34.4 (2020), 263–70, 263.

trouble now." The reference to "bowed down" spoke to familiar metaphors of aging and bodily decay, and Jacobs herself understood that whatever Horniblow's abstract hopes for her children and grandchildren's freedom, her personal fears of loss and suffering as she grew older overruled them. Horniblow "had an intense sympathy for runaways," but "she had known too much of the cruelties inflicted on those who were captured," and so "whenever I alluded to the subject, she would groan out, 'O, don't think of it, child. You'll break my heart.'"

After seven years spent hiding in an attic, and with the roof and walls figuratively and literally falling in on her, Jacobs realized her window for permanent escape was closing. However, "at this crisis, Providence," or perhaps more directly her friend Peter, "opened an unexpected way for [Jacobs] to escape," and arranged for her passage on a ship to the north. She was very nearly talked out of it by Horniblow, however, who "sobbed and groaned, and entreated me not to go." This once again diminished Jacobs's resolve and she gave her spot on the fleeing ship to another. As Horniblow was "breaking down under her weight of trouble," and in the aftermath of this abortive plan, though, she forgot to lock the door while visiting Jacobs and a known informant spotted the runaway. It was thus only with the knowledge that there was nowhere else to go that Jacobs finally received the reluctant blessing of her grandmother. Her final message, nonetheless, contained a dire warning about Jacobs's likely fate. Horniblow provided Jacobs with money, insisting, "while her tears were falling fast, that I should take the whole. 'You may be sick among strangers," she said, "and they would send you to the poorhouse to die.'" This parting message underscored Horniblow's love for Jacobs and reinforced her status as a respected elder. The language also suggests, however, that Jacobs saw the older woman's negative response as inevitable given her age and position: "Ah, that good grandmother!"[87]

* * *

Historians have done important work in highlighting the solidarity of enslaved people in the face of tremendous violence as well as in extending our understandings of what constituted resistance considering the overwhelming power of enslavers. There remains a risk, however, that in expanding our definitions to incorporate diverse, even conflicting responses to slavery, we underestimate the tensions and disagreements

---

[87] Jacobs, *Incidents in the Life*, 146, 225, 235.

enslaved people had over how to respond to oppression. In neglecting to explore the judgments enslaved people made about one another's actions and choices when navigating a life in bondage – both positive and negative – we flatten the necessarily complex relationships forged in slavery. We also minimize the significance of the dynamic and overlapping identities enslaved people constructed and understate the competing values that complicated social dynamics in slave communities. Whether stressing the harsh punishments that awaited potential rebels, recalling the tragic fates of previous runaways and resistors, or actively counselling against violence or escape, enslaved elders could be viewed as realistic truth-tellers of the horrors of slavery. They could, however, be portrayed by their peers who pushed for fight or flight in a negative light and be employed as symbols of resignation and defeat. These were people who had *survived* slavery but were not seen to have successfully escaped it. This distinction mattered for contemporaries: age operated as a vector of power in slave communities and in the broader politics and cultures of resistance.

Many of the representations discussed here clearly served a rhetorical purpose for fugitives and antislavery activists. Behind such representations – and unable to speak for themselves – were real people whose pain serves as a tragic reminder of the horrors of slavery. Notwithstanding the sympathy embedded in this discourse, the personal trauma of the aged became a necessary tool of antislavery activists pressing for direct action. The aged had lost their chance and could not turn back time, but it was not too late for others, who should do all they could to avoid such a fate. The negative depictions and recollections of elders in the context of resistance speak to the complex and contingent relationships enslaved people developed in slavery, but also to very real suffering. Enslaved people who were viewed as being unable or unwilling to resist after a lifetime of exploitation were represented by their peers with a mixture of sadness, support, shame, fear, and even disdain. Rather than view elders as people to follow, respect, or revere, enslaved and formerly enslaved people sometimes understood and interacted with them as people whose choices and paths were to be avoided at all costs. Enslaved elders might be portrayed by their peers as people who deserved support and respect on account of their age, but this respect could be predicated on pity, not parity.

PART II

ENSLAVERS

7

"Old God damn son-of-a-bitch, she gone on down to hell"

Elderly Enslavers and Enslaved Resistance

Leonard Black "lived a slave for more than twenty years" in Maryland before successfully escaping in 1837. Ten years later, Black published his antislavery memoir, in which he recounted the abuse he endured, the horrors of family separation, and the instability created by being "placed out" to different enslavers. Black's situation settled when he was returned to his first enslaver, a physician who resided in Anne Arundel County, but stability did not signify improvement. Black specifically noted how the advancing age of his "old master" led to worsening conditions for them all: "We were slaves yet, and the old man grew poorer and poorer the older he grew, and withal cross, much to our discomfort." With declining conditions, and fearing punishment from an ailing man, Black took flight while he still could. Although nearly captured by a search party made up of the "old master, his two sons, and many other people," Black was grateful to discover it was the old man who came closest to finding him: the ravages of aging had taken their toll on more than just his finances. Despite being just across the road from Black, he was unable to spot him: "the only reason the old man did not see me was because he was near-sighted, and forgot to pull his spectacles down over his eyes."[1] Black swiftly dropped to his knees, crawled to a safe location, and set out on the road to freedom.

In Black's description of his escape from bondage, the declining powers of his enslaver were framed as having given impetus to – and directly aiding – his resistance. In continually referring to his enslaver as "old," as

[1] Leonard Black, *The Life and Sufferings of Leonard Black, A Fugitive from Slavery* (New Bedford: Benjamin Lindsey, 1847), 5–6, 17, 23.

well as referencing his white hair, failing health, and poor vision, Black conjured up an image of a weak old man who was incapable of exerting control over a young and vigorous rebel. This would have been an image of declining power that was familiar to both Black and white Americans, North and South. In *Exum* v. *Canty*, 1857, the Mississippi Court of Appeals and Errors accepted that "feebleness and infirmity are the natural consequences of age," while another antebellum writer recorded sadly: "You can hardly bear to see a man, with whom you have been acquainted in his better days, after he has lost his bodily activity, his hearing, his seeing, his memory, and all of his sociability. These are the usual effects of old age, in a greater or less degree."[2] Black, however, was happy to see it was an "old man" who stood in his way to freedom.

The comparative framing of Bradford's diminishing force with Black's youthful activism reveals how enslaved people understood their enslaver's claims to mastery as dynamic and contestable on account of their descent down the "steps of life." Slaveholding authority in the antebellum South was based on public demonstrations of dominance and power, but enslaved people understood that the process of aging destabilized mastery and personally diminished "masters." Proslavery polemicists like Daniel Hundley proudly trumpeted the innate dominance of "honorable" enslavers, claiming that their "entire *physique* conveys to the mind an impression of firmness united to flexibility."[3] Black's depictions of a weak old man failing in business, and failing to see a runaway right in front of him, demonstrates that enslaved people recognized that mastery was never ordained but instead embodied. Bodies, Black or white, enslaver or enslaved, were all subject to what one antebellum doctor described as "the ravages of time ... the inevitable ruin to which all animated matter is incident."[4] Knowledge of this fact was applied when crafting individual and collective strategies for survival and forms of resistance.

Historians have long stressed the significance enslavers accorded to public demonstrations of authority, dominance, and independence, as well as the wider significance of these ideals to the dynamics of slavery itself. Recent work on the violence and exploitation of slavery has similarly reiterated the terrifying power enslavers wielded, both men and women, and the harm this wreaked on enslaved people. Walter Johnson, for example, describes enslaved people in the US South as having to

---

[2] *Exum* v. *Canty*, 34 Miss. 533 (1857), 548; Emmons, "Piety, a Peculiar Ornament to the Aged," 496.
[3] Hundley, *Social Relations*, 28.   [4] Riddlemoser, "Conception in the Human Female."

navigate the "carceral landscape" and the all-encompassing power of the slaveholding class, notwithstanding enslaved people's efforts to resist. Edward Baptist's work on the "pushing system" presents an image of constant and consistent exploitation by rapacious enslavers, while Stephanie Jones-Rogers has insisted that we recognize southern white women as enslavers in their own right. These women sought, and were able to, "acquire and exercise mastery over enslaved people."[5] This research is vital in ensuring the brutalities of slavery are fully appreciated. In presenting enslavers as such dominant figures, however, there is a danger that we confirm their own self-image as masterful even while rejecting their claims of benevolence. A more nuanced narrative becomes possible when we consider how the performance of mastery came under pressure – both internal and external – as enslavers aged. Enslavers could not stop time from marching on and the pressures associated with aging, both real and imagined, wreaked havoc on their public and private claims of dominance. The "inexorable hand of time" could render enslavers pitiful, if not pitiable; recognition of this fact shaped interpersonal relationships and the dynamics of power and resistance in the antebellum South.[6]

* * *

One of the most common occasions for enslaved people to comment on the age of their enslavers related to fears of sale or separation if the enslaver grew ill or died. As Lewis Clarke put it: "when master is sick we are in great trouble."[7] Charity Morris succinctly explained to her WPA interviewer why mortality mattered: "when de ole haid died out dey chillun got de property. You see we slaves wuz de property. Den we got separated. Some sent one way an some nother."[8] Death and ill health, of course, were not the preserve of the elderly: estate divisions, sale, or

[5] See, for example, Wyatt-Brown, *Southern Honor*; Greenberg, *Honor and Slavery*; Glover, *Southern Sons*; Friend and Glover (Eds.), *Southern Manhood*; Mayfield, *Counterfeit Gentlemen*; Wyatt-Brown, *A Warring Nation*; Baptist, *The Half Has Never Been Told*; Kirsten E. Wood, *Masterful Women: Slaveholding Widows from the American Revolution through the Civil War* (Chapel Hill: University of North Carolina Press, 2004); Rosenthal, *Accounting for Slavery*; Glymph, *Out of the House of Bondage*; Johnson, *River of Dark Dreams*, 222–3; Jones-Rogers, *They Were Her Property*, 62, 57–81.

[6] Starobin (Ed.), *Blacks in Bondage*, 34–5. Diane Miller Sommerville's work on suicide among white southerners in the Civil War era raises similar points in the context of self-destruction. See Sommerville, *Aberration of Mind*, 12.

[7] Clarke, *Narratives of the Sufferings of Lewis Clarke*, 77–8.

[8] Rawick (Ed.), *AS, 10.5, 150.*

separation could come at any point in enslaved peoples' lives.[9]
Contemporaries such as John S. Jacobs, however, applied a language of
temporality and embodied time to underscore how enslaved people understood that as their enslavers' age increased, so too did the likelihood of
death, sale, and separation: "Time passed swiftly on, and in due season
death smote down Mrs. H–, my mistress. The hungry heirs ordered us
slaves to mount the auction-block; and all of us, old and young, male and
female, married and single, were sold to the highest bidder."[10] Enslaved
people thus commonly viewed the advancing age of their enslavers, the
inevitable passing of time, and the ambition and advancement of "hungry
heirs" as the occasion of their own tragedies. As Peter Still told his brother
when discussing the ailing health of the "old man" who owned them, "if
he dies, we'll all be sold – they allers has an auction when folks dies – and
then their people's scattered all about. O 'pears like 'taint no use livin' in
this yer world. I sha'n't never see you no more!"[11]

Enslaved people sometimes hoped that older enslavers might rethink
their position as they neared the end of their mortal coil, fearful of eternal
judgment, with abolitionists and Black activists frequently connecting this
to their broader challenges to the proclaimed religiosity of American
slavers. James W. C. Pennington believed that as his former slaver "was
now an old man not far from his grave," he might be more willing to free
Pennington's parents. Sadly, age had not tempered the old man's avarice.
Even in instances where an enslaver's regret seemed sincere, enslaved
people knew that any intervention could occasion resistance from those
who sought to protect their future wealth in people. Historian Lorri
Glover has argued that southern parents "sought to inculcate in sons an
abiding sense of family loyalty," but white southerners hoping to rise in
a slave society could see the diminished force of aged parents as providing
the platform for their own success.[12] Jourden Banks recorded his disdain

---

[9] On sale, separation, and the internal slave trade, see Morris, *Southern Slavery and the Law*, 61–132; Tadman, *Speculators and Slaves*; Johnson, *Soul by Soul*; Deyle, *Carry Me Back*; Williams, *Help Me To Find My People*; Pargas, *Slavery and Forced Migration*.

[10] Jacobs, "A True Tale of Slavery," 86.

[11] Kate E. R. Pickard, *The Kidnapped and the Ransomed. Recollections of Peter Still and His Wife "Vina," after Forty Years of Slavery* (Syracuse: William T. Hamilton, 1856), 57–8.

[12] Glover, *Southern Sons*, 12–17, 12. On family structures, expectations, and obligations in the Old South, see James Oakes, *The Ruling Race: A History of American Slaveholders* (New York: W. W. Norton & Co., 1982); Wyatt-Brown, *Southern Honor*; Steven M. Stowe, *Intimacy and Power in the Old South: Ritual in the Lives of the Planters* (Baltimore: Johns Hopkins University Press, 1987); Joan E. Cashin, "The Structure of Antebellum Planter Families: 'The Ties that Bound us Was Strong,'" *Journal of Southern*

for his formerly powerful enslaver, Charles Yancey, who sickened and died in his fifties. Banks recalled that as Yancey "declined it became necessary for us slavemen to take our turns in watching with him at night," and that Yancey sought forgiveness for selling Banks's sister by claiming he would "make my will so that no more of you shall be sold out of the family." Banks gave short shrift to his ability to impose mastery in his weakened condition or to stand up to his ambitious heirs: "'Well,' said I, 'that may be your will, but how long will it stand with your children?'" Banks was proven correct and sold off, in his words, as fresh "meat" for the soul trade.[13]

Henry Blue, interviewed by abolitionist Benjamin Drew after escaping to Canada, believed his own enslaver to be a "kind and honorable man" who "used to say it was wrong to hold slaves." The end result remained the same: "a good many who hold them say the same. It's a habit – they mean, they say, to set them free at such a time, or such a time, – by and by they die, and the children hold on to the slaves."[14] A song recorded as "folklore" by the Indiana and Ohio branch of the WPA neatly summarized the cynicism many enslaved people held toward elderly enslavers' claims to regret or how they viewed their promises of freedom:

> My ole missus promise me
> When she died she'd set me free
> But she done dead this many years ago
> And here I'm a hoein' this same old row.[15]

Such cynicism was not misplaced. Lewis Clarke used the example of one "old gentleman ... a man of high standing in the church," to savagely undercut any hope that an enslaver's looming mortality might lead them to improve their treatment or to consider freeing their enslaved people. This pious "gentleman" informed George that "if he would wait upon him attentively, and do every thing for him possible, he would remember him in his will: he would do something handsome for him." George hoped that this meant freedom, but was soon disabused of this notion and was told instead "Well, George, I have made provision that when you die, you

---

History, 56.1 (February 1990): 55–70; Peter W. Bardaglio, *Reconstructing the Household: Families, Sex, and the Law in the Nineteenth-Century South* (Chapel Hill: University of North Carolina Press, 1995); Stevenson, *Life in Black and White*; V. Lynn Kennedy, *Born Southern: Childbirth, Motherhood, and Social Networks in the Old South* (Baltimore: Johns Hopkins University Press, 2010).

[13] Pennington, *A Narrative of Events of the Life of J. H. Banks*, 34–5, 39–40.
[14] Drew, *A North-Side View of Slavery*, 270.   [15] Rawick (Ed.), *AS, Supp.*, Ser. 1, 5, 69.

shall have a good coffin, and be put into the same vault with me. Will not that satisfy you, George?" Shockingly, it did not. George was confident enough in the declining powers of his enslaver to tell him as such, explaining that he did not want to share the space with this man because, whatever his claims of piety, George knew a reckoning was coming: "I afraid, Massa, when de debbil come take you body, he make mistake, and get mine."[16]

* * *

The death of an enslaver was an obvious and immediate rupture that had tremendous repercussions on enslaved peoples' lives. Even prior to this final movement down the "steps of life," however, advanced age affected the moods and actions of enslavers. Henry Gowens noted that his "master was kind at first, but as he grew older, he grew more and more severe, getting overseers who were harder and harder."[17] Louisa Picquet of Louisiana connected her enslaver's anxiety over his position, and attendant treatment of her, to his advanced age: "He was gray headed. That's the reason he was always so jealous. He never let me go out anywhere."[18] Leonard Black indicated how a loss of physical or mental acuity affected others' conditions of life: "the old man grew poorer and poorer the older he grew, and withal cross, much to our discomfort."[19] Similar issues were raised in Abram Harris's rendition of one of "dem old songs ... in de slabery times" in his WPA narrative. Its resemblance to the song quoted earlier reiterates the collective enslaved memory of the negative effects of enslavers' aging on their own lives:

> My old Mistis promised me
> Dat when she died, she gwine set me free,
> But she lived so long en got so po
> Dat she lef me digging wide r garden ho.[20]

White southerners likewise claimed that declining powers associated with aging could lead aged enslavers to fail to perform their duties as "masters." The concern rarely stemmed from sympathy for the enslaved people but instead spoke to self-interest and a desire to protect the so-called

---

[16] Clarke, *Narratives of the Sufferings of Lewis Clarke*, 82–3.

[17] Drew, *North-Side View of Slavery*, 138. See, also: Rawick (Ed.), *AS, Supp., Ser. 1, 2,* 134

[18] H. Mattison, *Louisa Picquet: The Octoroon: or Inside Views of Southern Domestic Life* (New York: Published by the Author, 1861), 20.

[19] Black, *The Life and Sufferings of Leonard Black*, 22–3.

[20] Rawick (Ed.), *AS,* 9.3, 175.

rights of the rising generation. These difficulties were acknowledged by enslavers themselves. Emma Taylor, enslaved in Mississippi, informed her WPA interviewer, "Marse, he gittin' old and 'cide he didn't need so many slaves, so he have de sale and a man come and put us all up on a big platform."[21] Ruth Riley of Anderson District, South Carolina, justified her sale of land and an enslaved man named Ephraim because, from her "extreme old age," she was "unable to govern, or dispose of the said negro advantageously."[22] These decisions might otherwise be taken out of an individual's hands. Thomas Miller, who had served as the agent for Elizabeth Marshall in Williamson County, Tennessee, explained in a legal petition that Marshall was "an aged woman and afflicted with bodily infirmities which prevented her from attending to her business with any degree of convenience." Miller used her lax treatment of her enslaved people to press his claims of her general incapacity: "The defendant was much inclined to be fickle and whimsical in the management of her affairs, some times insisting upon a strict performance of duty from her slaves, which your orator was called upon to enforce, at other times extending to them great indulgence." Miller insisted on his own capacity for control over that of the aged enslaver.[23]

Charges of submission and dependency in the antebellum South were gendered feminine and racially coded; such rhetoric – and the willingness of the court to accept Miller's claims – might simply reflect the power of these gendered norms. The transition toward dependency and bodily frailty in old age, however, operated alongside and sometimes overcame binaries of male/female and white/Black. Age was a relation of power, and the transition toward dependency – real or imagined – for women and men had real-world effects. In *Hill* v. *McLaurin*, 1854, the Mississippi High Court of Errors and Appeals heard contested testimony about the poor treatment of enslaved people by Duncan McLaurin as he moved "towards the decline of life." In the bill of complaint it was asserted that McLaurin was, "in his better or younger days, a liberal feeder of his negroes, a good planter and cropper." However, "he became so mentally and physically enfeebled by age and infirmities, as to cease making crops of any account, and so penurious and childish as not to feed his negroes,"

---

[21] Rawick (Ed.), *AS*, 5.4, 74.
[22] Petition of Ruth Riley, February 24, 1852, Anderson District, South Carolina, #21385208, Series 2, RSPP.
[23] Petition of Thomas Miller, February 23, 1852, Williamson County, Tennessee, #21485212, Series 2, RSPP.

and his sons determined to intervene. As they put it, "the childishness and dotage of their father" left them no choice: "something must be done with the old man and his affairs." The dispute itself revolved around the remaining heirs challenging two brothers' assumption of control and their manipulation of their old father, rather than out of any concern for the welfare of the enslaved. All parties accepted, however, that the aged McLaurin lacked the capacity to control himself or others.[24] The willingness of the court to accept the charges of undue influence over a dependent and submissive man, as well as the portrait of a fickle and inconsistent enslaver in his "dotage," suggests the broader social and cultural acceptance of the limitations of old age.

The heirs of James Luckett of Mississippi, who challenged his will in Claiborne County probate court in 1838 on account of aged incapacity, felt similarly emboldened to use his problematic actions as a "master" to argue for his "imbecility and want of mind." Luckett, who was "upwards of sixty," was described as "whimsical" and as having acted "more like a spoiled child than any thing else" on account of physical and mental decline. His flights of fancy were deemed permanent by one expert witness: "in advanced life recovery rarely takes place."[25] Luckett's failures were not described with sympathy for the enslaved people he owned, but instead, as in the *McLaurin* case, to challenge the distribution of his estate.

Irrespective of this purpose, the recorded testimony reveals the instability that enslaved people endured under ailing "masters." Alongside excessive violence for minor faults, Luckett mixed up names and orders; contemporaneous medical, social, and cultural commentators commonly accepted that "the act, in which the intellect of persons advanced in years, *first most frequently*, and *most troublesomely fails*, is that of *remembrance*."[26] Witnesses recalled that Luckett would "give orders to his servants to do things and if it did not please him he would swear he had never told the servants to do so." George Henderson described the punishment of those who failed to complete his impossible demands: "I went into his field with

---

[24] *Hill v. McLaurin*, 28 Miss. 288 (1854), 289. For the case files from the lower court, see Case File 125, Box 15, Lawrence County Chancery Court Cases, microfilm, reel 13317, MDAH.

[25] *Joseph Brock v. Legatees of James Luckett*, Case 641, Box 5803, Series 208, Case Files of the Mississippi High Court of Errors and Appeals, State Government Records Collection, MDAH; hereinafter cited as Luckett Case File.

[26] Caldwell, *Thoughts on the Effects of Old Age*, 25. Italics in original. On mid-nineteenth-century understandings of memory loss in age, see also Stanford, *The Aged Christian's Companion*, 6–7; van Oven, *On the Decline of Life*, 46; Lathrop, *The Infirmities and Comforts of Old Age*; *Potts v. House*, 6 Ga. 324 (1849), 355.

him once & he ordered his servants to quit ploughing and go to hoeing in an hour or two afterwards he flew into a great rage and ordered them to go to plowing again, and swore he had never told them to go to hoeing." While commenting on the legality of the document, the presiding judge's belief that the witnesses had "concur[red] in showing what was both natural & reasonable, in the decline of the old man under an incurable disease" suggests how Black and white southerners understood aging would shape the dynamics of mastery and interpersonal relations in slavery.[27]

In Anderson District, South Carolina, 1856, Hampton Stone petitioned in his role as committee to sell "the entire personal property" of Posey Trussell, "a very old man, and of extremely imbecile mind," because, in his infirmity, his land had been "neglected for some years past, dilapidated and worn out." The language of dilapidation extended to Trussell himself, whose neglect stretched to his performance of mastery. The slaves "have also been without a master for many years, and having been permitted to have their own way for so long a time, it must be with great inconvenience, difficulty and expense, that they can be managed in such way as to avoid serious loss." Trussell, the petitioner asserted, was approaching his end meekly and weakly; he was "phisically unable to help himself in any respect." The passage of time would bring only more suffering, and, as "there is not the slightest probability of any improvement hereafter," Stone and his supporters insisted that a takeover was required to protect the interests of the rising generation. They had no qualms in suggesting the enslaved peoples' lives were upended to serve this purpose: "I am decidedly of opinion, that it will be greatly to the interest of old Mr. Trussell and his heirs at law, that the entire personal property, except one or two negroes, to wait on the old man, should be sold, and the proceeds directed for their interests." The court agreed, and the sales occurred.[28] As enslavers moved down the steps of life, then, it was those whom they enslaved that might suffer the consequences.

* * *

[27] Luckett Case File. The will was eventually accepted to probate, with Chief Justice William L. Sharkey opining in the Mississippi High Court of Errors and Appeals that, while Luckett's "mind had not its original vigor" and "he was infirm from both age and disease," the will had been made during a "lucid interval." All parties, however, portrayed Luckett as frail, dependent, and submissive to others. *Brock v. Luckett's Executors*, 5 Miss. 459 (1840), 483.

[28] Petition of Hampton Stone, June 6, 1856; Affidavit of M. H. Brock, June 1856; "A Bill of Sale of the Goods and Chattels of Posey Trussell" and "A Bill of Sale of Four Negroes," August 7, 1856, Anderson District, South Carolina, #21385608, Series 2, RSPP.

The decline associated with aging, however, also demonstrated the limits to enslavers' corporeal powers. Israel Campbell described the cruelty of his elderly mistress: "she would swear, rant and beat the slaves as if they were brutes, and could never be pleased by any one – not only the slaves but her husband would feel the weight of her wrath if he dared to interpose a word in behalf of the slave." As she took sick her violence continued, but Campbell made clear to his readers that a reckoning was coming: "Old mistress died as she had lived – raving, swearing and screaming, nor would she listen even in her last moments to consolation or direct her mind to the great event which was fast approaching." Enslaved people looked to enslavers in late-life frailty and saw the limits of personal power in the face of the life cycle. As Campbell noted, "the dreaded and last enemy spares not the strong, and as the day passed away her spirit took its flight."[29]

Ailing enslavers who looked to their death with fear presented to some enslaved people a pitiful image that was the antithesis to the honor or respect antebellum enslavers so craved. White southern men were supposed to admire "a style of death that demonstrated mastery and control rather than fear and submission," but John Brown was clear that this rhetoric did not always match reality.[30] Brown's "old master Thomas Stevens" could not even match the violent fortitude of Campbell's old mistress. Stevens instead panicked every time he took ill and resorted to "begging and praying" for his enslaved nurse "to get the devil away from behind the door." The language of submission, frailty, and fear employed by Brown underscored how gendered norms associating masculinity with authority and autonomy were disrupted by the march of time. Stevens survived each of these episodes, but his terror – and the realization that enslavers could not command the temporal rhythms of life and death – showcased how these masters were mere mortals. Brown explained that enslavers tried to "make us believe that they are superior to us in every thing, and a different order of beings, almost next to God himself," but they could not keep this up in the face of aging, disease, and death. This clearly mattered to Brown: "when the masters die, we cannot but feel that somebody is stronger than they are."[31]

Plantation management manuals sagely explained that "the negro should feel that his master is his lawgiver and judge; and yet is his

---

[29] Campbell, *An Autobiography. Bond and Free*, 8, 10.
[30] Greenberg, *Honor and Slavery*, 91. See essays in Friend and Glover (Eds.), *Death and the American South*.
[31] Brown, *Slave Life in Georgia*, 203–4.

protector and friend, but so far above him, as never to be approached save in the most respectful manner."[32] Enslaved people knew, however, that rhetoric was not reality and that the hardships of aging might see enslavers become pitiful instead of powerful. When stating so, ex-slaves rubbished proslavery claims of Black dependency – claims that served to justify racist policies and practice well into the twentieth century – and demanded a rethinking of assumptions about just who was dependent on whom during slavery. Maggie Stenhouse, enslaved in South Carolina, explained that her "master" – "the old man" – was not the powerful patriarch of plantation legend, but instead a man meekly regressing to second infancy: "he had to be tended to like a child. He would knock his stick on the wall and some of the small children would lead him about where he wanted to go."[33] Henry Lewis of Texas similarly reversed the proslavery claim that enslaved people needed their masters and portrayed his enslaver as dependent, even degraded, in old age: "When he grow old he have de gout and he put de long mattress out on de gallery and lay down on it. He say, 'Come here, my li'l n***rs,' an den he make us rub he foots so he kin git to sleep."[34] Serena Mullberry Anndora Slate, enslaved in North Carolina, recalled that the slaves on her plantation mocked their mistress's delusions of youth, describing how "she try to dress like she was sixteen 'stead of sixty." The community laughed behind her back, but they still dared not say anything to her face: "Mis' Henrietta was ole an' she walked wid a cane. But you better not say she was ole, no suh, you sho hadn', an' you could tell by de way dat cane tap whether she was mad or glad."[35]

Historians have noted that jokes within the quarters were a form of collective cultural resistance for enslaved people, allowing them to puncture the self-importance and pride of those who enslaved them.[36] Mockery came at a risk, but some believed that the physical decline associated with age affected their oppressors' ability to apply discipline. In Ann Simon Deas's postbellum lament for the Lost South, she described how one "old lady" struggled accordingly: "I have found out why Mrs. Dalrymple spoils her servants so much – she is afraid of them! And

---

[32] "Management of Negroes," *De Bow's Review*, 19.3 (September 1855), 358–63, 361.
[33] Rawick (Ed.), *AS*, 10.6, 222.   [34] Rawick (Ed.), *AS*, 5.3, 9.
[35] Rawick (Ed.), *AS*, *Supp.*, Ser. 1, 11, 44, 43.
[36] Lawrence Levine, *The Unpredictable Past: Explorations in American Cultural History* (New York: Oxford University Press, 1993); Sterling Stuckey, *Going Through the Storm: The Influence of African American Art in History* (New York: Oxford University Press, 1994); Scott, *Domination and the Arts of Resistance*; Lussana, "Reassessing Brer Rabbit."

they know it, and tyrannize over her."[37] Male enslavers were equally recorded as weakened on account of age, whether in constitution or corporeal form. Frances Patterson of Mississippi described her "Old Marsa" as "sorter chicken hearted" and unwilling to spill blood.[38] Monroe Franklin Jamison explained how his enslaver, "an old man about seventy years of age," was "too old and frail to look after the farm." His incapacity did not benefit the slaves, however, with overseers being hired instead. The enslaver's frailty extended to being unable or unwilling to stop these overseers from going "beyond their limits" and punishing "those who were forbidden to be whipped." Jamison viewed this situation as evidence of the aged enslaver's "disregard for the feelings and rights of men," but it might plausibly have reflected his own submission to the overseers.[39]

Enslaved people sometimes understood that excessive punishment stemmed from the enslavers' fear that their powers were declining, and their belief that they needed to dominate while they still could. Henry "Box" Brown explained that his "old master" was increasingly "unable to attend to all his affairs himself," and that the white community were unnerved by his lax discipline: "I fancy the neighbours began to clamour about our masters mild treatment to his slaves, for which reason he was induced to employ an overseer."[40] Plantation advice given to antebellum enslavers confidently asserted that "no man should attempt to manage negroes, who is not perfectly firm and fearless; and who, moreover, has not entire control of his temper."[41] This rhetoric, however, relied on an image of mastery as innate, rather than embodied. Flesh-and-blood enslavers knew the limits to such discursive projections of power.

Enslaved people, too, understood that the pressures of aging undermined the identities and authority of enslavers. Eliza Coverton, enslaved in Missouri, had told her children that "Old man Coffman was a mean old slave holder. He was afraid of his slaves and had some one else to do the whipping."[42] Joe McCormick of Georgia believed that his enslaver, Hamilton, lived in fear of any decline in powers, with his anguish at this

---

[37] Deas, *Two Years of Plantation Life*, 110–11.

[38] Rawick (Ed.), *AS, Supp.*, Ser. 1, 9.4, 1679.

[39] Jamison, *Autobiography and Work of Bishop M. F. Jamison*, 23–4.

[40] Brown, *Narrative of the Life of Henry Box Brown*, 14.

[41] J. W. Randolph Plantation Rule Book, in Thomas Edward Cox Books, 1829–54, *Records of Antebellum Southern Plantations*, Series J: *Selections from the Southern Historical Collection*, Part 9, reel 16, 0356–66.

[42] Rawick (Ed.), *AS, Supp.*, Ser. 1, 2, 215.

thought intensifying his violence. McCormick claimed that Hamilton "was afraid the slaves might some day overpower him, and for this reason kept them under rigid subjection."[43] Rachel Cruze's memory of a violent encounter on her Tennessee plantation suggests that such fears were not unreasonable: "Ole Major said he'd do his own whipping right bravelike, but he really wasn't very successful at it . . . instead of ole Major punishing him he whipped ole Major. And that was the end of that."[44] The language of fear and failure used to describe these "masters" struck directly at the notions of honor and dominance that supposedly underpinned male enslaver identity; it reveals that enslaved people understood old age affected the application of white power.

* * *

In fact, such awareness of aging's effects might enable forms of resistance both covert and overt. Some enslaved people claimed that the advancing age of their enslavers influenced their plans to escape. John B. Meachum, who bought his freedom after hiring himself out, intensified his planned exit from slavery on account of his enslaver's advancing age. Meachum claimed his Kentucky enslaver was a "good man," but he could not be "satisfied" in this condition: "He was very old, and looked as if death was drawing near to him. So I proposed to him to hire my time, and he granted it. By working in a saltpetre cave I earned enough to purchase my freedom."[45] Some enslaved people thus took preemptive steps to avoid the dangers attendant upon the passing of an elderly master, with knowledge of the possibility of an intergenerational power struggle to come. Isaac Throgmorton of Kentucky was concerned his fate would worsen upon the death of his elderly enslaver, who had treated him "well enough" and made his plans accordingly: "when he got married, his wife and all her kin considered that I had been treated too well, and I knew directly that his head was laid low (and he was an old man) I would be done forever."[46] Throgmorton took flight while he still could and escaped to Canada.

A loss of power or status associated with aging thus influenced some enslaved people in making plans for resistance. Elijah Jenkins recalled that after his young enslaver died, he "fell to her mother, an old woman." Jenkins understood that she was not long for this world and, with the

[43] Rawick (Ed.), *AS, Supp., Ser. 1*, 4.2, 390.
[44] Rawick (Ed.), *AS, Supp., Ser. 1*, 5, 300–1.
[45] Meachum, *An Address to All the Colored Citizens*, 3.
[46] Blassingame (Ed.), *Slave Testimony*, 434.

knowledge that "on her death I would have to be sold," took flight. This was not difficult, Jenkins intimated, on account of her reduced powers: "I ran away, and did not meet with much difficulty in doing so."[47] The aging process gave some enslaved people the confidence to challenge, escape from, or overpower their enslavers. Isaac Suits recalled the time an abusive elderly white "done so bad that a colored man killed him – killed him right out in an open field with forty or fifty other men (negroes) 'round. He broke his neck, then doubled him over an' threw him on a stone." The pleasure he took in his actions was evident, as "when the men were carrying him out to hang him and they pass by the dead man, he called out, 'I've killed you once, old man, and I'm going now to where I can kill you again!'"[48] A sense that weakness was an accompaniment to old age challenged and occasionally overturned gendered presumptions of power. Sarah Wilson of Arkansas recalled the time her "old Marster," who was "mighty feeble" in his old age, utterly failed to overawe her aunt. Wilson described how her aunt, after being threatened with punishment, "just stood right up to him and never budged, and when he come close she just screamed out loud and run at him with her fingers stuck out straight and jabbed him in the belly." Wilson added, mockingly, "he had a big soft belly, too, and it hurt him."[49] A. J. Mitchell offered a similar tale, describing how his Aunt Susan simply told her elderly master, whose "head [w]as white as cotton," that she would not let him whip her and he, too, failed to physically overpower her.[50] For both aunts, however, the ultimate power of the slaveholding class was made clear. The women resisted physical punishment, but they were sold away.

Notwithstanding the broader structural force enslavers harnessed, individual slavers were aware of the dangers they faced if their powers faded with age. John Walker of North Carolina recorded in his plantation journal that, aged fifty-four, he felt "the infirmitys of age only in loosing my strength[.] I can't hold out to walk so far and as fast my Eye sight fails very much," while Robert F. W. Allston of South Carolina informed the daughter of a family friend that "in my declining years, it would be presumptuous to undertake the management of an insubordinate Slave."[51] Regardless of the proslavery claims that paternalism and reciprocal relations governed the master–slave relationship, enslavers

---

[47] Drew, *North-Side View of Slavery*, 113.   [48] Rawick (Ed.), *AS, Supp.*, Ser. 1, 11, 303.

[49] *FWP*, 13 (Oklahoma), 346.   [50] Rawick (Ed.), *AS, 10.6*, 103.

[51] Plantation Journal of John Walker, August 15, 1839, John Walker Papers #2300, SHC; Easterby and Littlefield (Eds.), *The South Carolina Rice Plantation*, 151–2.

understood the need for brute force. Emily Liles Harris, who recorded in her journal entry of November 1864 that "a few more years of this kind of life will wear me out. I feel old and miserable and ugly," struggled to maintain discipline in this condition just a few months later: "I had a fight with old Will and hurt myself worse than him. It is a painful necessity that I am reduced to the use of a stick but the negroes are becoming so imprudent and disrespectful that I cannot bear it."[52] Harris's slaves appeared to share the belief she, like the Confederacy, was declining in power and purpose and acted accordingly.

Advice manuals to enslavers explained that "slaves have no respect or affection for a master who indulges them over much, or who, from fear, or false humanity, fails to assume that degree of authority necessary to promote industry and enforce good order."[53] Lucinda Davis of Oklahoma described how this disrespect might play out for aged slave-holders if they lost power. Davis's enslaver, a Native American known as "Old man Tuskaya-hiniha," "was near 'bout blind before de War" and his condition only grew worse with the passage of time: "'bout de time of de War he go plumb blind." In his weakened condition he would simply "set on de long seat under de bresh shelter of de house all de time," and Davis would sometimes "lead him around de yard a little, but not very much."[54] Walter Johnson has noted how "the discipline that slaveholders exercised over their slaves on a daily basis was defined by visual power," but one's sight was shaped by the rhythms of the life cycle.[55] Notwithstanding the carceral landscape the slaveholding class created, individual decline occasioned individual resistance. Contemporaries who recorded that "sight is perhaps the first [sense] that gives warning of the course of time" would perhaps be unsurprised to learn from Davis that, with the "Old man" in this condition, it was "about de time all de slaves begin to slip out and run off."[56]

In his postbellum memoir of slave life, Isaac D. Williams recalled how an elderly white man failed to stop his flight. When setting the scene for his escape, Williams made a point of noting his own positionality at the prime of life by describing himself as "a heavy built man, over six feet in height, and weighing over two hundred and sixty pounds, yet there was no

[52] Racine (Ed.), *Piedmont Farmer*, 350, 365.
[53] Robert Collins, "Management of Slaves," *De Bow's Review*, 17.4 (1854), 421–6, 425.
[54] *FWP, 13* (Oklahoma), 54.   [55] Johnson, *River of Dark Dreams*, 166.
[56] Van Oven, *On the Decline of Life*, 43; *FWP, 13* (Oklahoma), 54. On declining eyesight see also Stanford, *The Aged Christian's Companion*, 7.

superfluous flesh on me – it was clear bone and sinew." Early in his escape effort he was confronted by "an old man with a gun and a large dog" looking to capture him. The man missed his shot, however, and Williams beat the dog until he "returned to his aged master howling piteously." The old man was left "shaking his fist in impotent rage." Despite the language of impotence and frailty, Williams "could not help but admire the courage of the old man." He also recognized that the man's individual failings did not mean Williams had reached safety: "As his frail body stood out in bold relief beneath the lengthening shadows of the evening I could but think of the power he represented."[57] The statement emphasizes the structural dominance of enslavers writ large, but Williams escaped because the old man who stood in his way was too frail to exert mastery. Power represented was not always power manifested, and enslaved people understood that the gap between rhetoric and reality worked in their favor. The fate of James H. Wood, a Mississippi enslaver, suggests that William's frail pursuer might have had a lucky escape in failing to catch a more vigorous runaway. In 1848, "James, a slave" was caught by Wood during his attempted flight and a fight ensued. Despite having a hunting dog with him, Wood was dominated by his young rival, with his advanced age understood by the court as shaping the encounter: "the boy made towards him, & he gave back, but being old & in the bushes he could not get out of the way, & the boy advanced & cut him once, & turned & left him." James was caught the next evening. When questioned, he was likewise aware that the advanced age of his pursuer had hindered him, dismissively responding to his captors that "he cut some old man but he did not know who it was."[58]

In Grace Lintner's postbellum paean to the antebellum order, she described how on the ascent up the steps of life white children were "to be reared rulers over their sable playmates, and [have] impressed on their unfolding minds ideas of superiority in birth." It was this inculcation in mastery that enabled "them to exercise authority to a degree inconceivable by those raised with different surroundings."[59] Those who were moving down the steps of life, however, could see their authority denied and receive a clear reminder of the limits to claims of innate superiority. One abolitionist author portrayed a scene where an enslaved man dealt a humiliating blow to an "elderly white man, a very ill-tempered fellow,"

---

[57] Williams, *Sunshine and Shadow*, 8, 26–7.
[58] *State of Mississippi* v. *James, a slave* (1848), Pontotoc County, Case 07, Box 21839, Series 1818, County Court Case Files, MDAH.
[59] Lintner, *Bond and Free*, ii.

who tried to chastise him on the streets of Charleston, South Carolina. This white man, who took pleasure in randomly beating Black people – enslaved or free – took his superiority for granted regardless of his advanced age. "Bob," however, understood this power to be illusory. After checking that no other white person was around to intervene, Bob "lifted the old fellow by the neck and the heels, as one would do an infant, and, carrying him deliberately over to the deepest part of the puddle, softly and cautiously laid him down upon his back in it." This humiliating reversal of mastery was a source of humor for both Black and white: "the redoubtable white man with the cudgel was much more cautious and peaceable in his walk thereafter; and Big Bob the carpenter, was much applauded by all his coloured acquaintances, and even many white gentlemen laughed at the exploit."[60]

Bob's abolitionist tale might, of course, be apocryphal. The message it conveyed, however – that aged enslavers risked having claims of honor and authority denied by both Black and white – indicates that antebellum southerners understood that aging had the potential to reshape the dynamics of mastery and interpersonal relations. Benjamin Johnson of Georgia offered a similar tale of the public humiliation of an old man who failed to maintain his dominance. "Ol' man Brady" tried to punish Johnson after catching him on his plantation without a pass, but Johnson turned the tables on the enslaver: "I stooped over to take off my coat I caught 'im in his pants an' throwed 'im in a puddle o' water an' den I lit out fer home. If you git home den dey couldn't do nuthin' to you." When Brady tried to punish him at "home" the next day, Johnson's enslaver insisted, in front of all and sundry, that his failure to exert mastery was final: "If he had you he shoulda whupped you an' dat woulda been his game but he let you git away an' so day wus yo' game." This public humiliation was witnessed with pleasure by the enslaved people. Nearly eighty years after slavery ended, Johnson still relished the memory: "Ol' man Brady's faced turned so red dat it looked like he wus gona bus.'"[61]

The failing force of old enslavers – once powerful figures now reduced to pathetic creatures – enabled some enslaved people to enact revenge for past abuses. Lewis Clarke recalled how enslaved peoples' hidden transcripts were a means of resistance:

They creep up to the bed, and with a very soft voice, inquire, "How is dear massa? O massa, how we want to hear your voice out in the field again." Well, this is what they say up in the sick room. They come down to their anxious companions.

[60] Neilson, *The Life and Adventures of Zamba*, 238–9.
[61] Rawick (Ed.), *AS*, 12.2, 322–3.

"How is the old man?" "Will he die?" Yes! yes! he sure to go this time; he never whip the slave no more. "Are you sure?" "Will he die?" O yes! surely gone for it now. Then they all look glad, and go to the cabin with a merry heart.

Clarke emphasized the depth of anger enslaved people held toward their oppressors by noting this dying man was being literally willed to hell. When explaining why he dug the grave so deep, the enslaved man tasked with the job replied: "he wanted to get the old man as near home as possible."[62]

Sometimes aged frailty allowed for physical revenge. One WPA respondent recalled how she was expected to take on the role of nurse when "Old mistress got sick." She took the opportunity to exact vengeance instead. While pretending to keep the flies off her mistress, this woman "would hit her all in the face," relying on the fact that she was too infirm to be able to communicate this to her husband. Indeed, "she would try to tell him on me," but the husband was unable to decipher her nonverbal communication and so the revenge continued unabated. The mistress died soon after, and the enslaved population rejoiced: "Old God damn son-of-a-bitch, she gone on down to hell."[63] Sojourner Truth likewise described how infirmity might see mastery, as well as gendered power dynamics, inverted and allow for wrongs to be righted. The enslaver Hasbrouck, who had taken cruel pleasure in tormenting a sick slave woman and her child, found himself reliant on an enslaved woman as he himself sickened over time. Truth claimed to take no pleasure in the story, explaining that "it was fearful to hear his old slave soon tell how, in the day of his calamity, she treated *him*," but this was clearly seen as a form of righteous revenge:

She was very strong, and was therefore selected to support her master, as he set up in bed, by putting her arms around while she stood behind him. It was then that she did her best to wreak her vengeance on him. She would clutch his feeble frame in her iron grasp, as in a vice; and, when her mistress did not see, would give him a squeeze, a shake, and lifting him up, set him down again, as hard as possible. If his breathing betrayed too tight a grasp, and her mistress said, "Be careful, don't hurt him, Soan!" her ever-ready answer was, "Oh no, Missus, no," in her most pleasant tone – and then, as soon as Missus's eyes and ears were engaged away, another grasp – another shake – another bounce. She was afraid the disease alone would let him recover, – an event she dreaded more than to do wrong herself. Isabella asked her, if she were not afraid his spirit would haunt her. "Oh, no," says Soan; "he was so wicked, the devil will never let him out of hell long enough for that."[64]

* * *

[62] Clarke, *Narratives of the Sufferings of Lewis Clarke*, 77–8.
[63] Rawick (Ed.), *AS*, *18*, *134*.   [64] Truth and Gilbert, *Narrative of Sojourner Truth*, 83–4.

Such accounts may seem like the narrative devices of abolitionists seeking to stress the punishment that awaited enslavers if they did not change their ways. White southerners, however, shared a belief that enslaved people might take control of aged enslavers and asserted as much in the court-room. Some claims of enslaved people's "influence" took dramatic forms, including manipulation, coercion, and even violence. As John Mayfield has noted, "in the highly symbolic structuring of Southern masculinity, to be manipulated and mastered was to be a slave, regardless of race."[65] In *Exum* v. *Canty*, 1857, the Mississippi Court of Appeals and Errors accepted that "feebleness and infirmity are the natural consequences of age," and heard that this might allow for inversions of mastery. During this dispute over the distribution of John Williams's estate, the court heard from several witnesses that he "was easily controlled and influenced" by his slaves, who had helped shape his will to partly suit their interests with a trusted local white. They also appeared to take pleasure in having tricked Williams's family out of their inheritance, with one witness report-ing that after the will was changed to acknowledge "that he did not intend to give old Ben and his boys anything [, h]e then laughed." Amy clearly shared the joke: "'Old Amy,' who was standing by, said "d – d old Ben." According to a number of witnesses, such behavior was not out of the norm: "Old Amy could control him, and get him to do whatever she wanted. His slaves, Jake and Elias, could also influence him."[66]

In Monroe County, Mississippi, 1854, Charles B. Lee actively looked to rid himself of two slaves because he was "old and feeble and said negroes [were] becoming fractious and troublesome to him."[67] Those who had not taken such steps risked a reversal of mastery, with reports ranging from fears of enslaved people exerting influence over weak elderly whites all the way up to fight and flight. On Henly Trussell's farm in Anderson District, South Carolina, his enslaved people were considered to have benefited from the eighty-three-year-old being "physically and men-tally incompetent to the government of his affairs." Trussell's administra-tors claimed "he was from his condition extremely liable to be imposed on, especially by his own slaves, who did pretty much as they pleased."[68] The enslaved people were apparently allowed to "take up goods, liquor,

[65] Mayfield, *Counterfeit Gentlemen*, 58.

[66] *Exum* v. *Canty*, 34 Miss. 533 (1857), 548, 542.

[67] Petition of Edward and Sarah Kemp, April 13, 1855, Monroe County, Mississippi, #21085518, Series 2, RSPP.

[68] Petition of Noah Reeves et al., May 8, 1854, Anderson District South Carolina, #21385440, Series 2, RSPP.

groceries, &c., both for use and sale; and the consequence was, as uniform experience proves in every like case, they idled away their time, dressed extravagantly, and laid the sure foundation of their master's ruin, and of their own sale into other hands." The court acknowledged Trussell was "enfeebled by age and infirmity" but, however much they disapproved of an "over fond master, perhaps an imprudent man" failing to enact vigorous measures on his farm, did not find improper influence and, in both cases, the enslaved people were spared sale or possession by the heirs.[69] Despite the failed challenges, and whether the inversion of power was true or false, these cases reveal that white southerners considered it *plausible* for aging to invert the relations between enslaver and enslaved. They show how age was an important factor in shaping hierarchies among white southerners and reveal the fluid and contested nature of mastery in the antebellum south.

Perceptions of enslavers as aged and infirm might thus serve as the launchpad for episodes of resistance. In *Belcher* v. *McKelvey*, 1859, the South Carolina Court of Appeals heard that George used his aged enslaver's infirmities to plot his escape to freedom. Robert Tucker, "about eighty years of age altogether unlettered, and of a mind, originally feeble, impaired by age and disease," hoped to emancipate his slaves at his death. George, "who had great influence over him," decided it was prudent not to wait and found a sympathetic white man who "would befriend him and the other negroes by taking them to a free State." He then organized his own bill of sale to W. W. Belcher, who would stand as his new "master." The attesting witness, John Johnson, "said to George, you are Belcher's property," but George was confident in his plans: "I am not afraid; Belcher is too good a man not to do what he has said, and he will contrive a way for my escape." Johnson came to believe the entire sale was orchestrated by George, who "seemed more interested than Tucker in having the deed drawn." George's confidence in Belcher was not misplaced: George escaped after Tucker's death and was "probably in Pennsylvania." It was not "contested that George left this State with the consent of Belcher," but he was clearly understood as the agent of his own freedom. Tucker's frailty made him "an easy subject of imposition and undue influence," and all witnesses believed this weakness eased George's flight.[70]

---

[69] *Reeves* v. *Gantt*, 8 Rich. Eq. 14 (S.C. 1855), 13. 18.
[70] *Belcher* v. *McKelvey; Tucker* v. *Belcher*, 32 S.C. Eq. 9, 11, Rich. Eq. 9 (1859), 11, 13, 14, 21, 22.

White southerners were clearly bothered by the idea that older enslavers might lack the ability to stand firm against their slaves. In Orange County, North Carolina, 1858, the heirs of Anne L. Woods, who died aged seventy and who had for the previous ten to fifteen years been "very feeble in mind and body, and almost entirely blind and deaf," claimed that her slaves had manipulated her in her dotage. According to one of her several wills, Woods conveyed her slaves, in trust, to Dr. Osmond F. Long, of Hillsboro, for one dollar, and instructed him to send them to Liberia or some free state following her death. If they did not wish to go, they should be turned over to Alexander Findley, who was known to be opposed to slavery. The heirs claimed that their exclusion from her estate was particularly egregious because "all the members of her family had been kind and attentive to her, as much so as her excluded mode of life enabled them to be." This "excluded" life, however, was said to have enabled an inversion of mastery: "she lived alone, as above stated, with said negroes, and in her old age and helplessness fell entirely under their influence and control, especially the influence of Major, who for many years before her death controlled her, and her affairs as he pleased." Some of her neighbors believed this influence was nothing more than dutiful care, with Samuel H. Hughes claiming that "[Major] managed her whole business or nearly so; and she had great confidence in him," but the heirs were adamant he applied more nefarious methods. They intimated she was afraid of Major and claimed that this conveyance was done "under the undue influence, whether of fear or not, they do not know, of the said slave Major. That this occurred so often, that it was notorious in the neighbourhood, and on these occasions it would be remarked that 'Major had made another will.'"[71] The court found that the trust, if not the proposed emancipation, was reasonable, and the slaves were eventually passed to Findley. While the heirs were unsuccessful, the fact that their challenge rested on the idea of enslaved people manipulating an old enslaver suggests this was deemed plausible – with aging thus a plausible site of danger to slavery's governance – by antebellum southerners. Regardless of political claims to the contrary, antebellum southerners understood that mastery was contingent rather than constant.

This type of manipulation over enslavers even allowed enslaved people to settle grudges among themselves. In Boyle County, Kentucky, 1844, an

[71] Petition of Robert Redding et al., December 24, 1847; Depositions, Alexander Anderson, Samuel Hughes, Allen Collins, Lemuel Wilkinson, August 12, 1858; Reports of Cases in Equity, Supreme Court of North Carolina, June 1858–August 1859, 216–20, Orange County, North Carolina, #21285822, Series 2, RSPP.

enslaved man named Dick claimed that his expected manumission upon the death of Benjamin Prall, aged sixty-three, was being circumvented by an enslaved woman named Becky. Dick alleged "that it was the cherished intention of his master to emancipate yr Petitioner by will and that he not only did so in his only true last will but spoke of it often whilst he retained his faculties as his decided intention and cherished wish." He was shocked upon Prall's death to note this was not the case. Prall had been sick for some time, as "his mind and body had both been failing him and gradually becoming weak and weaker," until he was finally hit with "a paralysis – which actively paralised [*sic*] his physical strength and greatly impaired, if it did not entirely destroy his mind." Dick believed that "Whilst in this weak, feeble and paralised [*sic*] condition, both as to body and mind," Prall "was prevailed upon" by Becky and her children to keep Dick enslaved while setting themselves free. Dick was adamant that revenge was her motive: "out of special ill will and malice towards yr Petitioner, the said Becky & children procured the said supposed will which has been recorded, wishing that he should be kept as a slave." In the "true will" that Becky had apparently persuaded the old man to discard, "she and her children and others were emancipated."[72] The only difference in Becky's "new" will was that Dick alone remained enslaved. Dick was, in fact, advertised for a public sale to be held two weeks after the petition was heard, but he was fortunate enough to be granted a partial stay and was eventually manumitted with bond. There was no record of why Becky took such action, but a lack of control from elderly enslavers sometimes allowed enslaved people space to settle grudges among themselves.

Enslaved people were accused of having exploited elderly and infirm enslavers both physically and mentally, with this reversal of mastery demonstrating the limits to any proslavery claims about the innate superiority of antebellum whites. Some cases suggested a degree of intimate manipulation, with an inversion of gendered power dynamics, and suggestions that aged men were particularly credulous in these cases, used to press home claims of incapacity. In Maryland, 1833, the heirs of Thomas Cramphin claimed that an enslaved woman named Caroline Calvert had formed "an illicit connexion and intercourse with said Cramphin, and live[d] with him as his mistress, from that time till his death, which happened in the ninety-second year of his age." Sexual relations between enslaver and enslaved typically spoke to the coercive and violent exploitation of enslaved women, but Cramphin's decline possibly provided

---

[72] Petition of Dick, May 22, 1844, Boyle County, Kentucky, #20784407, Series 2, RSPP.

Calvert some space to improve her material condition, both for herself and for the eleven children she apparently had with Cramphin in his "extreme old age." The heirs were utterly unconvinced of his paternity, stating that it was only "under this delusion, that he makes his will, leaving to the 'woman' by whom he has been induced to believe that he has children, a part, and to these children, almost the entire residue of his large estate, to the exclusion of his heirs."[73] The language of subjection and submission applied in these cases indicates how enslavers and enslaved alike might see the process of aging as upending the traditional operation of mastery. This terrified, disgusted, and angered white contemporaries. Enslaved people, however, might see their enslavers' descent down the steps of life as providing them with a limited window to adapt or even escape their circumstances.

White southerners thus argued that enslaved people might use the advanced age of their enslavers to serve their own interests and even to escape. Even if we are skeptical that petitions, depositions, and courtroom testimony speaks only to the dueling interests of the parties, the fact that complainants were willing to base their charges on such claims suggests the broader power of the discourse equating old age with submission and dependency. A dramatic reversal of the master–slave relationship was presented in *O' Neal* v. *Farr*, South Carolina, 1844. The Court of Appeals and Errors heard that Farr's decision to change his will to favor an enslaved woman named Fan – "his paramour" – was apparently shaped by "the threats and menaces of Fan." Fan was likely forced into this relationship as, while Farr was in the "vigor of health of manhood," she had been "respectful and submissive to his will." As he grew older and took sick, Fan reversed the dynamic and exerted control over Farr – and, indeed, over others on the plantation. According to one witness, "Fan could have sold, or prevented the sale of, any of Farr's negroes." This control took the form of words but also deeds. Fan "had even attempted violence on his person."[74] In *Potts* v. *House*, 1849, the Georgia Supreme Court further outlined the level of control Fan held over Farr when using the case as a comparator for their own discussion of "undue influence" by Charity, a woman enslaved by James Potts Snr. Potts, aged ninety, was at this point "rendered almost speechless by age and the loss of his health; was bedridden, and on account of his bodily infirmities at least, if not mental, rendered pretty much incapable of attending to and managing his

---

[73] *Davis* v. *Calvert*, 5 G & J, 269 (Maryland, 1833), 273, 275, 283.
[74] *O' Neal* v. *Farr*, 30 S.C.L. 80, 1 Rich. 80 (1844), 80–6.

ordinary business." Charity was argued to have taken advantage of this situation to "exercise a controlling influence over him," including making provisions for her family's manumission in the will. In earlier testimony that the court disallowed, one physician lamented the weak nature of Potts Snr after attending to him, claiming his "extreme old age" manifested itself in "a childishness that is not common to men of ordinary minds" and stressed the enslaved essentially did whatever they wanted with their "master."[75] With Charity in charge, another witness claimed, the community simply "obeyed or disobeyed his orders pretty much as they pleased."[76]

The court was disturbed by Pott's "miserable infatuation" with Charity, "which was shocking ... to our sense of decency and propriety, and proper subordination on the part of our negroes," but viewed it as "being immeasurably short ... on the score of unjust control, of that which accompanied Farr's will." In making this assessment, the court restated the depth of Fan's dominance:

She shook her fist in his face and threatened to knock his teeth down his throat; witness heard them quarrel in the night; heard her call Hannah, a servant, to bring her the whip and she would beat his skin off. They would get drunk together and she was insolent to him; told him to hush or she'd give him hell; cursed him for a d-ned rascal; rubbed her fist in his face and dared him to open his mouth; called him a d – ned old palsied rascal. Testator told Dawkins, that Fan had tried to kill him with a spear; she threw it at him and stuck it in the bed post ... Many other disgusting details were narrated on the trial, which need not be repeated.[77]

Fan's resort to violence marked her case as particularly transgressive, but both instances appalled the court. The cases reveal how southerners – Black and white – understood slaveholding authority as contingent and contestable, rather than innate. They demonstrate, moreover, how enslaved people might see the aging of their enslavers as opening a window for negotiation or acts of resistance.

Violence against enslavers was the most egregious upending of mastery, and in some cases advanced age marked some slavers as comparatively easy victims. In 1822, Tyrrel County, North Carolina, the General Assembly heard about the murder of Mary Wynn by several slaves. These men had apparently taken advantage of the limited white presence on her

---

[75] *Potts v. House*, 6 Ga. 324 (1849), 325, 357, 363; Rule of Exception, Troup County Superior Court, November term 1848, *Potts v. House*, Caveat, in Supreme Court – Clerk of Court, Criminal Appeals Case Files, 1846–1917, Case A-418, 12-4-1848, 14, GSA.

[76] *Potts v. House*, 6 Ga. 324 (1849), 363.

[77] *Potts v. House*, 6 Ga. 324 (1849), 360, 363, 361.

farm, with the court hearing that at the time she only "resided with her Grandfather John Gaskinton, an aged, infirm and helpless old man."[78] The specific reference to the man's age and infirmities suggest a belief that this made him incapable of defending himself, but also in fulfilling the gendered role of protector for others. Such phrasing suggests further how antebellum southerners understood age as undercutting supposedly masculine values.

The murder of Jesse Hassell by George, in Pasquotank County, North Carolina 1824, divided the community due to Hassell's illicit trading with slaves and the belief that his advanced age had, in fact, turned assault into murder. The petitioners who requested clemency for George noted that Hassel had "but one step between him & the grave," and argued that he had no intention to murder his victim. However, the counter-petition firmly rejected such reasoning, and stressed that condoning the murder of an "old," "emaciated," and "infirm" man risked demonstrating to *all* enslaved people the fragile nature of mastery. Regardless of the position for or against, the testimony in this trial, which included Hassel being heard to cry out and plead with his supposed "inferior" to "take all I have but spare my life," and vivid descriptions of a weak old man being choked to death by a dominant enslaved man, undermined any theoretical claims of white dominance.[79] The counter-petitioners presented a case that clemency here would inspire violence, theft, and even insurrection from the slave community who saw mastery inverted so.

In *Gilbert* v. *State*, 1847, the Supreme Court of Tennessee heard that two enslaved men beat their enslaver to death and set his barn on fire, hoping that the blaze would mask their actions. Gilbert had been helped by a younger man of seventeen, but this accomplice apparently did so under duress. This was perhaps the first time Gilbert had put his words into action, but he clearly did not fear his "master": Gilbert had already "threaten[ed] his master's life several times." A witness claimed, in fact, to have frequently "seen him with the hickory, which he called the peacemaker," that he later used to beat his enslaver to death. The comparative age and vigor of enslaved and enslaver was viewed as marking out the crime as particularly offensive. The ruling judge stressed that "the

---

[78] Petition of Joseph and Anne Wynn, December 17, 1823, Tyrrel County, North Carolina, #11282304, Series 1, RSPP.

[79] General Assembly, Session Records, November 1824–January 1825, Petitions and Papers Concerning Pardon of Negro, George, Charged with Murder, NCDAH. There are no records as to whether George was executed.

deceased was an old and very nearly blind man," and asserted that, even if their claim as to accidental fire was true, "it is not to believed that if the flame had got to the house and had risen beyond the control of the parties, two young athletic men could not have rescued the old man from the burning house." The comparative age and vigor of enslaved and enslaver was viewed as having directly shaped the contours of the act. The Supreme Court concluded: "It was a cruel murder, inflicted on a feeble old man."[80] These rebels, and the courts who judged them, understood their enslavers were "masters" in mere name. This knowledge directly shaped their decisions and actions in resisting slavery.

* * *

Antebellum enslavers presided over a cruel and violent system of exploitation, and enslaved people suffered horrendous abuse from white southerners, men and women, old and young. Recognition of this is fundamental to any understanding of slavery as an economic system and as a contested site of personal domination. Despite the violence of the slaveholding class and the structural force enslavers wielded, changes associated with age – both physical and mental, real and imagined – disrupted and denied enslavers' efforts to make this power real. Age was a vector of power for antebellum southerners, Black and white, and the aging process had the potential to shape and reshape social hierarchies and interpersonal relations in the Old South. Enslaved people might become pawns amidst intergenerational white conflict, but they could also see the advancing age of enslavers as providing them with a limited space to adapt, negotiate, or to resist their condition. Such a response was not inevitable nor even necessarily successful in the long or short term. Even small-scale acts of insubordination or temporary reversals of the dynamics of mastery, however, helped to demonstrate the limits of enslavers' powers and upend their claims to natural dominance. Enslaved people understood that mastery was not innate but instead embodied, and, that, as the body grew "withered by time," so too might their enslaver's pretensions of authority, dominance, and honor.[81] This knowledge shaped enslaved peoples' strategies for survival and forms of resistance both temporary and permanent.

---

[80] *Gilbert* v. *State*, 26 Tenn. 524, 7 Hum. 524 (1847), 525, 528, 531.
[81] Diary of Benjamin Leonard Covington Wailes, July 17, 1860.

8

"They are getting too old and weak"

Aged Mastery and White Conflict

Throughout the late 1850s, David Golightly Harris, a cotton farmer in Tennessee, recorded his struggles to make a profit and to manage the people he enslaved. Harris also outlined his resentment at the additional responsibilities foisted on him as his parents aged. On April 29, 1858, the thirty-seven-year-old Harris recorded that "Father & Mother came to see us to day." This had not been a pleasant experience: "They do not come often, they say they are getting too old and weak." His parents' growing infirmities affected their moods and health, which also limited their abilities as enslavers. Harris was annoyed at having to cover for these failings, bemoaning that "My fathers [*sic*] plantation takes much of my time & attention from my own." Harris knew he should be respectful to his elders, but he struggled with this: "I have been at much trouble [to] try to manage his business for him, but as I get no money and not much thanks, I think that I shall trouble myself less about them." After a particularly disagreeable visit, Harris recorded his frustration, but also tacit recognition that he would not have to deal with his parents' failings for too much longer, with reference to his mother's advanced age: "She is old and her ways and her days are nearly gone."[1]

The image Harris constructed of his aging parents was directly opposed to the portraits of masterful enslavers so beloved by proslavery writers of the antebellum period and beyond. If "the abstract idea of master is governing by one's own will, and that of slave is submission or subjection to such control," as William Smith put it, aged enslavers risked revealing to all the limits to such abstraction, and the invidious consequences of this

---

[1] Racine (Ed.), *Piedmont Farmer*, 81, 110, 184, 203.

for individual slavers and the slave system.[2] In Harris's telling, his elderly parents' enslaved people were neither submissive nor subjected to much control: "Fathers hands has done almost nothing this year. They are an expence to him and a vexation to me." Harris believed it was time for his father to step back from his duties entirely: "I do wish father would hire all his negroes to some man that would make them work."[3] If Harris's father could not enforce his will on those whom he enslaved or keep the respect of his peers, was he really a master at all?

Historians have noted that white men hoped to approach the end of their life "in control, never in a subservient position, marching and erect," with an emphasis on maintaining authority and power as they aged.[4] Brenda Stevenson argues that as white parents aged, "male children often assumed stewardship or patriarchal power, while daughters cared for elderly, sometimes ailing, parents and administered their domestic affairs," but with little attention to how this transition of power was experienced and understood. Harris's writings, however, suggest that real and imagined changes associated with the aging process might lead to tension and unsettle existing social dynamics. Stevenson shows that "the larger southern community was hierarchical," and that "race, class, gender, and culture, formed the basis of the South's stratification and traditionally placed planter status (Caucasian, wealthy, male) at its pinnacle."[5] Adding age as a factor in configuring relations of power among southern whites challenges the implied stasis of this framing.

John J. Clegg's fascinating work suggests that credit market discipline, and the structures of slavery itself, "*compelled* slave owners to compete via markets, whether they wanted to or not." Those who failed to adapt, specialize, or thrive in the competitive marketplace risked losing "their assets to those more willing or able to make the most cost-efficient use of them."[6] James Oakes argues that recent scholarship has destroyed "whatever was left of the mythical version of an Old South that resisted the money-grubbing values of the market." Instead, "southern slave society stood out by the extremity and ruthlessness of its exploitation. It was the

---

[2] William A. Smith; edited by Thomas O. Summers, *Lectures on the Philosophy and Practice of slavery: As Exhibited in the Institution of Domestic Slavery in the United States; With the Duties of Masters to Slaves* (Nashville: Stevenson and Evans, 1856), 41.

[3] Racine (Ed.), *Piedmont Farmer*, 175, 184.   [4] Greenberg, *Honor and Slavery*, 93.

[5] Stevenson, *Life in Black and White*, 138, xiii.

[6] John J. Clegg, "Credit Market Discipline and Capitalist Slavery in Antebellum South Carolina," *Social Science History*, 42.2 (2018), 343–76, 346, 347. Italics in original.

worst of all possible worlds."[7] This chapter shows how the push for dominance and profit, and the dynamics of slavery, affected white southerners' dealings with one another. Those considered as squandering their "assets" found themselves at risk of exploitation from those seeking to rise in a slave society; elderly enslavers, once "at the pinnacle," could be forced to fight against the rising generation who looked at them and saw dependency and submissiveness instead of autonomy and mastery.[8] These traits – and general binaries of power/powerlessness – were understood as bound up with the racializing discourse of slavery and the gendered dynamics of patriarchy.[9] Elderly enslavers – both men and women – sometimes came to believe that advanced age was a relation of powerlessness which marked them as closer to enslaved than enslaver, and which served to unsettle existing power relations in the community.

Those who fought against such depictions were forced to confront wider communal perceptions of their inability to enact mastery, and these battles had particular emotional effects. Cross-cultural scholarship argues that communal assumptions of incapacity associated with age can be humiliating. William E. May, for example, states that "the progressive loss of friends, job, bodily prowess, and energy; the passing look on the face of the young that tells us we are old – these experiences assault one's dignity; they humiliate."[10] In his final work on southern honor, Bertram Wyatt-Brown noted that "humiliation has only a thin bibliography"; this chapter adds to that bibliography by charting the challenges southern whites faced as they aged.[11] These old slavers are not objects of pity. Rather, this approach further reveals the culture of exploitation that drove life in antebellum slavery, and showcases the conflict that erupted among white southerners as a result of "Time's relentless hand."[12]

* * *

Antebellum enslavers commonly recorded their anguish at growing older, whether based on personal experience or in observing others. Diaries, letters, and other "ego documents" have long been understood by historians of medicine as providing insight into "the communal minds and

---

[7] Oakes, "Capitalism and Slavery," 216.   [8] Stevenson, *Life in Black and White*, xiii.

[9] See Glover, *Southern Sons*, 23; Merritt, *Masterless Men*, 121.

[10] William F. May, 'The Virtues and Vices of the Elderly', in Thomas R. Cole and Sally Gaddow (Eds.), *What Does It Mean to Grow Old? Reflections from the Humanities* (Durham: Duke University Press, 1986), 41–63, 52.

[11] Wyatt-Brown, *A Warring Nation*, 7.

[12] Lewis and Darley, *Odd Leaves from the Life of a Louisiana "Swamp Doctor,"* 141–3.

hearts of the sick" and as giving evidence of historical actors' "secret hopes and fears," including those related to the "experience of death, of being ill themselves or of tending an indisposed member of their family."[13] This included narratives relaying perceptions of the aging process; while not inevitably negative, slavers understood that they remained subject to "the ravages of time … the inevitable ruin to which all animated matter is incident," and recorded their responses to aging as such.[14] According to Puritan minister Joseph Lathrop, concern with aging as a comparative process, where people looked at others to understand their position on the steps of life, was common. The aged worried about how others perceived them, afraid alike of challenge and of being left behind: "Once our advice was sought and regarded; now we are passed by with neglect, and younger men take our place: even the management of our own substance has fallen into the hands of others, and they perhaps scarcely think us worthy of being consulted."[15]

Antebellum southerners prizing of independence and authority exacerbated their worries over status and respect. As Lorri Glover argues, an "intense – and racialized – zeal for independence was rooted in slaveholding, and it set southern elites on a course apart from their northern contemporaries."[16] Enslavers who had "reached the mid-day of [their] life, and basked for a time in the enjoyment of its sunlight," thus found their descent "through its afternoon and evening, to its night in the grave," with an attendant shift toward dependency, particularly unpleasant.[17] James Henry Hammond self-pityingly commented on the unstoppable march of time. On May 12, 1855, aged forty-eight, Hammond lamented being "now too old, too infirm, too heart broken to do any thing with spirit or look forward to any earthly enjoyments." As Kenneth Greenberg shows, when Hammond died aged fifty-seven, his son deliberately crafted a report of his final moment that articulated his father's "designs for mastery." Hammond Jnr recorded final words that apparently expressed undiminished vigor and a thirst for honor: "'As to a monument, I have nothing to say of that; you boys do as you think best. But, mind,' and he

---

[13] Roy Porter, "The Patient's View: Doing Medical History From Below," *Theory and Society* 14.2 (1985), 175–98, 183; Joan Lane, "'The Doctor Scolds Me': The Diaries and Correspondence of Patients in Eighteenth-Century England," in Roy Porter (Ed.), *Patients and Practitioners. Lay Perceptions of Medicine in Pre-Industrial Society* (Cambridge: Cambridge University Press, 1985), 205–48, 208.

[14] Riddlemoser, "Conception in the Human Female."

[15] Lathrop, *The Infirmities and Comforts of Old Age*, 6.   [16] Glover, *Southern Sons*, 23.

[17] Caldwell, *Thoughts on the Effects of Old Age*, 14.

uttered it with a thrilling earnestness, looking at me and pointing his finger, 'if we are subjugated, run a plow over my grave.'" But Hammond's long-term anguish over his failing health and weakened status tell a different story. On April 16, 1861, for example, Hammond lamented that reduced powers left him unable to fully express the momentousness of the attack of Fort Sumter: "my hand, my health, and my eyes fail me utterly." His children constructed a posthumous narrative of mastery, but Hammond's private writings resembled Lathrop's vision of aged anticipation of "the increase of infirmities and pains from month to month, – and the probable event of total decrepitude and confinement, and the entire loss of his feeble remains of sensibility and intellect."[18] Indeed, in Hammond's eyes, his reduced powers left him "little more than an imbecile."[19]

Benjamin Leonard Covington Wailes, a Mississippi enslaver, extensively detailed the negative effects of aging. Wailes hoped to approach his end with the stoicism expected of "honorable" men, recording in August, 1856:

Entered upon my sixtieth year. Blessed with a fair share of health and suffering under few of the infirmities of age. Somewhat bald and slightly gray. My eyes require glasses of higher power than is usual at my time of life, these organs having been most abused by reading and writing by candle light. My teeth are also much decayed, and many of them gone, the effects of salivation.[20]

On his birthday, Wailes often expressed his thanks for being blessed with "fewer infirmities than fall to most my age." His almost daily reports of ailing health between 1858 and 1862, including being "tortured with pain" and "excessively weak," suggest deeper concern with the troublesome march of time. Despite occasional gripes over his overseers and enslaved people, Wailes was generally able to assert his authority on the plantation and in the wider community. Yet his reflections on his health and frequently negative comments regarding other "old" people reveal his fears that this authority was tenuous and his concerns with how others saw him. In August 1858, for example, Wailes was dismayed to see a friend grown "exceedingly feeble and a mere skeleton; on the verge of the grave with consumption." His distress was compounded when his friend's "gay young wife told him laughingly that that she would never

---

[18] Lathrop, *The Infirmities and Comforts of Old Age*, 7.
[19] Carol Bleser (Ed.), *Secret and Sacred: The Diaries of James Henry Hammond, a Southern Slaveholder* (Columbia: University of South Carolina Press, 1988), 266–7, 300, 272.
[20] Diary of Benjamin Leonard Covington Wailes, August 1, 1856.

again marry a man with gray hairs in his head."[21] Wailes did not find the joke amusing.

Wailes was clearly concerned with the effects of aging on others. He acknowledged that most of his contemporaries were, as one antebellum commentator described it, "descending to old age, with great but insensible rapidity."[22] One friend "looks thin and begins to grow old – some gray in his hair," while another was "slow sluggish and decrepit in his movements ... his memory and mental activities greatly impaired."[23] Given the extensive descriptions of his own ailments, illnesses, and the "infirmities of age," it seems plausible that Wailes looked at his contemporaries and imagined his own fate. After recording how his friend Richard T. Archer, who had become "very irritable and dogmatic" as he aged, narrowly escaped "having his brains blown out" in a duel, Wailes acknowledged their shared movement down the steps of life: "He is becoming quite gray like myself."[24]

Beyond these personal reflections, Wailes was also disappointed at, to return to Harris's phrasing, the rising generation's apparent pleasure that his "ways and days" were "almost gone." After hearing the Natchez community planned to celebrate secession on George Washington's birthday, Wailes recorded sadness at "the destruction of our glorious Union and Republic" and the generational change this demonstrated: "A strange desecration of the day, but in this fast and enlightened age young America regards the purest and greatest patriot that ever lived nothing more than an old fogie." Wailes likewise understood himself to be a "fogie" and accepted that his best days were behind him:

Without suffering much painful desease in the last year I feel the infirmities of age growing upon me very sensibly, maladies not serious or formidable at the outset I find are becoming chronic, and of a graver aspect, and must, if they progress as they have latterly, seriously impair my vital organs. Perhaps I have had my share of the goods of this life, though I certainly have tasted deeply of its bitterness. But the will of God be done – what is, is best.[25]

Wailes died in November 1862, aged sixty-five. His diary suggests that he confronted his mortality with the stoicism expected of "masters."

---

[21] Diary of Benjamin Leonard Covington Wailes, August 1, 1858, August 5–6, 10, 1860, 29 August 1858.

[22] Emmons, "Piety, a Peculiar Ornament to the Aged," 499.

[23] Diary of Benjamin Leonard Covington Wailes, July 25, 1859.

[24] Diary of Benjamin Leonard Covington Wailes, January 7, 1860.

[25] Diary of Benjamin Leonard Covington Wailes, February 22, 1861, August 1, 1861.

Wailes's constant attention to health, his negative comments about how others treated aged contemporaries, and his concerns with wider intergenerational tension in antebellum society nevertheless reveal struggles with the changes age caused to health and self.

William Greenberg and Bertram Wyatt-Brown use the decision of famed Virginian firebreather Edmund Ruffin to kill himself rather than suffer the indignities of a dishonorable death to illustrate aged whites' concepts of honor and their efforts to maintain mastery. It is clear, also, that Ruffin had long struggled with declining powers on account of age. For several years prior to his death, Ruffin recorded his anguish, even anger, at "infirmities of body & mind," noting how in these "latter years, & more especially in the latest, my faculties & powers of mind, as well as of body, have been greatly impaired by age." In life and death, Ruffin was a powerful propagandist for slavery and the "Lost Cause," and Bertram Wyatt-Brown proclaimed that Ruffin demonstrated the power of the code of honor among southern whites when he "blew out his brains in rage against Confederate surrender": "Ruffin was no masquerader."[26] But Ruffin's choice to end his life also reflected fears of future suffering. By the coming of the Civil War, Ruffin was racked with pain and misery, could "see nothing before me but days & nights of decreasing capacity & means for enjoyment, & increasing sources & causes of pain," and longed for "a sudden, unexpected, & painless death."[27] Ruffin chose his end, but knew he had lost, and could only lose further, the ability to enact mastery elsewhere.

* * *

Antebellum southerners discussed the health and condition of friends, family, and members of the white community in both public and private settings, often sympathetically but sometimes disparagingly. Community judgments were important for subjective and functional understandings of age; people might not consider themselves old, but if friends, peers, and rivals did, tension could erupt. Court records and legal texts provide a window into these discussions. Ariela J. Gross notes that trials were a "forum for a man's neighbors to discuss not only his local reputation for slave treatment but all aspects of his plantation management: selling and

---

[26] Wyatt-Brown, *Southern Honor*, 35. Greenberg, *Honor and Slavery*, 93.

[27] William Kaufman Scarborough (Ed.), *The Diary of Edmund Ruffin, Vol. II: The Years of Hope, 1861–June 1863* (Baton Rouge: Louisiana State University Press, 1976), 139, 541, 673–4.

trading, the employment of overseers, growing crops, even breeding slaves."[28] This could include considerations of how age affected slave-holding authority.

During the trial over the distribution of Duncan McLaurin's Mississippi property, one witness claimed that McLaurin's "mind was declining with his age, but not more so than was usual for persons of his age." They "saw nothing in him that would indicate that he was more imbecile in his mind than men of his age would ordinarily be." Another, however, agreed with the counsel's contention that McLaurin demonstrated a degree of "fretful-ness and childish rage inconsistent with his solidity of mind as you had known him in other days and more reasonableness, which shewed the affects of old age on his mind."[29] Elisha Harrell of Gates County, North Carolina, seeking to prove his worth as a witness in a trial over the contested sale of a slave in 1831, acknowledged that at "seventy years old" he could not "recollect very minute things that passed many years ago." Nonetheless, Harrell forcefully insisted he recollected this case "very well."[30] In *Exum* v. *Canty,* 1851, however, the court accepted that "feeble-ness and infirmity are the natural consequences of age," and witnesses openly challenged the deceased's mental strength on this base:

All of the witnesses stated, as part of the grounds upon which they formed their opinion of his incompetency, that John Williams in conversation was disconnected and incoherent; that he would commence conversing on one subject, and before he got through with it would "skip" suddenly to another. Most of them stated that he would laugh "a childish," "foolish laugh," during his conversation, and without any "apparent cause," and would also "break off" his conversation on any subject "by cursing and abusing his brother Benjamin," without his name having been previously mentioned by any one.[31]

Antebellum contemporaries often referred to old age as a regression to infancy, with attendant negative loss of status. John Stanford wrote that "it is humiliating for a person to be subject to the trite adage, 'Once a man, and twice a child'; but in extreme old age it is seldom that the imputation can be avoided; and enfeebled humanity is compelled to submit."[32] W. A. Achenbaum argues that "being old and becoming older in

---

[28] Gross, *Double Character*, 98.

[29] *Hill* v. *McLaurin* (1856), Case File 125, Box 15, Lawrence County Chancery Court Cases, microfilm, reel 13317, MDAH.

[30] Gates County, Slave Records, 1783–1867, Civil Actions Concerning Slaves, 1783–1867, Box CR.041.928.003, Folder 1831, NCDAH.

[31] *Exum* v. *Canty*, 34 Miss. 533 (1857), 548, 540.

[32] Stanford, *The Aged Christian's Companion*, 53–4.

antebellum America did not connote loss of functionality."[33] Nevertheless, community observations on the changes associated with aging frequently appear in legal records and shaped social and legal disputes among southern whites. When Sandy Owens sought to prove that his aged father required appointment of a guardian because he was "physically helpless" and had a memory that was "at times extinct," he assured the court that extensive testimony from "neighbours & relations" could establish this truth.[34] Spartanburg enslaver David W. Moore was so disturbed by the frailties of a local white woman that he sought intervention (ostensibly) on her behalf. Moore requested a writ of lunacy to protect Mary McMakin's interests as she was "a verry aged lady and from her age and imbecility of mind & body is wholy incapable of governing & managing her own affairs." The doctors who examined McMakin agreed and stated plainly the frailties of age:

Her physical condition impaired by old age – her eyes dim – her hearing bad & she was continually in an uneasy, rocking motion; her mental faculties were very confused; her memory quite deficient ... with her extreme old age I am warranted in the belief, that her imbecility of mind would incapacitate her from transacting any business or even discharging the ordinary duties of life.

The court concurred and referred the petition to committee to find a suitable person to "have the lawful custody and charge of her person and property."[35]

In these cases, petitioners claimed to support their aged peers, and framed their discussions on aging sympathetically. North Carolina enslaver Ann Blount Pettigrew was equally supportive when recording her sadness at the declining health of "Old Forlaw," a "poor old man ... not long for this world I suspect." Such expressions of compassion toward ailing elderly enslavers, even if genuine, diminished the lingering shadow of their authority. Indeed, in Pettigrew's eyes, Forlaw was "a pitiable looking object."[36]

---

[33] Achenbaum, "Delineating Old Age," 303.

[34] Petition of Sandy Owens, September 28, 1858, Williamson County, Tennessee, #21485807, Series 2, RSPP.

[35] Petition of David Moore, February 21, 1846; Order, February 9, 1846; Affidavit, Dr. L. C. Kennedy, January 24, 1846; Testimony, John Brooke, Dr. L. C. Kennedy, Thomas Balinger, John Chapman, ca. February 9, 1846; Order, February 10, 1846; Jury's Report, ca. February 26, 1846; Commissioners' Report, February 26, 1846; Order, ca. 26 February 1846; Commissioner's Report, February 26, 1846, Spartanburg District, South Carolina, #21384623, Series 2, RSPP.

[36] Sarah McCulloch Lemmon (Ed.), *The Pettigrew Papers, Volume II, 1819–1843* (Raleigh: State Department of Archives and History, 1971), 78.

Pettigrew later reported that although ostensibly a "master," "the old man" had been deceived and victimized by his sons, who had illegally sold his enslaved people: "he is a child in intellect & therefore is not reproachble [*sic*] for any thing that is done but it is believed he knew nothing of this affair untill after." Forced to submit to his sons, Forlaw lost authority accordingly. His infantilization was underscored in Pettigrew's reporting that he "frequently cries immoderaly [*sic*]."[37] Antebellum contemporaries used tears to represent the elderly's loss of nerve and self-control: "So also in debilitated age, when the manly tone forsakes its hold, and the power of nerve has almost expired, we painfully observe the poor old man's tears silently flow down the channels of his furrowed cheeks."[38] Lorri Glover notes that "no quality mattered more to elite men or stood in starker contrast to the lives of slaves than independence."[39] Forlaw, however, barely controlled his bodily functions, let alone commanded the respect of others. His weakness attracted the vultures.

In the dispute over James Luckett's will, family, friends, and neighbors commented extensively on his physical frailties, and the embarrassment of all at his declining powers. Luckett, "about sixty years of age," suffered from palsy, apoplexy, and a loss of mental capacity as he aged. One witness recorded that Luckett continually returned "back to early life and reciting incidents, had partially lost his recollection of recent events." Some of his neighbors were unsympathetic, with Joseph Hennard claiming that he "generally found Mr. Luckett very irritable[;] he appeared more like a spoiled child than any thing else. He was whimsical." The physician Dr. Barnes attested that the changes were permanent, concluding that "from his age and the general symptoms of his case that there was not much probability" of improvement. David Gibson testified that Luckett resented his declining powers and self-isolated through fear of public mockery. Luckett, who "appeared as old men generally appear," needed his daughter to cut his food "up into mouth fulls." Luckett hoped for recovery and to "spend some time among his old neighbors & friends," but feared presenting an image of dependency in public: "in consequence of his not being able to feed himself ... he hated it, and ... felt ashamed to eat at the table." Such testimony vividly connects to wider theoretical literature on how "loss that is threatened with aging is not the sheer fact of physical decline, but the inevitable alienation from a body that is regarded as an imprisoning

---

[37] Lemmon (Ed.), *Pettigrew Papers*, 129.
[38] Stanford, *The Aged Christian's Companion*, 53–4.   [39] Glover, *Southern Sons*, 26.

object."[40] Luckett's response to this alienation was to withdraw from the company of his peers, perhaps fearing his bodily failings would inspire avarice instead of support.

Indeed, these comments on Luckett's age and infirmities were not neutral observations. Instead, they demonstrated the significance of age in the context of power, authority, and mastery. They were part of an explicit design to disregard Luckett's will. It was successful, with the court stating it was "quite impossible to believe, that James Luckett had any strength of understanding sufficient to qualify him deliberately & with fair judgment to will, with prudence & a settled purpose, the disposition of his estate." Luckett had hoped to have the power yet to "will something," but the aged man was publicly derided as "capricious & whimsical," and his decision-making as being fatally marked by "the fitful changes of his temper, jealousy, or sudden particulaties."[41] He had no mastery of mind or body, and the will was rejected. Luckett, as will be shown, was not alone in having his authority and identity challenged on account of age.

* * *

Proslavery commentators such as Patrick Hues Mell claimed that "slave-holders are more likely to be dignified in their intercourse with each other" because the assurance and self-respect gained through their shared position as "masters" made them "more likely to command respect from others."[42] Changes associated with old age, however, could see self-assurance dwindle and community respect disappear. Family and kin, as well as the wider white community, might diminish the aged person's claims to autonomy and authority to better their own position. Jason Miller of South Carolina understood that aging risked upending existing hierarchies, in both Black and white families, informing his WPA interviewer "I has seen many cases, where de head of de house turn over all his belongin's to de son who move in." Miller was clear that this change reflected a wider assumption of mastery: "In most of dese cases, de head of de house become no more pow'ful than a child and often when he give it all out, he get sent to de poorhouse, to boot."[43]

---

[40] Sally Gadow, "Recovering the Body in Ageing," in Nancy S. Jecker (Ed.), *Ageing and Ethics: Philosophical Problems in Gerontology* (New York: Springer, 1992), 113–20, 113; Coors, "Embodied Time," 133–5.

[41] *J. A. Brock v. Legatees of James Luckett*, Clairborne Co., 1838, Box 5803, Case 641, MDAH.

[42] Mell, *Slavery: A Treatise*, 35.   [43] Rawick (Ed.), *AS*, 3.3, 188.

Elderly enslavers were sometimes reduced to the dependency associated with childhood, or even slavery itself.[44] William Harper, a prominent southern politician and advocate for slavery, explained that social inequality was inevitable: "Man is born to subjection ... it is the very bias of [Man's] nature, that the strong and wise should control the weak and ignorant."[45] Such comments aimed to normalize the master–slave relation, and did not countenance enslavers' potential dependence and submission. Hierarchies, however, were more fluid than such rhetoric suggests, and legal records from across the US South reveal the susceptibility of elderly enslavers to abuse, deceit, and even violence from peers who saw the aged as easy victims, not as elders to be honored. Enslavers, taught "to resist every insult, every aggression upon his rights," could be stunned to find their failings on account of age.[46] Poor treatment meted out to aged enslavers reveals the contested and embodied nature of respect and authority in the antebellum south, and underscores the wider culture of exploitation that characterized slaveholding society.

Some enslavers, understanding that they were losing the powers required to maintain authority, acted first. Belinda R. Moseley of Virginia openly acknowledged that increased frailty impacted upon her ability to control her enslaved people and asked for trustees to be appointed: "from the turbulent temper of some of said slaves, and her advanced age and infirmities, she is made to feel the want of assistance in their management."[47] Such rhetoric might reflect gendered norms associating dependency with femininity, but male enslavers made similar admissions. Steve Johnson explained that his enslaver asked for assistance while on his descent: "[Master] wuz an old bachelor an' so he sent back to Missippi [*sic*] for his nephew James Boliver Billingsly to cum an' help him wid de plantation."[48] Benjamin Boulware of Fairfield, South Carolina, sought to offload his slaveholding responsibilities before it was too late. Boulware, who had assumed responsibility for raising his thirteen-year-old nephew John J. Neil and managing the eighteen slaves in his estate, wanted to sell them and save the money in a trust instead. He admitted the limits to his powers of endurance: "your Orator is now a man of feeble

[44] Glover, *Southern Sons*, 23.

[45] Chancellor Harper, "Memoir on Slavery, Part I," *De Bow's Review*, 8.3 (March, 1850), 232–43.

[46] Charles Grandison Parsons, *Inside View of Slavery; or, A Tour Among the Planters, with an Introduction by H. B. Stowe* (Boston: J. P. Jewett and Company, 1855), 238.

[47] Petition of Belinda Moseley, c. 1838, Lynchburg, Virginia, #21683803, Series 2, RSPP.

[48] Rawick (Ed.), *AS, Supp.*, Ser. 2, 6.5, 2055.

health in the decline of life, and ill suited to attend to hiring out these negroes from year to year."⁴⁹ The court agreed, and the enslaved people were sold at public auction.

Sometimes these decisions were taken out of the aged enslaver's hands. In 1859, Elijah Webb was granted trusteeship over the Terry estate because Nancy Webb Terry and Henry Terry were "both old, feeble and almost helpless, and are unable and have been for years past to provide for themselves necessary comforts." In his efforts to justify the transfer, Webb stressed the seemingly irreversible decline associated with age (and intoxication) and denigrated his dependents' prior handling of their affairs. Henry Webb Terry's "intemperate habits and his improvident management of the said lands" had worsened their conditions and necessitated his own assumption of control.⁵⁰ In 1857, the Parks family of Tennessee sought to remove Ezekiel Spriggs from his trusteeship of their property, including the slaves, because he was "advanced in years and has not as yet Invested" the money granted on their behalf. He was a liability, and the risks were worsening: "from his advanced age [Spriggs] might die and leave the money outstanding on precarious security." Spriggs meekly accepted their derogatory assessment, acknowledging he was "getting old, and is somewhat infirm," and a new trustee was hired.⁵¹ Elderly enslavers were sometimes thus depicted as necessary objects of public intervention, with the removal of agency indicating an inexorable transition toward dependency and submission – traits long understood as bound up with the racializing discourse of slavery and which risked positioning incapacitated elders as closer to enslaved than enslaver.⁵²

The heirs to the estate of William Edwards applied the discourse of a slide toward dependency as they sought to take control of the property from their aunt, Elizabeth Williams. Williams had been bequeathed twelve slaves and land in Southampton County, Virginia, with this property passing to the remaining heirs upon her death. The petitioners were concerned, however, that irreversible damage would be done to their future wealth before she died: "in consequence of the old age and extreme imbecility of the said Williams she is entirely incompetant [*sic*] to take care of

⁴⁹ Petition of Benjamin Boulware, July 12, 1859, Fairfield District, South Carolina, #21385955, Series 2, RSPP.
⁵⁰ Petition of Elijiah Webb, May 11, 1858, Anderson District, South Carolina, #21385846, Series 2, RSPP.
⁵¹ Petition of Louisa Parks et al., August 10, 1857; Answer, Ezekiel Spriggs, August 24, 1857, Bradley County, Tennessee, #21485742, Series 2, RSPP.
⁵² See Glover, *Southern Sons*, 23; Merritt, *Masterless Men*, 121.

herself or the said slaves in her possession." The enslaved people, who had "not been in the habit for sometime past of making a good support by their labour," had such laxity because there was "no person to make those work who are able." The petitioners warned the judges "that if something is not done in the premises by your worships, the said slaves and also the said Williams will become chargeable upon the County for their support or will die for the want of food."[53] They were worried about their own future wealth, but the problem was "solved" by Williams's death not long after the petition. Here, advanced age was more important than gender or other aspects of identity in establishing Williams's reduced capacity, as the petitioners implored the court to prioritize the interests of the rising generation over those on their way out. In doing so, they underscored how age, as much as race, gender, and class, was a relation of power that affected identities, personal relations, and social dynamics in the American South.

* * *

Proslavery writers suggested that "there is no relation, perhaps, unless it is that between father and son, in which a more decided influence is exerted, than that which exists between the master and his servant." However, age-related decline caused dramatic shifts in the supposedly natural, normal, and static hierarchies of parent and child.[54] In Davidson County, Tennessee, 1851, William M. Alexander sought court intervention to ascertain the mental state of his father. His petition was filed out of consideration for economic self-interest as much as any concern for his father's well-being: "Your petitioner is a son of said Thomas Alexander who is about to waste his estate for want of sufficient mental capacity to take care of and manage the same." The committee who assessed the elder Alexander acknowledged that though "neither an idiot nor a lunatic," he was no longer capable of mastery or even self-control. At upwards "of eighty years of age," Alexander's mind was "so much impaired from his extreme old age and physical debility that he is incapable of managing his affairs." The court granted William Alexander's request to assume control of his father's property and person.[55]

---

[53] Petition of Jonathan Darden et al., c. February 1850, Southampton County, Virginia, #21685015, Series 2, RSPP.

[54] Rev. A. T. Holmes, "The Duties of Christian Masters" in Nimmons McTyeire (Ed.), *Duties of Masters to Servants: Three Premium Essays,*" 145.

[55] Petition of William Alexander, October 1, 1851; Report of the jury, October 16, 1851; Court order, December 1, 1851, Davidson County, Tennessee, #21485136, Series 2, RSPP.

Similar dynamics were evident in Maury County, Tennessee, 1842, when Joseph Fagg asked for a Writ of Lunacy and the appointment of a guardian to protect his aged father from a vague but nefarious threat. Fagg Snr had "become very feeble and infirm, and from old age and imbecility of mind and body has become incapable of taking care of himself and his property, so as to provide for himself during his life and save his estate for his children." Joseph described the elder Fagg as "in his dotage" and "liable to be mislead [*sic*] as easily & controlled by others as a child."[56] Fagg Jnr claimed that his aim was to protect his father and safeguard his family, but in securing his family's wealth through a guardianship, the son publicly repudiated his father's claim to mastery and manhood and asserted himself as paterfamilias. The friends and families of those whose "ways and days" were done, to return to Harris's phrasing, could depict them as burdens whose authority must be ceded to protect the rising generation. Enslavers might expect to be respected by children, kin, and the wider community, but the decline that accompanied old age could see these dreams publicly denied.

These tensions occasioned no little strife for antebellum enslavers. Annie Row, interviewed for the Texas WPA project, witnessed one unwanted transition of power from her aging master to his son Billy: "'Tis a fine come to pass w'en de son goes 'ginst his father,' de Marster tells his boy." The son was clear over who was now in control: "'Jus' to protec' *my* property', Billy answers him."[57] Sarah Gudjer of North Carolina recalled that her "ole an' feeble" enslaver complained to her father about the lack of care or respect from his ungrateful heirs:

"Well, Smart (pappy, he name Smart), I's tard, wurried, an' trubble. All dese yeahs I wok foah mah chillun. Dey nevah do de right thing. Dey wurries me, Smart. I tell yo', Smart, I's a good mind t'put mahself away. I's good mind t' drown mahself right heah. I tebble worried, Smart."

Smart counselled his enslaver to be "content" for the time being, but "a few days aftah dat, Ole Marse Joe was found ahangin' in de ba'n by de bridle."[58]

Joseph Lathrop recorded his pity for "the aged man, who, when his strength fails, looks anxiously around, and sees not a son on whom he can lean."[59] But some white southerners saw their parents' advancing age as

---

[56] Petition of Joseph Fagg, September 19, 1842, Maury County, Tennessee, #21484207, Series 2, RSPP.

[57] Rawick (Ed.), *AS, Supp.*, Ser 2, 8.7, 3372. Italics mine.

[58] Rawick (Ed.), *AS, 14.1*, 352.

[59] Lathrop, *The Infirmities and Comforts of Old Age*, 8.

providing opportunities to take control and make their own way. In Newberry District, South Carolina, Charles Lile's children were so disturbed by his failing powers that they took to the courts to request a division of the estate before he destroyed their future. Liles had appointed James Ashford as trustee, aiming to ensure "a certain and suitable provision and support and to prevent them from coming to want and poverty by reason of the growing infirmities of the said Charles." Lile's inability to maintain oversight of his trustee's actions, however, was leading to ruin, with Ashford depicted as taking advantage of a weak man. Although "unable to point out any particular acts of mismanagement of the said James Ashford," the heirs insisted "the said Estate has not been so productive nor yielded so large a profit as it might otherwise have done had it been managed by private & self interest." They insisted that the problems resulted from their father's "age, infirmity & a confirmed habit of perpetual intoxication" that made him "entirely incapable of governing, or taking care of himself or his family." The children took charge instead, requesting new guardians for the minors, that Ashford account for the trust, and that the whole of the estate be divided between the children. These requests were granted. Charles Liles, publicly deemed unfit for self-governance, was given "a competent & fully adequate provision ... during life," but was made entirely submissive to his children.[60]

James Lane Sr. of Marion District, South Carolina, was another son who intervened to prevent the wasting of his father's estate. He insisted that his father, Osban Lane, had become weak in his old age, attracting invidious attention from local whites. James connected his father's reduced status to his advanced age and publicly insisted Osban was no longer a man or a "master," but instead a meek child needing protection from himself as much as others. James stated that his ninety-year-old father had long been "altogether unfit and unable to govern himself or manage his affairs," but had worsened in the past few years. His mind had "gradually become more and more impaired and weakened" until he had "grown completely childish and worn out in understanding," and thereby "in danger of becoming a victim to sharpers and swindlers." This was no abstract peril. John Deer Jnr, a family neighbor, had apparently "craftily worked upon the fears and weakness of the said Osban[,] inducing him to

---

[60] Petition of Lana Hancock et al., January 13, 1824; Orders, April 2, 1825, April 28, 1825; Commissioners' Report, November 28, 1826; Order, December 1826, Newberry District, South Carolina, #21382443, Series 2, RSPP.

believe that his near relations and friends were attempting to cheat and defraud him." After promising to provide Osban with "the necessaries of life," Deer Jnr gained control of his land, livestock, notes of purchase, and four enslaved people worth at least $2,000. James believed that Deer Jnr had seized upon the weakness of an old man and that he planned to remove the property beyond the court's jurisdiction, "and by these means to bring him in his old age to poverty."[61] The court granted James's request and he assumed mastery over his father and his estate.

* * *

The petitioners in these cases used the discourse of aging as a process of decline to rationalize their dominance, but asserted that they did so with respect to their elders' previous status. In some cases, however, elderly whites made claims of abuse and deceit because of their advanced age. Sarah Davenport, "an aged and infirm woman" from Newberry, South Carolina, asked her son-in-law Allen Pitts to live with her and "superintend her affairs" on account of her reduced powers. She promised Pitts four enslaved people upon her death as reward but he felt this was too long to wait and tricked her into signing a bill conveying them to him entirely. Pitts ignored the request to support his mother-in-law and clearly hoped that nature would soon take its course: "he has not as yet removed to the plantation of your oratrix nor has as yet taken upon himself any care or management of the business of your oratrix."[62] The courts rescinded the sale, but the case reveals the tenuous nature of Davenport's position, and the relative weakness of elderly whites in southern society.

In Adams County, Mississippi, 1849, a furious battle for control erupted over the slaves of the late John Henry, now enslaved by his widow, Emily. The case illustrates how ambitious heirs could marshal the discourse associating old age with decline to challenge the identity and reputation of elders. Henry's grandchildren stressed that "Emily is very aged and infirm, unable to use, manage, or control said property – and surrounded by and under the influence of advisers who are hostile to complainants and desirous to defeat their ultimate right to the enjoyment of said property." Their self-interest was clear: on account of Henry's lack of control, "there is great danger that in case said negroes should be

---

[61] Petition of James Lane Snr, January 20, 1840, Marion District, South Carolina, #21384012, Series 2, RSPP.

[62] Petition of Sarah Davenport, May 16, 1821, Newberry District, South Carolina, #21382121, Series 2, RSPP.

removed, they will be sold, carried away, or disposed of, so that they will be entirely lost to them."

Henry's grandchildren depicted an elderly widow controlled by shadowy advisors. Emily rejected this picture out of hand. Her response to the petition addressed the selfishness and disrespect of her grasping heirs, and asserted her personal mastery. Their claims that "she is unable to use, manage or control said property" were untrue: "On the contrary[,] she avers that she is now & always heretofore has been able to do so." Henry insisted that claims of incapacity were deliberate lies, made by those who were "impatient of the life of this respondent" and who "may have convinced themselves that she has already lived too long & ought not longer to stand in the way of their using said property." Impatience at her refusal to die animated their "notions about her infirmity." The challengers were "desperately bent, upon having the control, possession & use of said property, even during the life time of this respondent." Henry understood that they planned to use popular understandings of the limitations of old age against her: "presuming upon the old age of respondent, they & their aiders & advisers have stated that they intend to keep said property in litigation in this state until your respondent should die."[63] Henry defended herself from these charges and the parties reached a compromise. The case nevertheless reveals the depth of intergenerational divisions within some slaving families, with younger relatives willing to trample on the rights and belittle the reputations of those who had "lived too long."

In some cases, interested parties tried to hasten their elders' decline. In *Lehman* v. *Logan*, 1851, Henry R. Lehman, a remainderman to the property of the late John Logan, sought to secure his share before the death of John's wife, Mary Ann Logan, who had become sole executrix with possession of the whole estate. Lehman insisted Mary Ann was "old and infirm of mind, incapable of managing the estate, and that it has been greatly wasted," and painted a picture of slavery inverted: "the slaves have been so little kept in order that they have become idle and drunken; and that there is great danger, that the said slaves will not be forthcoming at the death of said Mary Ann." An injunction was initially approved but Logan's counsel fought back. The counsel admitted "that the defendant is very old, but denies, that the estate has been wasted and is now less valuable than when she received it." The North Carolina Supreme

---

[63] *Mary J. Henry et al.* v. *Emily Henry*, April 16, 1849, Records of the Vice-Chancery Court, Document Number 446, Adams County Courthouse, Natchez, Mississippi, HNF.

Court concurred. Justice Frederick Nash insisted "that the fears and apprehensions" of heirs that inheritable property would be wasted was not enough to usurp mastery, and expressed regret that "the only ground stated here is, that the defendant is a very aged lady, and labors, no doubt, under many of the infirmities incident to others at her time of life." Nash counseled patience, noting others were "content to risk their interests, until, in the course of nature, they shall come into its possession; and the plaintiff must be content, so far as this case is concerned, to bide his time."[64] Nash was clear that intergenerational transfer was inevitable. It simply should not be hastened.

Petitions and suits by those deceived, abused, or neglected on account of their age show significant levels of distress and demonstrate the problematic nature of aged mastery and contested hierarchies among antebellum southerners. Instead of support or respect, some aged enslavers came to realize their family keenly awaited their demise, while others believed they had been forced into dependency by unscrupulous heirs or others. Elegies for the antebellum order claimed that "generic characteristics" of the masterclass included "self-respect and consciousness of power," with "not a doubtful line in the face nor a doubtful tone in the voice."[65] Aged enslavers whose capabilities were dwindling, however, were wracked with doubt – and rightly so. Joshua Moody of Barnwell, South Carolina, for example, was in precarious health in 1837. While in a "state of great bodily and mental depression" following the death of his wife, Moody believed himself "altogether incapable of attending to his affairs." At this point, his son and son-in-law suggested "it would be better for him to divide the remainder of his estate among them with whom he might reside in more comfort than alone." Moody had little recollection of the events that took place but intimated that "he was induced to believe ... he was not capable of properly managing his affairs," and that he had little time left to live.[66]

Moody believed the document he signed allowed him to regain independence if he felt able. When he tried to enact this clause, however, he found that his loss of mastery was complete. The sons refused to return his property and instead installed him on a small plantation with three enslaved people, "with which scanty outfit, your Orator was obliged in

---

[64] *Lehman v. Logan*, 42. N.C. 296, 7 Ired. Eq. 296 (1851), 296, 297.
[65] Thomas Nelson Page, *Social Life in Virginia Before the War* (Cambridge, Mass.: John Wilson & Son, 1897), 44.
[66] Petition of Joshua Moody, July 14, 1841, Barnwell District, #21384109, Series 2, RSPP.

his old age to commence the world a new." Even more galling was the direct repudiation of his authority and autonomy – attributes so precious to antebellum southerners. John Mayfield notes that "by and large, Southern men were averse to admitting weakness," and that doing so meant renouncing claims of honor in the wider community.[67] Moody, however, was forced to publicly state that his sons denied him "the right to exercise ordinary acts of ownership" and claimed "the right to supervise and control [his] affairs, which pretensions are harassing to your Orator, inconsistent to his independence, and destructive of his comfort and happiness." Moody knew that "in the course of nature he could not live very long," but was desperate in his last years to "not be dependent even on his own children." The court concurred and restored Moody's property. He had, however, already suffered the indignity of public dishonor and abuse by children who rejected his claims of mastery, and was left with his reputation in tatters.[68]

In September 1839, John D. Young of Davidson County, Tennessee, outlined a similar struggle with family members who saw him as a problem to be removed, not a patriarch to respect. Young claimed that his sons Napoleon, Ferdinand, and William had manipulated him to gain the titles to certain land and slaves; he asked the court to restore the titles to him, and to grant compensation for monies they had earned by hiring out his slaves. Young, who admitted problems with intemperance, was outraged to find that his sons had "persuaded and procured him to make a conveyance of all his slavess [*sic*] and other property to his children in the form of a deed of gift, thereby stripping himself of the whole control of his property not even preserving a life estate." This action upended patriarchal norms, placing him "upon the mercy of his family who should have looked up to him for protection & support" – a mercy that was sorely lacking.

Young claimed that "Napoleon threatened to take violent possession of his negroes & sell them under pretence of the deed of 1826 or some other pretended claim." Young was left with no illusions about his newly subservient position: "so violent and preemptory had been the previous conduct of his son Napoleon that your Orator did not entertain the least doubt but he would forcibly take possession of said negroes and to prevent violence he peacibly gave possession thereof."[69] Elizabeth Fox-Genovese

---

[67] Mayfield, *Counterfeit Gentlemen*, 87.
[68] Petition of Joshua Moody, July 14, 1841, Barnwell District, #21384109, Series 2, RSPP.
[69] Petition of John Young, September 23, 1839, Davidson County, Tennessee, #21483906, Series 2, RSPP.

and Eugene Genovese argued that Southerners "despised submission," but Young knew that he could not defend himself and submitted accordingly.[70] Young's advanced age made this all the worse. His sons had "combined & confederated together to cheat & defraud yr Orator out all his property as well real as personal and to leave him in his infirmities and declining years upon the cold charities of a world of strangers." Although he received the court's support, Young had been forced to submit to his sons' usurpation of his mastery in his "declining years," and then to beg for assistance from the court.[71] Aggressive assertions of dominance were hallmarks of antebellum whites' relations with enslaved people, but this pursuit of power affected social relations in the white community too. Elderly whites cast in the position of dependents came to intimately understood how far age was a relation of power.

Some elderly enslavers were forced to publicly beg for protection from abuse, neglect, and deception from their slaveholding peers, including family members. Proslavery polemicists such as Daniel Hundley proudly stressed that all planters prioritized "the stoutest independence" and asked "no favors of either friend or foe."[72] As historian Lorri Glover states, dependency and submission were anathema to the desired image of enslavers: "Whites compelled submissiveness from their slaves and defined slaves as dependent and therefore debased; white men considered dependence and submission anathema for themselves."[73] Loss of power associated with aging, however, visibly contradicted such claims. North Carolina enslaver Pressley Holden was tricked out of his "property" by relatives who took advantage of his intemperance to get him to sign a deed of sale conveying his slaves to them. The "fraud was practiced" when Holden was in his seventies, but the criminals appeared to have had a change of heart. Holden recorded that "at first being ashamed to let your Petitioner know exactly what they had done [they] permitted the slaves to remain in his possession." As Pressley aged, however, they became emboldened; "taking advantage of his extreme age and feebleness," and in the expectation he had no power to resist, the fraudsters started "slipping from his possession slave after slave[,] transferring them to the defendants and others."[74] The fraudsters lost any remaining

[70] Fox-Genovese and Genovese, *Fatal Self-Deception*, 12.
[71] Petition of John Young, September 23, 1839, Davidson County, Tennessee, #21483906, Series 2, RSPP.
[72] Hundley, *Social Relations*, 28, 84.   [73] Glover, *Southern Sons*, 23.
[74] Petition of Pressley Holden, 1847, Surry County, Slave records, 1840–64, NCDAH.

caution in dealing with their aged mark and left him "stripped of all his property."

Some white southerners, then, exploited weakness in their elders, asserting mastery over them and both publicly and privately belittling their claims to authority. By emphasizing the incompetence of aged enslavers, rivals cut at their claims to honor and respect.[75] Such was the case for Wayne County enslaver Everitt Joyner, who, aged seventy, sought to recover an enslaved woman he had sold to Martha Woodward while drunk. To support his case, he was forced to detail his reduced status and infirmity: "he believes, that he was formerly and up to within a few years a good business man but that he has been for several years past very feeble and weak in both body and mind." Others in the community bore witness to these failings, with one witness informing the court: "He is nothing like the man he used to be."[76] The result of the petition is unclear, but to try and claim back his "property" Joyner was forced to publicly emphasize his weakness and lack of mastery. His deception by a woman undoubtedly further undercut Joyner's masculine identity and status among his peers. Disputes over aging, then, help pull away the self-serving mask of antebellum enslavers to reveal how mastery was embodied; bodies, as Joyner understood, risked growing "feeble and weak" over time.

Old age could also dramatically upend the claims of white superiority and reshape the expected dynamics of authority between Black and white southerners. In Tennessee, in 1838, William Slaughter, a man "far advanced in years," pleaded for the court's assistance in canceling a deed of conveyance to a free Black man named Richard Stuart. Slaughter had entered into a contract with Stuart, a former slave with the reputation for "honesty, sobriety, and industry," to supply the aged Slaughter and his wife with necessary goods and "other things that is common for folks of their age." Slaughter soon discovered how quickly power relations could shift: "not long after your Orator had placed himself in the power of said Stuart he discovered that the character & conduct of said Stuart were undergoing a total change – that he put off the bearing of a slave and put on that of a Master." Slaughter claimed that Stuart "soon became indiferent [*sic*] to the wishes and comfort of your Orator; and gradually insolent, neglectful, and almost utterly regardless of all the obligations imposed on him by said agreement," leaving Slaughter

---

[75] Welch, *Black Litigants*, 53.

[76] Petition of Everitt Joyner, July 14, 1863; Deposition, Blunt King, August 13, 1863, Wayne County, North Carolina, #21286320, Series 2, RSPP.

and his wife to fend for themselves. Slaughter was even frightened of this slave-turned-master: "The said Stuart has formed habits of drunkenness and utter indolence, and not only refuses to perform his agreement, but sets your orator at utter defiance; and distressing beyond endurance as is Your Orator's condition he dare not complain for fear of bodily injury." The court revoked the deed, but Slaughter's admission that in his advanced age he was "unable to protect himself" shows how aged-related decline could shape the dynamics of authority, power, and resistance in the antebellum south.[77] Joyner and Slaughter's experiences were inversions of the expected racial and gendered power dynamics in slavery; they both understood, and articulated to the court, that their advanced age had marked them as weak and that others saw and took advantage of this. In so doing, the cases further reveal the necessity of incorporating age as a category of analysis when interrogating power relations among antebellum southerners.

* * *

Elizabeth Fox-Genovese and Eugene Genovese detailed the significance attached to chivalry in the antebellum south, including how Southerners "credited slavery for providing the basis for southern respect and deference toward women."[78] Elderly women were also deceived by those seeking to profit from their decrepitude, presumed or real. Frances Claiborne was tricked into hiring out her slave when she "needed" him and directly referred to her age and gender to explain her lack of agency: "Yr oratrix being old infirm in her widowhood has no refuge from such doings save in the interposition" of the courts.[79] These interactions lend further weight to Stephanie Jones-Rogers argument that these women were "mistresses of the market," rather than "passive bystanders" to antebellum slavery.[80] They underscore women's significant role as slavers, and their desire to maintain this authority for as long as they could. When elderly white women complained of being deceived on account of age, they revealed their own role in the exploitative system of slavery – a system that shaped social conflict among white southerners, women and men, and in which age was an important relation of power.

---

[77] Petition of William Slaughter Sr., February 26, 1838, Washington County, Tennessee, #21483802, Series 2, RSPP.

[78] Fox-Genovese and Genovese, *The Mind of the Master Class*, 340.

[79] Petition of Frances Claiborne, November 1, 1819, Henrico County, Virginia, #21681905, Series 2, RSPP.

[80] Jones-Rogers, *They Were Her Property*, xiv–xv, 205.

These cases underline that white southerners were willing to trample on one another to profit from enslaved peoples' labors. Elders were often easy prey, whether women or men, but the manipulation of elderly women in particular gives the lie to the "moonlight and magnolias" myth of southern chivalry. In 1858, North Carolina enslaver Nancy Ward accused Malinda C. McCullough and Edward Houston of cheating her out of Lawrence, her enslaved "property." The two convinced Ward to sign a document she thought was a mortgage but was actually "an absolute Bill of Sale." Ward's illiteracy made her an easy mark, but she was convinced that her advanced age also put a target on her back. As "an old woman" she was "easily imposed on by the fraudulent representations of designing, cunning and dishonest persons."[81] South Carolina enslaver Rebecca Turner, "about seventy three years of age and very infirm and having lost in some degree her memory," similarly believed advanced age had marked her out as a victim. With infirmities ever increasing, Turner allowed her son to take stewardship of the farm, stock, and enslaved people. In return, "he would maintain support and clothe your oratrix and find her the common necessaries of life and feed and take care of her stock." Matthias took care of his ailing mother, but also claimed permanent ownership, not temporary stewardship, of the land and slaves. He convinced his mother to sign a bill of sale while she was "deranged," then refused her appeals to return the property in order to divide it among her children and instead "secure[d] unto himself the principal and most valuable part of her property." He eventually sold the slaves to Col. Wilson Nesbitt for $2,250, despite both parties knowing the fraud practiced. The case dragged on until 1842, by which time Matthias and Turner had both died, and so their respective heirs continued the fight.[82]

In 1822, Union District, South Carolina, Jane Boyd, a "very infirm old woman" in her seventies and "extremely imbecilic both of mind and body," was forced to plead for help against fraud and theft of her "property." After her husband's death, Boyd took ownership of an enslaved woman named Nancy and offered her freedom if she "produced" two children, who would remain enslaved. Under the pretense of companionship, however, an unscrupulous trickster named Thomas Lynum tricked

---

[81] Petition of Nancy Ward, February 6, 1858, Wayne County, North Carolina, #21285825, Series 2, RSPP.

[82] Petition of Rebecca Turner, May 21, 1818; –, c. 1823, Pinckney District, South Carolina, #21381821 and #21382308, Series 2, RSPP; *Wilson Nesbitt* v. *Nicey Price*, et al., June 1842.

the elderly Boyd into selling Nancy to him. Lynum executed this ruse with cold cunning, "pretending great friendship towards and strong anxiety for the welfare of your petitioner" who, Boyd was at pains to remind the court, was "a very infirm old woman." After worming his way into her confidence, Lynum "prevailed upon her by bill of sale to bargain sell and deliver unto him the said negro woman Nancy and her increase." Lynum then refused to pay for the sale or provide monies earned by his hiring of Nancy. He "openly and absolutely declared that he would make no further compensation for any other sum of money for the said negro." Boyd was a pitiful, if not pitiable figure, following this loss, declaring that "from age and infirmity [she] stands much in need of the labour and services of the said negro for her daily support."[83] In both cases, the court ordered compensation to the women, but they had been made aware that predators saw an aged persons' movement down the steps of life as providing space for their own ascent.

Eighty-five-year-old North Carolina enslaver Margaret Gittins was the victim of successive scams as two white men fought to take advantage of her weakness. Gittins had agreed to sign, as a witness, a deed that transferred several slaves from Drury Holcomb to Thomas A. Word. She soon discovered that she had in fact been swindled into transferring "all or some" of her own slaves to Word. In George Hauzer, Gittins believed she had found an ally to fight this fraud. Hauzer "informed her of the fraud" and "professed himself her friend in the warmest and most benevolent terms." He claimed to be disgusted by Word's actions, describing him as "a wicked crafty and designing man" who had "deceived her and intended to cheat and defraud her of her said slaves." Gittins, fearing that she was to be deprived "of all support and maintenance in her very advanced time of life," gratefully accepted Hauzer's offer to stand for her. Hauzer "insinuated himself into your Oratrix's favor and esteem in so much that she entertained a very high opinion as well of his honor and integrity as of his friendship for her and believed him a man warm in her interest and welfare from no other motive than pure Benevolence."[84] Hauzer convinced Gittins to sign a deed transferring her slaves to him at her death if he took up the case for her, but this deed actually provided for the immediate transfer of her slaves to Hauzer. The case eventually

[83] Petition of Jane Boyd, May 7, 1821, Union District, South Carolina, #21382115, Series 2, RSPP.

[84] Petition of Margaret Gittins, February 15, 1810, Surry County, North Carolina, #21281015, Series 2, RSPP.

concluded in Gittins's favor, but she spent her final years in a state of uncertainty, aware that when people looked at her they saw weakness to exploit and riches to be gained.

Unscrupulous persons could neglect or even aim violence against elders to hasten the transferal of property from the old to the young. Winny Allison of Laurens District, South Carolina, was forced to plead for protection from the cruelty of William Halbert. Halbert had agreed to support her and her late husband in return for the conveyance of their land, property, and slaves, and held to his bargain while Allison's husband lived, but saw the chance to profit when he died. "Since then she has experienced much cruel unkindness at his hands," with the aged widow even believing that Halbert had "procured arsenic with the intention of poisoning your oratrix." This reversal of her fortunes revealed the shifting and contested nature of hierarchies among white southerners: "she has from comparative opulence been thrown upon the charity of the world, in her seventy sixth year, in that most distressing poverty; destitute of a home, children and relations, and without one dollar to procure her subsistence."[85] The aggressive pursuit of profit structured antebellum slavery and inevitably bled into relations between white southerners, men and women.

Sometimes the targeting of elderly women extended to intimate exploitation. As Stephanie Jones-Rogers notes, "slave-owning women possessed the kind of wealth that prospective suitors and planters in training hoped to acquire or have at their disposal."[86] Margaret Hill of Alabama, "a very old woman," claimed that William Hill determined to marry her "with the sole intention of getting her property."[87] In 1842, Jane Rock of Maryland petitioned the court of equity for a divorce and relief on account of abusive treatment from her husband, James Rock. Jane entered her marriage to James in 1839 with a "considerable amount of property, real and personal, amply sufficient to support your petitioner in care and comfort during the brief residue of her life." She soon realized that James had married her for these worldly attractions: "your Petitioner believes and avers that her said husband married her for the base purpose of obtaining her property and not for the love of which he entertained for

---

[85] Petition of Winny Allison, January 1, 1842, Laurens District, South Carolina, #21384201, Series 2, RSPP.

[86] Jones-Rogers, *They Were Her Property*, xiv.

[87] Petition of Margaret Hill, December 15, 1846, Sumter County, Alabama, #20184616, Series 2, RSPP.

your petitioner as he induced her to believe." James treated his aged wife "with repeated and manifest cruelty, often compelling your petitioner to return to her bed in consequence of the severity of the blows inflicted," forcing her to flee from "her hitherto peaceful and happy home as the only sure means of preserving her life against the brutal tyranny & cruelty of her said husband."[88] In such encounters, ambitious enslavers saw advanced age as well as gender as the route by which they might seize power and assume mastery.

* * *

Elderly enslavers fought hard to protect themselves and drew on the legal system to secure their property and status. Nonetheless, appeals to the law meant publicly revealing their weakness and submitting to the court's mercy. One aged enslaver from Camden County, North Carolina, found out that "his favorite grandson" had tricked him into selling his property. The grandson manipulated his grandfather's "unlimited confidence" in him; he "signed [the papers] without having them read them, not having the slightest suspicion that they were drawn differently from his instructions," and admitted that "his mind as much as his body has been for several years much enfeebled."[89] In 1852, Texas, Travis County enslavers Benjamin and Isabella Grumbles received an injunction to prevent John Grumbles, their son, from seizing their slaves and removing them from the country. Scholars such as Nicholas Mirzoeff have argued that "visualized surveillance" was vital to enslavers' demonstrations of mastery, as well as to the significance of slave systems writ large, but individual claims of ocular power shifted with the passage of time.[90] Being "well stricken in years," the elderly Grumbles grumbled they were "not able to keep a constant watch over the entire described property."[91]

Some southerners preyed on the fears of elderly enslavers that their wills might be broken, speaking to a pervasive sense of insecurity for those who feared their time was running out. The daughter of Elinor Mackay of

---

[88] Petition of Jane Rock, c. 1842, St. Mary's County, Maryland, #20984214, RSPP, Ser 2.

[89] Answer of J. Morgan to the Bill of Complaint of David Sawyer, November 2, 1830, Camden County, Civil Actions Concerning Slaves and Freedmen of Color, 1819–1920 (Broken Series), NCDAH.

[90] Nicholas Mirzoeff, *The Right to Look: A Counterhistory of Visuality* (Durham: Duke University Press, 2011), 10. See also Teresa A. Goddu, "Anti-Slavery's Panoramic Perspective," *Melus* 39.2 (2014), 12–41.

[91] Petition of Benjamin and Isabella Grumbles, December 27, 1852, Travis County, Texas, #21585210, Series 2, RSPP.

McDowell County, North Carolina, expressed her "great fears" that the will Mackay had dictated "did not secure the negroes to her and her children," or protect them from sale. She emphasized that as "the wills of old persons were so frequently broken and declared void, that she would greatly prefer, that the said negroes should be settled upon her and her children by deed." Mackay's daughter continued to play up these fears, claiming to know "of some old person in Buncombe, whose will was broken, but that one of the children had a deed of gift for a negro which was held good, notwithstanding the bill was made void." Mackay insisted she did not want to gift the slaves before death as she feared "she would loose all control of the negroes, and the defendants might take them from her during her life," but her daughter and son-in-law "protested in the most solemn manner," swearing, "in the most sacred manner, never to molest or disturb the possession of the Plaintiff during her life." After repeated promises Mackay "finally" relented and, "confiding in their integrity, yielded" two slaves to Emily.[92] The "sacred" and "solemn" claims of her heirs were lies. The enslaved were hired out and even offered for sale, as the deed had been written to cede ownership to the children entirely. The courts granted Mackay's injunction and subpoena to support her claim, but not before she had been confronted with the disregard in which her family held her.

Wronged parties' beliefs that they had been targeted for deception and abuse because of aged weakness underscores that age was a significant vector of power for antebellum whites. Sarah Ray of Tennessee claimed to have "devoted her whole life to the care and attention of her Mother" Lydia, and self-righteously asserted that she had "worked harder than any slave on the place, and in all probability harder than any in the County of Smith." She was shocked when her position as favored heir was supplanted by a nephew, George Ray, who swooped in to take advantage "of the weak and fickle mind of an infirm mother of ninety years of age." George convinced Lydia, through the help of his "agent in the immediate neighborhood," to convey her slaves to him. Sarah's request to the court for support stressed the cruelty of using "false and corrupt practices over an aged and infirm mother whose mind is so far gone, as not to be able to resist such fraudulent practices." She was furious that her own service had been forgotten while "this man George Ray never staid one day in his life

---

[92] *Mackey* v. *Killian* (1857), McDowell County, Records of Slaves and Free Persons of Color, 1843–1873, Civil and Criminal Cases, Civil Actions, 1849–63, CR.064.928, NCDAH.

with her mother, and was never at her house more than some five or six times previous to her changing said conveyance." She hoped to receive the court's support as soon as possible on account of the dwindling power of her mother, who "in all probability may drop off at any time," but also lamenting that "her infirm and aged mother has been induced to turn against her, to order her from her home, to take her property from her, give it almost to a stranger and turn her upon the world to shift for herself."[93] The complaint and the appeal were dismissed without further evidence being provided, and Sarah was seemingly left to "shift for herself."

Of course, Sarah's presentation of her own virtue and George's avariciousness may have reflected her own desire for material reward. Elderly enslavers sometimes argued that those who claimed to "care" for them looked only to further their own interests. In 1843, Louisiana enslaver George Lagrange presented a pitiful image of the lack of care he had received. In 1834, Lagrange donated his land and slaves to Zephyrin Barre in return for the promise of support for the remainder of his life. Barre had done so "faithfully and religiously" up until his death, but his wife and heirs refused to accept any further responsibility while continuing to live off the donation. Legrange asserted he had been "treated with such ingratitude and contempt ... to be compelled, old and unfit for labour, to leave the premises of the widow of heirs and throw himself upon the charity of strangers."[94] The rising generation did not always show respect and support for elderly enslavers. Instead of seeing them as equals, some antebellum whites looked to elders and saw only exploitable dependency and weakness.

Proslavery writers such as George Fitzhugh concluded that "it is the duty of society to enslave the weak" and invoked seemingly static familial hierarchies to stress that inequalities were found everywhere: "Parents, husbands, guardians, teachers, committees, &c., are but masters under another name, whose duty it is to protect the weak, and whose right it is to control them."[95] When moving between life stages, enslavers confronted the dynamic nature of control, sometimes becoming targets for those happy to rise in the world at the expense of others. This can be seen in

[93] Petition of Sarah Ray, July 8, 1843, Sumner County, Tennessee, #21484223, Series 2, RSPP.

[94] Petition of George Lagrange, August 14, 1843, St. John the Baptist Parish, Louisiana, #20884327, Series 2, RSPP.

[95] George Fitzhugh, *Cannibals All! Or, Slaves without Masters* (Richmond: A. Morris, 1857), 278.

Kentucky enslaver William Page's dispute with his nephew, Benjamin Utterback. Utterback had convinced Page, who described himself as "of very advanced age being nearly 80 years old, of weak intellect and unhappily addicted to drink," that "he was in danger of being defrauded" out of his enslaved property. Utterback offered protection by taking on the slave himself. Only after the bill of sale had passed hands did Page realize he had been deceived. Utterback was now happily "appropriating to himself the value of [the slave's] labour" and refused "to deliver him to your orator."[96] In this and the Lagrange case, elderly enslavers publicly revealed the limits to aged mastery, and the avarice and exploitation of their presumed peers.

This offense was magnified when coming from family members. Kentucky enslaver William Davis, who had used slave labor to set up a "decent and comfortable support of himself and wife in their old & helpless age," was distraught to find himself tricked out of leisurely retirement by his own son. Davis acknowledged that "through his own imprudences and from the effects of old age" he had become too incompetent to transact "any kind of business whatsoever." Davis's son tricked him into signing over "every article of property that he possessed" through "an undue influence obtained over him by reason of his weak state of mind and by fraud ... and by false representations and by many other dishonourable and illegal acts." Davis's son knew his mark lacked the power to resist and threatened "to turn his Father & mother out of their house, to seize upon the negroes and send them to the southern market to be sold." Davis was forced to highlight his submissive status and plight in old age: "if permitted he will strip them of all their property, take from them their whole means of support and throw them in their old age and in their helplessness upon the charity of the world."[97] The petition was dismissed, and we are left to wonder how charitable the world was for this enslaver, but also for the enslaved now threatened with the auction block.

Occasionally the usurpation of elderly enslavers took more physical turns, with threats and violence underlining their loss of power in contests of mastery. William Dickinson of Albemarle County, Virginia, depicted advanced age as leaving him unable to defend his interests or himself. During a dispute over the hiring of three enslaved people, including Ralph,

[96] Petition of William Page, c. February 1807, Woodford County, Kentucky, #20780705, Series 2, RSPP.

[97] Petition of William Davis et al., Woodford County, Kentucky, October 24, 1832, #20783211, Series 2, RSSP.

who had run away, the plaintiffs took advantage of the fact that Dickinson was "totally disabled & hindered from attending the court both by sickness which then confined him to his house, & by the natural effects of old age." Dickinson tried to recover the runaway himself, notwithstanding his "advanced age & feeble health," but the men usurped his title of master and dramatically repudiated his claims to authority in front of his slaves. The men's agent "rode up into your Orator's yard ... in a noisy, boisterous manner, went round to the negro quarters, rushing into some or all of them, cursing the negroes for having[,] as he said, harboured Ralph, terrifying them, & threatening them violently if they did not produce him." Unsurprisingly, Ralph "ran off" at witnessing this turn of events. In asserting themselves on his land and over his "property," the men underscored their lack of respect for Dickinson and their disbelief in his capacity for control. Dickinson's enslaved people surely realized the precarity of their position if ambitious enslavers further challenged their "master."[98]

In Monroe County, Kentucky, 1858, William Martin was forced to confront his ever-dwindling power and the avarice this inspired from his peers. Martin, aged ninety, argued he had long maintained control over the twenty or thirty slaves on his farm and could continue to do so despite his age. His son, Hudson, disagreed and sought to take control of the property during his lifetime, enacting mental and physical abuse. Martin stated that "when no other white person was present [Hudson] cursed & abused & threatened pltf in a cruell manner – raised violent hands upon him, presented a pistol as he threatened to blow his brains out." Having frightened the old man into submission, Hudson "asserted then & there that he was the owner of every item of property the land & home of pltff and threatened to expel plftt from its possession." Both parties died before the case came to trial, but the court asserted that any changes to the direction of the property resulted from the disgraceful force applied to an ailing man:

the very advanced age of Wm. Martin, his feeble condition, the weakness & childishness peculiar to extreme old age & the peculiar circumstances with which he was surrounded force the conclusion that the parties did not contract upon an equal footing, but that the old man if capable of controlling at all was in a condition in which he was very liable to be overreached.[99]

[98] Petition of William Dickinson, September 26, 1834, Albemarle County, Virginia, #21683436, Series 2, RSPP.

[99] Petition of William Martin, June 29, 1858; Judgment c. 1861, Monroe County, Kentucky, #20785826, Series 2, RSPP.

The court ruled in Martin's favor posthumously, but if, as Lorri Glover has argued, southerners believed that a real man "was not controlled by anyone but himself," this ruling underscored that the whole community knew that in his decrepitude Martin was barely a man, let alone a "master."[100]

* * *

If slavery was a system characterized by dominance, then the overruling desire for supremacy extended into white southerners' dealings with one another, as shown by the eagerness to seize the property and wealth of elderly enslavers and to publicly assume mastery over them. In 1844, seventy-four-year-old James A. Pearson, of Lowndes County, Alabama, "became embarrassed in his pecuniary affairs" as a result of illness and age. To pay his medical bills, Pearson was forced to ask his son-in-law, Isaac T. Smith, for a loan. Smith's father stepped in and offered money on the condition Pearson put up three slaves for collateral. Over the next five years, "disregarding the dictates of honesty and fair dealing," Smith and his father conspired to "defraud" Pearson of the labor of his slaves and took profit far beyond the initial loan.[101] They were able to do so on account of Pearson's growing frailties, which were such that he had been forced to move in with his abusers. The court granted Pearson's appeal and the slaves were returned, but his lack of mastery had been displayed to the whole community.

The grasping nature of heirs hungry for profit was evident in the poor treatment of Elendor Price, a widow from Perry County, Alabama, in the late 1850s. Price, who described herself as "infirm in mind and body from old age and disease and uneducated and ignorant" and as "wholly unable to attend to her farm and the business appertaining thereto," had trusted her sons, Silas and James Price, to manage her business affairs. Over the years she had been asked to put her mark on several documents. While initially suspicious, Silas had "assured" her "that no harm would come of it and that she would not be thereby deprived of anything so long as she lived." Elendor clearly did not anticipate betrayal from her own kin: "being incapable of refusing anything he wished or demanded and being

---

[100] Lorri Glover, "'Let Us Manufacture Men': Educating Elite Boys in the Early National South," in Craig Thompson Friend and Lorri Glover (Eds.), *Southern Manhood: Perspectives on Masculinity in the Old South* (Athens: University of Georgia Press, 2004), 22–49, 29.

[101] Petition of James Pearson, April 2, 1848, Tallapoosa County, Alabama, #20184908, Series 2, RSPP.

entirely under his influence and in the habit for years of confidently relying upon him and yielding implicit obedience to his judgment she did at length sign said instrument as aforesaid." Price was eventually "astonished to find that if valid she is absolutely deprived of all right and title in the three slaves last mentioned & that she has been therein deceived and defrauded in her old age by her own son."[102] Price had planned to divest the "property" equally among her six children upon her death, but Silas seized what he could, when he could, and the old widow failed to stop him.

Tennessee enslaver William Gray, "old and infirm," was likewise victimized by his son, Andrew. William had set up the sale of an enslaved family but was forced to leave the negotiations due to ill health. The elder Gray trusted Andrew to complete on the terms he had specified but was disabused of this trust. A year passed before William realized anything was afoot. During this time he had been persuaded to move in with his son on account of his increasing infirmities. He did not find the expected support:

Your orator had not however lived long with said Andrew before he began to treat him badly – giving him diet not suitable to his age or the malady under which he laboured – and showing him none of that respect from a son your orator remonstrated with him, but to no effect. He insulted him after having attempted to injure him.

William was so upset by this poor treatment that he left and took with him the enslaved family he claimed ownership of. At this point, Andrew revealed his deception and threatened to sue his father to reclaim the "property." Any lingering pretense of William Gray's mastery collapsed entirely:

Your orator being old and infirm, and afflicted as aforesaid, considered himself little able to guard the vigilance and cunning of said Andrew; and believing from his conduct towards him previously, that he would stop at no means however base or underhand to regain the possession of said yellow woman slaves, Chaney and her said two children, while they remained with him; your orator thought it best to part with them to some person more able to watch the movements of the said Andrew.

A local white man William asked to take the slaves for him refused on account of the impending suit, leaving the old man to plead mercy and acknowledge his incapacity to the court. With no result recorded, it is

---

[102] Petition of Elendor Price, October 1, 1863, Perry County, Alabama, #20186330, Series 2, RSPP.

unclear whether he received it, but Gray himself saw the fraud as "an abuse of confidence scarcely parallelled [*sic*] in the annals of filial ingratitude."[103]

These cases reveal how old age was positioned as challenging existing power relations and social hierarchies and underline the necessity of incorporating age in our intersectional analyses of enslaver and enslaved alike. In December 1859, Susan Sillers Darden of Fayette, Alabama, recorded the "great excitement" of the community after hearing that a man named Sam Hartwell had tried to poison his father-in-law. The community gossip was that "he wanted the old man to be out of the way, so he could get his wife's share of the property." The father-in-law was saved from this fate but was furious at his betrayal, and he insisted to all and sundry he remained a man of strong will and purpose, rather than being a drain on the family's estate. He stressed, in fact, that "he was doing so much for him [Hartwell] & for him to be guilty of such an act & bring disgrace upon his family is too much to bear." The strength of these protestations suggests that it was no little concern to be considered dependent or a burden. Hartwell's actions further reinforce that the push for profit historians have identified as central to antebellum slavery extended into white southerners' inter-actions with one another.[104]

Enslavers who realized they were perceived as a burden or, even worse, an easy victim struggled to maintain their identities as "masters." Hannah Evans sued Etheldred Evans, her eighty-three-year-old hus-band, for maintenance, claiming he had abused and "gradually ceased to provide for" her, and had published a notice that he would not be responsible for her contracts. In his self-pitying defense, Etheldred was forced to reveal to the community that Hannah "desired [and was able to] ruin him by destroying the little property he had by owing him in debt," and that she had "abandoned him, leaving him for weeks & months at a time, when his age & infirmities required her society & assistance, until at length he had to live among his children, being too aged and decrepid" to live independently. Southern white men were expected to crave independence and to dominate dependents, physically

[103] Petition of William Gray, February 16, 1827, Maury County, Tennessee, #21482703, Series 2, RSPP.

[104] Susan Sillers Darden Diary, December 14, 1859 and December 15, 1859, *Records of Ante-bellum Southern Plantations from the Revolution through the Civil War*, Series N: *Selections from the Mississippi Department of Archives and History* (microfilm; Frederick, Md., 1985–), reel 6, frame 264.

if required, but Ethelred publicly claimed he was no longer capable of such force.[105] He meekly revealed to the court that "he had not the physical capacity to accomplish it, being now eighty three years of age, very infirm, & had been out of his bed for over twelve months, during all which time she has deserted him."[106] In this instance, age-related decline undercut expected gendered power dynamics; in challenging Hannah Evan's maintenance request, Ethelred had to publicly reveal to all and sundry his loss of manly mastery of self.[107]

Loss of face extended to financial failures and debt-induced dependency. Halifax County enslaver Jacob Lowry claimed that his physician abused him when he grew "advanced in years and unable to attend his business." In 1827, Lowry signed a bond as promise of payment for James Singleton's services for the "incorrect and exorbitant" sum of $1,000 for 126 visits over a 2-month period. Lowry believed he had succeeded in fighting this demand when the bond was called, but found that he had been sued for execution of the debt, leading to the seizure and sale of his enslaved man, Anderson. The suit was dismissed and the aged Lowry was left in ill health and a "master" of nothing.[108] Tennessee enslaver Joshua Hadly was similarly diminished, abused, and robbed. Hadly, aged seventy-six, fell out with his natal family, separated from his wife, and renounced his children. Into this void stepped Edward L. Douglass. Under "a promise that he should be made the sole heir," Douglass agreed to provide for Hadly until he died and to take "care" of his enslaved workers. Hadly quickly discovered his mistake: "instead of finding the affection and tenderness which this child of adoption had promised found in the short space of a month an enemy who was willing that the hoary head of 76 should seek a home from the charity of the world." Hadly's children, "when they found their Father was thus abandoned," took "him under their protection and tender[ed] him a home for life." However, the

---

[105] Edward Baptist, "'My Mind Is to Drown You and Leave You Behind': 'Omie Wise,' Intimate Violence, and Masculinity," in Christine Daniels and Michael V Kennedy (Eds.), *Over the Threshold: Intimate Violence in Early America* (London: Routledge, 1999), 94–110.

[106] Petition of Hannah Evans, April 1, 1844; Order, May 28, 1844; Answer, Etheldred Evans, May 28, 1844, Sumter District, South Carolina, #21384401, Series 2, RSPP.

[107] Some of the tensions surrounding the exercise of patriarchy, albeit not through an age-related lens, can be found in Laura Edwards, "Law, Domestic Violence, and the Limits of Patriarchal Authority in the Antebellum South," *Journal of Southern History*, 65.4 (1999), 733–70.

[108] Petition of Joseph Lowry et al., c. November 1834, Halifax County, Virginia, #21683425, Series 2, RSPP.

court dismissed his request that the bill of sale be rescinded and Hadly was left entirely dependent, a "master" no more.[109]

In the eyes of friends, families, and the wider community, enslavers who had once held power and status among their peers sometimes became in their old age inferiors to be tolerated, pitied, or even abused. In Rockingham County, North Carolina, Abner Thacker claimed that his mother, Mary Ann, owed him a slave. Thacker had taken in the elderly Mary Ann after she became "totally helpless" and required assistance. After building her an additional room and "attending to her business for several years," she abruptly left him, taking the slave he had been given as a reward for his kindness. Thacker believed that John Williams, Mary Ann's son-in-law, had taken advantage of the "impaired" mind of this "very old woman" to influence her actions. Mary Ann herself, however, rejected this portrait of a feeble and easily manipulated woman. In her response, Mary Ann claimed that she had suffered abuse and "great neglect" while in Thacker's care, receiving "nothing suitable to age & infirmities." Thacker's wife, Mary Ann's daughter-in-law, was "so rude, intolerant & turbulent, she could not bear it, & in order to increase her peace & comfort, she left the plaintiff's house & went to live with her only daughter the wife of the other Defendant, where she found a welcome reception, and the affections of a child." For this reason, Mary Ann decided to give Williams "the benefit of the services of her slaves, as compensation for the trouble and expense he was put to." In Mary Ann's view, the fact her son was deliberately "harassing her by warrants & suits" demonstrated his disrespect and disregard for his aged parent.[110]

Enslavers were thus sometimes viewed as burdens as they aged and were reduced to the status of dependents. In the case of Elizabeth Pickens, an enslaver from South Carolina, elder care became a proxy war for heirs. Pickens, who described herself as an old woman aged seventy-seven, "infirm, decrepid, and illiterate," moved in with her nephew, Andrew Smith, because of her declining powers. She granted him rights to the people she enslaved in exchange "for the proper support and maintenance of your oratrix during her natural life." Pickens "confidently hoped, from the large amount of property conveyed by her to the said defendant," even

---

[109] Petition of Joshua Hadly, c. November 1829, Smith County, Tennessee, #21482906, Series 2, RSPP.

[110] *Thacker v. Thacker and Williams* (1851), Rockingham County, Records of slaves and free persons of color, 1795–1867, Civil Actions re: slaves, Actions in equity re: slaves, NCDAH.

"if not from other considerations, that she would have received at his hands kind and gentle treatment, and a comfortable and generous maintenance." On the contrary, "for a long space of time, the said defendant and his family have treated her with the utmost indifference and neglect . . . she is not permitted to enjoy ordinary social privileges in the family of defendant, but kept secluded and almost isolated." The elderly woman found her situation entirely unacceptable: "the support and maintenance tendered her has been most meagre and straitened, and eked out with such manifest covetousness and reluctance as to render her situation, as a member of defendant's family, most unpleasant and intolerable."

Smith, on the other hand, maintained that Pickens "was provided for and taken care of," and instead cast aspersions on his uncle. Alongside protestations of his own innocence, Smith insisted on Pickens's general incapacity and dependency: "For two years he and his wife assisted her in getting out of and into bed. This painful and most laborious duty, for the complainant is a very large person, and will probably weigh two hundred and fifty pound, the defendant performed daily and constantly with cheerfulness and good will." Smith stressed that as an honorable man he was happy to perform such care, as "the complainant had taken him in his infancy and raised him, and he felt it was his sacred duty to take care of her in her old age and misfortune." For more than a decade she had been happy, but Smith claimed that her brother had then seized upon her growing weakness to enrich himself. It was Robert Pickens "who has caused all this disturbance between the complainant and defendant, to the old age and childishness of complainant, for the sole purpose, as this defendant believes, of dispossessing him and getting the complainant's property into his own hands."

In the process of defending himself, Smith had to denigrate his aunt's character on account of her age and incapacity. He offered a counter-narrative that demonstrates the difficulties historians have in assessing the treatment of the elderly when we have to balance the claims of the carer against those of the aged caree. Her version of events could not be trusted, Smith insisted, because "as the complainant advanced in age" she "began to lose the power of her mind," consequently becoming "harder to please, and more childish and whimsical in her notions." Smith agreed that she could move in with Robert Pickens if she liked but added that "she will soon be dissatisfied, and find herself more uncomfortable than she was at his house." The court supported Smith, finding the charges baseless and that Pickens owed him money. Even after she left, Smith asked to pay an allowance to the elderly woman, and the court agreed. This suggests that he was telling the truth with regards to his care for his aunt, but his motivations were still to some extent bound up with expectations of reward and advancement. Smith was "unwilling to see her in her old age become the means of gratifying the sordid and wicked purposes of others," but was equally honest about the self-interest that animated his own support for his aunt:

He is unwilling, too, after all the trouble and care and expense he has been put to in consequence of his agreement with complainant, to see it now revoked, not for her benefit, but for the benefit of one whom she did not prefer to defendant, for the last thirty or forty years of her life.[111]

Enslavers viewed as having one foot in the grave could thus become pawns in the conflict between competing and jealous heirs seeking to establish themselves above others. Enslavers' dominance was embodied, not innate, and those far advanced in years could find the distinction between rhetoric and reality to be a hard lesson.

* * *

Age was a significant factor in configuring relations of power among white southerners. This chapter has emphasized how the process of aging shaped and affected the manifestations of power and authority in the antebellum south, and the fluid and contested nature of slaveholding status. Enslavers of all classes hoped for respect and guarded their reputations jealously, but the ravages of time could render these efforts for naught. Age-weakened enslavers – men and women – were unable to defend their access to wealth and status built through the exploitation and abuse of enslaved people. Their susceptibility to deceit, neglect, and abuse reveals the extent to which mastery and slaveholding dominance were constructed and contested, not natural or static. Real or imagined loss of power associated with age saw the vultures come circling. Once at the apex of a system founded on domination, abuse, and violence, elderly southern slavers could be at the mercy of other whites willing to benefit themselves through taking advantage of others. The person stood atop the steps of life only had one place to go. Those who stood behind were eager to help them on their way down.

---

[111] Petition of Elizabeth Pickens, April 25, 1857; Answer, Andrew M. C. Smith, May 26, 1857; Decree, June 26, 1857; Notice of Appeal, ca. 1857, Anderson District, South Carolina, #21385747, Series 2, RSPP.

9

"Something must be done with the old man"

Dominion After Death

> It well bespeaks a man beheaded, quite
> Divested of the laurel robe of life,
> When every member struggles for its base,
> The head; the power of order now recedes,
> Unheeded efforts rise on every side,
> With dull emotion rolling through the brain
> Of apprehending slaves ...
>
> George Horton, "Division of an Estate"[1]

Advanced age affected the performance of mastery, and some slavers saw the declining fortunes of another as providing them with the opportunity to rise at their expense. Black activist George Horton's poem indicates that concerns with – and contests over – the authority of aged enslavers did not end at their death. Wealth generated by slaveholding needed to be passed on, and the quest for profit and status that animated southern enslavers saw ferocious disputes erupt over the transferal of property between generations. Contests over wills and inheritance help reveal the complex and contested relations between enslavers, intergenerational tension in the American South, and shifting social hierarchies shaped by the passage of time. As one lawyer put it in their challenge to the legitimacy of a will: "by nature, a man cannot have dominion, beyond the term of his own life, and that he cannot confer on another, an interest which he himself had not, that is an interest beyond his life."[2] Antebellum enslavers prized the presumption of authority and craved respect from family, kin,

---

[1] George M. Horton, *The Poetical Works of George M. Horton: The Colored Bard of North Carolina: To Which Is Prefixed the Life of the Author, Written by Himself* (Hillsborough: D. Heartt, 1845), 87–9.

[2] *Jane B. Ross et al.* v. *Vertner et al*, 5 How. Miss. 305, December 1840.

and community; Elizabeth Fox-Genovese and Eugene Genovese insisted that southerners were taught that "subversion of another's reputation was a criminal attack on his person."[3] And yet, in legal challenges to wills, deeds, and bills of sales recorded posthumously, antebellum southerners revealed the disregard they held for aged enslavers' claims of dominion, and their willingness to trash the reputation of fellow "masters" both before and after death.

* * *

The laws and customs surrounding inheritance have been the subject of much excellent historical work.[4] I am less interested in considering the legality or the process than in exploring how advanced age was used to unsettle claims of mastery in life and death, and the significance of this for white southern identities and social interactions. Nonetheless, it is worth setting the context for disputes surrounding inheritance and slavery. Historian Thomas Morris has noted that there were two ways for enslavers to "succeed to property under the common law." The first was by descent, "whereby title to property was acquired by right of representation as the heir at law, without any act of one's own. This concerned the succession to property of those who died without wills, the intestate succession. The other covered the succession to property through wills." Rules relating to the distribution of property of intestates were established in the English Statute of Distributions of 1670, and these rules crossed the Atlantic to cover the colonies then states, with the exception of Virginia, with only relatively minor changes through the antebellum period. The main provisions, as described by Morris, revolved around respecting the rights of bloodline heirs: "one-third of the estate would go to the widow, the residue in equal portions to the children, or if they were dead to their representations." If there were no children, "one half of the property would go to the widow and one-half to the 'next of kindred in equal degree and their representatives' and so on."[5]

---

[3] Fox-Genovese and Genovese, *The Mind of the Master Class*, 345.

[4] On inheritance laws with particular reference to antebellum slavery, see Adrienne D. Davis, "The Private Law of Race and Sex: An Antebellum Perspective," *Stanford Law Review*, 51.2 (1999), 221–88; Morris, *Southern Slavery and the Law*; Gross, *Double Character*; Jones, *Fathers of Conscience*; Pitts, *Family, Law, and Inheritance in America*. For more general work, see Lawrence Meir Friedman, *Dead Hands: A Social History of Wills, Trusts, and Inheritance Law* (Stanford: Stanford Law Books, 2009); Hendrik Hartog, *Someday All This Will Be Yours: A History of Inheritance and Old Age* (Cambridge, Mass.: Harvard University Press, 2012).

[5] Morris, *Southern Slavery and the Law*, 82.

Intestacy was bound by rules that sought to provide a "fair" distribution to bloodline heirs and their representatives, but wills were explicitly based around the notion of personal autonomy and "emphasized freedom" on the part of the testator.[6] This was the freedom of antebellum Southerners to express mastery from beyond the grave – to reward or to punish family, friends, or even the people whom they enslaved. The language applied by testators was bound by legal and cultural conventions where they directly stated their authority and intention to dispose of their "property" as they saw fit. The opening of Georgia enslaver James Smith's last will and testament provides the familiar refrain: "I, James Smith, of sound mind and memory ... being far advanced in age, and must shortly depart from this life, deem it right and proper, both as respects myself and family, I should make a disposition of all the property which a kind Providence has blessed me."[7]

The right to make a will was considered sacrosanct in a society that prioritized authority and autonomy. As the presiding judge in *Peeples v. Smith* noted when instructing the jury before deliberations over a contested will: "the right to make a will, was ... a very sacred right."[8] This was a right that was extended in most of the Southern states to all white men over twenty-one years of age and "being of sound mind and not a married woman."[9] Married women were theoretically not deemed competent to make a will due to the rules of coverture, and women of all ages faced myriad legal obstacles shaped by patriarchal structures and gendered power relations. Despite the entrenchment of masculine dominance in law across the antebellum South, there were loopholes and provisions in place that allowed white women to distribute (or to dispute) property after death, and many of the cases discussed here cover this.[10] The process of making a will is neatly summarized by historian Bernie D. Jones, who notes how testators constructed a will and "set forth the disposition of the property owned at the time of death." They named

---

[6] Pitts, *Family, Law, and Inheritance*, 40; Morris, *Southern Slavery and the Law*, 82.

[7] *Smith* v. *Dunwoody*, 19 Ga. 237 (1856), 238–9.

[8] *Peeples* v. *Smith*, 42 S.C.L., 8 Rich 90 (1854), 96.

[9] Pitts, *Family, Law, and Inheritance*, 11.

[10] Pitts, *Family, Law, and Inheritance*, 145 and ch. 5 in particular. See also Schweninger, *Appealing for Liberty*, 83–5; Wood, *Masterful Women*; Gwendoline M. Alphonso, "Naturalizing Affection, Securing Property: Family, Slavery, and the Courts in Antebellum South Carolina, 1830–1860," *Studies in American Political Development*, 35.2 (2021), 194–213, 204–7. On the ending of coverture, see Hendrik Hartog, *Man and Wife in America: A History* (Cambridge, Mass.: Harvard University Press, 2002), 287–309.

a trusted executor to carry out their wishes, who, after death, presented the will to the probate court. If the will was accepted the executor established the estates' assets, resolved any remaining debts, and made the bequests according to the testator's will. If there was a challenge, the process was "suspended while a will contest ensued."[11]

Alongside procedural complaints relating to the composition of a will, such as illegible handwriting and insufficient witnesses, antebellum southerners made more dramatic interventions by insisting undue influence – whether physical, mental, or both – and denied the testator's ability to make a will on account of mental incapacity. The very language applied when addressing mental competence – the charge of being non compos mentis ("not master of one's mind") – speaks plainly to the dynamic nature of mastery. Those who hoped to prove that, at time of death, the testator was "not master of one's mind" frequently sought to associate advanced age with bodily and mental infirmity and cast crude aspersions on their capacity in later life.[12] In his study on inheritance in the nineteenth-century North, Hendrik Hartog noted that to make such a challenge would require "having to talk – and be cross examined – about intimate 'dirty' aspects of care and life." According to Hartog, "few if any adult children would have found the prospect of such talk – making private matters public – anything but horrifying."[13] Robert Elder has similarly noted the importance among southern whites of posthumous respect, claiming that "those who lived by honor's tenets believed that a name was the most important thing one left behind when leaving the world."[14] To publicly claim a testator had been controlled by another was to force them into the relation of submission that white southerners identified with slavery; to suggest they had been unable to defend themselves against such imposition was to directly claim the testator lacked mastery at time of death. Challengers who seized upon the age and infirmity of testators thus deliberately traduced their name in seeking to rise at their expense. In doing so, this chapter demonstrates how ambitious heirs sought to establish dominance over their elders in death.

* * *

Testators were clearly aware that they might face challenges to their wills. The ubiquitous (and deliberate) reference to "sound and disposing mind and memory" in the opening lines was not always enough to convince

---

[11] Jones, *Fathers of Conscience*, 11.
[12] Schweninger, *Appealing for Liberty*, 73; Pitts, *Family, Law, and Inheritance*, 14–16.
[13] Hartog, *Someday All This Will Be Yours*, 171.   [14] Elder, *The Sacred Mirror*, 176.

skeptical or covetous challengers, and enslavers sometimes directly addressed their fears of such conflict when constructing the document.[15] In *Pace* v. *Mealing*, 1857, the Georgia Supreme Court heard of William Pace's concerns for his estate and legacy. Pace apparently informed his neighbor of his desire to construct an airtight will to avoid challenge:

I shall not live long and don't want to leave any unsettled business behind. I have made my will and had it executed. I have fixed my business as I have wished it to go. I have not made my will as your father did his, if you had been disposed to be contrary, you could have broken your father's will to atoms, into one thousand or ten thousand pieces ... that he knew that his boys were contentious, and that he had fixed his business so that there could be no mistake after his death.

Pace was correct to view "his boys" as contentious. He was incorrect about having fixed the will. Richard Dent, who examined the multiple, and conflicting, testamentary papers Pace left behind, heard his wife exclaim "poor old creature, he must have been deranged to leave his business in such a fix."

When Pace's wife heard the apparent last will propounded she rejected it entirely: "the old lady said 'this is not the will the old man read to me that night; that will cut out Stephen Pace, and this will (then being read) won't do.'" At this point Pace's widow interposed, changing the distribution of slaves to aid one of the sons over the others. Mary Pace asserted that the change was wished for by her husband prior to his death, but Justice Lumpkin dismissed her claim, noting not only "the discrepancy in dates" in her testimony but also the very clear handwriting of someone else: "one has only to inspect this paper to be satisfied that the addition at the end relative to Laney, was written at the same time with the body of the will, while the substitution of Chaney in the place of another name erased, was with a different ink and pen." Lumpkin acknowledged that Pace had hoped to establish a clear line of succession, but was adamant he had an "unsettled mind" and "was at a loss to know what disposition to make of his negroes, in order to do what was right and just."[16] Pace strongly desired to enact his final business as "he wished it to go," not only on a practicable level but also to avoid the shameful fate of his befuddled neighbor; his actions indicate the wider concern white enslavers had for their posthumous reputation. Pace failed to have his authority respected, however; he was cast as weak-willed and confused by family, friends, and

[15] John H. Pope will, November 4, 1859, Wilkes County Court of Ordinary, Estate Records, Wills, 1837–1877, Box 44, Reel 32, 288, GSA.

[16] *Pace v. Mealing*, 21 Ga. 464 (1857), 480–1, 484, 483, 502.

the wider community, and his authority was ultimately usurped by the courts.

Those who sought to challenge the actions of deceased enslavers often underscored the frailties associated with old age. They implicitly and explicitly framed aging as a transition toward dependency, even submission, to the will of another, and in doing so publicly diminished the reputation of the aged party. In 1843, the elderly Sarah Cate successfully asked for a bill of sale made by her late husband, William Cate, to be made void. Her reasoning for this was that Charles Cate, William's son, had used the "grossest fraud" to trick his father, who was "borne down by this excessive weight of years" and "extraordinary concomitant infirmities."[17] In Chester District, South Carolina, Isom Kirkpatrick, the administrator of the estate of the recently deceased John and Elizabeth McKelvy, insisted that a deed of conveyance made in his final years needed to be discarded because "at the time of the executions thereof the said John McKelvy was greatly advanced in years ... [his] understanding so impaired & weak as to be incapable of fully comprehending the nature & effect of such acts of execution." In both instances there was no result recorded, but friends, family, and neighbors publicly insisted that these "masters" had ended their life meekly and weakly. Historian John Mayfield has explained that white southern men were supposed to approach their declining years with "cool aplomb," but contemporaries understood the aging process could make a mockery of such rhetoric.[18] According to Kirkpatrick, this deceit was only possible because McKelvy was "too weak of understanding to resist."[19]

The advanced age of enslavers could thus be framed as having made them prone to deception and easy to control by unscrupulous family, friends, and neighbors. Historian David T. Moon Jr. noted that "the very notion of submission ran counter to manly liberty and honor in the South," and thus challengers who applied the language of submission and dependency to attack wills deliberately undermined the character, agency, and identity of the testator.[20] To serve their own interests, challengers expressly denied these individuals had been masterful at the end of life. In Sussex

---

[17] Petition of Sarah Cate, September 14, 1843, Bradley County, Tennessee, #21484315, Series 2, RSPP.

[18] Mayfield, *Counterfeit Gentlemen*, 100.

[19] Petition of Isom Kirkpatrick, May 12, 1857, Chester District, South Carolina, #21385741, Series 2, RSPP.

[20] David T. Moon Jr. "Southern Baptists and Southern Men: Evangelical Perceptions of Manhood in Nineteenth-Century Georgia," *Journal of Southern History*, 81.3 (2015), 563–606, 595.

County, Delaware, 1814, James Badley argued that his children had been tricked out of the rightful "property" due from their grandfather, Samuel Jackson Bailey, because of the "fraud and imposition" of Bailey Snr's son, Samuel Bailey. This fraud was only possible because of the advanced age of Samuel Jackson Bailey:

The said Samuel Bailey obtained the said instrument of writing from the said Samuel Jackson Bailey by imposing on his weakness and understanding, he being at that time about Ninety years of age or upwards, and for a long time before and at that time under great debility of both Body and Mind, addicted to the intemperate use of strong drink and almost blind & from such causes rendered incapable of knowing his own children, of attending to his business and unable to write his own name.

To further their own cause, family members openly and publicly dismissed any notion of authority and self-control on the part of the patriarch. Diane Miller Sommerville noted that, for southern white men, "mastery and honor were central" to their identities, but, in this instance, witnesses from across the community were invited to contribute to this public denial of Samuel Jackson Bailey's capacity for control.[21] George Moore asserted that for years prior to his death Jackson Bailey had been "blind and very subject to intoxication and did not contract or do any business during that time before his death," while Elisha Badley maintained that "his mind was weak and liable to be imposed on." The language of imposition and the emphasis on Jackson Bailey's total submission to his son reveals how contemporaries understood the claims of mastery to be dynamic, and that any such decline could be seized upon by another. Louday Goslin was utterly dismissive of Jackson Bailey here: "his mind was very weak and appeared to be in his dotage."

The challenge to the distribution of Jackson Bailey's enslaved people rested on publicly denying his claims to autonomy and authority. The "defense" offered by Samuel Bailey was hardly better in noting the limits to the old man's control. The petitioners had adamantly rejected the idea that "the said Samuel Bailey thought more of his son Samuel ... or that said Samuel paid or devoted more attention to his father than any the rest of his children," but Samuel and his witnesses clearly disagreed. William Elzey acknowledged that the process by which Samuel had received the slaves was somewhat sneaky, noting that the use of a bill of sale or deed was designed to avoid scrutiny: "if he was to send for [his will], it would

---

[21] Sommerville, *Aberration of Mind*, 3.

only make a noise between his children as they would be anxious to know what alteration was made in his said will." Elzey stressed, however, that Samuel deserved this additional recompense because he alone had supported his father when he "was very old and required great care and attention." The court ultimately agreed that this was a reasonable decision and rejected the challenge to the bill. They accepted, nonetheless, that Samuel Jackson Bailey was a weak man under the charge of another, and that the assumption of mastery by the strong over the weak was both natural and normal.[22]

The view that the experiences and process of aging would lead to an increased risk of dependency, and even exploitation, was central to the petition of Amy Clements in Halifax County, Virginia, 1840. Clements believed that her sister, who had a "considerable Estate in negro slaves & money," had spent the last years of her life a virtual slave of the family who became the sole beneficiaries of this upon her death. Clements was "informed & believes that a long time previous to her death she was confined to her bed or room & wholly subject to the government & control of the family in whose house she was domesticated." Such was the level of control they wielded, according to Clements, that "visitors of the family were seldom permitted to converse with her, & her own relations & others when addressing conversation or questions to her were not permitted to receive an answer from her own lips, but were generally replied to by some one of the family under whose care and control she was." She insisted that it was only "while in this state of imbecility & tutelage, and while residing in the house of the said John L Jennings," that they were able to exercise "for their own advantage the influence & control . . . to execute a paper purporting to be the will of the said Amy." This will, perhaps unsurprisingly, provided for "the whole of her estate to be equally divided between the aforesaid," and left Clements entirely adrift.[23] The petition was dismissed, but Clements sought to convince the court that the dependency of old age came at no small cost.

---

[22] Petiton of James Badley, June 21, 1814; Deposition, George Moore, June 5, 1815; Depositions, Jonathan Bailey, Elisha Badley, Louday Goslin, Leah Taylor, John Bennett, John Shehes, June 28, 1815; Depositions, Levin Moore, William Relph, Samuel Elliott, William Elzey, June 21, 1815; Depositions, William Hobbs, Isaac Phillips, Thomas Walker, Stephen D. Bailey, John Badley, June 22, 1815, Sussex County, Delaware, #20381401, Series 2, RSPP.

[23] Petition of Amy Clements, c. January 1840, Halifax County, Virginia, #21684007, Series 2, RSPP.

The son-in-law and grandchildren of the recently deceased Obadiah Johnson painted a portrait of an aged enslaver made submissive by grasping heirs, suggesting how this rhetoric of aged dependency ran alongside, but sometimes superseded, gendered binaries of power/powerlessness. The petitioners asserted that Johnson "was for many years previous to his death labouring under great bodily & mental [delirium], so much so that he became ... incapable of managing his affairs." They insisted the community would support them in proving Obadiah's lack of mastery, and witnesses duly agreed that "he exercised no kind of control over the slaves that worked upon his farm or those whose occupations confined them to his dwelling." Standing in his place, however, was the son, Monroe Johnson, who "exercised a complete control over all of the property" and made his father dependent "contrary to every filial & social duty." The patriarch was rendered submissive and controlled by another. The petitioners insisted that everyone knew he "had no mind of his own and no will unconnected with the wishes of the said Monroe Johnson." The heirs, who found themselves "cut off & entirely debased from their just rights & from sharing in the estate of their grandfather," stressed this would not have been done "had he have been in a state of mind competent to execute a will."[24] The petitioners in this case failed to convince the court, but they publicly revealed their final memories of the aged patriarch were of a weak and meek man, with no will of his own, and, in doing so, dragged his "name" through the mud.[25]

The challenge made to William Hunter's will underscored the common belief that advanced age limited the authority of the aged, as well as concerns that this weakness would elicit avarice from those seeking to rise at their expense. Proslavery writers used family analogies when defending the southern social order, with William Smith claiming "the head of the family is the *master*," but Hunter's case reveals the fluid and contested nature of these hierarchies.[26] Rather than respect for elders from kith and kin, a tremulous descent on the steps of life might occasion a feeding frenzy instead. Hunter, who died aged seventy-four, made a will that rendered all his property and slaves to Charles Walker, a neighbor not related by blood. Hunter's heirs-at-law, who were excluded, challenged the legality of the document by claiming Walker had practiced undue

---

[24] Petition of Reuban George et al., August 26, 1843, Goochland County, Virginia, #21684336, Series 2, RSPP.

[25] Elder, *The Sacred Mirror*, 176.

[26] Smith, *Lectures on the Philosophy and Practice of Slavery*, 40.

influence over an old man of "weak and unsound mind" and requested it be set aside. Hunter's diminished authority was repeatedly stressed by the complainants, with a consistent portrayal of a man "easily controlled and much under the influence of the said Charles Walker." Walker's counsel insisted, however, that this had been a conscious choice to reward Walker on account of his care for Hunter, and to punish his "family" for a shameful abandonment of their patriarch. Regardless of the different positions of the parties, witnesses shared an assessment of Hunter as a weak man who would only decline further with the passage of time. Hunter was "sad, serious, and melancholy," and in his advanced age "he lived secluded and had but little to do with the world."

Despite Walker's protestations that the care provided to Hunter was a measure of his altruism and honor, some witnesses portrayed his actions as a scheme to climb the social ladder at the expense of one on their way out. Artemetia J. Lyle testified that she had heard Walker conversing with Moses Wheat, a local white man, about their relative circumstances and asserting that there was an easy opportunity to make some money. Rather than move county, as Wheat intimated his plan was, Walker suggested he "stay by William Hunter and nurse him well, and secure his property; that it was a fortune ready made, and that it was in his power to secure it." Wheat piously asserted "that is not my way of doing business," but Walker insisted these actions were inevitable and that if not he, then someone else would take advantage of the aged man's ailing fortunes: "Walker then remarked that he, Wheat, was interested in the disposition of the property, and had more influence over [Hunter] than any one else, and when he moved away somebody would get it." Walker insisted that a contest for the "old" man's property was coming and that he would throw his hat into the ring:

He, Mr. Walker, has as much right to it as any one else, apart from the legal heirs, and he would, after the removal of Mr. Wheat, nurse the old man and get it if he could. Mr. Wheat then asked Walker if he would have property got in that way. To which Walker replied, I had as well have it as any one else, and my motto is, to keep all I have got and get all that I can.

The discourse applied by witnesses in this case clearly demonstrated that family, friends, and neighbors might look to white enslavers moving down the steps of life as enabling their own ascent in a slaveholding society.[27] Success was not guaranteed for those who sought to challenge last wills,

---

[27] *Walker* v. *Hunter*, 17 Ga. 364 (1855), 364, 366, 379, 368, 378.

but the cases collectively reveal how far southern contemporaries viewed aging as limiting the autonomy and authority of enslavers. Ambitious enslavers were willing and able to use charges of decrepitude to attack their peers in life and death, and even to secure their rise at the elder's expense.

* * *

Antebellum jurists were reluctant to intervene in the rights of testators, but cases heard frequently revolved around the presumption that old age would see mastery inverted and authority called into question. Some prospective slavers were said to have used subtle means to insinuate themselves into the favors of the aged in order to secure their own rise in society. In the late 1850s, Elisha and Mary Grant of Southampton County, Virginia, asserted that Nancy Miller, an elderly and childless widow who had "by thrift and economy ... accumulated a handsome estate mostly in negroes," had been tricked out of her final wishes. The sisters claimed that Lucy Bendall, who, alongside Mary, was "provided for in the will by the name of Elizabeth (a mistake of the draftsman)," became "dissatisfied with the provision made for her by the will and desired a change." She achieved this by using her son, Oliver Bendall, to tell the widow that the existing will "was of no value" because of the naming error and that he would assist her in redrafting the document. The Grants claimed that "he took the will away with him and it was never found until after Nancy Millers death and then in a mutilated condition."[28] They requested that the distribution be halted until the validity of the will was tried, but were unable to convince the court to do so. Whether the Bendalls had sought to deceive Nancy or to provide genuine assistance, their actions (and the Grants's response, too) involved convincing elderly whites that they were incapable of organizing their affairs, and of the necessity of having a stronger hand take charge instead.

The next of kin of Jacob D. Young, from Robertson County, Tennessee, were equally convinced of foul play when disputing the distribution of his property. In their petition they described the recently deceased Young as "a man of great excentricity," who died with 350 acres of land, 9 slaves, and $6,000 in cash, which he kept "locked up in a chest" alongside his will. Young, who died aged seventy-seven, had "been helpless and confined to his bed for some ten months previous"

[28] Petition of Elisha and Mary Grant, January 22, 1856, Southampton County, Virginia, #21685622, Series 2, RSPP.

and received dutiful care from the people he enslaved "when he was helpless." The next of kin insisted that Young had hoped to "reward" the three most prominent figures here by allowing them to choose their own enslavers after he died, but he failed to secure this in any meaningful way and death put paid to his plans. Indeed, the petitioners claimed that his nephew, Benjamin Roney, saw an opportunity for his own advancement and took it. Roney seized the keys to the chest and, when he eventually "delivered up the keys, $3500 and the will were missing."[29] Roney then filed petition to have all the property sold, including the three men due their limited freedom, and to have the proceeds divided equally. He was able to convince a significant number of the other legatees to support him in foiling the patriarch's plan. The initial request to prevent the sale was dismissed, and was only reversed on appeal.

In the case of *Hill* v. *McLaurin*, 1854, the Mississippi Courts accepted that an aged enslaver had been controlled by two of his sons to the detriment of the remaining heirs. The Supreme Court's summation of the case noted how Duncan McLaurin had "amassed a large estate, real, personal, and mixed," and "was, in his better or younger days, a liberal feeder of his negroes, a good planter and cropper." The conflation of younger with better emphasizes the negative connotations contemporaries attached to aging and, indeed, the inexorable hand of time led to a decline in fortune. This reduced capacity led two of his sons to take control, but the nature of their "control" became the subject of a dispute from the remaining heirs, who complained this was a ruse to further the brothers' interest exclusively, rather than protect the patriarch or the wider family. It was agreed, however, that "towards the decline of life about 15 years before his death [Duncan] entrusted to his sons Daniel McLaurin and John McLaurin, men in the vigor of manhood (and of great shrewdness and energy of body mind and character) the chief supervision and general direction of his business." The complainants were adamant that this supervision was not done out of benevolence or with respect for the father. Daniel and John McLaurin were framed by the petitioners as having viewed their father as a burden who needed to be sidelined for the

---

[29] Petition of Samuel Gilbert et al., February 16, 1859; Order, ca. January 28, 1859; Last Will and Testament, Jacob F. Young, March 3, 1858; Recollection of the Will, John Hutchison, December 11, 1858; Final Decree and Notice of Appeal, December 20, 1860; Bond, December 22, 1860; Supreme Court Decree, ca. January 14, 1861, Robertson County, Tennessee, #21485904, Series 2, RSPP.

good of the future, and in using their father's inevitable descent to enrich themselves at the expense of others:

About four or five years before his death [McLaurin] became so enfeebled by age and infirmities as to cease making the crops he had been accustomed to and finally became so mentally imbelice [*sic*] and so thoroughly in his dotage that the said Daniel McLaurin in August in the year 1847 declared to members of the family that something must be done with the old man.

The "something" that the sons referred to, was, in this instance, the usurpation of their father's control. They claimed willingness to cooperate here, telling "members of the family that something must be done with the old man and his affairs[,] meaning some disposition of his property beyond his control . . . [to prevent] the said property from being wasted & misman-aged." The complainants discovered that Daniel and John McLaurin had no plans to share their father's wealth evenly, and instead claimed the brothers had convinced their father to sign the property over to them alone. This charge was explicitly predicated on casting aspersions on the McLaurin family patriarch's authority, identity, and mastery. The com-plainants charged (and the courts accepted) that "the said Duncan was the mere instrument in the hands of such men, his said sons, and subject to their management and undue influence." It was only "with the old man thus circumstanced, laboring under a loss of memory and understanding, bor-dering on idiocy, incapable of disposing of his property with reason or due reflection as to amounts or the various objects of his bounty," that the sons took over. The abuse of their "decayed parent" was, the complainants charged, utterly "unjust and unconscionable." The language of decay and submission they utilized reveals their own dismissal of McLaurin's agency.

Daniel and John McLaurin insisted that any "assistance, aid and service" they provided to their father was "always cheerfully rendered as ordinary duties from children to a parent," but the court ultimately dismissed this claim and underscored how far the power dynamics between "child" and "parent" were utterly reversed. Gwendoline M. Alphonso has recently shown how "naturalized hierarchies and dependencies based on family and race, between parents and children and between whites and blacks" governed proslavery ideologies and the antebellum social order, but the McLaurin brothers were understood as having seen the advancing age of their father as providing them the chance to overturn these hierarchies – to seize control and advance their interests instead.[30] The court declared the

---

[30] Alphonso, "Naturalizing Affection, Securing Property," 197.

titles they had established while controlling the deceased McLaurin null and void and set the distribution of the property to be done by the probate court instead. The case revealed, nonetheless, how far aged enslavers could become mere pawns in the contests between ambitious heirs.[31]

* * *

Challenges to wills and distributions sometimes spoke to concerns with foul play after remarriage, with both the children from the first marriage and those from later couplings suggesting that aged enslavers had been manipulated into benefiting one at the expense of others. Mattie Fannen recalled how her enslaver was pressured by his new (and younger) wife to change his will to avoid favoring one set of children over her own: "His young wife cried till he destroyed it. She said, 'You kept the old ones here and me and my children won't have nothing.'"[32] Some ambitious sorts went beyond tears and persuasion. In 1840, Writty Hassell of Tennessee asked for maintenance from the estate of her recently deceased husband, Zebulon Hassell. Writty claimed that Zebulon's children from his first marriage had preyed upon the fact he was "old and infirm" and convinced him to convey his property to them, including eight slaves, without making any provision for her. Writty, who was also "old infirm and poor," believed this to be a "fraud" upon her rights. The court, however, dismissed the case after hearing that Writty and Zebulon had signed a contract that the property each brought to the marriage "was to belong at their death to their respective children & grandchildren by their former marriage and that the same was not to pass out of the respective families to which it belonged."[33] Writty, it seemed, was the one trying to fraudulently deny her late husband's mastery.

Barsheba and John Burns of Union District, South Carolina, in 1834, argued for a similar case of manipulation from competing heirs. Barsheba Burns claimed that the children from Thomas Burn's first marriage had intentionally turned Thomas against her and John, the child they had together. Burns insisted the children had "used all means in their power by misrepresentations promises and inducements of all kinds to engender an unkind and immaterial feeling on the part of Thomas Burns towards

---

[31] *Hill* v. *McLaurin* (1856), Case File 125, Box 15, Lawrence County Chancery Court Cases, microfilm, reel 13317, MDAH; *Hill* v. *McLaurin*, 28 Miss. 288 (1854), 289, 290, 293.

[32] Rawick (Ed.), *AS*, 8.2, 265.

[33] Petition of Writty Hassel, February 10, 1842; Answer, John Hassell, Zebulon Hassell, March 25, 1840, Dickson County, Tennessee, #21484019 Series 2, RSPP.

your Oratrix and her children." This left Burns, "an aged and infirm widow ... without the shadow of a provision for her support when he had ample means for doing so and would doubtless have done so but for the unholy influences which was exercised over him by the children of his former marriage." The court partially granted Burns request to nullify the deed and divide the property evenly. The image Burns presented of her recently deceased husband spoke directly to understandings of old age as a regression to the frailty and dependency of infancy: "like most other persons who have arrived at that advanced stage of life [Thomas Burns] had become jealous childish, suspecting and easily practiced on."[34] The court clearly accepted such regression was possible, that mastery was temporary, and that elderly enslavers might not expect to be accorded respect or honor by their peers. They should instead fear the avarice of ambitious enslavers.

Some of the challenged wills spoke to lurid tales of intimate exploitation. The image of aged people being tricked by the young in intimate affairs has long been a powerful cultural trope, and antebellum southerners clearly believed that reality lay behind such representations.[35] Meta Morriss Grimball of South Carolina witnessed a neighbor with "his new young wife" and sardonically noted "she is much taller than her old husband; and looks like his daughter; she was poor, or I am sure she could never have married that blear-eyed old creature."[36] Some challenges to wills thus stressed that the aged had been tricked into giving up their property and damaging the rightful heirs. The distributees and heirs-at-law of the late John Garrett, from Laurens District, South Carolina, looked to void a deed of gift executed by Garrett to Nancy Hughes, with whom he "lived in a state of concubinage," by claiming that she had exerted undue influence over him while he was "far advanced in years and of great imbecility of mind and body and utterly incompetent to do anything." Hughes furiously rejected the claim she had sexually manipulated the older man, insisting "that it was a just and proper compensation for her industry care and attention, not only in the management of the affairs and property of the said John Garretts, but in attending upon and

---

[34] Petition of Barsheba and John Burns, February 14, 1834, Union District, South Carolina, #21383426, Series 2, RSPP.

[35] See, for example, Tim Parkin, *Old Age in the Roman World: A Cultural and Social History* (Baltimore: Johns Hopkins University Press, 2003), 193–273; Angus McLaren, *Impotence: A Cultural History* (Chicago: University of Chicago Press, 2008); Helen Yallop, *Age and Identity in Eighteenth-Century England* (London: Routledge, 2016), 107–21.

[36] Journal of Meta Morris Grimball, December 1860–February 1866, 1, SCL.

ministering to him, when disease and sickness rendered such kindness and attention necessary."[37] The petition was left unresolved, but the intimation that an older man was tricked into giving up his property indicates how advanced age was viewed as reducing autonomy and authority, as well as allowing for reversals of gendered power dynamics among white couples.

In Grayson County, Texas, 1865, Sally Hudson's efforts to probate Isaac Hudson's will were challenged by the grandchildren from his first marriage. John Mayrant, the grandchildren's guardian, charged that Isaac "was not of a sound and disposing mind and memory at the time and long before said will was made, and that he had not the mental capacity and discretion to make a will & that said will was obtained by undue influence and fraud." This fraud was explicitly predicated on Isaac's age and infirmities. Maynard insisted that Isaac "was an old man more than seventy years old and very frail when said pretended will was executed" and that his "unsound mind and memory" was "caused by old age and disease." Isaac was left in the state of second infancy contemporaries associated with advanced old age, being described as "extremely childish and therefore wholly unable and incapacitated to resist the influences that designing and artful persons practiced upon him as hereinafter stated." Maynard made clear that Isaac's weakness was well known, and his reputation for mastery denied: "All the foregoing facts viz: the old age, frailty, mental incapacity, and unsoundness of mind and memory were notorious in the neighborhood." Rather than respect her aged husband, "Sally Hudson and her relations and friends" were charged with seeing this as an opportunity "to overreach the said Isaac of unsound mind as aforesaid and thereby get hold of the property of the said Isaac wrongfully and fraudulently and to obtain possession of the same."[38] Sally's request was rejected and the trope of the aged being tricked and made submissive by their intimate partners, including an inversion of the trope of masculine dominance, was well acknowledged by the court and community.

This was a problem that affected women too. In 1841, Rutherford County, North Carolina, the explosive testimony of Squire Simmons destroyed Benjamin Logan's efforts to claim ownership of Phebe Simmons's

[37] Petition of Beverley Garrett et al., November 29, 1850; Answer, Nancy Hughes, January 24, 1851, Laurens District, South Carolina, #21385045, Series 2, RSPP.
[38] Petition of Sally Hudson, August 25, 1865; Copy of Answer, John Mayrant, August 25, 1865; Copy of Amended Answer, John Mayrant, October 30, 1865; Amended Answer, John Mayrant, November 27, 1865, Grayson County, Texas, #21586504, Series 2, RSPP.

property. Phebe, an aged widow, had surprised the neighborhood with her marriage to the much younger Logan in 1818. Squire, who was Phebes's son, claimed that "he had no knowledge, or belief that his mother intended ever again to marry, and least of all did he imagine that she would ever marry a man young enough to be her own child." The affair was, in fact, conducted to the "utter astonishment of the neighbourhood." However, Logan, described by his rival as "younger than her oldest son; a man notoriously intemperate and drunken, poor and indebted beyond his ability to pay his Debts," was apparently only one of many who had been eyeing up the wealthy widow. Phebe was aware of this interest and, after Logan intimated his intentions, stated that "she did not know what any young man would want with a sickly old woman like herself, unless it was to get her negroes!" She insisted any suitor would fail here, for "she intended them for her son Squire Simmons."

Simmons apparently knew the risks of exploitation, but she married Logan still. Squire was adamant this was not done in good faith, however, and that Logan "wished to deceive and defraud an old decrepit grand mother out of her property under the pretext of marriage." His machinations involved having "concealed the marriage until he bound his victim fast," and only inviting as witnesses "a picked set, the cronies and conspirators who went to cheat one old woman out of two negroes." Squire could do nothing now but fear for the future, stating he "forsaw, or thought he foresaw, that his sickly old mother would live a most unhappy life with a drunken young man. Sad experience proved he was not mistaken." Logan refused to help his aged wife as she grew sick, "whiped and struck her with the butt of the waggon whip," and "supported himself out of her estate." Logan clearly hoped that the marriage would be short lived and that he would inherit the land and slaves, but while Phebe "was expected to die several years before she did ... she lingered on in much suffering in body and mind." This suffering was alleviated by Squire, and not Logan, who "exercised the exclusive & uninterrupted dominion & ownership over the said negroes" for his own benefit instead.[39] Phebe died in 1829 after years of mistreatment. Squire, at this point, seized the slaves and successfully defended his actions in court after her death. Any sense of pity for Phebe must, of course, be reconciled with the fact she had built her wealth as a slaver; the end result was simply that the "rightful" enslaver won. More important than sympathy is that the case reveals how the rapacious desire

[39] Petition of Benjamin Logan, May 1, 1841; Answer, Squire Simmons, November 6, 1841, Rutherford County, North Carolina, #212841061, Series 2, RSPP.

for profit, and exploitation built into slavery, extended into antebellum enslavers' dealings with one another. Advanced age was seen as a weakness that could be exploited to further one's ascent in society.

* * *

Some elderly enslavers were depicted as having been made to change their wills in the face of abuse, intimidation, and even violence. The final memories and representations of these aged individuals, from family, friend, or foe, and openly discussed in petitions, depositions, and antebellum courtrooms, emphasized their weakness, as well as their meek submission to the authority of another. Bertram Wyatt-Brown noted the importance for antebellum southerners of being able to defend one's honor and that "an insult, verbal or otherwise, damaged the psyche as surely as a slap on the face, and required a violent response." For some elders, however, this response was no longer possible in the face of their weakened powers and this reduced status came at a cost both physical and mental. Brown's contention that, in the context of honor and conflict, "winners humiliate losers," is amply demonstrated in this final section.[40] This humiliation sometimes came in life and extended after death, with aged enslavers' characters and reputations being dragged through the mud to better serve the interests of the living.

In 1839, the Supreme Court of Kentucky struggled to agree over the legality (and morality) of Jeconias Singleton's will. This was an explosive family dispute which demonstrates the ferocity of intergenerational conflict when white southerners believed they were losing the chance to profit from slavery. "Old man" Singleton, as he was described by practically all the witnesses, had cut off his youngest son, William, to favor the remaining brothers in his last will and testament. William and his supporters, including Singleton's widow, insisted this will be set aside as the "old man . . . was of insane mind and memory, at and before it was published, and was laboring under an unfounded prejudice against, and insane aversion to, his son William." More troubling still was the claim that he was left in his dotage as no master at all. The "pretended will," they insisted, was only "produced by the undue and controlling influence of the principal devisees, the defendants."

This was an extremely bitter dispute. Extensive testimony was produced by all parties to the suit, who, notwithstanding their competing

<hr>

[40] Wyattt-Brown, *A Warring Nation*, 54, 6.

aims, agreed that Singleton had lost control of himself and others, and that this had manifested in intergenerational tension and internecine strife. Jeconias, it was claimed, "labored under extraordinary delusions for years before the will was made," and at times believed "that persons were in pursuit of him to kill him; at others, that they were about to take him to the lunatic asylum; that he was ruined, and his whole family were ruined." The court heard that this "unnatural feeling would some-times fall on One son, and then on another, but eventually settled on William ... [and] continued till his death." William and his supporters, principally his mother, insisted that this was no coincidence. The jealous brothers "operated upon [Singleton's] excited or disordered mind, by their conduct and conversations, to keep alive his inveterate feelings against his son, and to make the impression that he ought not to make William and Mrs. Brown equal with them, in the division of his estate."[41]

Witnesses recalled their shock at the extent of Jeconias's fury at his son, as well as their belief in the unjust nature of it. The pastor of their church recalled Jeconias "was passionate, vehement and unnatural in his conduct to William, and flew into a violent rage because the church would not hear the evidence of a slave against him, and though he and others made every effort to reconcile him, they could do nothing with him." Throughout, they insisted, William had "behaved humbly and respectfully to his father," obeying the cultural expectation of filial obedience, and, in fact, "to gratify him, withdrew from the church." Jeconias's rage continued unabated, however, and was argued to consti-tute evidence of insanity: "Whenever, afterwards, the name of William was mentioned, which happened on various occasions, up to his death, he would fly into a violent ungovernable rage, and act like a madman." The court heard extensively from Jeconias's widow. She stressed how the other sons had turned their father against William and how such charges wormed their way into his mind as he grew older and weaker. In his better days he might have stood up to such influence, with the widow noting, "his conduct was very different in the fore part of his life." As he declined, however:

Any little thing would put him in a violent rage and passion. His sons had a very great influence over him. The boys, when they came to see us, would ask if Will had quit drinking yet, and that the old man had better give his property to them – they had families and children, and Will had none.

---

[41] *Singleton's Will*, 38 Ky. 315, 8 Dana 315 (1839), 315, 322, 325, 322–33.

In the eyes of the plaintiffs, the beneficiaries of the will had resented William's position as the family favorite and sought to and succeeded in poisoning their father's mind against him. The widow recalled hearing "the old man say that the boys said, that he ought not to give Will and Brown much of his property," and that this had worked on his enfeebled mind. Their strategy included provocatively charging that William had a child by one of Jeconias's slaves. "She heard John Singleton say, in the presence and hearing of the old man, when he was lying on his settee, do you see the striking likeness of Harriet's child to Will; the old man said – Oh Jonny, Jonny."

Jeconias's widow insisted that the boys' dealings were fraudulent from first to last and were the culmination of a long-standing plan to disinherit their brother. "After the old man's death," she asked for the will to be read to her, and "when [John] read that part which said that [Jeconias] was of sound and disposing mind, but weak of body, the witness said, now John, don't you know that is not so, that the old man was not in his right mind." Rather than deny it, John practically smirked back to her: "John replied, 'yes I do know that he has not been in his right mind for four or five years past, and was not able to make a will.'" The brothers had more pressing concerns, though: "Lewis has said to me that William should not have any more of his father's estate." The court found against the will and clearly disapproved of the extended efforts the brothers applied to disinherit William, believing they had fraudulently exploited the weakness of a man who, "if not actually insane, was subject to violent excitements and inveterate passions and was, moreover, greatly impaired by age, by excessive drink, and by habitual subjection to the most extravagant delusions." These shocking acts were "contrary to their duty to a brother" and relied on exploiting the submissive nature of an elderly man.[42]

The court ruled in a majority decision that the will be discarded on account of undue influence and because Jeconias Singleton was non compos mentis. It is worth dwelling, however, on the stinging dissent from Justice Robertson and the lengthy appeal from the defendant's counsel. Both of these presented an alternative family history which, while not compelling to the majority, offers insight into the ferocity of intergenerational strife when property and profit were at stake, the contested nature of mastery for antebellum slavers, and how social hierarchies were shaped by understandings of aging as a process of decline. In this alternative reading, William was portrayed as having disgraced himself

[42] *Singleton's Will*, 38 Ky. 315, 8 Dana 315 (1839), 326, 328, 332.

and his family, with the disrespect shown toward the patriarch of the family particularly repugnant. They were adamant that although drink had impaired Jeconias's capacity, there had been no lasting debility; claims to the contrary were simply designed to embarrass the recently deceased and provide an acceptable excuse to override his will. They insisted that a number of witnesses described him as "industrious, economical, and enterprising" until the very end of his life and that the only ones who charged otherwise had a direct interest in making the case. The most significant witness here was Jeconias's widow, one of the few to directly state he was in a permanent manic state. The counsel insisted this was shaped entirely by self-interest: William was "the darling of her heart," and so she "felt a strong leaning against the will."

Robertson was unconvinced that Jeconias's treatment of William had been irrational or constituted evidence of insanity, instead painting a picture of an aged patriarch betrayed by a feckless son: "the testator suspected his son William of conduct which he looked on with peculiar indignation and horror. I do not know that his suspicions were without rational foundation." In Robertson's eyes, any usurpation of mastery had come from William himself, with this filial disrespect particularly egregious. William had "deported himself rudely and rebelliously towards his passionate and venerable father" and was even charged with having "told his mother that he would cut [Jeconias's] throat if he was not his father." William's disrespect was not kept private, but he instead took his complaints public, denigrating his father as a "damned rascal" and "spoke of his father to others, in a manner equally profane and contemptuous." Robertson was deeply concerned with the interjection of the courts in this family matter. If, having heard about such shocking disrespect toward an aged testator, the court rejected the idea it might influence them to change their will, the decision would have wider repercussions. It would:

render insecure and comparatively delusive the cherished right given by law to every free man of sound mind and legal discretion, to dispose, at his death, of the estate which he had acquired while living, and the chief end of toiling for which, may have been – as with many – the luxury of giving it, at his death, to those he loves or prefers.[43]

Robertson's language was cloaked in judicial restraint, but John M. Hewitt had no such qualms. In a furious rebuttal of the ruling against them and a request for a new trial, Hewitt denigrated William on account

---

[43] *Singleton's Will*, 38 Ky. 315, 8 Dana 315 (1839), 336, 334, 339–41.

of his disrespect to his aged father. He explicitly compared the upstanding reputation of the patriarch with his ungrateful son, noting he had built up his wealth and fortune through "half a century's toil and economy." William, meanwhile, was "an old bachelor, upwards of thirty-three, with a strong attachment to a negress" and with little personal success. According to Hewitt, "If ever Col. Singleton did a righteous deed, it was in disinheriting William." A significant part of Hewitt's appeal revolved around the concern that the trial had sullied the reputation of a man no longer able to defend himself. The counsel plainly asked "what good then can result from fixing a stigma upon the memory of Col. Singleton, Lewis, John and Elijah – all of whom have many boys and girls just coming into active and useful life – by declaring the first a madman, and the others fraudulent and traitorous?"

Having noted the injustice of this posthumous destruction of a man's honor, the counsel went on the attack. Mrs. Singleton, to whose testimony "so much importance is very undeservingly attached," was depicted as having abused her husband in life and in death. Alongside stressing her aim to protect her "favorite" son at the expense of Jeconias's will, the counsel weaponized her own advanced age. If they were expected to take as given the aged infirmity of Singleton as acting against him, they must also acknowledge that his widow, whose testimony in their view had "so much importance ... undeservingly attached," was "further in the wane of life, than her husband" and "subject to all the imperfections and infirmities of age." Having cast Mrs. Singleton as the weak link, they reasserted the masterful nature of "Col. Singleton" in comparison. Even up to his final moments, Jeconias was "a man of fixed purposes, independent in his sentiments and judgment, not to be influenced by wife, children, or friends." This was a determined effort to reject the image of a frail old man that the court had accepted in ruling against the will in the first instance. It was impossible to imagine, the counsel thundered, that such an authoritative and honorable man could be the subject of undue influence: "he was the last man that ever lived who could be subjugated to the wishes of another." With a rhetorical flourish, the counsel expounded "How few such men!"[44]

As part of the appeal, however, Hewitt provided contradictory comments about Jeconias's state of mastery. Despite his efforts to portray Jeconias as commanding right to the end, Hewitt nonetheless insisted that the "venerable father" had been intimidated by William and that he felt

---

[44] *Singleton's Will*, 38 Ky. 315, 8 Dana 315 (1839), 352, 341, 352, 354, 356, 357.

unable to defend himself. After having publicly derided his father, tres-
passed on his plantation, and threatened him in front of others, William's
disrespect turned physical. William visited his father's plantation with a gun
and threatened to shoot those who had been "telling damned lies upon"
him. Upon seeing his father in the field, he apparently "pointed the gun at
the old man." At this point, "all of them took fright and fled – his father
with them." The presumption of mastery from son over father was near
total, and the language of fright and flight was anathema to claims of
southern manhood. Despite their hopes to protect Jeconias's will and
reputation, the image Hewitt conjured of an elderly man forced to flee
from his son, alongside his slaves, equally accepted his reduced capacity
and character. Hewitt insisted, however, that William's reprehensible
actions must be taken into account: "This is the son, who commands the
sympathy of the Court – and this the father who has received their denunciation for continued persecution." William's actions were degrading at
a personal and familial level, but also risked undercutting wider social
hierarchies. Was it not "as apparent that William's treatment to his father
induced him to disinherit him, as that it brought his grey hairs with sorrow
to the grave? And shall he not be permitted there to rest without the blight
upon his reputation – that while living, he persecuted his immaculate son
William"? In Hewitt's rendition, filial ingratitude deserved nothing but
scorn, and to challenge Jeconias's will was to challenge the fabric of society.
It required acknowledging the contested nature of mastery and social
hierarchies, to the harm of all: "The statute of wills ought to be repealed,
if men shall be prevented from disinheriting such scoffing and rebellious
sons as William Singleton is proved before this Court to have been. William
broke his father's heart, and is now about to squander his estate!" Despite
John M. Hewitt's extraordinary pleading, the petition was overruled without response. Jeconias Singleton's last will was broken, and his reputation
was too.[45] The competing testimony and disputed ruling shows how explosively intergenerational strife might erupt between antebellum enslavers
when property, profit, and mastery itself were at stake.

* * *

When challenging the legitimacy of wills, some southern whites went so
far as to claim aged enslavers had been controlled by enslaved people.
John Mayfield has noted that "in the highly symbolic structuring of

---

[45] *Singleton's Will*, 38 Ky. 315, 8 Dana 315 (1839), 340, 377–8, 380, 382, 397.

Southern masculinity, to be manipulated and mastered was to be a slave, regardless of race," and such arguments were applied by rivals seeking to supplant the aged testator.[46] Dependency, which historian Diane Miller Sommerville has described as resembling an "assault on Southern manhood," was yet more shameful if it involved an inversion of the claims to white superiority that justified antebellum slavery.[47] The willingness of southern whites to use this discourse to denigrate deceased friends, family, and other enslavers to better secure their own wealth reinforces the ruthless competitiveness of antebellum slavers, and their combined emphasis on dominance and productive exploitation of slaves as necessary components of mastery.

One such case was presented in the challenge to John Williams's will in South Carolina. Williams was portrayed as a weak and infirm man by family members who sought to contest the distribution of his property after death. Williams, who was born in South Carolina, had moved to Mississippi and then left after encountering health problems and falling out with family members. Upon his return, Williams cut his heirs-at-law from the will entirely, making the sole beneficiaries the neighboring Canty family. This led to a furious response after his death, with his brother leading the charge: "the said deed is null and void, because at the time of its execution John Williams was non compos mentis; that from excessive dissipation and drunkenness, and other causes, his mind had become so impaired, weakened, and destroyed, as wholly to disqualify and incapacitate him to execute said deed." More explosively, they asserted that "on account of his weakness of intellect, he was wholly and perfectly under the control, and subject to the influence of an old negress (belonging to him) named Amy" and "that the influence of this negress was unduly and fraudulently used by the Cantys to procure the execution of this deed."

The court ultimately discarded the complaints and accepted that the Cantys had stepped up to support Williams when he needed it most. This support was, in fact, only necessary because his brother had taken advantage of Williams's weakness and "induced him to remove to Mississippi, under a promise that he, Benjamin, would furnish him a plantation on which to live; ... Benjamin Williams failed to do this, and turned him out of house and home." Benjamin used his brother's money to pay his own debts and had, in fact, "gotten all that he, John Williams, made while in Mississippi." The Cantys asserted that they had simply stepped up after Williams ignominiously returned to South Carolina, presenting themselves

---

[46] Mayfield, *Counterfeit Gentlemen*, 58.   [47] Sommerville, *Aberration of Mind*, 186.

as having cared for an aged and frail man and "furnished him every comfort," and were thus deserving of his gratitude: "for six months before his death he was very feeble, almost as helpless as an infant, and that they then showed him every kindness, and supplied his every want."[48] Despite the extensive claims of Williams's incapacity – both physical and mental – and the lurid claims of enslaved people controlling him, the court found that his will was a rational act done in a rational mind and ruled in the Cantys' favor.

In *Etheridge* v. *Corprew*, December 1855, the North Carolina Supreme Court heard about a disturbing lack of control over the enslaved people residing on John Wheatly's farm. His heirs challenged Wheatly's will by claiming that this inversion of mastery was directly related to frailties caused by his advanced age: Wheatly was "very old, and his mind so much impaired as to subject him to the entire control of his slaves." The lack of mastery here was a problem, but it mainly served to further the complainants' claims of Wheatly's incapacity in order to challenge the division of property after death. The heirs were adamant that Wheatly had been controlled not only by his enslaved people, but by his scheming executor too. Wheatly's heirs believed that Wilson Corprew had manipulated the old man into signing over his entire estate to him in his "last moments, when no white person was near." Corprew took the whole property and then cut off the rest of the family. According to the heirs, this was not a decision Wheatly would have made in his right mind. By this point, however, "John was too weak from old age and sickness, to know what he was doing."[49] The Supreme Court ultimately refused to adjudicate on the matter of motive and, focusing solely on procedural questions, allowed the will to probate. Regardless of the result, Wheatly's character, conduct, and final expression of authority were openly denied by his family on account of a weakness of body and mind associated with old age. It was publicly stated that he had been controlled by others, and had been made subservient to those he ostensibly enslaved. The case underscored how far efforts to rise in a slave society, and the desire for mastery itself, revolved around the dominance of others, white and Black.

The shame attached to this type of reversal of power was clearly utilized by the challengers to James Potts's will in Georgia, 1849.[50] Potts had died in

---

[48] *Exum* v. *Canty*, 34 Miss. 533, October 1857. See also *Ben Exum et al.* v. *Zach Canty et al.*, 1855, Carrollton District Chancery Court Minutes, Microfilm 38382, Case 51.8, MDAH.

[49] *Etheridge* v. *Corprew*, 48. N.C. 14 (1855), 14–15.

[50] Mayfield, *Counterfeit Gentlemen*, 58.

his nineties and his heirs contested his distribution of property to Alonzo P. House on account of his incapacity to make a will. They focused heavily on the undue influence of his enslaved woman, Charity. During the initial trial, witnesses provided extensive (but contested) testimony on how they perceived his failing powers on account of age, painting an image of a man made dependent, submissive, and a master in name only.[51] Potts, who "had lost his teeth & could not talk as distinctly as previously," was portrayed as being nearly entirely reliant on Charity to conduct business or even to be understood. Historians have long stated how dependency was anathema to notions of honor and authority for southern whites, with Robert Elder noting that "a lack of self-mastery could turn the potential for fame into ill repute."[52] This was certainly the case for Potts, with witnesses openly voicing their disgust at the submissive state he was reduced to. John Hill recalled going to see Potts about business and coming away with the belief that he was "[. . . utterly incapable of transacting any business whatever, with anything like prudence or reason. In fact I believe he had no reason]. He seemed to be stupid, & dull & entirely so. I do not know what the cause of his mental inactivity was, [but suppose age was one reason]." Hill claimed he took no pleasure in observing these failings, but felt the need to observe and record them for posterity: "[. . . I remained some time watching him after I had despaired transacting business with him, & I had melancholy impressions of the weakness of the man.]."

Other witnesses provided more troubling detail about how Potts's slaves exerted control over him, with Jesse Kaisey claiming that "his negroes did pretty much as they pleased; and especially did his principal house woman exercise a controlling influence over him." This extended to working on their own behalf, Kaisey argued, with the claim that Lucy, his interpreter, "would frequently misinterpret for him, in business not pertaining to the house, and which did not belong to her line of business." Kaisey was adamant, even if the court rejected elements of his testimony, that age had rendered Potts incompetent: "[. . . he would say that he (Potts) was wholly incompetent to make a will for several years before his death, states that his imbecility great out of old age.]." Another witness emphasized the lax control and state of semi-freedom for those enslaved on his farm, portraying a world where mastery had been inverted by claiming

---

[51] The testimony bookended with [ ] was disallowed by the court. I include it here, nonetheless, as it was openly stated by witnesses and recorded, and thus reveals further insight into contested perceptions of aging.
[52] Elder, *The Sacred Mirror*, 189.

that "they obeyed or disobeyed his orders pretty much as they pleased." James Hewart spoke of a man entirely absent of the force necessary for control: "[Pott's] bodily health was very much impaired . . . [his mind was also weak & very changeable]." An attending physician lamented the weak nature of Potts, claiming his "extreme old age" manifested itself in "a childishness that is not common to men of ordinary minds" and stressed the enslaved did whatever they wanted with their "master":

[Witness saw them] putting on the old man a pair of socks contrary to his will, but they persisted in it until he finally became willing or yielded to them. [Witness thinks the old man was to a considerable extent entirely in the hands of those who nursed him, as they appeared to do with & for him pretty much as they pleased with the exception] that he would not suffer his feet washed nor his head shaved.

Several witnesses disputed the accounts of senility and incompetence, but accepted the latitude provided to the enslaved people on the farm, and the court initially found for the will. The plaintiffs appealed, however, with Potts's age and presumed dependency central to their case. Their counsel was adamant: "the law does recognize degrees in mind . . . And when the mental debility of a testator is the consequence of age, there is less presumption of the sanity of the testator at the time of the execution of the will, then [sic] when the mental malady is ordinary lunacy."[53]

Regardless of their extensive pleas over the important connection between old age and infirmity, the complainants were firmly swatted down by the Supreme Court. Justice Joseph Henry Lumpkin specifically asserted that "*Old age* does not deprive a man of the capacity of making a testament," and went on to use precedent from a New York trial to underline the importance of protection from avaricious heirs. The judge here (with Lumpkin's affirmation) recorded a fear that negative treatment of the elderly was near inevitable absent the self-interest of heirs:

It is one of the painful consequences of extreme old age, that it ceases to excite interest, and is apt to be left solitary and neglected. The control which the law still gives to a man, over the disposal of his property, is one of the most efficient means which he has, in protracted life, to command the attention due to his infirmities. The will of such an aged man ought to be regarded with great tenderness, when it appears not to have been procured by fraudulent acts, but contains those very dispositions which the circumstances of his situation, and the course of the natural affections dictated.

---

[53] Rule of Exception, Troup County Superior Court, November term 1848, *Potts v. House*, Caveat, in A.418, *William E. Potts et al.* v. *Alzono P. House*, exr., in Supreme Court – Clerk of Court, Criminal Appeals Case Files, 1846–1917, Case A-418, GSA.

Lumpkin also addressed the claims of undue influence on the part of the slaves. Despite his personal disgust at the inversion of mastery, he insisted that "miserable infatuation, however shocking it might be to our sense of decency and propriety, and proper subordination on the part of our negroes" was not enough to discount Potts's will unless he had been made "to do that which he was unable to refuse, by importunity or threats, or any other way by which one person acquires dominion and control over another." Lumpkin was unimpressed by the control (or lack thereof) of Potts's slaves, but insisted it was "only necessary to advert for a moment to the brief of the testimony in the case before us, to see how immeasurably short it comes on the score of unjust control." Despite the lurid claims of submission to the will of his slaves, Lumpkin asserted that their transfer to Alonzo P. House, "who resided in the State of Alabama, and between whom and the slaves of the deceased no intimacy, much less *conspiracy*," held out no personal benefit to the named parties and there was no evidence of foul play.[54] Despite acknowledging Potts had the right to distribute his property as he saw fit, the final public image presented of Potts was not that of a masterful patriarch, but of a meek, weak, and submissive child. Lumpkin's justification further savaged, rather than salvaged, Potts's name and reputation, and his rhetoric revealed a wider recognition of the declining powers associated with aging and the potential disrespect and disregard that awaited the aged.

* * *

Southern courts clearly sought to protect the rights of testators, even in the most lurid challenges to their wills. As the South Carolina Court of Appeals and Errors insisted in *O' Neal v. Farr*, "When a sane man, with legal solemnities, executes a will, the law presumes, in the absence of proof to the contrary, that it was done voluntarily, and that it contains truly his wishes and intentions in relation to the disposition of his property." They also insisted that "the burden of proof lies on him who alleges the existence of undue influence, and its exercise in the procurement of the will."[55] Legal niceties, however, could not save testators from having their names dragged through the mud after death, nor prevent the public airing of the disrespect family, friends, and neighbors held for aged enslavers in the final stages of life. Much of the testimony discussed here, whether defending testators or challenging them, operated under – and reified – the

---

[54] *Potts v. House*, 6 Ga. 324 (1849), 355, 360, 363, 364.
[55] *O' Neal v. Farr*, 30 S.C.L. 80, 1 Rich. 80 (1844), 85.

assumption that old age increased the likelihood of dependency and frailty, both mental and physical. The cases vividly reveal how far this discourse could motivate and legitimate the assumption of mastery by the young over the old, underscoring the contentious social relations present in white communities of the antebellum South.

Southerners craved "the esteem of their peers" and worked hard to "secure their position in society," with their last will and testament serving as a final expression of their mastery and position among their peers.[56] Those seeking to rise in the world, however, were willing to publicly traduce the reputation of the dead to achieve their aims, and they could use the physical and mental effects of aging – whether perceived or real – to make their case. Courts were reluctant to interfere with wills, and respect for the wishes of testators was important to southern whites who prized their independence and authority, even after death. Nonetheless, cases heard across the antebellum South detailed how far age was understood to limit and direct the actions and identities of enslavers, the ferocity of intergenerational tension as slavers (or those who sought to be) fought to ensure their elders did not waste their "property," and how age shaped social conflict and hierarchies in white communities. Whether successful or not, the challenges to the wills discussed in this chapter reveal how the declining force associated with aging – and the inevitability of death itself – was viewed by some white southerners as providing them with a springboard for their own success. As William Robinson recalled of his own enslaver's death: "About three weeks later they began to look up the will, for boys then were like a good many are today, just waiting for the old man to die, so they could run through with what he had accumulated."[57] Enslavers hoped to meet their end with communal affirmation of their mastery, and with their reputation upheld by the wider community. A loss of power associated with age, however, could see the vultures circling and, as the next chapter reveals, after death, the carcass picked clean.

---

[56] Glover, "Let Us Manufacture Men," 31.
[57] Robinson, *From Log Cabin to the Pulpit*, 28.

10

"Let our women and old men . . . be disabused of the false and unfounded notion that slavery is sinful"

Emancipation Contested

Intergenerational disputes shaped by white southerners' hopes to profit from slavery did not end with the death of an enslaver. These contests became particularly virulent when the matter revolved around manumissions, and this chapter shows how elderly enslavers who sought to posthumously emancipate enslaved people had their actions challenged by rivals who utilized the discourse that conflated old age with weakness, both of body and mind, to diminish their reputation and deny their mastery. Justice Joseph Henry Lumpkin of Georgia's comments when he rejected one such proposed emancipation spoke to the connections contemporaries drew between old age and weakness: "Let our women and old men, and persons of weak and infirm minds, be disabused of the false and unfounded notion that slavery is sinful, and that they will peril their souls if they do not disinherit their offspring by emancipating their slaves."[1] Lumpkin's comments reveal how the aging process had public and political ramifications in a slave society. A focus on emancipation and age serves as a fitting end to this study, which underlines the wider importance of age as a vector of power in the antebellum South.

Chapter 1 noted the range of laws passed across the slave states to limit or manage manumission in the antebellum period. Hardening racism and proslavery attitudes, combined with a fear that white communities would be "flooded with a population of paupers, sinking under the weight of years and a life of hardships and labour," helped shape such measures.[2] By

---

[1] *American Colonization Society* v. *Gartrell*, 23 Ga. 448 (1857), 464–5.

[2] *Manns* v. *Given*, 35 Va. 689, 7 Leigh 689 (1836), 773. See Eric Burin, *Slavery and the Peculiar Solution: A History of the Colonization Society* (Gainesville: University Press of Florida, 2005), 126–31; Alejandro De La Fuente and Ariela J. Gross, *Becoming Free,*

the 1830s most Southern states had passed laws that meant all manumissions had to be approved at a judicial or legislative level. In the decades that followed, a number of states passed bans on manumission entirely or mandated that emancipated slaves leave the state immediately upon pain of re-enslavement. Much of the legislation here grappled with how to best manage, or even to prevent, enslavers from posthumously freeing enslaved people. Thomas Morris notes that "special conceptual problems were presented" through such arrangements, as judges and juries had to balance the respect for a testator's wishes with concerns that the public "good" was harmed by freeing enslaved people. Manumission "fell within the bounds of public policy even when it was seen in private rights."[3]

The balancing act that required respecting the rights of the individual while upholding the collective "good" allowed for a degree of latitude on a state-by-state, and even case-by-case, basis. Notwithstanding the aforementioned restrictions, there were avenues for freedom for slaves across the antebellum South. Much excellent work has explored the legislative and political elements of manumission, and the experiences of, and attitudes toward, the process from both white and Black southerners.[4] This chapter takes as its analytical focus the attention contemporaries paid to age when looking to challenge testamentary efforts to free enslaved people. I explore how those who sought to challenge manumissions – and sometimes emancipation itself – believed that casting aspersions on the character of those who sought to manumit their slaves on account of their age was an effective way to do so. I thereby emphasize the significance of intergenerational tension in the antebellum South, the significance of age in white southern communities, and the dynamic and contested nature of mastery itself.

* * *

Enslavers of all ages attempted to manumit their slaves and clearly did so for a variety of reasons. Requests that came in final wills, or in petitions referencing the advanced age of the petitioner, typically applied language that suggested this must be regarded as a final expression of mastery and

---

Becoming Black: Race, Freedom, and Law in Cuba, Virginia, and Louisiana (New York: Cambridge University Press, 2020), ch. 4; Fox-Genovese and Genovese, *Fatal Self-Deception*, 98–110.

[3] Morris, *Southern Slavery and the Law*, 373; Jenny Bourne Wahl, "Legal Constraints on Slave Masters: The Problem of Social Cost," *American Journal of Legal Theory* 41.1 (1997), 1–24.

[4] For the wider literature on manumission and the law, see Chapter 3.

respected accordingly. Some aged enslavers expressed concerns that slave-holding would affect their passage past the pearly gates and they wished to absolve themselves before death. In Gaspar Sinclair's petition to free his two slaves, he explained how, being "a very old man," he was "now disposed to close his affairs in this world, and by a proper provision, prepare for a better – to this conscientiously, your petitioner is disposed to discharge all debts due by him, and more especially his debts of gratitude." His "gratitude" entailed freedom to those enslaved people who, through their labors, had "furnished those comforts which all desire in this world."[5] There was no recorded result for the request but, as Sinclair's proposal went against Mississippi law, it is reasonable to assume he failed.

Enslavers who attempted to free enslaved people commonly detailed the particular care they received in advanced age, with "meritorious service" an important threshold to cross when attempting to legitimate such actions. John Ryan of Edgefield Parish, South Carolina, "being far advanced in life," expressed his desire to emancipate his "aged and faithful Slave of good character," while in 1841, Peggy Rankin, of Montgomery County, Texas, asked permission to set free three slaves who had "been remarkably kind and attentive to your memorialist in her infirm old age." Rankin, aged eighty-six, knew that "ordinary to the course of nature she cannot long survive" and wanted to fulfill her wishes before it was too late.[6]

Executors and heirs sometimes expressed their hopes of fulfilling the last expression of mastery from testators who willed emancipation. Joel Battle of North Carolina wanted to set free the fifty- or sixty-year-old Jolly because it was "the dying request of the said Amos."[7] Marshal Jameson recorded how his push to emancipate his father's slave Jacob related to his sense of "filial affection and reverence for his Father's memory."[8] Many executors and heirs honored the wishes of their testators. Those who sought to manumit enslaved people, however, recognized the problems they faced in so doing. This could relate to legal restrictions but, more

---

[5] Petition from Gaspar Sinclair, Emancipations: 1820s, State Government Records, Series 2370, Box 6813, Folder 9, MDAH.

[6] Petition of John Ryan, November 25, 1823, Edgefield District/Parish, South Carolina, #11382311, Series 1, RSPP; Petition of Peggy Rankin, October 25, 1841, Montgomery County, Texas, #11584102, Series 1 RSPP.

[7] Petition of Joel Battle, c. May 1817, Edgecombe County, North Carolina, #21281703, Series 2, RSPP.

[8] Petition of Marshal Jameson, April 7, 1828, Williamson County, Tennessee, #21482804, Series 2, RSPP.

nefariously, could also indicate a fear of jealous or greedy heirs disrupting their plans. Some testators prepared for precisely this. Peter Corn explained that his aunt's enslaver sought to posthumously support his slaves, and that "before he died he put down in a way dat his daughters and sons-in-laws could not break it 'cepting dey would raise several thousand dollars."[9] In 1828, Samuel Miller of Jackson, Mississippi, stressed his desire to set Martha Tyler free while he could, noting that this would serve as his final expression of authority and that he was all too aware the clock was ticking: "he is now advancing in years and knows not at what hour the hand of death, may prevent his paying this last act of benevolence and kindness to a servant endeared to him by years of faithful servitude." Miller was clearly fearful that his "act of benevolence" might be prevented after his death and informed the court of his determination "to attempt the consummation of a purpose, which might be defeated by longer delay."[10] Miller, as will be shown, was right to fear the defeat of his purpose.

Some emancipations were foiled simply because of legal technicalities, as noted earlier. Manumission was, however, the subject of public concern and came with specific technicalities and legal provisions. A failure to abide by state law, even including laws passed after the death of the testator, saw some manumissions foiled and the "dead hand" denied. In *Robinson* v. *King*, 1849, Elisha King's executor expressed his own reservations about the proposed manumission of King's slaves. He was, according to one witness, "afraid the community would think hard of him." This problem was taken out of his hands as the plan was in conflict with the Act of 1818 that expressly forbade manumission by will.[11] In *Lea* v. *Brown*, 1857, the North Carolina Supreme Court rejected Nathaniel Lea's convoluted efforts to free his slaves. Lea, who died aged sixty-seven without children, had bequeathed to his executor Thomas J. Brown the slaves who had "been faithful to me and served me well, attended and nursed me in my long and painful sickness." He instructed Brown to "take care of the said slaves, treat them kindly and humanely" and provided him with $3,000 to pay them expenses, as well as land and personal property. The heirs-at-law insisted that the bequest was void because this was, in fact, a deliberate "attempt to emancipate slaves & provide for them,

---

[9] *FWP, 10* (Missouri), 90.
[10] Petition from Samuel Miller, Emancipations: 1830s, State Government Records, Series 2370, Box 6813, Folder 12, MDAH.
[11] *Robinson* v. *King*, 6 Ga 539 (1849), 541.

without complying with the laws of the state and against public policy."
The case made its way up to the State Supreme Court and, in *Lea
v. Brown*, 1857, Justice Pearson was clear that the measures applied
were unacceptable:

> In our case had the testator tried on purpose, he could not have more directly
> violated the provisions of this Statute, or more effectually contravened the fixed
> policy of the State. Here we have a family of negroes with two hundred acres of
> land, and three thousand dollars in money, to provide for their support, so that
> they may not be made to work like other negroes. The result, if his intentions are to
> be carried out, will be to establish in our midst a set of privileged negroes, causing
> the others to be dissatisfied and restless, and affording a harbor for the lazy and
> evil disposed.[12]

Despite rejecting the proposed emancipation, the court refused to accept
the heir's proposed plan to sell the slaves and distribute the monies among
themselves. They asserted that Brown and his kin still had rights to the
slaves, while the heirs-at-law held the land in trust. Juggling the rights and
wishes of testators alongside public policy and broader concerns with
emancipation was clearly a delicate balancing act for southern judges
and juries.

In *Smith v. Dunwoody*, 1856, avowedly proslavery Justice Joseph Henry
Lumpkin of Georgia was forthright about his personal disdain for manumission, alongside affirming the legal restrictions on manumission.[13]
Lumpkin was clear that James Smith's plan for the gradual emancipation
of his slaves was against the law and rejected it entirely. He was equally
disturbed to think that such a plan would harm the property rights of his
heirs, describing it as being "repugnant to the rights of the property in the
legatees."[14] While insisting that the Court had no "intention of making
a will for Mr. Smith or any other one else," they would, with "God and the
law helping us, do all we can in this and every other case, to give that
direction to property which is agreeable to the best feelings, affections and
reasons of mankind." In this ruling, mankind was synonymous with

[12] Petition of John Lea and Sidney Lea, October 10, 1855, Caswell County, North Carolina,
#21285533, Series 2, RSPP; Reports, May 15, 1858, January 4, 1860; North Carolina
Reports, Cases in Equity, Supreme Court of North Carolina, December Term 1856–
December Term 1857, 141–51; *Lea v. Brown*, 58 N.C. 379 (1860).

[13] On Lumpkin and manumission, see Alfred L. Brophy, *University, Court, and Slave:
Proslavery Academic Thought and Southern Jurisprudence, 1831–1861* (New York:
Oxford University Press, 2016), ch. 9.

[14] *Smith v. Dunwoody*, 19 Ga. 237 (1856), 260, 261.

whiteness and the court pushed Smith's "dead hand" firmly back down into the grave.

* * *

Those who wanted to challenge emancipation and the concomitant loss of property were able to make use of the widespread legal restrictions on the practice, as well as the broader social and cultural antipathy toward emancipation, to make their case. The basic principle of respecting the wishes of testators remained significant, however, even in cases relating to emancipation. Even the ardently proslavery Lumpkin's dismissal of Thomas Beall's planned emancipation in 1857 included the grudging acceptance "that a testator may by his will direct his Executor to remove his negroes to some other country, where they may acquire, as well as enjoy their freedom, and that the performance of such trust, will be permitted, if not enforced against such Executor." Beall's executors had, however, erred by allowing the emancipated slaves to remain on the plantation in a state of freedom while money was raised to send them to California or Liberia. Lumpkin was happy to conclude, then, "that the bequest of freedom to slaves in this case is void, as it was to take effect in this State, and the slaves are made the legatees of their own freedom, a boon they are incapable of taking."[15]

Courts were reluctant to intervene in emancipations that followed the law and frequently shut down those who sought to overrule the last expression of mastery from enslavers. Nathan Miller of Arkansas recalled how, despite fierce challenge from the deceased enslaver's heirs, his grandfather's freedom was upheld by the Supreme Court, which "said they couldn't break the dead man's will."[16] In *Cromartie* v. *Robison*, 1855, the North Carolina Supreme Court upheld the emancipation of James McKay's enslaved people despite concerns over the document's legality from the executor, who worried (perhaps self-interestedly) that the loose wording of the will meant only two named slaves should be freed. The court concluded that the provisions for freedom must be read in the most capacious light given McKay's known emancipatory wishes and that "A decent regard for the memory of the testator" forbade any efforts to limit his will's reach: to do so would make "a mockery" of McKay's wishes. In protecting McKay's plans, however, Justice Pearson underlined that the

[15] *Drane* v. *Beall*, 21 Ga. 21 (1857), 43.
[16] Rawick (Ed.), *AS, 10.5*, 93. See also *Gilbert* v. *Ward*, 10 Fed. Cas. 348, 4 Cranch C. C. 171 (1831).

process of contesting a will risked – perhaps even required – undermining the reputation of the dead.[17]

In 1841, the Court of Appeals in Kentucky was equally adamant of the need to protect the rights and reputations of testators in rejecting the challenge to Alexander Reed Snr's manumissions in his will. His heirs vigorously disputed his capacity to make a will, but, alongside stressing his "attachment to and [planned] emancipation of his slaves" and his favoritism of two children, the court stated that "the only negative facts" the complainants brought up were "the testator's age and physical infirmities." This was not enough, and the presiding judge chided the complainants' extensive efforts to diminish the memory of the deceased patriarch. Reed, the court asserted, had been in full control of his mind and was able to determine the distribution of his property irrespective of any bodily frailties: "the liberation of his slaves at his own death, had been his settled purpose for many years, and when there could be no question as to his capacity." The insidious attempts to convince the court that Reed's advanced age inevitably equated with incapacity seemed a point of contention, with the judgment tersely ruling that "not one fact proved in this Court tend[s] to show that his will was procured, or controled, or modified, in any respect, by improper influence of any kind."[18] Despite their failures, the extensive efforts of Reed's heirs to connect advanced age with a lack of mastery was a common tactic for white southerners seeking to challenge manumission. It was frequently depicted as the act of the weak and infirm, and one that reduced the rights of the rising generation as well as harmed the wider public. The concern over aged mastery was both personal and political.

*   *   *

Challenges to wills and posthumous emancipations were frequently rejected by antebellum courts, where even proslavery judges (begrudgingly) upheld the "cherished principle" of respecting the rights of testators. The fact that appellate and higher courts heard these cases at all, however, reveals how much white southern claims of mastery in old age were contestable. Enslaved people were all too aware of the challenges and limits to freedom promised. Robert Burns of Tennessee recalled how his enslaver set free his slaves but that his mastery did not extend beyond death: "After his death his son-in-law enslaved dem again by breaking de

---

[17] *Cromartie v. Robison*, 55 N.C. 218, 2 Jones Eq. 218 (1855), 221–2.
[18] *Reed's Will*, 41 Ky. 79, 2 B. Mon. 79 (1841), 79–80.

will of his father-in-law."[19] Formerly enslaved people insisted that freedom promised in wills was reliant on the goodwill of heirs and executors, and that, when set against self-interest, this could rarely be relied on. As Peter Wheeler claimed, "as soon as old master died, I was free by law – but pity me if slavery folks regard law that ever I see: for slavery is a tramplin' on all laws."[20] Friends, family, and foe sometimes saw in emancipation plans the folly of weak whites whose ways and days were done, and sought to frustrate them accordingly. Mary McCray recalled the fury of her aged enslaver's family members after hearing her plans to emancipate had been set in the will: "A short time after her estate was settled, some of her relations were enraged because Aunt Polly Adams, as they called her, had set her slaves free." They did not keep their concerns private or respect her wishes, but instead "kept the slaves there for three years while they were trying to break the will."[21]

When challenging the aged emancipators plans, some complainants publicly portrayed the testator's last will as evidence of their descent into decrepitude. In *Gass v. Gass*, 1842, the Supreme Court of Tennessee heard that John Gass, "at an advanced age, and infirm health," made a will that manumitted his slaves upon the death or remarriage of his wife, as well as established a school for children in the neighborhood. He did so because of a belief "that the state of pre-eminence he would acquire in his future existence depended in some measure upon the amount of estate he should acquire, and the charitable purpose to which he should contribute it." That the targeted audience of his largesse included his enslaved people, however, was framed by the complainants as revealing the "general decay of body and mind" from "old age and disease." Despite finding his actions "eccentric," the court refused to accept that Gass's concern with his immortal soul in his advanced age constituted evidence of insanity. It insisted, moreover, that when making a will, "old age alone is no disqualification."[22] Gass's fear of death and concern over the morality of slavery, however, spoke to his family as weakness of character.

The Tennessee courts were equally fair-minded in the consideration of Joshua Hadley's will some ten years earlier. Hadley had conveyed his slaves to George Latimer, who subsequently removed them to Illinois,

[19] Rawick (Ed.), *AS, Supp.*, Ser. 1, 12, 78.   [20] Wheeler, *Chains and Freedom*, 37.
[21] Mary McCray, *Life of Mary F. McCray: Born and Raised a Slave in the State of Kentucky* (Lima, Ohio: [s.n.], 1898), 17–18.
[22] *Gass's Heirs v. Gass's Ex'r's*, 22 Tenn. 278, 3 Hum. 278 (1842), 278–9, 286, 279, 281.

a free state, and this occasioned a long-drawn-out legal battle which eventually concluded in favor of the will. While the court explicitly noted, when considering Hadley's will, that "old age does not disqualify a person from making a voluntary conveyance of property, without proof showing that the donee imposed upon the donor or exercised some improper influence," the complainants worked extremely hard to try and prove that there was "improper influence." They were adamant that advanced age had diminished Hadley's authority and autonomy to the point of being mastered by another. Hadley's natal heirs claimed that George Latimer was no true friend but had instead exploited Hadley as he descended the steps of life. Hadley was described as "old feeble and childish, and worn down with sickness," and it was in this diminished state, the heirs insisted, that Latimer convinced him to sign a will "by which the whole estate was devised to him." The family had apparently had a falling out prior to this because the heirs refused to emancipate his slaves. They insisted their reluctance here was purely due to the legal restrictions on manumission in Tennessee, and nothing to do with the prospective loss of income this entailed for them. At this point, however, Hadley's "resentment fell upon them & that in its most bitter form," to the extent they "were literally driven out from home." The heirs-at-law painted a portrait of an unstable man whose growing antislavery urges revealed the decaying mind of a man made submissive. Although "he was by nature a man of strong passions," the complainants insisted that the inexorable march of time meant these urges "gained more perfect & absolute dominion over him."

This language of possession and compulsion – of Hadley as being feeble and childish – spoke directly to a discourse of aged infirmity and was deliberately used by the complainants to cast aspersions on his character and identity. The heirs-at-law insisted that in his dotage Hadley had been mastered, not masterful, and that his descent on the steps of life was hastened by one seeking to rise at his expense. According to the petitioners, Latimer saw Hadley's frailties and "pursued his own interest in it." Latimer sought to isolate and control the "old gentleman," taking Hadley into his house where "no one could interpose." This ensured "his dominion over the old man was as absolute as that which he had exerted over the property." As Hadley's health worsened, however, "the ties of nature prevailed over the brandishments of cupidity & Capt Hadley was restored once more to his family." At this point, Hadley seemingly realized the folly of emancipation and "looked upon his former delusion apparently with mortification and regret, at his best moments he was desirous to revoke any will he might have made, & also to have a bill filed to recover back the home place." It was too late for the complainants, as Hadley died before any revision or revocation took place. The battle thus moved into the courtroom.

Latimer's defense accepted the aged infirmities of Hadley, but insisted it was the natal heirs who had exploited their weak patriarch. Latimer portrayed Hadley's family as having looked to hasten his demise with the hopes of preventing emancipation and enriching themselves accordingly. Hadley had been abandoned "at an advanced age without any member of his family to attend upon him," precisely because he had sought to emancipate his slaves and thus rob his family of their inheritance. Latimer insisted that this plan was of paramount importance to Hadley and not the product of infirmity, derangement, or his own undue influence: "[Hadley] was averse to slavery and often expressed himself so. He had applied to the Legislature to the courts to have them freed but his application had been denied and because it was he employed Respondt. to convey them to a free state that they might be emancipated." The court found Latimer's testimony compelling. Justice Jacob Peck, in fact, was displeased by the complainants' extensive efforts to diminish their father's reputation: "thirty or forty depositions have not only repeated, what five or six had proved as well, but they are loaded with much impertinent and irrelevant matter, making in the whole a most burthensome record." All the complainants had achieved was to prove that there were bad feelings between Hadley and his family, and that Latimer's support had filled a void only worsened by Hadley's advanced age: "in the moments of gloom, which his desertion, his age and disease brought upon him, it was natural for him to seek new objects for his affection." Latimer was the deserving recipient of any such revision, with "few men [having] sustained a better character than creditable witnesses give him." The court definitively asserted that Latimer did not act fraudulently in conveying the slaves to Illinois, and the extensive efforts of the petitioners to discredit their father seemingly worked against them. In the opinion of the court, Peck insisted, "It is said he was old; that of itself will not do."[23]

---

[23] Petition of Hannah Hadley et al., April 12, 1832; Answer [Incomplete], George Latimer, April 12, 1830; Opinion, ca. August 20, 1832; Order, August 20, 1832; Deposition [Incomplete], William Douglass, n.d.; Examination of J. H. Hadley, n.d., Smith County, Tennessee, #21483007, Series 2, RSPP; *Hadley* v. *Latimer*, 3 Yerg Tenn. 537 (1832), 537, 541, 542, 543–4, 545.

In *Manns* v. *Givens*, Virginia, 1838, the challenge to Thomas Reynold's
character came not from his heirs, but from his executor – the very man he
had entrusted to enact his will. After Givens refused to set Reynolds's
slaves free, the enslaved people themselves brought a freedom suit. In his
defense of keeping the slaves in chains, Givens used the discourse of aged
decline to render Reynolds as weak and meek in his old age, with any such
emancipation reflecting his lack of mastery. These actions, they insisted,
could not constitute evidence of his true will, with the defendant's counsel
pointedly challenging Reverend Samuel Mitchell, one of the subscribing
witnesses, by noting "was not *Thomas Reynolds* very old, superannuated
and in his dotage, when he signed said deed?" They also openly questioned whether Mitchell – an antislavery Methodist – had unduly influenced Reynolds in warning of eternal damnation and that "slavery was
a moral evil," and, in doing so, implied that Reynolds had been made
submissive to his will.[24] Such a tremulous approach to death was anathema to southern notions of mastery and was used to paint a portrait of
a man not in control of his mind, let alone others. The Virginia courts
heard and saw a public dismissal of Reynold's character by those seeking
to profit from his estate, but they eventually upheld his final wishes and
stressed that the rights of the "master" had to be respected at all costs. The
extended efforts to frustrate Reynold's will, and the insidious references to
his advanced age, religious fervor, and submission to others, failed.
Nonetheless, they reveal how the discourse of age and infirmity was
used by white southerners to speak directly to matters of authority and
identity. White southerners knew that mastery, and the power this
entailed, was not innate, but instead something contingent and, in fact,
contestable.

* * *

Southern whites may have been raised in a culture that "taught them to
respect their patriarchal elders," as well as confronted models of "chivalry" that supposedly governed interactions between men and women,
but they also balanced these messages with the competing demand that
they assert themselves and look to rise in the world.[25] When threatened
with the loss of their expected property from aged patriarchs looking to

---

[24] *Manns v. Given*, 35 Va. 689, 7 Leigh 689 (1836), 767.
[25] Stevenson, *Life in Black and White*, 119. On "chivalry," see Fox-Genovese and Genovese,
The Mind of the Master Class, 329–64. On parent–child dynamics, see Glover, *Southern
Sons*; Glover, "Let Us Manufacture Men"; Stevenson, *Life in Black and White*.

emancipate "their" slaves, respect for elders could be jettisoned in favor of aggressive self-interest. Lewis Clarke explained why his mother and her children were not set free as her deceased enslaver had insisted:

Ten persons in one family, each worth three hundred dollars, are not easily set free among those accustomed to live by continued robbery . . . We did not, therefore, by an instrument from the hand of the dead, escape the avaricious grab of the slaveholder. It is the common belief that the will was destroyed by the heirs of Mr. Campbell.[26]

Sometimes this usurpation of control occurred while the testators who proposed manumission were still alive. In Maury County, Tennessee, 1858, Samuel Caruthers, who was in his sixties and suffering "greatly with p[h]ysical debility and mental infirmity," complained to the court that "his most cherished desire" to free his slaves was taken from him. Caruthers, who described himself as being "in his decrepid & infirm old age," claimed that in his reduced state he had fallen "victim to the cupidity & avarice of a set of persons who beset him on all sides." These fraudsters "preyed upon his substance" like "vultures." Caruthers's nephews, Samuel and Thomas Love, rode to the rescue at this point, informing their uncle that they would pay Caruthers's debts and "save his slaves from Executions." This was a lie: the nephews saw in their uncle's descent to decrepitude a chance to enrich themselves. The Loves sold several of his slaves and even looked to hasten his decline by refusing to supply him with "the necessities of life." Caruthers asked for assistance from the court to regain whatever property his nephews had not yet squandered.[27] But Caruthers's appeal was too late for several enslaved people who, having already been sold, were the true losers of this intergenerational power struggle.

Samuel Richardson of Tennessee was likewise distressed to find that his strong "inclination to emancipate his slaves" was taken from him (and from the enslaved people) on account of his declining powers. Richardson was "hostile to slavery" and hoped "to rid himself of the perplexity incident to the government & controll" of his enslaved people. He thus conveyed them to Thomas Hopkins, "a man of excellent character, of a gentle disposition, humane & Kind to his slaves." Richardson believed this conveyance was conditional on Hopkins not selling them, and "that he should during his life if he saw proper emancipate said slaves but that if

---

[26] Clarke, *Narratives of the Sufferings of Lewis Clarke*, 10.
[27] Petition of Samuel Caruthers, March 15, 1858, Maury County, Tennessee, #21485814, Series 2, RSPP.

he should fail to emancipate said slaves in his life time, then they were at his death to be returned to your orator." Hopkins, however, died "without having emancipated any of said slaves" and his executor, James Thompson, claimed the twenty slaves as his own "absolute property." Thompson also asserted "an utter disbelief" of the existence of any clause compelling him to return them.[28] Richardson fought hard to regain control of, and seek the emancipation for, the twenty enslaved people, but to no avail. His mastery, once lost, could not be restored.

The connection contemporaries drew between old age and weakness, and the willingness of some whites to exploit this to their best interest, was revealed to Henry Chiles of Tennessee in 1841. Chiles, who described himself as "aged and infirm," was a bachelor whose fourteen slaves had "cared much for him in his old age." As reward for this care, Chiles wanted to "manumit all the slaves, at his death if not before." With no children, and "being exempted, from age, disease, and want of education, to transact much of his business," Chiles had increasingly been forced "to confide in others to do it for him." Jesse Williams and William Rodgers, two local whites, saw their chance. After advising Chiles that state law prevented this planned manumission and noting his increased frailties, Williams and Rodgers suggested that he convey the slaves to them and they would enact his wishes. Chiles agreed but, after hearing of no progress and finding that Williams "studiously avoided having any conversation with him on the subject in the presence of any person who could be a witness," he realized his trust had been misplaced and sought to restore title to the slaves. Chiles's precarious health made "him the more anxious and solicitous to have his matters all arranged for death," but this precarity only encouraged the fraudsters: "This is all well known to the said Williams, and still he refuses to come up and have a settlement."[29] With no result recorded, it is hard to be optimistic about the proposed manumission. Historians have long identified the rapacious desire for profit among southern whites in shaping the mistreatment of enslaved people, but abuse in the name of wealth and status extended into enslavers' dealings with one another, and age shaped the dynamics of mastery and power in the antebellum South. Elderly enslavers here were

---

[28] Petition of Samuel Richardson, December 5, 1837; Answer, James Thompson, December 25, 1837; Supplemental Bill, March 28, 1838; Answer, James Thompson, June 16, 1838, Ward County, Tennessee, #21483705, Series 2, RSPP.

[29] Petition of Henry Chiles, May 30, 1853, Knox County, Tennessee, #21485331, Series 2, RSPP.

publicly derided by the rising generation, who looked at them and saw dependency, submission, and weakness to exploit.

* * *

Court cases from across the US South reveal how far "hungry heirs" would insult the reputations and memories of others when looking to further their own ascent in a slave society.[30] In 1846, Edward Butts of Southampton County, Virginia, fought hard to prevent several enslaved people who had been willed their freedom from being sold after the death of their enslaver. These slaves had been mortgaged out but, upon hearing of the death of the master, the temporary owners simply moved to sell them as their own property.[31] Grace, a "free woman of Colour" from Charleston, South Carolina, struggled to prevent the administrator of James Ryan's estate from selling her after his death, insisting that "for many years previous to his death [Ryan] was very infirm and subject to frequent fits of severe disposition" and that during this time she had "acted as nurse for him and as his most Confidential Servant." For this "meritorious service," she was to be rewarded with freedom and Ryan recorded as much in his will. After Ryan died, however, his executor claimed that he had died intestate and, upon receiving letters of administration, "endeavoured to Sell and dispose of your Oratrix, and threatens to sell her as a Slave in the Country."[32]

In Tennessee, 1852, seven enslaved people petitioned for their freedom after noting that their aged enslaver, who "for many years prior to his death ... was anxiously engaged upon the subject of emancipating your petitioners," had been tricked out of so doing in his dotage. The petitioners explicitly noted how, in his weakened state, William Crouse "fell into the hands of false and pretended friends." These "friends" recognized Crouse was not long for this world and "gave him false advice" on the laws of emancipation. They "took a conveyance of your petitioners absolutely under a verbal promise to emancipate them," but, instead, upon his death, "set up absolute title to your petitioners, land and other property conveyed."[33] The slaves received their freedom, but were back in the

---

[30] Jacobs, "A True Tale of Slavery," 86.

[31] Petition of Edward Butts, February 24 1846, Southampton County, Virginia, #21684611, Series 2, RSPP.

[32] Petition of Grace, July 9, 1817, Charleston District, South Carolina, #21381708, Series 2, RSPP.

[33] Petition of Bob, Reynolds, and Jacob, January 17, 1852, Stewart County, Tennessee, #11485504, Series 1, RSPP.

courts only a year later attempting to prevent their forced removal to Liberia.

White southerners were willing to publicly deny the final expressions of mastery from testators, and to try and prevent enslavers from emancipating enslaved people they hoped to profit from instead. The rising generation refused to accept this abrogation of their "rights" from those on their way out. The naked self-interest in these cases saw competing claims among southern whites looking to rise at another's expense. In 1823, the failed efforts of Georgian enslaver John Querns to free his slaves led to a falling out among the disputed claimants to the will. As the presiding judge recorded, "The negroes thus attempted to set free, have been claimed by one John Spear ... also by the Complainants [Arnetts] ... and also by these defendants [Thomas Talbot and Thomas Lasley]." Spear's claim seemed to be particularly egregious, with his positioning of himself as Quern's half-brother and only next of kin deemed dubious by both the Talbots and the Arnetts, who joined forces to try to defeat this. To Tablot's chagrin, however, the union proved fragile in the face of future wealth, with "said Arnetts being avariciously disposed to grasp the whole of said Negores [*sic*]." As the cases and countersuits multiplied, the Talbots and Arnetts renewed their agreement "for the purpose of defeating and setting aside the claim of said Spear and bringing the contest between themselves to a decision." This covenant was accepted by the jury, and the eighteen people who had hoped for freedom remained enslaved. The winners allowed the enslaved people to remain in families for as long as this was deemed "practicable."[34]

Enslaved people who had expected emancipation from their enslaver were confronted with the limits of mastery in death. In Sumner County, Tennessee, deceased enslaver Peter Fisher's last will was denied first by his executor and, eventually, by the courts. Fisher had provided for the emancipation of his slaves, but following his death the will was contested. Ninety-nine of Fisher's peers signed on to a challenge that traduced his character and denied his final will was an expression of mastery at all, given "the imbecile and deranged state of the old gentleman's mind as well as the fraud practiced in obtaining it."[35] In Charleston, 1847, an enslaved woman named Phillis found that her late mistress's "last wish" that she "should enjoy as the reward of her former usefullness and fidelity ...

[34] February 1823, Wilkes County Superior Court, Records of Writs, 1822–23, Box 43, Reel 6, 274–289, GSA.
[35] Combined petition, c. 1831, Sumner County, Tennessee, #11483104, Series 1, RSPP.

exemption from bodily labour" did not extend past her deathbed. Phillis had lived in a state of quasi-freedom in Georgetown with her husband and daughter for nearly a decade prior to this emancipation, but the limits to enslaver benevolence were starkly revealed. After the death of their bene-factor, a man named Hasford Walker entered their home "and forcibly seized and took possession of her daughter Martha and child William, lodged them in the George Town goal and hurried them off the next day by Steam Boat to Charleston," ready for sale.[36] This quasi-freedom had not followed the law and, despite the support of some local whites, Phillis's young children were sold away from her.

Enslaved people understood that they faced trouble when aged enslavers' promises of freedom were weighed against the avarice of ambi-tious heirs. In 1843, Nancy was forced to petition the Tennessee courts for her family's freedom after finding her mistress had been prevented from manumitting them by the deceit of her brother, James Mahon. The elderly Sally Mahon had attempted to make her will accordingly, but was told by James that the best chance of success would be to convey the family to him: "He then could and would take them to a free state and set them free." It did not take long after Sally's death for his true intention to come to light. The slaves not only were kept enslaved but also, according to Nancy, were being used by James to secure the repayment of debt. One witness called on Nancy's behalf believed there was a coordinated deceit of the aged woman; the witness had asked the executor if he was "ready to attend business" on Nancy's behalf. He cynically replied "not in the way she wanted it done." James had, by this point, already tried to sell one of Nancy's children.[37]

Such treatment might speak to gendered norms that associated femin-inity with submission and normalized male control over women regard-less of age. The extended efforts of Barbara to protect her children after her enslaver's death, however, reveal how the dependency associated with old age operated alongside and challenged gendered norms. The case underscores the disrespect and disregard aged enslavers might suffer from those who saw them as a burden, as well as the trauma of enslaved people caught amidst intergenerational conflict. Barbara insisted that Stephen Osborne had promised that neither she nor her children would

---

[36] Petition of Benjamin King, April 7, 1847, Charleston District, South Carolina, #21384740, Series 2, RSPP.

[37] Petition of Nancy, March 10, 1843, Sumner County, Tennessee, #21484330, Series 2, RSPP.

ever serve his children, but his promises of freedom were not recorded legally. As Osborne grew older, his children took control of his affairs, and Barbara's family suffered the consequences. The heirs attempted to convince Osborne to sell either the children or Barbara, but failed. They did not take this failure lightly and took active steps to destroy Barbara's family. First, they got rid of Barbara's husband, a free Black man, "by cursing and abusing of him, pissing on him, and threatening him with Horrid imprecations and ruin, if he did not leave their said fathers plantation and give up all claim to those your oratrixes children as free persons." Barbara specifically understood that the frailties of the eighty-year-old Osborne left him unable to protect her family. She explained that "the said Stephens children seemed so determined to destroy him [Barbara's husband] or drive him off, and that the said Stephen had become so old and infirm that he could not prevent it (being about 80 years old)." The Osbornes's mastery of their father extended over his deathbed, with Barbara insisting that the eldest son, Jonathan Osborne, "would not let him speak knowing what he intended to say." Barbara was granted the opportunity to defend her children's right to freedom, but Jonathan Osborne fought against her by playing up the associations between age and incapacity. He insisted that "if any such contract as that alleged ever was made he contends that it was absolutely void because from mental imbecility [Stephen Osbourne] was for many years before his death incapable to contract." Barbara did, eventually, receive freedom for herself and her children, but only after enduring horrendous abuse from those who understood that the declining powers of an aged enslaver might occasion their own ascent and acted accordingly.[38]

* * *

Some complainants insisted that wills that proposed emancipation were fraudulent, obtained through deceit, threats, and violence, or were shaped by the inevitable frailties – both physical and mental – associated with old age. The challengers to Virginia enslaver Benjamin Whitfield's will in 1799 contended it was only through "the undue influence of some persons who pretended friendship to him he had an instrument prepared

---

[38] Petition of Barbara, May 1826; Answer of Jonathan Osborne, December 27, 1827, Scott County, Virginia, #21682613, Series 2, RSPP. Further details on Barbara's struggles can be found in Petition of Jonathan Osborne, September 2, 1831, Scott County, Virginia, #21683111, Series 2, RSPP; and Petition of Barbara, Senah, and Wesley to the Virginia General Assembly, December 17, 1836, #11683624, Series 1, RSPP.

purporting to be a deed of emancipation" for his twenty-five slaves. In his will, Whitfield claimed to have become "fully persuaded that freedom is the natural right of all mankind and that it is my duty to do to others as I would desire to be done by." He decided to emancipate his enslaved people, but his heirs were skeptical that this spoke to anything beyond the delusions of an infirm mind. They insisted this rhetoric was not matched by his actions when in his prime. According to Reuben Whitfield, "he did his utmost to keep the said Negroes in subjection and possession[,] often causing them to be brought home and severely corrected for disobeying his orders." Despite the skepticism, the court accepted the will for probate and the enslaved people were emancipated.

While not promising success, challengers frequently applied the discourse of aging as a process of decline and compared the aged testator's actions in their prime with their decline in old age. Others summoned up an idealized image of what an enslaver *should* be like alongside a forthright defense of slavery, indicating that those who supported emancipation simply were not masterful or deserving of respect – in life or death – from their peers. In so doing, the complainants asserted themselves over the aged enslaver and sought to gain power at their expense. In Putnam County, Florida, 1855, George Oliver's children fought against his will, wherein the sixty-one-year-old Oliver had cut off his "unruly and disobedient son" Henry. He also looked to connect an enslaved woman named Isabella and her two children with agents of the American Colonization Society to precipitate their removal to Liberia. Both actions were challenged by his heirs, who claimed that Oliver had only done so under duress. During the trial, the court heard that the elderly George had long been "impaired by disease and suffering." More explosively, his children claimed that the changes to his will were only "made under the undue and improper influence of a slave of the deceased named Isabella," who "had great influence over the Testator." Arguments raged over whether this was the result of the "natural affection" George developed based on Isabella's care for him or was reflective of a weak man bowled over in his dotage, as well as whether Henry had deserved disinheriting.[39]

---

[39] Petition of Sarah Oliver et al., November 10, 1855; Copy of Last Will and Testament and Codicil, George Oliver, November 21, 1853; Jury Verdict and Judgment, February 9, 1855; Depositions, James Oliver, Thomas Purse, John Macpherson Perrieu, Joseph Ganahl, May 1, 1855; Appeal, May 1, 1855; Decision, ca. 1855; Inventory and Appraisement, Estate of George Oliver, December 25, 1855, Putnam County, Florida, #20585509, Series 2, RSPP.

Eventually, the court found for the petitioners and discarded the final expression of George's mastery.

Enslavers who sought to emancipate their slaves faced challenges before and after death, with complainants using the language of infirmity and dependency to cast doubt on the legitimacy of their actions and to raise suspicions about their character and conduct. During their escape effort, William Craft recorded how a white woman told Ellen Craft, while disguised as the enslaver "Mr. Johnson," of how she had altered her late husband's will to prevent the emancipations he proposed. This, she insisted, was out of respect for the man he had once been, and not the pitiful character left at time of death: "I and all our friends knew very well that he was too good a man to have ever thought of doing such an unkind and foolish thing, had he been in his right mind, and, therefore we had the will altered as it should have been in the first place."[40] In cases where the wills had been put to probate, claimants publicly undercut elderly enslavers' claims of mastery in life and death and, in doing so, revealed the fluid and contested hierarchies among southern whites where aging was understood as a relation of power. In St. Tammany Parish, Louisiana, 1849, the children of Nathan Maples petitioned the court to regain control of "slaves" who were now acting as free people. They asserted that their father had sold two women named Mitty and Sarah to their mother, Jenny Broxton, a free person of color, who had promptly emancipated them. Jenny and her husband had themselves been emancipated by Maples in 1826, but Maples's children argued that these emancipations were a "sham of a sale" that only occurred because Maples "was old & infirm in body & mind and was over persuaded to execute the same." Accordingly, "all subsequent acts of pretended ownership on the part of the said Jenny Broxton and particularly the said act of emancipation executed aforesaid in favor of the said Milly & Sarah are likewise null & void."

Maples's children were furious that they had been "robbed" of property and inheritance, arguing that this scheme was all designed "to interrupt the regular and natural decent of his property." They were careful to frame their challenge as relating to an aged and ailing man becoming dependent and, indeed, submissive, in order to play up the notion this was an example not of mastery but of meekness. It was through "various persuasions and entreaties," the heirs insisted, and not as master of his

---

[40] William Craft, *Running a Thousand Miles for Freedom; or, the Escape of William and Ellen Craft from Slavery* (London: William Tweedie, 1860), 61–6.

mind, that the old man was tricked into doing this. The children were initially successful, but, on appeal, witnesses argued that this had been the deliberate decision of a man who simply disliked his children. One witness claimed they "heard Nathan Maples frequently say that there were three of his children who should never enjoy any of his property," while another heard Maples adamantly defending his right, as master, to "be allowed to do as he pleased with his property." The court eventually accepted Maples's right to free the slaves. The most compelling testimony here seemed to be his daughter's assertion this had not related to abolitionist leanings. Instead, it was a rational decision based on economic self-interest and a desire to get one over his ungrateful children: "[she] heard him say, that his slaves should get their freedom, but they should pay him his price."[41]

Challengers elsewhere insisted that any proposed emancipation was out of character, implying or outright stating that the decaying effects of age had weakened the testator to the extent they had lost their way. In *Redford v. Peggy*, 1828, the proposed "immancypation" of George Redford's slaves became a contest "between the slaves seeking Probate, and the Administrator resisting it." Redford's executors called a number of witnesses to state that he had, prior to his decline in fortunes, always expressed "his opposition to the emancipation of negroes." One stated they heard him say "that he never would set free his negroes, and expressed considerable hatred against free negroes." They insisted that at the time the new will was drawn up, Redford "was very deaf, and from the debility of his body and mind, he was scarcely able to have made and written a Will in the year 1818." Any new will, they insisted, must have been fraudulent, and their suspicions were aroused further (or they sought to further arouse the suspicions of the jury) because the new document "was brought to the witness by Tarlton, one of the negroes included in the Will in controversy, shortly after the Testator's death, who said he found it near the Testator's house."[42] The executors fought hard to cast doubt on Redford's state of mind and stressed his physical debility and shameful dependency on the enslaved people he freed, but the court allowed for the emancipation provided the slaves left the state immediately.

[41] Petition of John Maples et al., September 17, 1849; Transcript of Court Records, September 25, 1849–November 15, 1856, including: Order, September 24, 1849; Verdict, November Term 1856; Supplemental Petition, June 4, 1855; Testimonies, William B. Addison, et al., December 27, 1854, St. Tammany Parish, Louisiana, #20884945, Series 2, RSPP.

[42] *Redford v. Peggy*, 27 Va. 316, 6 Randolph 316 (1828), 704, 703, 702, 703.

In Kentucky, 1848, Edmund Talbot's proposed emancipation of his enslaved people was denied by the Court of Appeals after a challenge from his children. The court determined that Talbot, who "was old and feeble, both in body and mind," had "no will of his own" at time of death. He had instead, in his dotage, become subservient to and "submitted implicitly to the dictation of a colored woman whom he had emancipated, and whose familiar intercourse with him, had brought him into complete and continued subjection to her influence."[43] David T. Moon Jr. has noted that "the very notion of submission ran counter to manly liberty and honor in the South," but in this case all (white) parties publicly asserted and agreed that Talbot's descent to decrepitude marked a loss of authority, autonomy, and honor.[44] Talbot had become humiliatingly dependent and "undisguisedly yielded to an influence of such a character, and lost, under its exercise, apparently all independence of thought and action." This circumstance, the judge insisted, proved "that his mental faculties had given away, before the combined operation of old age and disease; and that he no longer retained that degree of intellect and mental capacity, which would have enabled him to make a valid disposition of his estate by will."[45] Connections of advanced age to dependency, submission, and frailty – whether of body or mind – provided ambitious enslavers with a discourse that normalized their dominance of elders who stood in their way.

* * *

In 1825, the Supreme Court of North Carolina rejected the efforts of Nathaniel Jones's executor to emancipate one of his slaves, despite their best efforts to stress that his mastery extended beyond death. Jones had hoped to emancipate his slaves "whenever the laws of the state would allow it," and expressly noted the antislavery impulses that motivated him here. As Jones explained, "The golden rule directs us to do unto every human creature, as we would wish to be done unto; and sure I am, that there is not one of us would agree to be kept in slavery during a long life." Before the 1830s, however, North Carolina only allowed for emancipation for meritorious services, and so when Jones's executor appealed in 1823 on behalf of a man named Allen who was about to be sold, contrary to Jones's express directions in his will, the dispute escalated. The

---

[43] *Denton v. Franklin*, 48 Ky. 28, 9 B. Mon 28 (1848), 30.
[44] Moon Jr., "Southern Baptists and Southern Men," 595.
[45] *Denton v. Franklin*, 48 Ky. 28, 9 B. Mon 28 (1848), 30.

challenge here indicated how far decisions relating to "property" spoke to wider intergenerational tensions and shifting power dynamics between the young and the old. The opposing counsel was adamant that to keep Allen enslaved was an abject repudiation of "the wishes of the owner declared in his will." Allens's heirs actions, they insisted, were utterly contemptible:

who sacrifices to a mean avarice every consideration of humanity and mercy; who regards neither the welfare of the living, nor the declared intention of the dead; who holds the former in slavery without right, and robs the latter of property which he did not intend he should enjoy; whose bosom is inaccessible to the emotions of kindness; who remembers without regard the dying wishes of him on the fruits of whose industry he fattens; and makes a base advantage to himself by trampling on what the barbarous and the refined, the ancients and the moderns, have united in esteeming sacred; whose callousness to moral considerations exceeds that of the robber on the highway, and can be likened only to that of him who robs a tenant of the grave.

The court was unmoved by this thunderous rhetoric and calmly swatted away the planned emancipation. Jones had not "continued the trust in his executors to see to the liberation of his slaves, at any indefinite period of time," and so, "when they were delivered over to his representatives by the assent of his executors, the trust would seem to cease in the latter, and attach to the former."[46] Jones's will had passed with the passage of time, and the enslaved people lost out.

Antebellum southerners thus understood – or were willing to claim – that depredations of aging cut across categories of race and gender and undermined normative hierarchies of power. An inversion of gendered power dynamics on account of old age was evident in Susannah Langdon's efforts to annul three decisions her father, David Roper, made toward the end of his life. Roper, an enslaver in Kentucky, provided deeds of land and money to his neighbor, David James, and, more shockingly, "bequeathed all his personal estate to two of the slaves whom he had emancipated" in his will. Langdon insisted that these acts be made void on account of the "fraud, influence and imposition practised upon him, in his advanced age, and feeble state of body and mind, by those in whose favor those instruments were executed." The court heard that James had taken "advantage of [Roper's] confidence and perfect submission to his opinions and will," and, by "alarming his fears and increasing his dread and apprehension," convinced Roper to give James the land and

---

[46] *Pride v. Pulliam*, 4 Hawks 49 (N.C. 1825), 50, 59.

money. The court rejected this conveyance: "A deed thus extorted from the excited fears and terrors of a feeble-minded old man ... ought not and cannot be permitted to stand."[47] The last image of Roper presented by family and friends, and one upheld by the wider white community, was of a man entirely absent of authority, honor, and mastery.

The challenge to the proposed emancipation was trickier to adjudicate. The justices agreed that Roper had long expressed "that those slaves should serve no one after his death," and that the deeds he had executed to this effect were done during his more active period of life. They were plainly disturbed about the distribution of his estate to the slaves, however, and viewed this decision as evidence of his declining powers. This action came during "his last illness, and not long before his death, at a time when his body and mind, naturally weak, were both much enfeebled by age and disease." More shocking for contemporaries was that Lucy and Hector, the two named slaves, had apparently directed this action: Roper "was much under their influence and control, and there is good reason to believe that Lucy used means to prejudice and embitter his mind against his children ... Indeed it is proven that he was induced to believe that his children visited him for the purpose of plundering him of his property, and there is grounds to believe that this impression was made on his mind by the tales of Lucy." The court believed that such reversals of mastery were, in fact, common, noting that "it is not surprising that an aged man like Roper, suffering under the pains of disease, and of a weak mind naturally, should become alienated from his children" and instead "have his affections concentrated upon those who were daily around his person, and plying him with tales calculated to excite and prejudice his mind."[48] The normative narrative of aged decline provided a rationale for rejecting Roper's wishes as a true final expression of mastery; the court canceled the conveyance of property while allowing the emancipation.

Some of the more lurid challenges to emancipation cast aspersions on the legitimacy of the act by claiming it to be the product of an inverted master–slave relationship. In claiming that the enslaved people emancipated had, in fact, taken advantage of their aged and infirm "masters" to further their own interests, the testator was explicitly portrayed as submissive and weak. In *Minor's Heirs* v. *Thomas (of color)*, 1851, the Court of Appeals of Kentucky heard that a group of enslaved people were emancipated and given a tract of land by the will of Jeremiah Minor.

[47] *James* v. *Langdon*, 46 Ky. 193 (1846), 193–5.
[48] *James* v. *Langdon*, 46 Ky. 193 (1846), 196–7.

The heirs contended this document was fraudulent on account of the "undue influence of the emancipated slaves ... upon the mind of the deceased, when enfeebled by illness and extreme old age." Their "influence" extended to exploiting his "sense of utter helplessness" and "feeling of complete dependence upon these slaves." The court heard that Minor, a widower in his nineties, "lived alone with his slaves, that they had unbounded influence over him, and controlled him at discretion." The language used to describe Minor – a man in "second childhood and complete dotage," with "the exhausted faculties and expiring intellect of an old man" – and the rejection of his will indicate how white southerners believed that aging destabilized the performance of mastery and risked inverting the power dynamics of slavery. In his dotage, it was Minor who was deemed incapable of "resisting" his enslaved people.[49] This discourse was applied by white southerners hoping to further their own interests at the expense of others.

If some challengers sought to argue that testators had been shamefully controlled by their slaves, others claimed that their efforts to manumit enslaved people reflected a fearful and tremulous approach to death. Rather than meet their end as "masters," the testators were considered to have bowed to the forces of those who portrayed slavery as an evil out of fear for their souls. In *Townshend* v. *Townshend*, 1854, George Townshend's supposed fear for his immortal soul was derided by some of his peers as evidence of his descent toward decrepitude. The Maryland Court of Appeals heard one witness state that Townshend's efforts to emancipate his slaves was animated by his belief that "he was commanded by Almighty God, to free his negroes and to give them his property, and if he failed to do this, would incur everlasting damnation." The challengers had earlier depicted this as absurd in itself, with his heirs charging "that by reason of the insane delusions of said John Townshend, especially in reference to his negroes, he was wholly incapable of executing these pretended deeds of manumission."[50] In *Gordon* v. *Blackman*, 1844, the South Carolina Court of Appeals and Errors likewise struck down Samuel McCorkle's efforts to manumit his slaves, who, as it turned out, were his own children from Lydia, another slave named. There was some dispute in the lower courts about the legality of the plan, with the Chancellor of the Court of Equity, David Johnston, believing that, although his

---

[49] *Minor's Heirs* v. *Thomas (of color)*, 51 Ky. 106 (1851), 106, 111, 109.

[50] *Townshend* v. *Townshend*, 5 Md. 287 (1853), 289; *Townshend* v. *Townshend*, 6 Md. 295 (1854), 300.

"repugnance" toward emancipation was "stronger than I can express," he could not declare it void and instead hoped the appellate court would do so.

This is precisely what happened, and Johnston's portrayal of McCorkle as a weak and frail man, barely a master at all, on account of his proposed emancipation, speaks directly to themes explored in this chapter. McCorkle, who was in his late sixties by the time he died, was mastered by his slave *and* by his fear of death. This was anathema to the notion of honor, and the language applied by Johnston struck directly at the reputation and legacy of the departed:

> This is another of those cases, multiplying of late with a fearful rapidity, in which the superstitious weakness of dying men, proceeding from an astonishing ignorance of the solid moral and scriptural foundations upon which the institution of slavery rests, and from a total inattention to the shock which their conduct is calculated to give to the whole frame of our social polity, induces them, in their last moments, to emancipate their slaves, in fraud of the indubitable and declared policy of the State.[51]

The language employed by Johnston to describe McCorkle – language that was tacitly approved by the higher courts – cast aside entirely the masterful identity expected of antebellum slavers. He openly derided McCorkle and portrayed him as having approached his death weakly and meekly. This mattered most, of course, to his illegitimate children. They were sold at a public auction on February 2, 1846.[52]

The extended challenge to Mississippi enslaver Isaac Ross's efforts to manumit and send his slaves to Liberia from his heirs, while unsuccessful, reveals how far contemporaries saw advanced age as impacting upon mastery and authority, and how these ideas were applied by those looking to make their own way as slavers. The Mississippi Supreme Court upheld the legality of emancipation, provided it was accompanied by removal out of the state, but the plaintiff's counsel, the Hon. D. Mayes, ferociously appealed against the will and emancipation more generally. Mayes expounded on the inevitable weakness of the aged – both in body and mind – and the necessity of seizing power from them before they damaged the interests of the rising generation. Mayes portrayed manumission as contrary to the sectional, if not national, interest, and that it arose from a lack of fortitude on the part of these so-called "masters." Mayes

---

[51] *Gordon* v. *Blackman*, 1 Rich. Eq. 61 (S.C. 1844), 64, 61.

[52] Alexia Jones Hesley and Patrick McCawley, *The Many Faces of Slavery: South Carolina Department of Archives and History* (S. C. State Library, 1999), 80.

expended significant energy on noting that the intergenerational transfer of wealth was both natural and necessary to society's best interests, and went even further when noting that "it has never been understood by jurists, that the power to make a will, conferred on the dead, the ability to deprive the living of the use of that property, which the laws of the country had protected him in the enjoyment of, and of which death had deprived him." Ross's plans for emancipation were thus a direct abuse of his personal heirs *and* of the rising generation of slavers: "the manumission of a slave is as distinctly the destruction of property, as is the casting of money into the ocean." Mayes pointedly recalled how these apparent antislavery urges had not affected Ross's earthly behavior: "Besides, this is not a case of a master manumitting his slaves by sending them to Liberia; but the case of a master who retained his slaves as such, until the moment of his death, but who attempts to prevent their becoming the slaves of his heirs."[53]

Outside of the challenges to the will on account of intergenerational and societal fairness, Mayes portrayed emancipation as being an affront to the proslavery position of Mississippi and a "strike at the institution itself." Any affirmative decision on the part of the will, Mayes insisted, would inspire greater support for emancipation and harm the "policy of Mississippi." It provided "inducements to abolitionists and emancipators to visit our state, and inculcate and disseminate their principles." Most significantly for this book was just *who* Mayes believed most likely to break ranks. It was the aged and infirm, Mayes insisted, who could not resist such pressure:

And can we more effectually invite them to come amongst us, than we will do by a determination that if they succeed in making such impressions on the minds of our aged and infirm citizens, or others in the prospect of death, as to produce a will directing their slaves to be carried to Ohio, Indiana, or any other non-slave holding state or country, they can thereby effect their emancipation?

Is it not part of the policy of Mississippi, to protect her citizens against fanaticism in religion, and a morbid sensibility on the subject of slave holding! And does it, not war with this end to proclaim to the world, come here, all ye who seek the destruction of slavery, address yourselves to, and endeavor to disturb the consciences of our women, our old men, and others, whose sickly sensibilities are easily operated on. Impress upon them in the closet, and by the fireside, your false and unfounded tenets, of the sinfulness of slavery, and the peril in which their souls stand if they do not disinherit their offspring by emancipating their slaves!

---

[53] *Jane B. Ross et al.* v. *Vertner et al.*, 5 How. Miss. 305, December 1840. Appendix 770–808, 787, 789, 795.

Mayes's position, and the position of Ross's heirs, was that the present and growing threat to slavery would be hastened by abolitionists looking to exploit the inevitable weakness of the aged and infirm. The unstoppable descent toward dependency and submission for elders was, Mayes argued, a universal law that necessitated the transfer of wealth and power from one generation to the next. All white southerners needed to be conscious of this transition and be proactive in asserting control over those who had lost the power to control themselves. Mastery was fluid and contested because enslavers knew it could not last forever; southern whites were constantly testing one another's character and capacity for control, and any sign of "sickly sensibilities" and a loss of power might provide the chance for another's ascent. The global history of legislation surrounding inheritance, Mayes insisted, was admonishing "us of the safe-guards necessary to be thrown by law around property to protect it, when in the possession of the infirm, the diseased, and the dying, against the varied assaults of those who lie in wait for the weak, and prowl around the bed of the expiring!"[54] Maye's fiery rhetoric did not sway the court, but the arguments made reveal how antebellum southerners challenged one another over the idea that aging entailed a necessary decline, and on the necessary impact of this on mastery itself. Mayes was referring to abolitionists preying on, and prowling around, "the weak," but he might well have been referring to how white southerners in general perceived their aging peers.

By way of conclusion, I return to Justice Joseph Henry Lumpkin of Georgia. The sense that emancipatory impulses from the aged, who were losing authority and their very identity as "masters," must be rejected by those still in their prime was clearly exemplified in Lumpkin's denunciation of the American Colonization Society's efforts to emancipate Francis Gideon's slaves in 1857. Gideon had left his slaves in trust to the ACS in order to be transported to Liberia, and Lumpkin seemed to take pleasure in frustrating this plan on a technicality. Lumpkin despised the "wild, fanatical, and destructive" plans of emancipation and insisted that a corporation could not inherit slaves like a natural person, making the will void. He also asserted that the state was not obliged to respect the wishes of an organization whose policies were "so especially ruinous to

---

[54] *Jane B. Ross et al.* v. *Vertner et al.*, 5 How. Miss. 305, December 1840. Appendix 770–808, 790, 792. The emancipated slaves went on to establish the famous "Mississippi in Africa" settlement in Liberia. Two years after this case Mississippi banned manumission by last will entirely.

the prosperity, importance and political strength of the Southern States." Lumpkin clearly took great pleasure in attacking the ACS, and in promoting slavery more generally. His derisive commentary on the character and conduct of those who sought to emancipate their slaves underlines the prevalence of the discourse that portrayed aging as a process of decline and decay. In Lumpkin's eyes, emancipation was the act of the aged and the weak, and must be rejected by all true masters: "Let our women and old men, and persons of weak and infirm minds, be disabused of the false and unfounded notion that slavery is sinful, and that they will peril their souls if they do not disinherit their offspring by emancipating their slaves."[55] The discursive construction of old age as a form of emasculation, alongside the connections to infirmity and weakness, underlines how age operated alongside and interconnected with categories of class, gender, and race. It reveals a concern that aging was a period of decline with both personal and political consequences. Age was a vital factor in configuring relations of power in the American South and understandings of aging as a period of declining force led to conflict between white southerners looking to rise at another's expense. White enslavers looked to their aged peers and saw weakness they must reject, but which they also might exploit for themselves.

[55] *American Colonization Society* v. *Gartrell*, 23 Ga. 448 (1857), 462, 464–5.

Conclusion

In 1937, Violet Guntharpe, then aged eighty-two, told her WPA interviewer about the horrendous violence of the US Civil War and the dangers that accompanied "freedom." She vividly described "de air full of de stink of dead carcasses and de sky black wid turkey buzzards" that ushered in the new era of emancipation. Newly freed people, abandoned in a warzone, were thrown back on their own resources. Some could "scour de woods for hickory nuts, acorns, cane roots, and artichokes, and seine de river for fish," but the most vulnerable could not even do this: "Lots of de chillun die, as did de old folks."[1] Recently, historians have urged us to "disrupt" the history of emancipation by reflecting on the generational violence of slavery, the sickness and deprivation that followed the war, the lack of structural changes to secure genuine freedom, and the racist violence of white southerners determined to deny the promise of Reconstruction.[2] Guntharpe's memories underscore the urgency of this injunction.

Emancipated people understood that their former enslavers and even their supposed allies would not make it easy for them to claim their freedom. The desperation of their position in the desolate landscape of the "conquered" south was evident in the immediate aftermath of the war. As one Black author reported:

Money is very scarce, and numbers of the ex-slaves have been driven from plantations, or left rather than submit to cruelty. Even where the master has made a contract and hired his slaves, it has generally occurred that he would turn out on the highway to starve, suffer and die, the old, infirm, sick, blind, lame, and halt, even though these had been enriching him for nearly half a century.[3]

[1] Rawick (Ed.), *AS*, 2.2, 217.   [2] Downs and Blight (Eds.), *Beyond Freedom*.
[3] James Lynch, "Letter from the Rev. James Lynch," *The Christian Recorder* (July 1, 1865).

More than half a century later, the promises of "freedom" still seemed broken to many. Some WPA respondents negatively compared their experiences as elders in freedom to the lives of the aged enslaved. Granny Cain lamented: "My mistress was so good I wish I was living with her now, I sho' wouldn't have such a hard time getting something to eat. I am old and have rheumatism and can't get about good now."[4] In a more reflective mood, Smith Simmons mused that "sometimes I thinks freedom is better and sometimes I don't. In slavery times the old folks was cared for and now there ain't no one to see to them."[5]

Well into the twentieth century, many white Americans saw such narratives as legitimating enslavers' claims of paternalism, and used them to reify proslavery images of a leisurely retirement for enslaved elders.[6] Against these readings, historians have pointed to the severely problematic status of "positive" discussions of slavery captured in interviews with Black southerners by white people in the era of the Great Depression, "Jim Crow," and the terrors of lynching. Alongside these crucial contexts, and argued in the Introduction to this book, we must consider the positionality of interviewees. Respondents may have truly believed enslaved elders had this type of care; they may even have witnessed individual cases of such care for "key slaves"; but they had never been elderly in slavery themselves.[7] They spoke *for* their elders in claiming that previous generations had it better. What these testimonies vividly show is the continued toll of racism, poverty, and exploitation, and the constraints that structural inequalities put on paper "freedom."

Bettie White Irby's testimony illustrates these tensions. Irby recalled the joy of her Aunt Lizzie upon emancipation:

"Oh", she shouted, "thank God dat we is free – dat we is free! De yoke of bondage is done off'n our necks."

I looked at her and I couldn't unnerstand.

"But Aunt Lizzie," I say, "yo' ain't got no yoke on yo' neck."

"Yo' jes' don't know," she shouted. "dat yoke has been took off our necks fo' good. Thank God fo' dat, Oh, thank god!"

And she kept on shoutin' and cuttin' up fo' a long time.

---

[4] Rawick (Ed.), *AS*, 2.1, 168. [5] Rawick (Ed.), *AS*, *Supp.*, Ser. *1*, 10.5, 1942.

[6] Burwell, *A Girl's Life in Virginia*, 10–14; Rebecca Latimer Felton, *Country Life in Georgia In the Days of My Youth; Addresses Before Georgia Legislature Woman's Clubs, Women's Organizations and other Noted Occasions* (Index Printing Company, Atlanta, Ga., 1919), 55–6; Ulrich B. Phillips, *Life and Labor in the Old South* (Boston: Little, Brown, & Co., 1929), 197.

[7] Tadman, *Speculators and Slaves*, xxi.

Aunt Lizzie did not live into the 1930s – but it is difficult not to wonder if she would have equally told those who claimed they would "jest as soon be back in slavery as I am now," as they had "nothing and have to work so hard," that "dat yoke has been took off our necks fo' good."[8] To say as such is adamantly not to minimize the very real suffering people such as Cain, Simmons, and others recorded in their WPA interviews. It is instead to reflect on the violence and suffering that came *after* slavery, and to reinforce the continued injustices Black Americans faced in the postbellum period and beyond. As Barney Alford put it, "When de slaves wus sot free, dey had nuffin an' ole Marse didnt give 'em anything. All uf us had a mi'ty hard time."[9]

Black elders suffered in slavery; they toiled in the first days of freedom; and their descendants struggled for decades afterwards. The legacies of slavery lingered long and linger still. This book has charted one part of that story – the sufferings of enslaved people under slavery and in their first days of "freedom." The poisonous cocktail of pursuit of profit and desire for dominance that animated white southern enslavers led to the abuse, exploitation, and neglect of the aged enslaved. After years immersed in this material, I return continually to the open expressions of self-interest of white enslavers in bills of sale, petitions, and demands to get rid of those "in the decline of life" before they became "worthless and a charge upon their owners."[10] No further evidence is needed of the hideousness of enslavers taking the "best years and the best strength" from enslaved people to further their profit line than their willingness to dispense of these same individuals once they might become a charge on the estate.[11] As one antislavery author recorded, white southerners could, and did, "see human forms, from infancy to grey hairs, sold under the hammer."[12] Slavery was a cruel and violent system of exploitation, and enslaved elders suffered tremendously in bondage.

---

[8] Rawick (Ed.), *AS, Supp.*, Ser. 2, 5.4, 1861; Rawick (Ed.), *AS, Supp.*, Ser. 1, 9.4, 1873.

[9] Rawick (Ed.), *AS, Supp.*, Ser.1, 6.1, 43. Outstanding work on this topic includes Glymph, *Out of the House of Bondage*; Downs, *Sick From Freedom*; Kidada E. Williams, *I Saw Death Coming: A History of Terror and Survival in the War Against Reconstruction* (New York: Bloomsbury Academic, 2023).

[10] Petition of Abram Childress, November 5, 1855, Franklin County Virginia, #21685519, RSPP, Series 2.

[11] Douglass, *My Bondage and My Freedom*, 112–14.

[12] Aaron, *The Light and Truth of Slavery*, 16.

FIGURE 11.1 Dorothea Lange, photographer. *Ex-Slave and Wife on Steps of Plantation House Now in Decay.* Greene County, Georgia. United States Greene County Georgia, 1937. July. Courtesy of the Library of Congress.

* * *

The cruelty and violence of this system of exploitation affected all aspects of the lives and relationships of those enmeshed within it. The tensions of slavery also played out in intergenerational encounters within the enslaved community. While scholars generally agree that enslaved people respected their elders and sought to protect them from the worst excesses of bondage, the evidence addressed here suggests that those deemed elderly by their peers and enslavers did not always benefit from these formal codes of behavior. As people were forced to confront community perceptions that they were losing physical or mental power, they also lost roles and responsibilities, whether in work, leisure, or community organization, that they might once have valued. This caused tension, and sometimes even violence. Younger enslaved people who wanted to secure these roles sometimes undermined or usurped their elders, demonstrating their willingness to secure their own ascent by pushing another off of the perch.

Undoubtedly, many enslaved people supported their elders, and many of the aged enslaved surely found solace in this solidarity in the face of oppression. At the same time, we need to interrogate claims of respect from people who were not themselves old in slavery. In the WPA narratives, a near-constant refrain is the complaint that the rising Black generation does not respect its elders. One unnamed respondent informed the all-Black interview unit of Fisk University that "young people don't pay enough respect to old gray-headed folks." Silas Dothrum was less circumspect: "the young people today ain't worth a shit."[13] Such statements were frequently preceded by discussions on children leaving parents isolated or ignoring their guidance, the vexations of childcare, being looked over or replaced for work, on younger members of the community's disrespect for elders in social affairs, or simply on the physical and mental ailments associated with aging.

In fact, as this book has shown, similar intergenerational dynamics existed in slavery. Indeed, the structural violence of slavery exacerbated such tensions, not least because of enslavers' deliberate efforts to divide and control their coerced workers. Against this backdrop, many testimonies might read differently than when conditioned by unquestioned acceptance of belief in respect for elders, including Solomon Northup's gentle mockery of "patriarch" Abram for his forgetfulness, Frederick Douglass's distrust of Sandy's root-work and dismissal of Uncle Isaac's "remedies," and Jacobs's reflections on Horniblow's unwillingness to accept the risks of fight or flight and her counsel to remain in bondage instead. Understanding the wider contexts of the lives of elders such as Abram, Sandy, and Horniblow, including the difficulties they faced because of their age, helps us to center their perspectives – an endeavor all the more important because their own, unmediated voices are lost forever.

Much contemporary Black writing *about* the aged enslaved is clearly sympathetic and demonstrates genuine feeling for them. But it is typically not their voices we hear, and it is not their eyes through which we look. In so many narratives, enslaved elders have no independent existence, thoughts, or emotions. Instead, as foil characters who elevate the heroism of fugitives, rebels, and resistors, they are the necessary tools of antislavery activists pressing for direct action. In many of these renditions, the aged had lost their chance to escape and could not turn back time; they are depicted in ways that emphasize that is not too late for others to avoid the horrors of this fate. In the context of resistance, negative depictions and recollections

---

[13] Rawick (Ed.), *AS*, *18*, 47; Rawick (Ed.), *AS*, *8.1*, 185.

of elders illustrate the complexity and contingency of relationships forged between enslaved people, but also testify to very real suffering and pain. These portraits of enslaved people perceived as unable or unwilling to resist after a lifetime of exploitation were shot through with sadness, support, shame, and fear, but sometimes also disdain. These were not people to follow or unquestionably revere, but instead people whose choices and paths were to be avoided at all costs. Even if peers did deem enslaved elders as deserving support and respect on account of their age, this respect could be predicated on pity, not parity; and the aged enslaveds' responses to this diminishment further complicate narratives of solidarity and unified resistance in slave communities of the antebellum South.

* * *

The exploitative culture of slavery also turned its talons on those who exerted control over and abused enslaved people for as long as they were able. Enslavers, men and women, were animated at the personal and political levels by the pursuit of profit. In this quest, they sought domination of those they enslaved. But against their deepest-held wishes, elderly enslavers were not always able to command the control they craved. In revealing the limits to the dominion of elderly enslavers, we are able to reject their self-image of total "mastery," just as we reject their claims of benevolence. The pressures associated with aging, whether real or imagined, could wreak havoc on enslavers' public and private claims of dominance. The "inexorable hand of time," in North Carolina slaver William Pettigrew's phrase, could render enslavers wretched and pathetic; recognition of this fact shaped interpersonal relationships and the dynamics of power and resistance in the antebellum South.[14]

Ultimately, the exploitative nature of slavery structured interactions between white southerners. As they grew older, enslavers struggled to find their place within a society that prized autonomy and expressions of dominance. Rather than respect one another as "masters" or "mistresses," white southerners could see in elders weakness to exploit and "dependents" to master. Even in hierarchical white southern society, "time's relentless hand" diminished slavers' hopes for control and their presumptions of mastery, whether over enslaved people or other whites.[15] One enslaver's motto was "to keep all I have got and get all that I can," and such ideologies helped to shape southern social interactions. Elderly

---

[14] Starobin (Ed.), *Blacks in Bondage*, 34–5.
[15] Lewis and Darley, *Odd Leaves from the Life of a Louisiana "Swamp Doctor,"* 141–3.

enslavers once "at the pinnacle" could be forced to fight against the rising generation who did not fear or respect them; they did not always succeed in defending what they had "got," let alone their reputations and identities here.[16] Old slavers are not the object of pity, but their fates further reveal the all-encompassing effects of the culture of exploitation that drove life in antebellum slavery.

Old Age and American Slavery has revealed how antebellum southerners adapted to, resisted, or failed to overcome changes associated with age, both real and imagined, and the extent to which these struggles intersected with wider concerns over control, exploitation, resistance, and survival in a slave society. In doing so, it asks future scholars to rethink static hierarchies among Black and white southerners, to incorporate age into their work as a category of analysis and as a relation of power, and to address the contingent and contested networks of solidarity and support among enslavers and enslaved in the American South. Age shaped slavery, both as a system of economic exploitation and a contested site of personal domination, in crucial ways. Albeit never on equal terms, both Black and white southerners had to grapple with the realization that "old age [was] creeping on me so fast," and their efforts to do so were entwined in the wider struggles within and against slavery.[17] The "ravages of time" came for all; recognition of this simple fact shaped the dynamics of American slavery, and the lives of enslaved people and enslavers alike.[18]

---

[16] *Walker* v. *Hunter*, 17 Ga. 364 (1855), 378; Stevenson, *Life in Black and White*, xiii.
[17] Racine (Ed.), *Piedmont Farmer*, 426.
[18] Riddlemoser, "Conception in the Human Female."

Bibliography

ARCHIVAL SOURCES

Library of Virginia

Auditor of Public Accounts, Condemned Blacks Executed or Transported Records, Condemned Slaves, Court Orders, and Valuations, 1810–22.
Executive Papers, Henry A. Wise.
Executive Papers, James Barbour.
Executive Papers, John Letcher.
Executive Papers, Joseph Johnson.
Executive Papers, William Smith.
Rockbridge County Minute Book, Reel 43, November 1853, 189–202.

Georgia State Archives, Morrow

Archibald Smith Family Papers.
Elbert County, Superior Court Minutes & Records.
Glynn County, Court of Ordinary, Estate Records.
Troup County Superior Court Records.
Wilkes County Court of Ordinary, Estate Records, Wills, 1837–77.
Wilkes County Superior Court, Records of Writs, 1822–3.

Library of Congress, Washington DC

Kenneth Stampp (Ed.), *Records of Antebellum Southern Plantations from the Revolution through the Civil War* (Frederick: University Publications of America, c. 1985–2000).
Series A: James Henry Hammond Papers.
Series B: Alonzo White Slave Auction Book.
Series J: John Nevitt Diary.
Series J: Thomas Edward Cox Books.

Series N: Benjamin Leonard Covington Wailes Diary.
Series N: Susan Sillers Darden Diary.
Joseph Meredith Toner Collection of Manuscripts, Box 150, Part II.
W. A. Riddlemoser, "Conception in the Human Female," 1843–4.

Louisiana and Lower Mississippi Valley Collections, LSU Libraries, Baton Rouge

Bennet H. Barrow Papers.
Eliza L. Magruder Diary.
James Stewart McGehee Collection.
Priscilla Munnikhuysen Bond Papers.

Mississippi State Archives, Jackson

Carrollton District Chancery Court Minutes.
Case Files of the Mississippi High Court of Errors and Appeals.
County Court Case Files, Pontotoc County.
Duncan (Stephen Jr.) Papers.
Emancipations, State Government Records.
Lawrence County Chancery Court Cases.

Natchez Historic Foundation, Mississippi

Dr. John Carmichael Jenkins Journal, Elgin Plantation Records.
Records of the Vice-Chancery Court, Adams County Courthouse.

North Carolina Department of Archives and History, Raleigh.

Camden County, Civil Actions Concerning Slaves and Freedmen of Color, 1819–1920 (Broken Series).
Gates County, Slaves Records, 1783–1867.
General Assembly, Session Records, November 1824–January 1825, Petitions and Papers Concerning Pardon of Negro, George, Charged with Murder.
McDowell County, Records of Slaves and Free Persons of Color, 1843–73.
North Carolina Slave Collection, 1748–1922, Slavery Papers, Conspiracy, 1802.
Pasquotank County, Records of Slaves and Free Persons of Color, 1733–1866, 1892.
Perquimans County, Slave Records, 1759–1864.
Rockingham County, Records of Slaves and Free Persons of Color, 1795–1867.
Surry County, Slave Records, 1840–64.
Wilkes County, Slave Papers, 1830–60.

South Carolina Department of Archives and History, Columbia

Court of Magistrates and Freeholders, Kershaw District, South Carolina. *Gantt* v. *Venning*, City Ct. of Charleston, Box 34, Jan 1840, S.C., Sup. Ct. Records.

South Caroliniana Library, Columbia

Andrew Flinn Plantation Book, 1840.
Anne Simon Deas, *Two Years of Plantation Life* (1910).
Baptist Church, Welsh Neck, Society Hill, Records, 1737–1935.
Journal of Meta Morris Grimball.
Mary Esther Huger Reminiscences, MS vol. bd., 1890–92.

Southern Historical Collection, University of North Carolina, Chapel Hill

Ben Sparkman Plantation Journal.
David Gavin Diary.
Edmonia Cabell Wilkins Papers.
Everard Green Baker Papers.
John Walker Papers.
Robert Ruffin Barrow Papers.
Roswell Elmer Diary.

Census and Quantitative Material

Berry, Daina Ramey, *"Berry Slave Value Database"* (Ann Arbor: Inter-University Consortium for Political and Social Research [distributor], 2017-10-30). https://doi.org/10.3886/E101113V1.
Carter, Susan B., Scott Sigmund Gartner, Michael R. Haines, et al. (Eds.), *Historical Statistics of the United States, Earliest Times to the Present: Millennial Edition* (New York: Cambridge University Press, 2006).
United States Census Bureau, *Census for 1820* (Washington, DC: Gales & Seaton, 1821).
United States Census Bureau, *1840 Census: Compendium of the Enumeration of the Inhabitants and Statistics of the United States, as Obtained at the Department of State, from the Returns of the Sixth Census* (Washington, DC: Thomas Allen, 1841).
United States Census Bureau, *1850 Census: Compendium of the Seventh Census* (Washington, DC: Beverley Tucker, Senate Printer, 1854).
United States Census Bureau, *1860 Census: Recapitulation of the Tables of Population, Nativity, and Occupation* (Washington, DC: Beverley Tucker, Senate Printer, 1864).

Court Records

American Colonization Society v. *Gartrell*, 23 Ga. 448 (1857).
Belcher v. *McKelvey*; *Tucker* v. *Belcher*, 32 S.C. Eq. 9, 11, Rich. Eq. 9 (1859).
Brock v. *Luckett's Executors*, 5 Miss. 459 (1840).

Caldwell v. *Porcher*, 27 S.C.L. 138, 2 McMullan 329 (1842).
Chambers v. *Davis*, 62. N.C. 152 (1867).
Cromartie v. *Robison*, 55 N.C. 218, 2 Jones Eq. 218 (1855).
Davis v. *Calvert*, 5 G & J, 269 (Md, 1833).
De Tollenere v. *Fuller*, 8 S.C.L. 117, 1 Mill 117 (1817).
Denton v. *Franklin*, 48 Ky. 28, 9 B. Mon 28 (1848).
Drane v. *Beall*, 21 Ga. 21 (1857).
Etheridge v. *Corprew*, 3 Jones N.C. 14 (1855).
Exum v. *Canty*, 34 Miss. 533 (1857).
Gass's Heirs v. *Gass's Ex'r's*, 22 Tenn. 278, 3 Hum. 278 (1842).
Gilbert v. *State*, 26 Tenn. 524, 7 Hum. 524 (1847).
Gilbert v. *Ward*, 10 Fed. Cas. 348, 4 Cranch C. C. 171 (1831).
Gordon v. *Blackman*, 1 Rich. Eq. 61 (S.C. 1844).
Hadley v. *Latimer*, 3 Yerg Tenn. 537 (1832).
Hart v. *Powell*, 18, Ga. 635 (1855).
Heirs of Potter v. *Potter's Widow*, 3 N.J.L. 415 (1808).
Hill v. *McLaurin*, 28 Miss. 288 (1854).
Inhabitants of Winchendon v. *Inhabitants of Hatfield*, 4 Mass. 123 (1808).
James v. *Langdon*, 46 Ky. 193 (1846).
Jane B. Ross et al. V. *Vertner et al.*, 5 How. Miss. 305 (1840).
Lawrence v. *McFarlane*, 7 Mart. (n.s) 558 (1829).
Lea v. *Brown*, 58 N.C. 379 (1860).
Lehman v. *Logan*, 42. N.C. 296, 7 Ired. Eq. 296 (1851).
Manns v. *Given*, 35 Va. 689, 7 Leigh 689 (1836)
Minor's Heirs v. *Thomas (of color)*, 51 Ky. 106 (1851).
Mooney v. *Evans*, 6 Ired. Eq. 363 (N.C. 1849)
O'Neal v. *Farr*, 30 S.C.L. 80, 1 Rich. 80 (1844).
Pace v. *Mealing*, 21 Ga. 464 (1857).
Peeples v. *Smith*, 42 S.C.L., 8 Rich 90 (1854).
Peers v. *Davis' Administrators*, 29 Mo. 184 (1859).
Potts v. *House*, 6 Ga. 324 (1849).
Pride v. *Pulliam*, 4 Hawks 49 (N.C. 1825).
Redford v. *Peggy*, 27 Va. 316, 6 Randolph 316 (1828).
Reed's Will, 41 Ky. 79, 2 B. Mon. 79 (1841).
Reeves v. *Gantt*, 8 Rich. Eq. 14 (1855).
Robinson v. *King*, 6 Ga 539 (1849).
Scott v. *Clarkson*, 4 Ky. 277, 1 Bibb 277 (1808).
Selectmen v. *Jacob*, 2 Tyler 192 (Vt. 1802).
Singleton's Will, 38 Ky. 315, 8 Dana 315 (1839).
Smith v. *Dunwoody*, 19 Ga. 237 (1856).
State v. *Duckworth*, 1 Winston 243 (1864).
State v. *Robbins*, 48. N.C. 249 (1855).
Tallahassee Railroad Co. v *Macon*, 8 Fla. 299 (1859).
Townshend v. *Townshend*, 5 Md. 287 (1853).
Townshend v. *Townshend*, 6 Md. 295 (1854)
Venning v. *Gantt*, 25 S.C.L. 87 1 Chev. 87 (1840).

Walker v. *Hunter*, 17 Ga. 364 (1855).
Wallingsford v. Allen, 35 U.S. 10 Pet. 583 (1836).
William (a slave) v. *State*, 18 Ga. 356 (1855).

Legislation

Georgia. General Assembly, "An Act To Compel Owners of Old or Infirm Slaves to Maintain Them," in *Acts of the General Assembly of the State of Georgia ... 1815* [Vol. 1], 34–5.

Georgia. General Assembly, "An Act to Establish an Infirmary for the Relief and Protection of Aged and Afflicted Negroes, in the State of Georgia," in *Acts of the General Assembly of the State of Georgia ... 1832* [Vol. 1], 176–7.

Maryland. General Assembly, "An Act to Repeal Certain Parts of an Act, Entitled, An Act to Prevent Disabled and Superannuated Slaves Being Set Free, or the Manumission of Slaves by Any Last Will and Testament," in *Laws of Maryland, Made and Passed at a Session of Assembly ...* (Annapolis: Frederick Green, 1790).

Maryland. General Assembly, "An Act Relating to Negroes, and to Repeal the Acts of Assembly Therein Mentioned," in *Laws of Maryland, Made and Passed at a Session of Assembly ...* (Annapolis: Frederick Green, 1796).

Virginia. General Assembly, "An Act to Amend an Act, Entitled 'An Act to Reduce Into One Act, The Several Acts Concerning Slaves, Free Negroes, and Mulattoes,' and For Other Purposes," in *Acts Passed at a General Assembly of the Commonwealth of Virginia ...* (Richmond: Thomas Ritchie, 1824), 34.3.

"North American Slave Narratives," *Documenting the American South* (University Library, University of North Carolina at Chapel Hill), https://docsouth.unc.edu/neh/texts.html

Aaron, *The Light and Truth of Slavery: Aaron's History* (Worcester: The Author, 1845).

Aleckson, Sam, *Before the War, and After the Union* (Boston: Gold Mind, 1929).

Allen, William Francis, Charles Pickard Ware, and Lucy McKim Garrison, *Slave Songs of the United States* (New York: Timpson & Co., 1867).

Anderson, Robert, *The Anderson Surpriser: Written after He Was Seventy-Five Years of Age. An Account of His Florida and Northern Trip* (Macon: Printed for the Author, 1895).

Anderson, William, *Life and Narrative of William J. Anderson, Twenty-four Years a Slave; Sold Eight Times! In Jail Sixty Times!! Whipped Three Hundred Times!!! or The Dark Deeds of American Slavery Revealed ...* (Chicago: Daily Tribune Book and Job Printing Office, 1857).

Armistead, Wilson, *A Tribute for the Negro: Being a Vindication of the Moral, Intellectual, and Religious Capabilities of the Colored Portion of Mankind; with Particular Reference to the African Race* (Manchester: W. Irwin, 1848).

Ball, Charles, *Fifty Years in Chains or, The Life of an American Slave* (New York: H. Dayton; Indianapolis: Asher & Co, 1859).

Ball, Charles, *Slavery in the United States: A Narrative of the Life and Adventures of Charles Ball, a Black Man* ... (New York: John S. Taylor, 1837).

Bibb, Henry, *Narrative of the Life and Adventures of Henry Bibb, An American Slave Written by himself* (New York: Published for the Author, 1849).

Black, Leonard, *The Life and Sufferings of Leonard Black, A Fugitive from Slavery* (New Bedford: Benjamin Lindsey, 1847).

Bradford, Sarah, *Harriet, the Moses of Her People* (New York: Geo. R. Lockwood and Son, 1886).

Branham, Levi, *My Life and Travels* (Dalton: A. J. Showalter Co. Printers and Publishers, 1929).

Brown, Henry, *Narrative of the Life of Henry Box Brown, Written by Himself* (Manchester: Published by the Author, 1851).

Brown, John, *Slave Life in Georgia: A Narrative of the Life, Sufferings, and Escape of John Brown, A Fugitive Slave, Now in England* (London: L.A. Chaemerovzow, 1855).

Brown, Sterling N., *My Own Life Story* (Washington, DC: Hamilton Printing, 1924).

Browne, Martha Griffith, *Autobiography of a Female Slave* (New York: Redfield, 1857).

Bruce, Henry Clay, *The New Man: Twenty-Nine Years a Slave. Twenty-Nine Years a Free Man* (York: P. Anstadt & Sons, 1895).

Campbell, Israel, *An Autobiography. Bond and Free: Or, Yearnings for Freedom, from My Green Brier House. Being the Story of My Life in Freedom. By Israel Campbell. Minister of the Gospel* (Philadelphia: Published by the Author, 1861).

Chesney, Pharaoh Jackson, and John Coram Webster, *Last of the Pioneers: Or, Old Times in East Tenn., Being the Life and Reminiscences of Pharaoh Jackson Chesney (Aged 120 Years)* (Knoxville: S. B. Newman & Co., Printers & Book Binders, 1902).

Clarke, Lewis Garrard, *Narratives of the Sufferings of Lewis Clarke, During a Captivity of More Than Twenty-Five Years Among the Algerines of Kentucky, One of the So Called Christian States of America. Dictated by Himself* (Boston: David H. Ela, Printer, 1845).

Clarke, Lewis Garrard, and Milton Clarke, *Narratives of the Sufferings of Lewis and Milton Clarke, Sons of a Soldier of the Revolution, During a Captivity of More than Twenty Years Among the Slaveholders of Kentucky, One of the So-Called Christian States of North America* (Boston: Bela Marsh, 1846)

Cook, Fields, and Mary Jo Jackson Bratton, "Fields's Observations: The Slave Narrative of a Nineteenth-Century Virginian," *Virginia Magazine of History and Biography* (1980), 75–93.

Cox, Mary L., and Susan H. Cox, *Narrative of Dimmock Charlton, a British Subject, Taken from the Brig "Peacock" by the US Sloop "Hornet," Enslaved while a Prisoner of War, and Retained Forty-Five Years in Bondage* (Philadelphia: The Editors, 1859).

Craft, William, *Running a Thousand Miles for Freedom; or, the Escape of William and Ellen Craft from Slavery* (London: William Tweedie, 1860).

Curry, James, "Narrative of James Curry, A Fugitive Slave," *The Liberator*, January 10, 1840.

Douglass, Frederick, *Life and Times of Frederick Douglass, His Early Life as a Slave, His Escape from Bondage, and His Complete History to This Time* ... (Hartford: Park Publishing Co., 1881).

Douglass, Frederick, *Life and Times of Frederick Douglass, Written by Himself. His Early Life as a Slave, His Escape from Bondage, and His Complete History to the Present Time* ... (Boston: De Wolfe & Fiske Co., 1892).

Douglass, Frederick, *My Bondage and My Freedom: Part* I. – *Life as a Slave. Part* II. – *Life as Freeman* (New York: Miller, Orton & Mulligan, 1855).

Douglass, Frederick, *Narrative of the Life of Frederick Douglass, an American Slave. Written by Himself* (Boston: Anti-Slavery Office, 1845).

Fedric, Francis, *Slave Life in Virginia and Kentucky; or, Fifty Years of Slavery in the Southern States of America* (London: Wertheim, McIntosh, and Hunt, 1863).

Grandy, Moses, *Narrative of the Life of Moses Grandy; Late a Slave in the United States of America* (London: C. Gilpin, 5, Bishopsgate-street, 1843).

Green, Jacob, *Narrative of the Life of J. D. Green, A Runaway Slave, from Kentucky, Containing an Account of His Three Escapes, in 1839, 1846, and 1848* (Huddersfield: Henry Fielding, 1864).

Green, William, *Narrative of Events in the Life of William Green (Formerly a Slave). Written by Himself* (Springfield: L. M. Guernsey, Book, Job, & Card Printer, 1853).

Grimes, William, *The Life of William Grimes, the Runaway Slave, Written by Himself* (New York: W. Grimes, 1825).

Hawkins, William G., *Lunsford Lane; or, Another Helper from North Carolina* (Boston: Crosby & Nichols, 1863).

Henry, George, *Life of George Henry. Together with a Brief History of the Colored People in America* (Providence: The Author; H. I. Gould, 1894).

Henson, Josiah, *"Uncle Tom's Story of His Life." An Autobiography of the Rev. Josiah Henson (Mrs. Harriet Beecher Stowe's "Uncle Tom")* ... (London: Christian Age Office, 1876).

Hildreth, Richard, *The Slave: or Memoirs of Archy Moore. Vol. I* (Boston: John H. Eastburn, Printer, 1836).

Hildreth, Richard, *The White Slave; or, Memoirs of a Fugitive* (Boston: Tappan and Whittemore, 1852).

Horton, George M., *The Poetical Works of George M. Horton: The Colored Bard of North Carolina: To Which Is Prefixed the Life of the Author, Written by Himself* (Hillsborough: D. Heartt, 1845).

Hughes, Louis, *Thirty Years a Slave: From Bondage to Freedom. The Institution of Slavery as Seen on the Plantation and in the Home of the Planter* (Milwaukee: South Side Printing Co., 1897).

Jackson, Andrew, *Narrative and Writings of Andrew Jackson, of Kentucky; Containing an Account of His Birth, and Twenty-Six Years of His Life While a Slave; His Escape; Five Years of Freedom, Together with Anecdotes Relating to Slavery; Journal of One Year's Travels; Sketches, etc. Narrated by Himself; Written by a Friend* (Syracuse: Daily and Weekly Star Office, 1847).

Jackson, John Andrew, *The Experience of a Slave in South Carolina* (London: Passmore & Alabaster, 1862).

Jacobs, Harriet, *Incidents in the Life of a Slave Girl. Written by Herself* (Boston: Published for the Author, 1861).

Jacobs, John S., "A True Tale of Slavery," *The Leisure Hour: A Family Journal of Instruction and Recreation*, 476 (February 7, 1861), 85–7.

Loguen, Jermain Wesley, *The Rev. J. W. Loguen, as a Slave and as a Freeman. A Narrative of Real Life* (Syracuse: J. G. K. Truair & Co., 1859).

Jamison, Monroe Franklin, *Autobiography and Work of Bishop M. F. Jamison, D.D. ('Uncle Joe') Editor, Publisher, and Church Extension Secretary; a Narration of His Whole Career from the Cradle to the Bishopric of the Colored M. E. Church in America* (Nashville: M. E. Church, 1912).

Lowery, Irving E., *Life on the Old Plantation in Ante-Bellum Days, or, A Story Based on Facts* (Columbia: The State Co., Printers, 1911).

Matthews, James, "Recollections of Slavery by a Runaway Slave," *The Emancipator*, August 23, September 13, September 20, October 11, October 18, 1838.

Mattison, H., *Louisa Picquet: The Octoroon: or Inside Views of Southern Domestic Life* (New York: Published by the Author, 1861).

McCray, Mary, *Life of Mary F. McCray: Born and Raised a Slave in the State of Kentucky* (Lima, Ohio: [s.n.], 1898).

Meachum, John B., *An Address to All the Colored Citizens of the United States* (Philadelphia: King & Baird, 1846).

Neilson, Peter, *The Life and Adventures of Zamba, an African Negro King; and His Experience of Slavery in South Carolina. Written by Himself. Corrected and Arranged by Peter Neilson* (London: Smith, Elder & Co., 1847).

Northup, Solomon, *Twelve Years a Slave: Narrative of Solomon Northup, a Citizen of New York, Kidnapped in Washington City in 1841, and Rescued in 1853* (Auburn: Derby & Miller, 1853).

O' Neal, William, *Life and History of William O'Neal, or, The Man Who Sold His Wife* (St. Louis: A. R. Fleming, 1896).

Parker, Allen, *Recollections of Slavery Times* (Worcester: Chas. W. Burbank & Co., 1895).

Pennington, James W. C., *The Fugitive Blacksmith; or, Events in the History of James W. C. Pennington, Pastor of a Presbyterian Church, New York, Formerly a Slave in the State of Maryland, United States* (London: Charles Gilpin, 1849).

Pennington, J. W. C., *A Narrative of Events of the Life of J. H. Banks, an Escaped Slave, from the Cotton State, Alabama, in America* (Liverpool: M. Rourke, Printer, 1861).

Peterson, Daniel H., *The Looking-Glass: Being a True Report and Narrative of the Life, Travels, and Labors of the Rev. Daniel H. Peterson, a Colored Clergyman; Embracing a Period of Time from the Year 1812 to 1854, and Including His Visit to Western Africa* (New York: Wright, 1854).

Pickard, Kate E. R., *The Kidnapped and the Ransomed. Recollections of Peter Still and His Wife "Vina," after Forty Years of Slavery* (Syracuse: William T. Hamilton, 1856).

Pierson, Emily Catharine, *Jamie Parker, the Fugitive* (Hartford: Brockett, Fuller and Co., 1851).

Robinson, William H., *From Log Cabin to the Pulpit, or, Fifteen Years in Slavery* (Eau Clair: James H. Tifft, 1913).

Roper, Moses, *A Narrative of the Adventures and Escape of Moses Roper, from American Slavery* (Philadelphia: Merrihew & Gunn, 1838).

Simpson, John Hawkins, *Horrors of the Virginian Slave Trade and of the Slave-Rearing Plantations. The True Story of Dinah, an Escaped Virginian Slave ...* (London: A. W. Bennett, 1863).

Steward, Austin, *Twenty-Two Years a Slave, and Forty Years a Freeman; Embracing a Correspondence of Several Years, While President of Wilberforce Colony, London, Canada West* (Rochester: William Alling, 1857).

Stroyer, Jacob, *Sketches of My Life in the South. Part I* (Salem: Salem Press, 1879).

Thompson, John, *The Life of John Thompson, a Fugitive Slave; Containing His History of 25 Years in Bondage, and His Providential Escape. Written by Himself* (Worcester: John Thompson, 1856).

Truth, Sojourner, and Olive Gilbert, *Narrative of Sojourner Truth, a Northern Slave, Emancipated from Bodily Servitude by the State of New York, in 1828* (Boston: The Author, 1850).

Walker, William, *Buried Alive (Behind Prison Walls) for a Quarter of a Century: Life of William Walker* (Saginaw: Friedman & Hynan, 1892).

Ward, Samuel Ringgold, *Autobiography of a Fugitive Negro: His Anti-Slavery Labours in the United States, Canada, & England* (London: John Snow, 35, Paternoster Row, 1855).

Watkins, James *Narrative of the Life of James Watkins, Formerly a "Chattel" in Maryland, US; Containing an Account of His Escape from Slavery, Together with an Appeal on Behalf of Three Millions of Such "Pieces of Property," Still Held Under the Standard of the Eagle* (Bolton: Kenyon & Abbot, 1852).

Watkins, James, *Struggles for Freedom; or the Life of James Watkins, Formerly a Slave in Maryland, US; in Which Is Detailed a Graphic Account of His Extraordinary Escape from Slavery, Notices of the Fugitive Slave Law, the Sentiments of American Divines on the Subject of Slavery, etc., etc.* (Manchester: A. Heywood, Oldham Street, 1860).

Watson, Henry, *Narrative of Henry Watson, A Fugitive Slave. Written by Himself* (Boston: Bela Marsh, 1848).

Wells Brown, William, *My Southern Home: or, The South and Its People* (Boston: A. G. Brown & Co., Publishers, 1880).

Wells Brown, William, *Narrative of Williams Wells Brown, A Fugitive Slave Written by Himself* (Boston: The Anti-Slavery Office, 1847).

Wheeler, Peter, *Chains and Freedom: Or, The Life and Adventures of Peter Wheeler, a Colored Man Yet Living. A Slave in Chains, a Sailor on the Deep, and a Sinner at the Cross*, ed. Charles Edwards Lester (New York: E. S. Arnold & Co., 1839).

Williams, Isaac, *Aunt Sally: Or, The Cross the Way of Freedom. A Narrative of the Slave-Life and Purchase of the Mother of Rev. Isaac Williams of Detroit, Michigan* (Cincinnati: American Reform Tract and Book Society, 1858).

Williams, Isaac D., *Sunshines and Shadow of Slave Life: Reminiscences as told by Isaac D. Williams to "Tege"* (Michigan: Evening News Printing and Binding House, 1885).

Williams, James, *Life and Adventures of James Williams, a Fugitive Slave, with a Full Description of the Underground Railroad* (San Francisco: Women's Union Print, 424 Montgomery Street, 1873).

Williams, James, *Narrative of James Williams, an American Slave, Who Was for Several Years a Driver on a Cotton Plantation in Alabama* (New York: American Anti-Slavery Society; Boston: Isaac Knapp, 1838).

Collected Slave Testimony

Abrahams, Roger D. (Ed.), *African American Folktales: Stories from Black Traditions in the New World* (New York: Pantheon Books, 1985).

Blassingame, John (Ed.), *Slave Testimony: Two Centuries of Letters, Speeches, Interviews, and Autobiographies* (Baton Rouge: Louisiana State University Press, 1977).

Brewer, John Mason (Ed.), *American Negro Folklore* (Chicago: Quadrangle Books, 1968).

Federal Writers' Project: Slave Narrative Project, Vol. 7, Kentucky, Bogie-Woods with combined interviews of others. 1936. Manuscript/Mixed Material. www .loc.gov/item/mesn070/.

Federal Writers' Project: Slave Narrative Project, Vol. 9, Mississippi, Allen-Young. 1936. Manuscript/Mixed Material. www.loc.gov/item/mesn090/.

Federal Writers' Project: Slave Narrative Project, Vol. 10, Missouri, Abbot-Younger. 1936. Manuscript/Mixed Material. www.loc.gov/item/mesn100/.

Federal Writers' Project: Slave Narrative Project, Vol. 13, Oklahoma, Adams-Young. 1936. Manuscript/Mixed Material. www.loc.gov/item/mesn130/.

Federal Writers' Project: Slave Narrative Project, Vol. 17, Virginia, Berry-Wilson. 1936. Manuscript/Mixed Material. www.loc.gov/item/mesn170/.

Georgia Writers' Project, *Drums and Shadows: Survival Studies among the Georgia Coastal Negroes* (Athens: University of Georgia Press, 1986).

Perdue Jr., Charles L., Thomas E. Barden, and Robert K. Phillips (Eds.), *Weevils in the Wheat: Interviews with Virginia Ex-Slaves* (Charlottesville: University of Virginia Press, 1992).

Rawick, George P. (Ed.), *The American Slave: A Composite Autobiography, Series 1–2.* 19 Vols. (Westport: Greenwood Press, 1972).

Rawick, George P. (Ed.), *The American Slave: A Composite Autobiography, Supplement, Series 1.* 12 Vols. (Westport: Greenwood Press, 1977).

Rawick, George P. (Ed.), *The American Slave: A Composite Autobiography, Supplement, Series 2.* 10 Vols. (Westport: Greenwood Press, 1979).

Saxon, Lyle, Edward Dreyer, and Robert Tallant (Eds.), *Gumbo-Ya-Ya: A Collection of Louisiana Folk Tales* (Baton Rouge; Louisiana State University Press, 1945).

Starobin, Robert (Ed.), *Blacks in Bondage: Letters of American Slaves* (New York: New Viewpoints, 1974).

Newspapers

The Charlotte Observer.

The Christian Recorder.
The Liberator.
The North Star.
Provincial Freeman.
Weekly Advocate.
Weekly Anglo-African.

PUBLISHED PRIMARY SOURCES

Agricola, "Management of Negroes," *Southern Cultivator*, 13 (1855), 171–4.

[Anon], "Editorial," *Southern Medical and Surgical Journal*, 12 (1856), 21–36.

[Anon], "Growing Old," *The Ladies' Repository: A Monthly Periodical, Devoted to Literature, Arts, and Religion*, 18.5 (May 1858), 276–82.

[Anon], "Management of Negroes," *De Bow's Review*, 19.3 (1855), 358–63.

[Anon], "Management of Negroes upon Southern Estates," *De Bow's Review*, 10.6 (1851), 621–7.

[Anon], "Premature Old Age," *The Magazine of Domestic Economy*, 1 (London: W. S. Orr and Co., Paternoster Row, September 1842), 127.

Avirett, James Battle, *The Old Plantation: How We Lived in Great House and Cabin Before the War* (New York: F. Tennyson Neely Co., 1901).

Baillie, James, *The Life and Age of Man: Stages of Man's Life from the Cradle to the Grave* (New York, c. 1848).

Baillie, James, *The Life and Age of Woman: Stages of Woman's Life from the Cradle to the Grave* (New York, c. 1848).

Ball, Erica L., "To Train Them for the Work: Manhood, Morality, and Free Black Conduct Discourse in Antebellum New York," in Timothy R. Buckner and Peter Caster (Eds.), *Fathers, Preachers, Rebels, Men: Black Masculinity in US History and Literature, 1820–1945* (Columbus: Ohio State University Press, 2011), 60–80.

Baldwin, Joseph G., *The Flush Times of Alabama and Mississippi. A Series of Sketches* (New York: D. Appleton and Co., 1854).

Barnum, P. T., *The Life of Joice Heth, the Nurse of Gen. George Washington (the Father of Our Country,) Now Living at the Astonishing Age of 161 Years and Weighs Only 46 Pounds* (New York: Printed for the Publisher, 1835).

Bleser, Carol (Ed.), *Secret and Sacred: The Diaries of James Henry Hammond, a Southern Slaveholder* (Columbia: University of South Carolina Press, 1988).

Burwell, Letitia, *A Girl's Life in Virginia Before the War* (New York: Frederick A. Stokes, 1895).

Caldwell, Charles, *Thoughts on the Effects of Old Age on the Human Constitution: A Special Introductory* (Louisville: John C. Noble Printer, 1846).

Clay, Thomas, *Detail of a Plan for the Moral Improvement of Negroes on Plantations* (Printed at the request of the Presbytery, Georgia, 1833).

Clifton, James M. (Ed.), *Life and Labor on Argyle Island: Letters and Documents of a Savannah River Rice Plantation, 1833–1867* (Savannah: The Beehive Press, 1978).

Collins, Robert, "Management of Slaves," *De Bow's Review*, 17.4 (1854), 421–6.

Deedes, Henry, *Sketches of the South and West or Ten Month's Residence in the United States* (Edinburgh and London: William Blackwood & Sons, 1869).

Drew, Benjamin, *A North-Side View of Slavery. The Refugee: or the Narratives of Fugitive Slaves in Canada. Related by Themselves, with an Account of the History and Condition of the Colored Population of Upper Canada* (Boston: J. P. Jewett and Company, 1856).

Easterby, James H., and Daniel C. Littlefield (Eds.), *The South Carolina Rice Plantation, as Revealed in the Papers of Robert F. W. Allston* (Columbia: University of South Carolina Press, 2004).

Emerson, Ralph Waldo, "Old Age," *The Atlantic Monthly* (January, 1862), 134–40.

Emmons, Nathanael, *The Works of Nathanael Emmons, D. D., Late Pastor of the Church in Franklin, Mass., with a Memoir of His Life, Vol. II* (Boston: Crocker & Brewster, 1842).

Felton, Rebecca Latimer, *Country Life in Georgia In the Days of My Youth ALSO Addresses Before Georgia Legislature Woman's Clubs, Women's Organizations and other Noted Occasions* (Atlanta: Index Printing Company, 1919).

Fitzhugh, George, *Cannibals All! Or, Slaves without Masters* (Richmond: A. Morris, 1857).

Franklin, "Overseers," *The Southern Cultivator*, II (1847), 107–8.

Gilman, Caroline, *Recollections of a Southern Matron* (New York: Harper & Brothers, 1838).

Harper, Chancellor, "Memoir on Slavery, Part I," *De Bow's Review*, 8.3 (1850), 232–43.

Horace, *The Odes and Carmen Saeculare of Horace*. John Conington, trans. (London: George Bell and Sons, 1882): Book 3, Poem 6.

Holmes, Rev. A. T. "The Duties of Christian Masters," in Holland Nimmons McTyeire (Ed.), *Duties of Masters to Servants: Three Premium Essays* (Charleston: Southern Baptist Publication Society, 1851), 129–51.

Hundley, Daniel, *Social Relations in Our Southern States* (New York: H. B Price, 1860).

Jefferson, Thomas, *Notes on the State of Virginia* (Philadelphia: Richard and Hall, 1788).

Kemble, Frances Ann, *Journal of a Residence on a Georgian Plantation in 1838–1839* (Athens: University of Georgia Press, 1984: originally published New York, 1863).

Lathrop, Joseph, *The Infirmities and Comforts of Old Age: A Sermon to Aged People* (Springfield: Henry Brewer, 1805; 2nd ed., 1806).

Lemmon, Sarah McCulloch (Ed.), *The Pettigrew Papers, Volume II, 1819–1843* (Raleigh: State Department of Archives and History, 1971).

Lewis, Henry Clay, and Felix Octavius Carr Darley, *Odd Leaves from the Life of a Louisiana "Swamp Doctor." In "The Swamp Doctor's Adventures in the South-West. Containing the Whole of the Louisiana Swamp Doctor; Streaks of Squatter Life; and Far-Western Scenes; in a Series of Forty-Two Humorous Southern and Western Sketches ..."* (Philadelphia: T. B. Peterson, 1858).

Lintner, Grace, *Bond and Free: A Tale of the South* (Indianapolis: C. B. Ingraham, 1882).

Mallard, Robert Q., *Plantation Life Before Emancipation* (Richmond: Whittet & Shepperson, 1892).

McTyeire, Holland Nimmons (Ed.), *Duties of Masters to Servants: Three Premium Essays* (Charleston: Southern Baptist Publication Society, 1851).

Mell, Patrick Hues, *Slavery: A Treatise, Showing That Slavery Is Neither a Moral, Political, nor Social Evil* (Penfield: Printed by Benj. Brantly, 1844).

Merrill, A. P., MD, "An Essay on some of the Distinctive Peculiarities of the Negro Race," *Southern Medical and Surgical Journal*, 12 (1856), 21–36.

Nott, Josiah Clark, "Statistics of Southern Slave Population," *De Bow's Review*, 4.3 (1847), 275–89.

Olmsted, Frederick Law, *A Journey in the Seaboard Slave States; With Remarks on Their Economy* (New York; London: Dix and Edwards; Sampson & Low, 1856).

Olmsted, Frederick Law, *Journeys and Explorations in the Cotton Kingdom of America. A Traveller's Observations on Cotton and Slavery in the American Slave States. Based upon Three Former Volumes of Journeys and Observations* (London: Sampson, Low, Son & Co., 1862).

Page, Thomas Nelson, *Social Life in Virginia Before the War* (Cambridge, Mass.: John Wilson & Son, 1897).

Parsons, Charles Grandison, *Inside View of Slavery; or, A Tour Among the Planters, with an Introduction by H. B. Stowe* (Boston: J. P. Jewett and Company, 1855).

Racine, Philip N. (Ed.), *Piedmont Farmer: The Journals of David Golightly Harris, 1855–1870* (Knoxville: University of Tennessee Press, 1990).

Redpath, James, *The Roving Editor: Or, Talks with Slaves in the Southern States* (New York: Negro Universities Press, 1968; originally published in 1859 by A. B. Burdick).

Roles, John, *Inside Views of Slavery on Southern Plantations* (New York: John A Gray & Green, Printers and Stereotypes, 1864).

Rosengarten, Theodore (Ed.), *Tombee: Portrait of a Cotton Planter* (New York: Quill, William Morrow, 1986).

Rush, Benjamin, "An Account of the State of the Body and Mind in Old Age and Observations upon Its Diseases and Their Remedies," in *Medical Inquiries and Observations* (Philadelphia: Thomas Dobson, 1793), 293–321.

Scarborough, William Kaufman (Ed.), *The Diary of Edmund Ruffin, Volume II: The Years of Hope, 1861–June 1863* (Baton Rouge: Louisiana State University Press, 1976).

Smith, William A. (Ed.), *Thomas O. Summers, Lectures on the Philosophy and Practice of slavery: As Exhibited in the Institution of Domestic Slavery in the United States; With the Duties of Masters to Slaves* (Nashville: Stevenson and Evans, 1856).

Stanford, John, *The Aged Christian's Companion* (New York: Stanford & Swords, 1855).

Stowe, Harriet Beecher, *Uncle Tom's Cabin or, Life Among the Lowly, with an Introduction by David Bromwich* (Cambridge, Mass.: Belknap Press of Harvard University Press, 2009; originally published Boston: John P. Jewett, 1852).

Thorpe, Thomas Bangs, *The Master's House; A Tale of Southern Life, by Logan* (New York: T. L. McElrath, 1854).

Van Oven, Barnard, MD, *On the Decline of Life in Health and Disease, Being An Attempt to Investigate the Causes of Longevity; And the Best Means of Attaining a Healthful Old Age* (London: John Churchill, 1853).

Weld, Theodore Dwight, *American Slavery As It Is: Testimony of a Thousand Witnesses* (New York: American Anti-Slavery Office, 1839).

Online Database

Race and Slavery Petitions Project, Series 1 and 2 (University Libraries, University of North Carolina at Greensboro), accessed via the "Slavery and the Law (1775–1867)" module of the subscription database ProQuest History Vault.

SECONDARY SOURCES

Abosede, George, Clive Glaser, Margaret D. Jacobs, et al., "*AHR* Conversation: Each Generation Writes Its Own History of Generations," *American Historical Review*, 123.5 (December 2018), 1504–46.

Achenbaum, W. Andrew, "Delineating Old Age: From Functional Status to Bureaucratic Criteria," in Corinne T. Field and Nicholas L. Syrett (Eds.), *Age in America: The Colonial Era to the Present* (New York: New York University Press, 2015), 301–20.

Achenbaum, W. Andrew, *Old Age in the New Land: The American Experience since 1790* (Baltimore: Johns Hopkins University Press, 1978).

Alphonso, Gwendoline M., "Naturalizing Affection, Securing Property: Family, Slavery, and the Courts in Antebellum South Carolina, 1830–1860," *Studies in American Political Development*, 35.2 (2021), 194–213.

Anderson, Jeffrey E., *Conjure in African American Society* (Baton Rouge: Louisiana State University Press, 2005).

Anderson, Ralph V., and Robert E. Gallman, "Slaves as Fixed Capital: Slave Labor and Southern Economic Development," *Journal of American History*, 64.1 (1977), 24–46.

Anderson, William L., *Slavery and Class in the American South: A Generation of Slave Narrative Testimony, 1840–1865* (New York: Oxford University Press, 2019).

Ayers, Edward L., *Vengeance and Justice: Crime and Punishment in the 19th-Century American South* (New York: Oxford University Press, 1984).

Bailey, David Thomas, "A Divided Prism: Two Sources of Black Testimony on Slavery," *Journal of Southern History*, 46.3 (1980), 381–404.

Baptist, Edward E., *The Half Has Never Been Told: Slavery and the Making of American Capitalism* (New York: Basic Books, 2014).

Baptist, Edward E., "'My Mind Is to Drown You and Leave You Behind': 'Omie Wise,' Intimate Violence, and Masculinity," in Christine Daniels and Michael V. Kennedy (Eds.), *Over the Threshold: Intimate Violence in Early America* (London: Routledge, 1999), 94–110.

Baptist, Edward E., "'Stol' and Fetched Here': Enslaved Migration, Ex-slave Narratives, and Vernacular History," in Edward E. Baptist and Stephanie M. H. Camp (Eds.), *New Studies in the History of American Slavery* (Athens: University of Georgia Press, 2006), 243–74.

Barclay, Jenifer L., *The Mark of Slavery: Disability, Race, and Gender in Antebellum America* (Urbana: University of Illinois Press, 2021).

Bardaglio, Peter W., *Reconstructing the Household: Families, Sex, and the Law in the Nineteenth-Century South* (Chapel Hill: University of North Carolina Press, 1995).

Beckert, Sven, *Empire of Cotton: A Global History* (Cambridge, Mass.: Harvard University Press, 2014).

Berner, Julia W., "'Never be free without trustin' some person': Networking and Buying Freedom in the Nineteenth-Century United States," *Slavery & Abolition*, 40.2 (2018), 341–60.

Berry, Daina Ramey, *"Swing the Sickle for the Harvest is Ripe": Gender and Slavery in Antebellum Georgia* (Urbana: The University of Illinois Press, 2007).

Berry, Daina Ramey, *The Price for Their Pound of Flesh: The Value of the Enslaved from Womb to Grave in the Building of the Nation* (Boston: Beacon Press, 2017).

Berry, Stephen, *Princes of Cotton: Four Diaries of Young Men in the South, 1848–1860* (Athens: University of Georgia Press, 2007).

Blassingame, John, *The Slave Community: Plantation Life in the Antebellum South* (New York: Oxford University Press, 1972).

Blassingame, John, "Status and Social Structure in the Slave Community: Evidence From New Sources," in Harry P. Owens (Ed.), *Perspectives and Irony in American Slavery* (Jackson: University of Mississippi Press, 1976), 137–51.

Blassingame, John, "Using the Testimony of Ex-Slaves: Approaches and Problems," *Journal of Southern History*, 41.4 (1975), 473–92.

Blight, David W., *Race and Reunion: The Civil War in American Memory* (Cambridge, Mass.: Harvard University Press, 2001).

Boster, Dea H., *African American Slavery and Disability: Bodies, Property, and Power in the Antebellum South, 1800–1860* (New York: Routledge, 2013).

Boydston, Jeanne, "Gender as a Question of Historical Analysis," *Gender & History*, 20.3 (2008), 558–83.

Breen, Patrick H., *The Land Shall Be Deluged in Blood: A New History of the Nat Turner Revolt* (New York: Oxford University Press, 2015).

Brophy, Alfred R., *University, Court, and Slave: Proslavery Academic Thought and Southern Jurisprudence, 1831–1861* (New York: Oxford University Press, 2016).

Brown, Vincent, *Tacky's Revolt: The Story of an Atlantic Slave War* (Cambridge, Mass.: Harvard University Press, 2020).

Bruce Jr., Dickson D., *Violence and Culture in the Antebellum South* (Austin: University of Texas Press, 1979).

Buckner, Timothy R., "A Crucible of Masculinity: William Johnson's Barbershop and the Making of Free Black Men in the Antebellum South," in Timothy R. Buckner and Peter Caster (Eds.), *Fathers, Preachers, Rebels, Men: Black*

Masculinity in US History and Literature, 1820–1945 (Columbus: Ohio State University Press, 2011), 41–60.

Burin, Eric, *Slavery and the Peculiar Solution: A History of the Colonization Society* (Gainesville: University Press of Florida, 2005).

Calomoris, Charles W., and Jonathan B. Pritchett, "Preserving Slave Families for Profit: Traders' Incentives and Pricing in the New Orleans Slave Market," *Journal of Economic History*, 69.4 (2009), 986–1011.

Camp, Stephanie M. H., *Closer to Freedom: Enslaved Women and Everyday Resistance in the Plantation South* (Chapel Hill: University of North Carolina Press, 2004).

Camp, Stephanie M. H., "Pleasures of Resistance: Enslaved Women and Body Politics in the Plantation South, 1830–1861," *Journal of Southern History*, 68.3 (2002), 533–72.

Carter Jackson, Kellie, *Force and Freedom: Black Abolitionists and the Politics of Violence* (Philadelphia: University of Pennsylvania Press, 2020).

Cashin, Joan E., "The Structure of Antebellum Planter Families: 'The Ties that Bound us Was Strong,'" *Journal of Southern History*, 56.1 (1990), 55–70.

Chireau, Yvonne P., *Black Magic: Religion and the African American Conjuring Tradition* (Berkeley: University of California Press, 2003).

Chireau, Yvonne P., "The Uses of the Supernatural: Toward a History of Black Women's Magical Practices," in Susan Juster and Lisa MacFarlane (Eds.) *Religion and American Culture* (Ithaca: Cornell University Press, 1996), 171–88.

Chudacoff, Howard P., *How Old Are You?: Age Consciousness in American Culture* (Princeton: Princeton University Press, 1989).

Clegg, John J., "A Theory of Capitalist Slavery," *Journal of Historical Sociology*, 33.1 (2020), 74–98.

Clegg, John J., "Credit Market Discipline and Capitalist Slavery in Antebellum South Carolina," *Social Science History*, 42.2 (2018), 343–76.

Close, Stacey, *Elderly Slaves of the Plantation South* (London: Routledge, 1997).

Coclanis, Peter, "Slavery, Capitalism, and the Problem of Misprision," *Journal of American Studies*, 52 (2018), 1–9.

Cole, Thomas R., *The Journey of Life: A Cultural History of Aging in America* (New York: Cambridge University Press, 1992).

Cooper Owens, Deirdre, *Medical Bondage: Race, Gender, and the Origins of American Gynecology* (Athens: University of Georgia Press, 2017).

Coors, Michael, "Embodied Time: The Narrative Refiguration of Aging," in Mark Schweda, Michael Coors, and Claudia Bozzaro (Eds.), *Aging and Human Nature: Perspectives from Philosophical, Theological, and Historical Anthropology* (Cham: Springer Nature, 2020), 129–41.

Covey, Herbert C. and Paul T. Lockman Jr., "Narrative References to Older African Americans Living in Slavery," *Social Science Journal*, 33.1 (1996), 31–2.

Davis, Adrienne D., "The Private Law of Race and Sex: An Antebellum Perspective," *Stanford Law Review*, 51.2 (1999), 221–88.

Davis, Charles T. and Henry Louis Gates Jr. (Eds.), *The Slave's Narrative* (New York: Oxford University Press, 1985).

Davis, Natalie Zemon, *Fiction in the Archives: Pardon Tales and Their Tellers in Sixteenth-Century France* (Stanford: Stanford University Press, 1987).

De La Fuente, Alejandro, and Ariela J. Gross, *Becoming Free, Becoming Black: Race, Freedom, and Law in Cuba, Virginia, and Louisiana* (New York: Cambridge University Press, 2020).

Desch Obi, T. J., *Fighting for Honor: The History of African Martial Arts in the Atlantic World* (Columbia: University of South Carolina Press, 2008).

Deyle, Steven, *Carry Me Back: The Domestic Slave Trade in American Life* (Oxford: Oxford University Press, 2005).

Doddington, David Stefan and Elizabeth Maeve Barnes, "Engaging with Sources: Slave Narratives," *Bloomsbury History: Theory and Methods* (London: Bloomsbury Publishing, 2021). http://dx.doi.org/10.5040/9781350970892 .089.

Doddington, David Stefan, *Contesting Slave Masculinity in the American South* (New York: Cambridge University Press, 2018).

Dolan, Frances E., *True Relations: Reading, Literature, and Evidence in Seventeenth-Century England* (Philadelphia: University of Pennsylvania Press, 2013).

Downs, Jim, *Sick From Freedom: African-American Illness and Suffering During the Civil War and Reconstruction* (New York: Oxford University Press, 2015).

Downs, Jim, and David Blight (Eds.), *Beyond Freedom: Disrupting the History of Emancipation* (Athens: University of Georgia Press, 2017).

Dusinberre, William, "Power and Agency in Antebellum Slavery," *American Nineteenth Century History*, 12. 2 (2011), 139–48.

Dusinberre, William, *Strategies for Survival: Recollections of Bondage in Antebellum Virginia* (Charlottesville: University of Virginia Press, 2011).

Dusinberre, William, *Them Dark Days: Slavery in the American Rice Swamps* (New York: Oxford University Press, 1996).

Eden, Jason, and Naomi Eden, *Age Norms and Intercultural Interaction in Colonial North America* (Lanham: Lexington Books, 2017).

Edwards, Laura, "Law, Domestic Violence, and the Limits of Patriarchal Authority in the Antebellum South," *Journal of Southern History*, 65.4 (1999), 733–70.

Elder, Robert, *The Sacred Mirror: Evangelicalism, Honor, and Identity in the Deep South, 1790–1860* (Chapel Hill: University of North Carolina Press, 2016).

Ernest, John (Ed.), *The Oxford Handbook of the American Slave Narratives* (New York; Oxford: Oxford University Press, 2014).

Escott, Paul D., *Slavery Remembered: A Record of Twentieth Century Slave-Narratives* (Chapel Hill: University of North Carolina Press, 1979).

Fede, Andrew, *Homicide Justified: The Legality of Killing Slaves in the United States and the Atlantic World* (Athens: University of Georgia Press, 2017).

Fede, Andrew, "Legal Protection for Slave Buyers in the U.S. South: A Caveat Concerning Caveat Emptor," *American Journal of Legal History*, 31.4 (1987), 322–58.

Ferguson, Lydia, "Pro-slavery Appropriations and Inadvertent Agencies: The Elder(ly) 'Uncle' in Plantation Fiction," *American Studies*, 58.1 (2019), 49–72.

Fett, Sharla, *Working Cures: Healing, Health, and Power on Southern Slave Plantations* (Chapel Hill: University of North Carolina Press, 2002).

Field, Corinne T., "Antifeminism, Anti-Blackness, and Anti-Oldness: The Intersectional Aesthetics of Aging in the Nineteenth-Century United States," *Signs*, 47.4 (2022) 843–83.

Field, Corinne T., "Old-Age Justice and Black Feminist History: Sojourner Truth's and Harriet Tubman's Intersectional Legacies," *Radical History Review*, 139 (2021), 37–51.

Field, Corinne T., *The Struggle for Equal Adulthood: Gender, Race, Age, and the Fight for Equal Citizenship in Antebellum America* (Chapel Hill: University of North Carolina Press, 2014).

Field, Corinne T., and Nicholas L. Syrett (Eds.), *Age in America: The Colonial Era to the Present* (New York: New York University Press, 2015).

Field, Corinne T., and Nicholas L. Syrett (Eds.), "AHR Roundtable: Chronological Age: A Useful Category of Historical Analysis," *American Historical Review*, 125 (2020), 371–459.

Finder, Gabriel N., "Introduction: Interrogating Evil," *Journal of Holocaust Research*, 34.4 (2020), 263–70.

Fischer, David Hackett, *Growing Old in America* (New York: Oxford University Press, 1978).

Fogel, Robert and Stanley Engerman, *Time on the Cross: The Economics of Negro Slavery* (New York: W. W. Norton, 1989 [1974]).

Follett, Richard, "Heat, Sex, and Sugar: Pregnancy and Childbearing in the Slave Quarters," *Journal of Family History*, 28.4 (2003), 510–39.

Follett, Richard, Sven Beckert, Peter Coclanis, and Barbara Hahn, *Plantation Kingdom: The American South and Its Global Commodities* (Baltimore: Johns Hopkins University Press, 2017).

Ford, Lacy, *Deliver Us from Evil: The Slavery Question in the Old South* (New York: Oxford University Press, 2009).

Forret, Jeff, *Race Relations at the Margins: Slaves and Poor Whites in the Antebellum Southern Countryside* (Baton Rouge: Louisiana State University Press, 2006).

Forret, Jeff, *Slave Against Slave: Plantation Violence in the Old South* (Baton Rouge: Louisiana State University Press, 2015).

Forret, Jeff, *William's Gang: A Notorious Slave Trader and His Cargo of Black Convicts* (New York: Cambridge University Press, 2020).

Franklin, John Hope and Loren Schweninger, *Runaway Slaves: Rebels on the Plantation* (New York: Oxford University Press, 1999).

Fraser, Rebecca, *Courtship and Love among the Enslaved in North Carolina* (Jackson: University Press of Mississippi, 2007).

Friedman, Lawrence Meir, *Dead Hands: A Social History of Wills, Trusts, and Inheritance Law* (Stanford: Stanford Law Books, 2009).

Friend, Craig Thompson, and Lorri Glover (Eds.), *Death and the American South* (New York: Cambridge University Press, 2014).

Friend, Craig Thompson, and Lorri Glover (Eds.), *Southern Manhood: Perspectives on Masculinity in the Old South* (Athens: University of Georgia Press, 2004).

Fuentes, Marisa J., *Dispossessed Lives: Enslaved Women, Violence, and the Archive* (Philadelphia: University of Pennsylvania Press, 2016).

Gadow, Sally, "Recovering the Body in Ageing," in Nancy S. Jecker (Ed.), *Ageing and Ethics: Philosophical Problems in Gerontology* (New York: Springer, 1992), 113–20.

Gaines, Kevin K., *Uplifting the Race: Black Leadership, Politics, and Culture in the Twentieth Century* (Chapel Hill: University of North Carolina Press, 1996).

Genovese, Elizabeth Fox and Eugene Genovese, *Fatal Self-Deception: Slaveholding Paternalism in the Old South* (New York: Cambridge University Press, 2011).

Genovese, Elizabeth Fox and Eugene Genovese, *The Mind of the Master Class: History and Faith in the Southern Slaveholder's Worldview* (New York: Cambridge University Press, 2005).

Genovese, Eugene, *Roll, Jordan, Roll: The World the Slaves Made* (New York: First Vintage Books Edition, 1976).

Glover, Lorri, "'Let Us Manufacture Men': Educating Elite Boys in the Early National South," in Craig Thompson Friend and Lorri Glover (Eds.), *Southern Manhood: Perspectives on Masculinity in the Old South* (Athens: University of Georgia Press, 2004), 22–49.

Glover, Lorri, *Southern Sons: Becoming Men in the New Nation* (Baltimore: Johns Hopkins University Press, 2007).

Glymph, Thavolia, *Out of the House of Bondage: The Transformation of the Plantation Household* (New York: Cambridge University Press, 2008).

Goddu, Teresa A., "Anti-Slavery's Panoramic Perspective," *Melus*, 39.2 (2014), 12–41.

Greenberg, Kenneth S., *Honor and Slavery: Lies, Duels, Noses, Masks, Dressing as a Woman, Gifts, Strangers, Humanitarianism, Death, Slave Rebellions, the Proslavery Argument, Baseball, Hunting, and Gambling in the Old South* (Princeton: University of Princeton Press, 1996).

Griffin, Rebecca J., "Courtship Contests and the Meaning of Conflict in the Folklore of Slaves," *Journal of Southern History*, 71 (2005), 769–802.

Griffin, Rebecca J., "'Goin' Back Over There to See That Girl': Competing Social Spaces in the Lives of the Enslaved in Antebellum North Carolina," *Slavery and Abolition*, 25.1 (2004), 94–113.

Gross, Ariela J., *Double Character: Slavery and Mastery in the Antebellum Southern Courtroom* (Princeton: Princeton University Press, 2000).

Gutman, Herbert, *The Black Family in Slavery and Freedom, 1750–1925* (Oxford: Basil Blackwall, 1976).

Haber, Carole, *Beyond Sixty-Five: The Dilemma of Old Age in America's Past* (Cambridge: Cambridge University Press, 1983).

Haber, Carole and Brian Gratton, *Old Age and the Search for Security: An American Social History* (Bloomington: Indiana University Press, 1994).

Haber, Carole and Brian Gratton, "Old Age, Public Welfare and Race: The Case of Charleston, South Carolina 1800–1949," *Journal of Social History*, 21.2 (1987), 263–79.

Hartog, Hendrik, *Man & Wife in America: A History* (Cambridge, Mass.: Harvard University Press, 2002).

Hartog, Hendrik, *Someday All This Will Be Yours: A History of Inheritance and Old Age* (Cambridge, Mass.: Harvard University Press, 2012).

Hesley, Alexia Jones and Patrick McCawley, *The Many Faces of Slavery: South Carolina Department of Archives and History* (Columbia: SC State Library, 1999).

Hilliard, Kathleen M., *Masters, Slaves, and Exchange: Power's Purchase in the Old South* (New York: Cambridge University Press, 2014).

Holden, Vanessa, *Surviving Southampton: African American Women and Resistance in Nat Turner's Community* (Urbana: University of Illinois Press, 2021).

Horton, James Oliver and Lois E. Horton, "Violence, Protest, and Identity: Black Manhood in Antebellum America," in Darlene Clark Hine and Earnestine Jenkins (Eds.), *A Question of Manhood. "Manhood Rights": The Construction of Black Male History and Manhood, 1750–1870* (Bloomington: Indiana University Press, 1999), 382–95.

Hunt-Kennedy, Stefanie, *Between Fitness and Death: Disability and Slavery in the Caribbean* (Urbana: University of Illinois Press, 2020).

Ingle, Sarah Elizabeth, "Conjured Memories: Race, Place, and Cultural Memory in the American Conjure Tale, 1877–1905" (PhD Dissertation, College of William and Mary, 2004: https://libraetd.lib.virginia.edu/public_view/zw12z565t).

Johnson, Michael P., "Denmark Vesey and His Co-Conspirators," *William and Mary Quarterly*, 58.4 (2001), 915–76.

Johnson, Michael P., "Forum: The Making of a Slave Conspiracy, Part 2," *William and Mary Quarterly*, 59.1 (2002), 135–202.

Johnson, Michael P., "Runaway Slaves and the Slave Communities in South Carolina, 1799 to 1830," *William and Mary Quarterly*, 38.3 (Jul., 1981), 418–41.

Johnson, Paul, "Historical Readings of Old Age and Ageing," in Paul Johnson and Pat Thane (Eds.), *Old Age from Antiquity to Post-Modernity* (London: Routledge, 1998), 1–18.

Johnson, Walter, "A Nettlesome Classic Turns Twenty-Five," *Common-Place*, 1.4 (2001).

Johnson, Walter, *River of Dark Dreams: Slavery and Empire in the Cotton Kingdom* (Cambridge, Mass.: Harvard University Press, 2013).

Johnson, Walter, *Soul by Soul: Life Inside the Antebellum Slave Market* (Cambridge, Mass.: Harvard University Press, 2001).

Jones, Bernie D., *Fathers of Conscience: Mixed-Race Inheritance in the Antebellum South* (Athens: University of Georgia Press, 2009).

Jones-Rogers, Stephanie, *They Were Her Property: White Women As Slave Owners in the American South* (New Haven: Yale University Press, 2019).

Joyner, Charles, *Remember Me: Slave Life in Coastal Georgia* (Athens: University of Georgia Press, 2011).

Kallio, Kirsi Pauliina, and Mary E. Thomas, "Intergenerational Encounters, Intersubjective Age Relations," *Emotion, Space, and Society*, 32 (2019), 1–4.

Katz, Stephen, Kavita Sivaramakrishnan, and Pat Thane, "'To Understand All Life as Fragile, Valuable, and Interdependent': A Roundtable on Old Age and History," *Radical History Review*, 139 (2021), 13–36.

Kay, Marvin L. Michael and Lorin Lee Cary, "Slave Runaways in Colonial North Carolina, 1748–1775," in Darlene Clark Hine and Earnestine Jenkins (Eds.), *A Question of Manhood. "Manhood Rights": The Construction of Black Male History and Manhood, 1750–1870* (Bloomington: Indiana University Press, 1999), 130–65.

Kaye, Anthony, *Joining Places: Slave Neighborhoods in the Old South* (Chapel Hill: University of North Carolina Press, 2007).

Kennedy, V. Lynn, *Born Southern: Childbirth, Motherhood, and Social Networks in the Old South* (Baltimore: Johns Hopkins University Press, 2010).

Kennington, Kelly M., *In the Shadow of Dred Scott: St Louis Freedom Suits and the Legal Culture of Slavery in Antebellum America* (Athens: University of Georgia Press, 2017).

Kennon, Raquel, "Slavery and the Cultural Turn," in David Stefan Doddington and Enrico Dal Lago (Eds.), *Writing the History of Slavery* (London: Bloomsbury Academic, 2022), 399–416.

King, Wilma, *Stolen Childhood: Slave Youth in Nineteenth-Century America* (Bloomington: Indiana University Press, 1995).

King, Wilma, "'Suffer with them till death': Slave Women and Their Children in Nineteenth-Century America," in David Barry Gaspar and Darlene Clark Hine (Eds.), *More Than Chattel: Black Women and Slavery in the Americas* (Bloomington: Indiana University Press, 1996), 145–68.

Klebaner, Benjamin Joseph, "American Manumission Laws and the Responsibility for Supporting Slaves," *Virginia Magazine of History and Biography*, 63.4 (1955), 443–53.

Kleijwegt, Marc (Ed.), *The Faces of Freedom: The Manumission and Emancipation of Slaves in Old World and New World Slavery* (Boston: Leiden University Press, 2006).

Knight, Benjamin, "Black Women, Eldership, and Communities of Care in the Nineteenth-Century North," *Early American Studies*, 17.4 (2019), 545–61.

Kolchin, Peter, "Re-Evaluating the Antebellum Slave Community," *Journal of American History*, 70.3 (1983), 579–601.

Lane, Joan, "'The Doctor Scolds Me': The Diaries and Correspondence of Patients in Eighteenth-Century England," in Roy Porter (Ed.), *Patients and Practitioners. Lay Perceptions of Medicine in Pre-Industrial Society* (Cambridge: Cambridge University Press, 1985), 205–48.

Levine, Lawrence, *Black Culture and Black Consciousness: Afro-American Folk Thought From Slavery to Freedom* (New York: Oxford University Press, 1977).

Levine, Lawrence, *The Unpredictable Past: Explorations in American Cultural History* (New York: Oxford University Press, 1993).

Livesey, Andrea, "Conceived in Violence: Enslaved Mothers and Children Bborn of Rape in Nineteenth-Century Louisiana," *Slavery & Abolition*, 38.2 (2017), 373–91.

Lockley, Timothy J., *Lines in the Sand: Race and Class in Lowcountry Georgia* (Athens: University of Georgia Press, 2001).

Lussana, Sergio, *My Brother Slaves: Friendship, Masculinity, and Resistance in the Antebellum South* (Lexington: University Press of Kentucky, 2016).

Lussana, Sergio, "Reassessing Brer Rabbit: Friendship, Altruism, and Community in the Folklore of Enslaved African-Americans," *Slavery & Abolition* (2017), 1–24.

Lussana, Sergio, "To See who was Best on the Plantation: Enslaved Fighting Contests and Masculinity in the Antebellum Plantation South," *Journal of Southern History* 76.4 (2010), 901–22.

Martin, Jonathan D., *Divided Mastery: Slave Hiring in the American South* (Cambridge, Mass.: Harvard University Press, 2004).

Martin, Kameelah L., *Conjuring Moments in African American Literature: Women, Spirit Work, and Other Such Hoodoo* (New York: Palgrave Macmillan, 2013).

May, William F., "The Virtues and Vices of the Elderly," in Thomas R. Cole and Sally Gaddow (Eds.), *What Does It Mean to Grow Old? Reflections from the Humanities* (Durham: Duke University Press, 1986), 41–63.

Mayfield, John, *Counterfeit Gentlemen: Manhood and Humor in the Old South* (Gainesville: University of Florida Press, 2009).

McCandless, Peter, *Slavery, Disease, and Suffering in the Southern Lowcountry* (New York: Cambridge University Press, 2012).

McElya, Micki, *Clinging to Mammy: The Faithful Slave in Twentieth Century America* (Cambridge, Mass.: Harvard University Press, 2007).

McLaren, Angus, *Impotence: A Cultural History* (Chicago: University of Chicago Press, 2008).

Merritt, Keri Leigh, *Masterless Men: Poor Whites and Slavery in the Antebellum South* (New York: Cambridge University Press, 2017).

Miller, Albert G., *Elevating the Race: Theophilus G. Steward, Black Theology, and the Making of an African American Civil Society, 1865–1924* (Knoxville: University of Tennessee Press, 2003).

Mintz, Steven, "Reflections on Age as a Category of Analysis," *Journal of the History of Childhood and Youth*, 1.1 (2008), 90–4.

Mirzoeff, Nicholas, *The Right to Look: A Counterhistory of Visuality* (Durham: Duke University Press, 2011).

Moon Jr., David T., "Southern Baptists and Southern Men: Evangelical Perceptions of Manhood in Nineteenth-Century Georgia," *Journal of Southern History*, 81.3 (2015), 563–606.

Morgan, Jennifer L., *Laboring Women: Reproduction and Labor in New World Slavery* (Philadelphia: University of Pennsylvania Press, 2004).

Morgan, Jennifer L., *Reckoning With Slavery: Gender, Kinship, and Capitalism in the early Black Atlantic* (Durham: Duke University Press, 2020).

Morgan, Philip D., *Slave Counterpoint: Black Culture in the Eighteenth-Century Chesapeake & Lowcountry* (Chapel Hill: University of North Carolina Press, 1998).

Morris, Thomas D., *Southern Slavery and the Law, 1619–1860* (Chapel Hill: University of North Carolina Press, 1996).

Murphy, Sharon Ann, "Securing Human Property: Slavery, Life Insurance and Industrialization in the Upper South," *Journal of the Early Republic*, 25.4 (2005), 615–52.

Murray, David, *Matter, Magic, and Spirit: Representing Indian and African American Belief* (Philadelphia: University of Pennsylvania Press, 2007).

Murray, John E., Alan L. Olmstead, Trevon D. Logan, Jonathon B. Pritchett, and Peter L. Rousseau, "The Half Has Never Been Told: Slavery and the Making of American Capitalism," *Journal of Economic History*, 75.3 (2015), 919–31.

Musher, Sharon Ann, "Contesting 'The Way the Almighty Wants It': Crafting Memories of Ex-Slaves in the Slave Narrative Collection," *American Quarterly*, 53.1 (2001), 1–31.

Mustakeem, Sowande' M., *Slavery at Sea: Terror, Sex, and Sickness in the Middle Passage* (Urbana: University of Illinois Press, 2017).

Nelson, Scott Reynolds, "Who Put Their Capitalism in My Slavery?" *Journal of the Civil War Era*, 5.2 (2015), 289–310.

Oakes, James, "Capitalism and Slavery and the Civil War," *International Labor and Working-Class History*, 89 (2016), 195–220.

Oakes, James, *The Ruling Race: A History of American Slaveholders* (New York: W. W. Norton & Co., 1982).

Ottaway, Susannah R., *The Decline of Life: Old Age in Eighteenth-Century England* (Oxford: Oxford University Press, 2004).

Ottaway, Susannah R., "Medicine and Old Age," in Mark Jackson (Ed.), *The Oxford Handbook of the History of Medicine* (Oxford: Oxford University Press, 2013), 338–55.

Ottaway, Susannah R., Lynn A. Botelho, and Katharine Kittredge, *Power and Poverty: Old Age in the Pre-Industrial Past* (Westport: Greenwood Press, 2002).

Owens, Leslie Howard, *This Species of Property: Slave Life and Culture in the Old South* (Oxford: Oxford University Press, 1976).

Pargas, Damian Alan, "From the Cradle to the Fields: Slave Childcare and Childhood in the antebellum South," *Slavery & Abolition*, 32.4 (2011), 477–93.

Pargas, Damian Alan, *Slavery and Forced Migration in the Antebellum South* (New York: Cambridge University Press, 2016).

Parkin, Tim, *Old Age in the Roman World: A Cultural and Social History* (Baltimore: Johns Hopkins University Press, 2003).

Parry, Tyler D. and Charlton W. Yingling, "Slave Hounds and Abolition in the Americas," *Past & Present*, 246.1 (2020), 69–108.

Patterson, Orlando, *Rituals of Blood: Consequences of Slavery in two American Centuries* (Washington, DC: Civitas/Counterpoint, 1998).

Patterson, Orlando, *Slavery and Social Death: A Comparative Study* (Cambridge, Mass.: Harvard University Press, 1982).

Penningroth, Dylan, *The Claims of Kinfolk: African American Property and Community in the Nineteenth-Century South* (Chapel Hill: University of North Carolina Press, 2003).

Phillips, Ulrich Bonnell, *Life and Labor in the Old South* (Boston: Little, Brown, & Co., 1929).

Pitts, Yvonne, *Family Law, and Inheritance in America: A Social and Legal History of Nineteenth-Century Kentucky* (New York: Cambridge University Press, 2012).

Pollard, Leslie, "Aging and Slavery: A Gerontological Perspective," *Journal of Negro History*, 66.3 (1981), 228–34.

Porter, Roy, "The Patient's View: Doing Medical History From Below," *Theory and Society* 14.2 (1985), 175–98.

Pritchett, Jonathan B., and Herman Freudenberger, "A Peculiar Sample: A Reply to Steckel and Ziebarth," *Journal of Economic History*, 76.1 (2016), 139–62.

Protzko, John and Jonathan W. Schooler, "Kids These Days: Why the Youth of Today Seem Lacking," *Science Advances* 5.10 (2019).

Raboteau, Albert J., *Slave Religion: The Invisible Institution in the Antebellum South* (Oxford: Oxford University Press, 2004; 1st published 1978).

Rawick, George P., *The American Slave: A Composite Autobiography. From Sundown to Sunup: The Making of the Black Community* (Westport: Greenwood Press, 1972).

Ritterhouse, Jennifer, "Reading, Intimacy, and the Role of Uncle Remus in White Southern Social Memory," *Journal of Southern History*, 69.3 (2003), 585–622.

Rosenthal, Caitlin, *Accounting for Slavery: Masters and Management* (Cambridge, Mass.: Harvard University Press, 2018).

Roth, Sarah, *Gender and Race in Antebellum Popular Culture* (New York: Cambridge University Press, 2014).

Rucker, Walter, "Conjure, Magic, and Power: The Influence of Afro-Atlantic Religious Practices on Slave Resistance and Rebellion," *Journal of Black Studies*, 32.1 (2001), 84–103.

Rüegger, Heinz, "Beyond Control. Dependence and Passivity in Old Age," in Mark Schweda, Michael Coors, and Claudia Bozzaro (Eds.), *Aging and Human Nature: Perspectives from Philosophical, Theological, and Historical Anthropology* (Cham: Springer Nature, 2020), 47–57.

Ruiz, Dorothy Smith, *Amazing Grace: African American Grandmothers as Caregivers and Conveyors of Traditional Values* (Westport: Praeger 2004).

Sandy, Laura, *The Overseers of Early American Slavery: Supervisors, Enslaved Labourers, and the Plantation Enterprise* (London: Routledge, 2020).

Savitt, Todd L., *Medicine and Slavery: The Diseases and Health Care of Blacks in Antebellum Virginia* (Urbana: University of Illinois Press, 1981).

Schneider, Eric B., "Children's Growth in an Adaptive Framework: Explaining the Growth Patterns of American Slaves and Other Historical Populations," *Economic History Review*, 70.1 (2017), 3–29.

Schwall, Alexander R. "Defining Age and Using Age-Relevant Constructs," in Walter C. Borman and Jerry W. Hedge (Eds.), *The Oxford Handbook of Work and Aging* (Oxford: Oxford University Press, 2012), 170–86.

Schwartz, Marie Jenkins, *Birthing a Slave: Motherhood and Medicine in the Antebellum South* (Cambridge, Mass.: Harvard University Press, 2006).

Schwartz, Marie Jenkins, *Born in Bondage: Growing Up Enslaved in the Antebellum South* (Cambridge, Mass.: Harvard University Press, 2000).

Schweda, Mark, "The Autumn of My Years: Aging and the Temporal Structure of Human Life," in Mark Schweda, Michael Coors, and Claudia Bozzaro (Eds.), *Aging and Human Nature: Perspectives from Philosophical, Theological, and Historical Anthropology* (Cham: Springer Nature, 2020), 143–59.

Schweninger, Loren, *Appealing for Liberty: Freedom Suits in the South* (New York: Oxford University Press, 2018).

Scott, James C., *Domination and the Arts of Resistance: Hidden Transcripts* (New Haven: Yale University Press, 1990).

Scott, James C., *Weapons of the Weak: Everyday Forms of Peasant Resistance* (New Haven: Yale University Press, 1985).

Scott, Joan, "Gender: A Useful Category of Analysis," *American Historical Review*, 91.5 (1986), 1053–75.

Shaw, Stephanie, "Using the WPA Ex-slave Narratives to Study the Great Depression," *Journal of Southern History*, 69.3 (2003), 623–58.

Silkenat, David, *Scars on the Land: An Environmental History of Slavery in the American South* (New York: Oxford University Press, 2022).

Smith, Theophus Harold, *Conjuring Culture: Biblical Formations of Black America* (Oxford: Oxford University Press, 1994).

Snyder, Terri L., *The Power to Die: Slavery and Suicide in British North America* (Chicago: Chicago University Press, 2015).

Sommerville, Diane Miller, *Aberration of Mind: Suicide and Suffering in the Civil War-Era South* (Chapel Hill: University of North Carolina Press, 2018).

Spindel, Donna, "Assessing Memory: Twentieth-Century Slave Narratives Reconsidered," *Journal of Interdisciplinary History*, 27.2 (1996), 247–61.

Steckel, Richard H. "A Peculiar Population: The Nutrition, Health, and Mortality of American Slaves from Childhood to Maturity," *Journal of Economic History*, 46.3 (1986), 721–41.

Steckel, Richard H., "A Dreadful Childhood: The Excess Mortality of American Slaves," *Social Science History*, 10.4 (1986), 427–65.

Steckel, Richard H., "Biological Measures of the Standard of Living," *Journal of Economic Perspectives*, 22.1 (2008), 129–152.

Steedman, Carolyn, *Dust* (Manchester: Manchester University Press, 2001).

Stevenson, Brenda, "Distress and Discord in Virginian Slave Families," in Carol Bleser (Ed.), *In Joy and Sorrow: Women, Family, and Marriage in the Victorian South, 1830–1900* (New York: Oxford University Press, 1991), 103–25.

Stevenson, Brenda, *Life in Black and White: Family and Community in the Slave South* (New York: Oxford University Press, 1996).

Stevenson, Brenda, "Marsa never sot Aunt Rebecca down": Enslaved Women, Religion, and Social Power in the Antebellum South," *Journal of African American History*, 90.4 (2005), 345–67.

Stevenson, Brenda, "'What's love got to do with it': Concubinage and enslaved women and girls in the Antebellum South," *Journal of African American History*, 98.1 (2013), 99–125.

Stevenson, Brenda, "Gender Conventions, Ideals and Identity among Antebellum Virginia Slave Women," in David Barry Gaspar and Darlene Clark Hine (Eds.),

More Than Chattel: Black Women and Slavery in the Americas (Bloomington: Indiana University Press, 1994), 169–93.

Stowe, Steven M., *Intimacy and Power in the Old South: Ritual in the Lives of the Planters* (Baltimore: Johns Hopkins University Press, 1987).

Stuckey, Sterling, *Going Through the Storm: The Influence of African American Art in History* (New York: Oxford University Press, 1994).

Stuckey, Sterling, *Slave Culture: Nationalist Theory and the Foundations of Black America* (New York: Oxford University Press, 2013. 2nd ed., originally published 1987).

Stuckey, Sterling, "Through the Prism of Folklore: The Black Ethos in Slavery," *Massachusetts Review* 9 (1968), 417–37.

Sundquist, Eric, *To Wake the Nations: Race in the Making of American Literature* (Cambridge, Mass.: Harvard University Press, 2003).

Tadman, Michael, "The Reputation of the Slave Trader in Southern History and the Social Memory of the South," *American Nineteenth Century History*, 8.3 (2007), 247–71.

Tadman, Michael, *Speculators and Slaves: Masters, Traders, and Slaves in the Old South* (Madison: University of Wisconsin Press, 1996 [1989]).

Thane, Pat, *Old Age in English History: Past Experiences, Present Issues* (Oxford: Oxford University Press, 2000).

Thompson, Cheryl, *Uncle: Race, Nostalgia, and the Politics of Loyalty* (Toronto: Coach House Books, 2021).

Trouillot, Michel-Rolph, *Silencing the Past: Power and the Production of History* (Boston: Beacon Press, 1995).

Wahl, Jennie Bourne, "Legal Constraints on Slave Masters: The Problem of Social Cost," *American Journal of Legal Theory* 41.1 (1997), 1–24.

Walker, Alice, "Uncle Remus, No Friend of Mine," *The Georgia Review*, 66.3 (2012), 635–7.

Weiner, Marli F., *Sex, Sickness, and Slavery: Illness in the Antebellum South* (Urbana: University of Illinois Press, 2012).

Welch, Kimberly M., *Black Litigants in the Antebellum American South* (Chapel Hill: University of North Carolina Press, 2018).

Wells-Oghoghomeh, Alexis S., "'She Come Like a Nightmare': Hags, Witches and the Gendered Trans-Sense among the Enslaved in the Lower South," *Journal of African Religions*, 5:2 (2017), 239–74.

Wells-Oghoghomeh, Alexis S., *The Souls of Womenfolk: The Religious Cultures of Enslaved Women in the Lower South* (Chapel Hill: University of North Carolina Press, 2022).

West, Emily, *Chains of Love: Slave Couples in Antebellum South Carolina* (Urbana: University of Illinois Press, 2004).

White, Deborah Gray, *Ar'n't I A Woman? Female Slaves in the Plantation South* (New York: W. W. Norton & Company, 1999 [1985]).

Whitman, T. Stephen, *The Price of Freedom: Slavery and Manumission in Baltimore and Early National Maryland* (Lexington: University Press of Kentucky, 1997).

Wiethoff, William E., *Crafting the Overseers Image* (Columbia: University of South Carolina Press, 2006).

Williams, Eric, *Capitalism and Slavery* (Chapel Hill: University of North Carolina Press, 1944).

Williams, Heather A., *Help Me To Find My People: The African American Search for Family Lost in Slavery* (Chapel Hill: University of North Carolina Press, 2012).

Williams, Kidada E., *I Saw Death Coming: A History of Terror and Survival in the War Against Reconstruction* (London: Bloomsbury Academic, 2023).

Windon, Nathaniel, "A Tale of Two Uncles: The Old Age of Uncle Tom and Uncle Remus," *Common-Place* 17.2 (2017).

Windon, Nathaniel, "Superannuated: Old Age on the Antebellum Plantation," *American Quarterly*, 71.3 (2019), 767–77.

Witham, Miles D. and Avan Ahie Sayer (Eds.), "Introduction to the Age and Ageing sarcopenia collection," *Age and Ageing*, 45.6 (2016), 752–3.

Wood, Gregory, *Retiring Men: Manhood, Labor, and Growing Old in America, 1900–1960* (Lanham: Lexington Books, 2012).

Wood, Kirsten E., *Masterful Women: Slaveholding Widows from the American Revolution through the Civil War* (Chapel Hill: University of North Carolina Press, 2004).

Wright, Gavin, "Slavery and Anglo-American Capitalism Revisited," *Economic History Review*, 73.2 (2020), 353–83.

Wyatt-Brown, Bertram, *The Shaping of Southern Culture: Honor, Grace, and War, 1760s–1890s* (Chapel Hill: University of North Carolina Press, 2001).

Wyatt-Brown, Bertram, *Southern Honor: Ethics and Behavior in the Old South* (New York: Oxford University Press, 1982).

Wyatt-Brown, Bertram, *A Warring Nation: Honor, Race, and Humiliation in America and Abroad* (Charlottesville: University of Virginia Press, 2014).

Yallop, Helen, *Age and Identity in Eighteenth-Century England* (London: Routledge, 2016).

Yarbrough, Fay, "Power, Perception, and Interracial Sex: Former Slaves Recall a Multiracial South," *Journal of Southern History*, 71.3 (2005), 559–98.

Young, Robert, *Domesticating Slavery: The Master Class in Georgia and South Carolina, 1670–1837* (Chapel Hill: University of North Carolina Press, 1997).

Index

"Mammy," 41
"Uncle Remus," 141

abolitionists
  preying on weak enslavers, 343–5
  and resistance, 115, 200, 202, 214
  rejection of paternalism, 23, 50
  rhetoric of, 25, 66, 243
  support of Black elders, 79
Achenbaum, W. A, 8, 21, 258
aging. *See* old age
Alabama, 8, 12, 42, 51, 70, 74, 83, 148, 149,
  158, 174, 178, 182, 184, 185, 214, 276,
  282, 284, 316
Anderson, William, 60
Arkansas, 8, 12, 106, 149, 172, 177, 238
auction. *See* sale

bald, 58, 179, 255
Baldwin, Joseph, 12
Ball, Charles, 38, 39, 44, 56, 141, 147, 209
Banks, Jourden, 201, 210, 214, 228
Baptist, Edward, 227
Barclay, Jenifer, 119, 137
Berry, Daina Ramey, 4, 105, 110, 140
Bibb, Henry, 82, 192
Black, Leonard, 225, 230
Boster, Dea, 128
Boydston, Jeanne, 20
Branham, Levi, 121
Brown, Henry "Box," 96, 140, 236
Brown, John, 59, 81, 84, 124, 234
Bruce, Henry Clay, 188–9

Caldwell, Charles, 9
Campbell, Israel, 115, 234
cancer, 88, 100
caveat emptor, 82
Chesney, Pharoah Jackson, 136
childcare
  by elders, 26, 33–43, 76, 101, 175
  elders violent, 114–16, 120
  favorites, 118–19
  intergenerational tension, 110–12, 114
Chireau, Yvonne P, 190
Clarke, Lewis, 50, 81, 93, 96, 98, 227, 229,
  241, 329
Clay, Thomas, 57
Clegg, John J, 252
Close, Stacey, 122, 158, 181
conjure
  "African" knowledge, 165, 171, 192
  and intergenerational tension, 177–9
  and resistance, 190–2
  as revenge of elder, 172–7
  failure of, 181–3
  hag, 167, 168
  intergenerational tension, 184–5, 189
  white perceptions of, 167
  witches, 167–70
conjurers
  and Christianity, 178, 185, 187–94
  as deceitful, 183–4, 188, 192
  as deluded, 193–4
  disbelief in, 181–3
  intimate exploitation, 174
  mockery of, 188

271, 274, 275, 277, 278, 286, 304, 313,
320, 321, 323, 338, 351
Northup, Solomon, 4, 108, 147–8, 195–7,
214, 350
Nott, Josiah Clark, 69
nursing mothers, 39

O' Neal, William, 211
Oakes, James, 252
old age
 as infancy, 99, 199, 232, 235, 241, 248,
 258, 260, 266, 287, 303, 304, 313, 315,
 326, 341
 cultural representations, 9, 11, 204
 deception, 267–76, 277–80, 285–6,
 287–8, 298, 299–300, 307–11, 326,
 329–31, 333
 decline associated with, 4, 11, 35, 58,
 122, 125, 129, 131, 134, 138, 144, 146,
 149, 150, 151, 152, 153, 159, 179, 180,
 199, 226, 232, 233, 238–9, 253–7, 260,
 281, 307, 314, 324, 325, 328, 336, 338,
 340, 343
 dependency in, 108, 235, 261–4, 270,
 279, 282, 284, 287, 296, 314, 338
 efforts to hide, 81, 85
 enabling resistance, 225, 233, 237–42,
 243–5, 247–50, 311–17
 financial losses, 225, 230, 251, 266, 285,
 300
 financial value, 5, 35, 36, 38, 67, 77, 78,
 87, 88, 90, 91, 92, 93, 99, 216
 intimate exploitation, 277, 303–6
 isolation, 79, 144–7, 148, 168, 245, 260,
 315, 341
 jealousy, 116, 120, 122, 180, 230, 261,
 303
 lack of mastery, 2, 127, 226, 231–3, 234,
 235–7, 243–5, 246–50, 252, 257–61,
 262–4, 265–7, 268–73, 282, 283, 294,
 295–9, 300–2, 304, 306–17, 325–8,
 333–8, 339–45
 physical violence, 280–2, 284, 305,
 309–11
 political and personal, 318
 premature, 18, 58, 85, 196, 213
 relational and subjective, 145
 sadness, 145, 298, 327
 stereotypes, 168, 206, 210, 217, 221, 243
 theories on, 16–19

Olmsted, Frederick Law, 52, 78
overseer, 41, 53, 59, 60–3, 115, 201, 206,
214, 230, 236

Pargas, Damian Alan, 120
Parker, Allen, 143, 144
Parker, Jamie, 44, 49, 98, 202
paternalism, 28, 34, 52, 73, 76, 273, 279, 347
 rejection of, 54, 60, 64, 69, 90, 99, 103,
 253
Pennington, James, 125, 210, 228
Pettigrew, William, 2, 351
Picquet, Louisa, 230
punishment
 and resistance, 213–15
 of elders, 51–6, 58, 60, 61, 66–9, 86, 114

Raboteau, Albert J, 181
racial uplift, 172, 187
Redpath, James, 77, 204
reproductive exploitation, 36, 53, 92, 93, 99
resistance
 and fatalism, 203–5, 207, 211, 214, 218
 and youth, 205–7, 212
 betrayal of, 207–10
 dangers of, 199
 demographics of, 198
 elders counsel against, 216–21
 elders support, 201–2, 220
 intergenerational tension, 18, 115, 116,
 118, 133, 169, 170, 205, 210–13,
 216–17
respect
 claims of, 1, 3, 98, 106, 107, 110, 113,
 118, 119, 140, 142, 158, 162, 167, 170,
 171, 176, 181, 189, 191, 196, 201, 228,
 320
 lack of, 27, 106–7, 108, 112–13, 132,
 147, 148, 160, 191, 350
reverence. *See* respect
rheumatism, 88, 91, 103, 144, 170, 347
Robinson, William, 202, 317
Roper, Moses, 53, 201
Ruffin, Edmund, 257
Rush, Benjamin, 138

sale
 as enslaver old, 227–8, 231, 233, 238,
 243, 262
 challenged on account of age, 48, 86–9